Stakeholders

Stakeholders
Theory and Practice

Andrew L. Friedman

and

Samantha Miles

OXFORD

UNIVERSITY PRESS

Great Clarendon Street, Oxford OX2 6DP

Oxford University Press is a department of the University of Oxford.
It furthers the University's objective of excellence in research, scholarship,
and education by publishing worldwide in

Oxford New York

Auckland Cape Town Dar es Salaam Hong Kong Karachi
Kuala Lumpur Madrid Melbourne Mexico City Nairobi
New Delhi Shanghai Taipei Toronto

With offices in

Argentina Austria Brazil Chile Czech Republic France Greece
Guatemala Hungary Italy Japan Poland Portugal Singapore
South Korea Switzerland Thailand Turkey Ukraine Vietnam

Oxford is a registered trade mark of Oxford University Press
in the UK and in certain other countries

Published in the United States
by Oxford University Press Inc., New York

British Library Cataloguing in Publication Data

Data available

Library of Congress Cataloging in Publication Data

Friedman, Andrew L.
  Stakeholders : theory and practice / Andrew L. Friedman and Samantha Miles.
      P. cm.
  ISBN-13: 978-0-19-926987-7 (alk.paper)
  ISBN-10: 0-19-926987-4 (alk.paper)
  ISBN-13: 978-0-19-926986-0 (alk.paper)
  ISBN-10: 0-19-926986-6 (alk. paper)
 1. Strategic planning. 2. Business ethics. 3. Stockholders. I. Miles, Samantha,
1969- II. Title.
  HD30.28.F73 2006
  306.3–dc22   2005032362

Typeset by SPI Publisher Services, Pondicherry, India
Printed in Great Britain
on acid-free paper by
Antony Rowe Ltd., Chippenham, Wiltshire

ISBN 0-19-926986-6   978-0-19-926986-0
ISBN 0-19-926987-4 (Pbk.)   978-0-19-926987-7 (Pbk.)
1 3 5 7 9 10 8 6 4 2

For Carla and Jon

☐ PREFACE

The stakeholder field of theory, practice, and policy has reached a crossroads. Leading up to where we are now, there has been enormous growth in the popularity of the concept among academics and policymakers and this has encouraged managers, stakeholders, and their representatives to develop practices informed by the stakeholder concept. One clear path ahead is that the development of theory, practice, and policy continue to reinforce each other, leading to greater and wider influence of the concept on practice and policy. However, as the concept has become more popular, the path has become tangled with the many different ways the concept has been used. For example, different practices have come to be called stakeholder activities, particularly by those seeking to use the label to legitimize their actions. Also, a range of different definitions as to what a stakeholder is has emerged. Concentrating on these issues encourages a view of a second future path of the stakeholder field: as a fad that is rapidly passing its time of influence, which peters out as a future marker for progress. Already we notice a reluctance to use the word stakeholder among managers because of their concern that its meaning is unclear.

Aims and Approach

The primary aim of *Stakeholders: Theory and Practice* is to encourage the field along the first path. This book analyses, classifies, and critiques the diffused strands of the stakeholder literature. The authors believe that such a 'sorting' is necessary because of the widely recognized 'muddle' that has accompanied the popularity of the stakeholder concept. Major theoretical contributions are placed in the context of their philosophical underpinnings and are discussed along with literature aimed at recommending, describing, and analysing practical strategies and specific policies. Though the stakeholder concept is fairly new it has developed substantially, particularly since Freeman's landmark book of 1984. One important aspect of this development has been a decentring of the concept away from exclusive focus on corporate strategy and/or corporate morality. Although the overwhelming majority of the stakeholder literature is concerned with publicly owned corporations, some have sought to open space for other kinds of organizations to be considered (Smillie and Helmich 1999). More radically, rather than being limited to stakeholder management, representing how organizations ought to behave (for their own strategic good or for a wider social good), the concept has been widened by some to embrace stakeholders' own perspectives as complementing, and sometimes opposing, the organization perspective (Calton and Lad 1995; Frooman 1999). In this book we allow for a broad perspective by considering theories in relation the *organization–stakeholder relationship*. The design of this book supports this perspective. It reflects distinctions, which we believe have been key to the historical development of the stakeholder concept, and will be important for the future influence of the concept, and the agenda of those who see the concept as encouraging a change in how organizations and stakeholders interact. These distinctions are:

1. Among theory, practice, and policy. These are the subjects of distinct literatures that often show a surprising lack of appreciation of each other. A major purpose of this book is to bring these literatures together while emphasizing common themes. For each of these subjects a framework or model is presented to allow different contributions to be compared (Sections 3.2.4, 6.5, and 9.2).

2. Between normative and analytical approaches. This distinction is commonly expressed as a three-way classification: normative, instrumental, and descriptive. The term normative is generally used in the stakeholder literature in what would be thought of as the philosophic sense: as a prescriptive and categorical provision of guidance for actions and policies in all circumstances because it is the 'right' thing to do. Elsewhere in management literature it is used in a hypothetical sense in the form of 'If you want to achieve X, then do Y'. Donaldson and Preston (1995) refer to this as 'instrumental'. Here we use the term analytic to cover both instrumental theory and descriptive theory (Section 2.6).

3. Between organization-centred and stakeholder perspectives. This is one aspect of a general sensitivity to the social construction of the concept, i.e., sensitivity to differing perspectives on the concept by different people, affected by their social position. The stakeholder relation is dynamic and potentially highly contested and this can be reflected in the very concept of stakeholders being contested as well (Chapter 5).

Limitations

We concentrate on organization–stakeholder relations more than on macropolitical issues of governance and the broader use of the concept of stakeholders such as the idea of stakeholder pensions. Both are important, but this book is mainly aimed at readers interested in stakeholder management within organizations and the ways that stakeholders influence organizations. Macro issues are approached in terms of their relevance for these more micro-level (or meso-level) theories and practice. We also do not concentrate on detailed review of evidence for specific hypotheses in the literature, although we do briefly review the evidence for the fundamental instrumental stakeholder proposition in Chapter 5.

How to use *Stakeholders: Theory and Practice*

This book is distinctive in that it deals with theory, practice, policy, and education. There are four types of books that specialize in the stakeholder field:

1. Theoretical monographs that comprehensively deal with a single theory or a narrow collection of theories. Other theories are dealt with primarily as background leading up to the theory being proposed, or are only summarized in order to point out their failings and how the proposed theory is an improvement (Clarkson 1994; Post, Preston, and Sachs 2002; Phillips 2003*b*). These books may present recommendations for practice and policy but do not attempt a comprehensive review of either.

2. Practical guides and presentation of examples of good and bad practice. These are intended more for managers in practice (Svendsen 1998; Andriof et al. 2002, 2003), rather than managers in education where more reflective approaches are called for.

3. Collections of articles focused around a specific theme within the stakeholder field (Clarkson 1998; Sharma and Starik 2004) or a collection of papers given at a themed conference (Näsi 1995; Kelly, Kelly, and Gamble 1997). These are limited to the aspect of the stakeholder field that the editors or conference organizers believed to be new or important.

4. Applications of the stakeholder concept to specific fields: financial reporting (Stittle 2003), corporate governance (Alkhafaji 1989), business ethics (Weiss 1998, 2003), and marketing (Duncan and Moriarty 1997).

Beyond these relatively few types of books, the vast majority of stakeholder literature is to be found in articles in a wide range of academic journals, as can be seen in the References to this book. *Stakeholders: Theory and Practice* is unlike all the above types of books in that it presents many theories, each in its own terms and not as part of building up to a single theory or as foils to the preferred theory. It is not primarily aimed at management practitioners and is intended to guide students of management and management strategy, as well as students studying business ethics, organization behaviour, and related fields such as corporate governance, environmental management, sociology, and politics.

Stakeholders: Theory and Practice deals with the stakeholder field in a comprehensive manner. In this the only comparable book is Freeman (1984). Freeman surveyed use of the stakeholder concept up to the writing of his book. He expressed the concept clearly, emphasized the way the concept could be implemented by management in practice, discussed consequences of taking the concept seriously for business success and indeed survival, and issued warnings of the consequences of ignoring stakeholders for corporate survival. What emerged from Freeman (1984) was a clear statement of the stakeholder concept, but what we would regard as a narrow statement in that it was written from the perspective of management and, more narrowly, of management strategy. It was also strongly slanted towards a descriptive and instrumental approach, rather than a normative approach (which Freeman himself took up with vigour subsequent to his 1984 book).

We regard *Stakeholders: Theory and Practice* as 'updating' Freeman (1984) in that we provide a summary of the development of the stakeholder concept up to 2005. This involves much more attention being devoted to developments of the concept, particularly since 1984, and to an assessment of the extent to which the concept has been put into practice and has influenced policymaking and management education. The latter issues were not addressed by Freeman (1984) largely because they postdate his book. What emerges from *Stakeholders: Theory and Practice* is a complex statement of a multifarious stakeholder concept, replete with different philosophical underpinnings, many definitions of the term stakeholder, diverse implications for management practice, as well as implications for stakeholder strategies and actions and for policymakers. The contribution of *Stakeholders: Theory and Practice* is not, as for Freeman (1984), to provide a clear statement of the concept with clear implications for management strategy, but rather to provide a clear statement of this fundamental variety, via various methods and models, which allow the field to be ordered and more easily understood, and allow more considered judgements to be made on the diverse components of the field.

An underlying reason for *Strategic Management: A Stakeholder Approach* was the turbulence Freeman detected in the situation of US business in the early 1980s: accelerated mergers and acquisitions; recognition of new and powerful competitors from abroad, particularly Japan; and increased pressures at home on US corporations from employees, environmentalists, the media, consumer groups, and other special interest groups. The stakeholder concept was presented as an important potential remedy for these ills. An underlying reason for *Stakeholders: Theory and Practice* is turbulence in the stakeholder field, due to the variety of competing and complementary formulations and of derived implications from different contributors (due to the popularity of the stakeholder concept). This popularity has been driven not only by further development of many of the issues 'on the ground' that Freeman was responding to (continued globalization and sensitization of stakeholders, and particularly the media, to organization–stakeholder relations), but also by new issues in practice, arising from the manner in which organizations have responded to the call for stakeholder management. In consequence, the stakeholder concept is presented here as a relatively mature field of thought, practice, and policy where clarity in ordering the field is what we believe is required and what we have attempted to provide.

The plethora of stakeholder theories and practices are classified along specific dimensions using models in the form of figures. Concepts underlying the many stakeholder theories, as well as brief examples of stakeholder practice, are clearly set out in the form of vignettes. We have emphasized exposition at the expense of critique of existing stakeholder theory and practice. However, occasionally we have provided a critical perspective, such as on the convergence debate (Section 5.3). Finally, at the end of each chapter we have provided a set of questions/exercises. By and large, these are broad and rather difficult questions to answer. We offer them as possible essay and dissertation topics for students as well as pointers towards future directions of stakeholder research.

☐ CONTENTS

☐ LIST OF FIGURES

◻ LIST OF TABLES

☐ LIST OF VIGNETTES

☐ LIST OF ABBREVIATIONS

ABI	Association of British Insurers
ACCA	Association of Chartered Certified Accountants
AGM	Annual general meeting
AI	Amnesty International
AICPA	American Institute of Certified Public Accountants
AIDS	Acquired immunodeficiency syndrome
ALPA	Airline Pilots Association
ASAP	As soon as possible
ASSC	Accounting Standards Steering Committee
AT&T	American Telephone and Telegraph Company
BBC	British Broadcasting Corporation
BiC	Business in the Community
BiE	Business in the Environment
BITF	Business Impact Task Force
BP	British Petroleum
BSC	Balanced scorecard
BSE	Bovine spongiform encephalopathy
BT	British Telecom
CAFÉ	Coffee And Farmer Equity
CalPERS	California Public Employees' Retirement System
CBS	Columbia Broadcasting System
CEFIC	European Chemical Industry Council Reporting
CEO	Chief executive officer
CERES	Coalition for Environmentally Responsible Economies
CESER	Corporate Environmental, Social, and Ethical Reporting
CFC	Chlorofluorocarbons
CFO	Chief financial officer
CFS	Co-operative Financial Services (UK)
CICA	Canadian Institute of Chartered Accountants

CII	Council of Institutional Investors
CRPB	Caux Roundtable Principles for Business
CSP	Corporate social performance
CSR	Corporate social responsibility
CSX	Chessie Seaboard Multiplier (railroad transportation company)
CTC	Centre for Tomorrow's Company
DEFRA	Department for the Environment and Rural Affairs
DTI	Department for Trade and Industry
EDF	Environmental Defense Fund
EFQM	Excellence For Quality Management
EII	Earth Island Institute
EIRIS	Ethical Investment Research Information Services
EMAS	Eco-Management Audit Scheme
EPA	Environmental Protection Agency
EPE	European Partners for the Environment
ERA	Environmental Reporting Awards
ESS	Enron Energy Services
ETI	Ethical Trading Initiative
EU	European Union
GEC	General Electric Company
GEMI	Global Environmental Management Initiative
GM	Genetically modified
GMB	General Municipal Boilermakers, a British trade union
GRI	Global Reporting Initiative
GSK	GlaxoSmithKline
GSP	Global Sullivan Principles
FTSE	Financial Times Stock Exchange
HRM	Human resource management
IAM	International Association of Machinists (US trade union)
IASB	International Accounting Standards Board
IASC	International Accounting Standards Committee
IBM	International Business Machines
ICC	International Chamber of Commerce
IFA	Independent Financial Advisers
IiP	Investors in People

ILO	International Labour Organization
ISCT	Integrative Social Contracts Theory
ISEA	Institute for Social and Ethical AccountAbility
ISO	International Organisation for Standarisation
JEDI	Joint Energy Development Initiative
KLD	Kinder, Lydenberg, Domini, and Company
KPI	Key performance indicator
LBG	London Benchmarking Group
LJM	A Special Purpose Entity created at Enron
M&S	Marks & Spencer
MBA	Masters in Business Administration
MEB	Management Institute for Environment and Business
MIT	Massachusetts Institute of Technology
MNE	Multinational enterprise
NGO	Non-governmental organization
OECD	Organization for Economic Co-operation and Development
OFR	Operating and Financial Review
ORR	Office of the Rail Regulator
OXERA	Oxford Economic Research Associates
PCAOB	Public Company Accounting Oversight Board
P/E	Market Price to Earnings Ratio
PERI	Public Environmental Reporting Initiative
PESTEL	Political, Economic, Social, Technological, Environmental and Legal
PIRC	Pensions & Investment Research Consultants
PP	Pollution Probe
PR	Public Relations
RADP	Reactive–accommodative–defensive–proactive
RSA	Royal Society for Arts
SA8000	Social Accountability 8000
SEC	Securities and Exchange Commission
SIGMA	Sustainability Integrated Guidelines for Management
SME	Small and medium-sized enterprises
SPE	Special Purpose Entities
SRI	Socially responsible investment
SWOT	Strengths, weaknesses, opportunities, and threats

TNS   The Natural Step
UK   United Kingdom
UKSIF   United Kingdom Social Investment Forum
UN   United Nations
UNCTAD   United Nations Conference on Trade and Development
UNEP   United Nations Environmental Programme
UNGC   United Nations Global Compact
WBCSD   World Business Council for Sustainable Development
WWF   World Wide Fund for Nature (formerly World Wildlife Fund)

☐ ACKNOWLEDGEMENTS

The authors would like to thank Penelope Simons and Christina Willliams who read all or parts of the manuscript and made useful suggestions. We would also like to thank our 'public' offices in Bristol: the Boston Tea Party, Cattleman Restaurant, J. J. Bean and Quartier Vert.

1 Introduction

1.1 **The stakeholder concept**

The classic definition of a stakeholder is 'any group or individual who can affect or is affected by the achievement of the organization's objectives' (Freeman 1984: 46).[1] At its broadest and most ambitious the stakeholder concept represents a redefinition of all organizations: how they should be conceptualized and what they should be. The organization itself should be thought of as a grouping of stakeholders and the purpose of the organization should be to manage their interests, needs and viewpoints. In so doing, a particular group of stakeholders—(top-level) managers—are thought of as the focal group, charged with fulfilling the role of stakeholder management. The concept was elaborated by Evan and Freeman (1993: 82) as the following two principles:

1. *Principle of corporate legitimacy.* The corporation should be managed for the benefit of its stakeholders: its customers, suppliers, owners, employees, and local communities. The rights of these groups must be ensured, and, further, the groups must participate, in some sense, in decisions that substantially affect their welfare.

2. *The stakeholder fiduciary principle.* Management bears a fiduciary relationship (Vignette 1.1) to stakeholders and to the corporation as an abstract entity. It must act in the interests of the stakeholders as their agent, and it must act in the interests of the corporation to ensure the survival of the firm, safeguarding the long-term stakes of each group.

Vignette 1.1 WHAT ARE FIDUCIARY DUTIES?

Fiduciary duties are duties of one who holds something in trust, according to the *Oxford English Dictionary*. The duties required are honesty, adequate care for that which is entrusted, and transparency and trust that the fiduciary will avoid personal gain or harm to the beneficiary (Marens and Wicks 1999). This is most commonly associated with the relationship between management and shareholders. Unlike other agents who provide the corporation with various types of capital, contracts or other forms of safeguards do not protect shareholders (due to their claim being residual and not relating to specific assets) rendering their investment open to greater risk. Consequently, fiduciary duties are imposed on managers to protect the shareholders as legal owners who are not in a position to manage their own affairs. Legally, the relationship is not with the shareholder but with the shareholder's investment.

The definition of a stakeholder, the characterization of the organization and its purpose, characterizations of the role that managers do take on or should take on are all contested, even within the 'camp' of those who would consider themselves to be proponents of the stakeholder concept. Freeman uses a different definition of stakeholders as 'those groups who are vital to the survival and success of the corporation' (2004: 58) in later work in which the two principles are altered and renamed (2004: 64):

1. *The stakeholder-enabling principle.* Corporations shall be managed in the interests of stakeholders.
2. *The principle of director responsibility.* Directors of the corporation shall have a duty of care to use reasonable judgement to define and direct the affairs of the corporation in accordance with the stakeholder-enabling principle.

He adds a further principle, which reflects a relatively new tendency in stakeholder theory, i.e. to consider the stakeholder concept from the perspective of the stakeholders themselves and their activities (2004: 64):

The principle of stakeholder recourse. Stakeholders may bring an action against the directors for failure to perform the required duty of care.

These elaborations of the stakeholder concept are versions of *normative* stakeholder theory, meaning theories of how managers (and sometimes stakeholders) should act and should view the purpose of the organization, based on some ethical principle. There are other approaches to the stakeholder concept. Some are concerned with how managers and stakeholders actually behave and how they view their actions and roles. These have been labelled as *descriptive* stakeholder theory. Some are concerned with how managers should act if they are to further their own interests or what theorists conceive as the interests of the organization, usually viewed as (long-run) profit maximization or maximization of stockholder value. This strategic approach is generally based on what has been called *instrumental* stakeholder theory, which is the proposition that if managers treat stakeholders in line with the stakeholder concept, then the organization will be more successful or more likely to be sustainable. This three-way categorization of approaches to the stakeholder concept was popularized by Donaldson and Preston (1995). Relations among these ways of elaborating the stakeholder concept have been subject to considerable debate in the academic literature. This is discussed in Chapters 2 and 5. A discussion of the range of stakeholder definitions and the range of groups included in the definition follows in Section 1.3.

1.2 Context of the stakeholder concept and its popularity

Interest in the concept of stakeholders among academics has burgeoned in recent years. Donaldson and Preston (1995: 65) noted that a dozen books and more than 100 articles primarily concerned with the stakeholder concept had appeared. Since then interest in the stakeholder concept has quickened even further. Simply type out the word stakeholders in a search engine such as Google Scholar and you will find more than 100,000 references.[2] Several issues of notable journals have been devoted to elaborating and debating the stakeholder concept (*Business Ethics Quarterly*, 1994: 4/4; 2002: 12/2; *Critical Perspectives in Accounting*, 1998: 9/2; *Academy of Management Review*, 1999: 24/2; *Academy of Management Journal*, 1999: 42/5). The stakeholder concept has also grown in popularity among policymakers, regulators, non-governmental organizations (NGOs), business, and the media (Section 2.5).

Many contributors to the stakeholder concept have made their contributions (particularly normative contributions) in debate with those who promote the chief rival vision of the corporation and the role of its top managers: the stockholder (shareholder)[3] model, based on ownership. The objective of the corporation is to maximize stockholder value expressed either as maximizing long-run profits, growth, or dividends (though how long this long run should be is debatable). Friedman (1962: 74) argued that this is the 'one and only social responsibility of business' as long as companies keep to the rules of the capitalist game, i.e. 'engage in open and free competition without deception or fraud'. However, this view appears to be giving way to the view that business has wider responsibilities and that those responsibilities are best expressed in terms of the stakeholder concept. A further measure of the popularity of the stakeholder concept has been the recent proliferation of literature broadly contesting the concept and reiterating the view that stakeholder concept promoters have been specifically trying to replace (Argenti 1993, 1997; Sternberg 1997, 2000; Marcoux 2000, 2003) (Section 5.2).

1.3 Stakeholder definitions: profusion and some confusion

Partly in consequence of its popularity, the stakeholder concept has come to be used in a variety of contexts, often with somewhat different definitions of stakeholders. This has led to the concept being criticized as:

- A 'muddling of theoretical bases and objectives' (Donaldson and Preston 1995: 73).
- 'A rather vague and cryptic concept that is open to a wide variety of rather divergent political interpretations' (referring to a vision of a stakeholder society, Hay 1996: 47).
- A 'slippery creature ... used by different people to mean widely different things which happen to suit their arguments' (Weyer 1996: 35).
- The term stakeholding becoming 'content free' meaning 'almost anything the author desires' and the stakeholder debate becoming 'confused' and 'often shallow' in nature (Stoney and Winstanley 2001: 650).

Different literatures adopting different definitions have hampered cross-discipline research and debate. This may be thought of as an example of negative consequences of the elaboration of discourse. Groups of writers come to coalesce around particular social constructions of reality, leading to writers referring to stakeholders without being aware of relevant theoretical issues that have been raised in other literatures. For example, Roberts and Mahoney (2004: 400) criticized accounting researchers who either 'fail to incorporate stakeholder research published in business ethics literature' or 'rely on different versions of stakeholder theory'. They examined 125 accounting studies that use stakeholder language and found that nearly two-thirds 'use the term stakeholder without reference to any version of stakeholder theory'. Writers use the same label to refer to substantially different concepts, for example some use the term 'stakeholders', but are clearly referring only to legitimate stakeholders, without defining legitimacy (Section 5.4.3). Others use a much broader definition. This distinction can have substantial consequences on ethical, strategic, and policy conclusions.

1.3.1 WHAT IS A STAKEHOLDER?

Table 1.1 presents a summary of fifty-five definitions covering seventy-five texts arranged in chronological order.[4] The earliest definition is often credited to an internal memo produced in 1963 by the Stanford Research Institute: 'those groups without whose support the organization would cease to exist'[5] (Freeman, 1984: 31). Similar definitions have been advocated by Bowie (1988), Freeman and Reed (1983), and Näsi (1995). Freeman (2004: 58) has continued to use this definition in a modified form: 'those groups who are vital to the survival and success of the organization'. Clearly, this definition is entirely organization-centric. It is also a stringent definition; it excludes categories of agents that other definitions include.

In what is commonly regarded, at least in academic circles, as seminal stakeholder text, stakeholders are defined as 'any group or individual who can affect or is affected by the achievement of the organization objectives' (Freeman 1984: 46). Table 1.1 gives an indication of the popularity of this definition. This definition is more balanced and

Table 1.1 Stakeholder definitions: chronological

Date	Author	Stakeholder definition
1963	1. Stanford Research Institute	Those groups without whose support the organization would cease to exist
1964	2. Rhenman adopted by: 3. Steadman and Green (1997)	Are depending on the firm in order to achieve their personal goals and on whom the firm is depending for its existence
1965	4. Ansoff (1965a: 34)	The objectives of the firm should be derived balancing the conflicting claims of the various 'stakeholders' in the firm.... The firm has a responsibility to all of these and must configure its objectives so as to give each a measure of satisfaction
1971	5. Ahlstedt and Jahnukainen	Driven by their own interests and goals are participants in a firm, and thus depending on it and for whose sake the firm is depending
1983	6. Freeman and Reed (1983: 91)	Wide: can affect the achievements of an organization's objectives to who is affected by the achievement of an organization's objectives Narrow: on which the organization is dependent for its continual survival
1984	7. Freeman (1984: 46) adopted by: 8. Berman et al. (1999) 9. Burton and Dunn (1996) 10. Calton and Kurland (1995) 11. Frooman (1999) 12. Goodpaster (1991) 13. Greenley and Foxall (1997) 14. Heugens, Van den Bosch, and Van Riel (2002) 15. Jawahar and McLaughlin (2001) 16. Jones and Wicks (1999a) 17. Kujala (2001) 18. Metcalfe (1998) 19. Page (2002) 20. Roberts (1992) 21. Rowley and Moldoveanu (2003) 22. Rowley (1997) 23. Sternberg (1997) 24. Wood and Jones (1995)	Can affect or is affected by the achievements of the organization's objectives
1987	25. Cornell and Shapiro (1987: 5) 26. Freeman and Gilbert	'Claimants' who have 'contracts' Can affect or is affected by business
1988	27. Bowie (1988: 112) 28. Evan and Freeman	Without whose support the organization would cease to exist Have a stake or claim in the firm Benefit from or are harmed by, and whose rights are violated or respected by, corporate actions

(contd.)

Table 1.1 (*contd.*)

Date	Author	Stakeholder definition
1989	29. Alkhafaji (1989: 36)	Groups to whom the corporation is responsible
	30. Carroll	Asserts to have one or more of these kinds of stakes, which range from an interest to a right (legal or moral) to ownership or legal title to the company's assets or property
1990	31. Freeman and Evan	Contract holders
1991	32. Low (1991: 336)	All those who have an interest in the firm's survival
	33. Miller and Lewis (1991: 55)	Stakeholders are people who can help or hurt the corporation
	34. Savage et al. (1991: 61)	Have an interest in the actions of an organization and have the ability to influence it
	35. Thompson, Wartick, and Smith (1991: 209)	In 'relationship with an organization'
1992	36. Hill and Jones (1992: 133)	Constituents who have a legitimate claim on the firm . . . established through the existence of an *exchange relationship*. They supply 'the firm with critical resources (contributions) and in exchange each expects its interests to be satisfied (by inducements)'
	37. Palgrave et al. (1992)	Those whose welfare is tied with a company
1993	38. Brenner (1993: 205)	Having some legitimate, non-trivial relationship with an organization (such as) exchange transactions, action impacts, and moral responsibilities
	39. Carroll (1993: 22)	Individuals or groups with which business interacts who have a stake or vested interest in the firm. Asserts to have or may have more of the kinds of stakes in business . . . may be affected or affect. Power and legitimacy
	40. Starik (1993: 22)	Any naturally occurring entity that affects or is affected by organizational performance
1994	41. Clarkson (1994: 5)	Bear some form of risk as a result of having invested some sort of capital, human or financial, something of value, in a firm . . . [or] . . . are placed at risk as a result of a firm's activities
	42. Freeman (1994 a: 415)	Participants in 'the human process of joint value creation'
	43. Langtry (1994: 433)	The firm is significantly responsible for their well-being or they hold a moral or legal claim on the firm
	44. Mahoney	Passive stakeholders who have a moral claim on the company not to infringe liberties or inflict harm and active stakeholders those whose claims are more in the nature of welfare rights
	45. Schlossberger	Investors who provide specific capital or opportunity capital to a business
	46. Starik (1994: 90)	Can and are making their actual stakes known . . . or might be influenced by, or are potentially influencers of, some organization whether or not this influence is perceived or known
	47. Wicks, Gilbert, and Freeman (1994: 483)	Interact with and give meaning and definition to the corporation

Table 1.1 (*contd.*)

Date	Author	Stakeholder definition
1995	48. Blair	All parties who have contributed inputs to the enterprise and who, as a result, have at risk investments that are highly specialized to the enterprise
	49. Brenner (1995: 76)	Are or which could impact or be impacted by the firm/organization
	50. Calton and Lad	Legitimate claims
	51. Clarkson (1995: 106)	Have, or claim, ownership rights, or interests in a corporation and its activities
	52. Donaldson and Preston (1995: 85)	Those individuals with explicit or implicit contracts with the firm. Identified through the actual or potential harms and benefits that they experience or anticipate experiencing as a result of the firm's actions or inactions
	53. Jones (1995: 407)	Groups and individuals with (*a*) the power to affect the firm's performance and/or (*b*) a stake in the firm's performance
	54. Näsi (1995: 19)	Interact with the firm and thus make its operation possible
1996	55. Gray, Owen, and Adams (1996: 45)	Any human agency that can be influenced by, or can itself influence, the activities of the organization in question
1997	56. Carroll and Näsi (1997: 46)	Any individual or group who affects or is affected by the organization and its processes, activities, and functioning
	57. Mitchell, Agle, and Wood adopted by: 58. Agle, Mitchell, and Sonnenfeld (1999)	Legitimate or urgent claim on the corporation or the power to influence the corporation
	59. Phillips (1997: 63–4)	Voluntary members of a cooperative scheme for mutual benefit . . . partners for the achievement of mutual advantage. A claim (norm) can only be justifiable in the case that it can be approved of by all those affected by the norm
1998	60. Argandoña (1998: 1099)	Those who have an interest in the company (so that the firm, in turn, may have an interest in satisfying their demands)
	61. Frederick (1998: 361)	Everyone in the community who has a stake in what the company does
1999	62. Clarkson Centre for Business Ethics (1999: 257) Adopted by: 63. Whysall (2000)	Parties that have a stake in the corporation: something at risk, and therefore something to gain or lose, as a result of corporate activity
	64. Leader	Have rights that are internally linked to the constitution of the company, which gives them constitutional powers
	65. Reed	Those with 'an interest for which a valid normative claim can be advanced'
2000	66. Gibson (2000: 245)	Those groups or individuals with whom the organization interacts or has interdependencies and any individual or group who can affect or is affected by the actions, decisions, policies, practices, or goals of the organization

(*contd.*)

Table 1.1 (*contd.*)

Date	Author	Stakeholder definition
	67. Kochan and Rubinstein	Contribute valued resources . . . which are put at risk and would experience costs if the firm fails or their relationship with the firm terminates and . . . have power over an organization
	68. Scott and Lane (2000: 53)	A direct influence on organizational performance and survival
2001	69. Hendry	Moral actors . . . relationships cannot be reduced to contractual or economic relations. Include social characteristics such as interdependence
	70. Lampe (2001: 166)	Parties affected by an organization
	71. Ruf et al. (2001: 145)	Constituencies who have explicit or implicit contracts with the firm
2002	72. Cragg	The corporation impacts . . . individuals and collectivities whose interests are thereby affected both negatively and positively
	73. Orts and Strudler (2002: 218)	Participants in a business (who) have some kind of economic stake directly at risk
	74. Reed	Basic stake, whereby stakes can be that of fair economic opportunity, a stake of authenticity, or one of political equality
2003	75. Phillips (2003*a*: 30–1)	Normative stakeholders: for whose benefit should the firm be managed. Derivative stakeholders: potential to affect organization and its normative stakeholders

much broader than that of the Stanford Research Institute. The symmetrical phrase 'can affect or is affected by' opens the idea that 'outside' individuals or groups may consider themselves to be stakeholders of an organization, without the organization considering them to be stakeholders. A group or individuals may consider themselves to be affected by the achievement of organization objectives without 'insiders' in the organization noticing or acknowledging these affects. This definition is also broader in that it specifies individuals as well as groups. In addition, there are many groups that are affected by the achievement of the organization's objectives, but that would not be thought of by anyone as having their support required for the organization to continue to exist. For example, a few individual consumers may be affected by an organization withdrawing an unpopular product from a market in terms of the range of their choice being reduced, or in terms of their real wealth being reduced by having to replace the product with a more expensive item. A few individual employees will certainly be affected by an organization deciding to outsource a small part of its operations. Withdrawal of support for the organization by these relatively small numbers, who would be stakeholders under the Freeman definition, would not cause the organization to cease to exist (unless these groups were joined by a large proportion of the rest of the organization's customers or employees). Similar arguments could be made about suppliers and competitors.

An even broader definition was proposed by Gray, Owen, and Adams (1996: 45): 'any group or individual that can be influenced by, or can itself influence, the activities of the organisation'. Here the activities of an organization can be much more comprehensively considered to be the touchstone to trigger an organization–stakeholder relationship, rather than the more restrictive 'achievement of organization objectives'. This then allows individuals and groups who are affected by unintended consequences of goal-directed activity of the organization, or even by activities that are not related to organization objectives at all, to be embraced as stakeholders. Employees of an organization, for example, may act in ways that are even counter to the organization objectives (as when going on strike or working to rule), and this, in turn, can influence or affect others.

Starik (1994) pushes the definition of stakeholders far beyond that considered by all others. He distinguishes a narrow definition by taking the intersection of a Freeman definition and Carroll's definition (1993: 22): 'individuals or groups with which business interacts who have a 'stake', or vested interest, in the firm'. The resulting narrow definition would limit stakeholders to those who are making their actual stakes known (referring to Hirschman's idea of 'voice' (1970)) *and* who actually influence the organization (Starik 1994: 90). Starik's contribution is in his definition(s) of stakeholders at the broadest end of the spectrum. This he suggests could be 'any naturally occurring entity which affects or is affected by organizational performance' (Starik 1994: 92). Not only does this include living entities: animals and plants; it also includes non-living environmental forms such as rocks and water, as well as systems of such entities including the Sun–Earth system (Gaia) and the cosmos.

Even more imaginatively Starik proposes other non-living entities that can be considered as stakeholders, such as people who have died and those not yet born. Future generations are often brought into discussions of environmental impacts. Starik notes that founders of businesses are often described as having left 'spirits' or legacies and he notes that many non-Western cultures revere dead ancestors. These entities may be said to affect current organizations through this spiritual medium. Another set of non-living entities may be human-transformed objects, such as one's house or 'personal products' in the sense that we give such objects human names and often communicate with them as though they were alive. Here the relation is based on a subjective or value-oriented nature of what may potentially be a stakeholder. Finally, and perhaps most unconventionally, Starik notes that stakeholders may refer to entities that may have no physical form at all. Mental images or archetypes can affect and be affected by our perceptions of the world. He pushes this further to suggest that concepts such as love, honesty, and community could be considered stakeholders in that they can be embodied in physical forms and can affect organizations and people beyond physical form 'as mental–emotional constructs' (Starik 1994: 94). Ideas of success and failure affect organizational morale and behaviour. In this, Starik's definition could be connected to recent work in evolutionary biology on 'memes' (Vignette 1.2).

Vignette 1.2 MEMES

Richard Dawkins is well known for proposing that natural selection proceeds in the interests of genes, rather than the species or the individual organism: the selfish gene. Genes are the true 'replicators' that compete for survival and it is this that drives the evolution of biological design. At the end of his book Dawkins (1976) went further to suggest that there are other 'self-replicating' entities and he suggested a new kind of replicator has recently emerged on Earth: memes. Memes are units of *cultural* transmission. Memes are one of a class of 'slightly inaccurate self-replicating entities'. Given the right conditions they 'automatically band together to create systems, or machines, that carry them around and work to favour their continued replication' (Dawkins 1989: 322). Genes are one kind, memes are another. Genes are instructions for building proteins, stored in cells and passed on by reproduction. Memes are instructions for producing behaviour, stored in a brain and passed on to other brains by imitation (Blackmore 1996). Examples of memes are 'tunes, ideas, catch-phrases, clothes fashions, ways of making pots or of building arches' (Dawkins 1989: 192). Memes propagate by jumping from brain to brain, like parasites or viruses, infecting a host. They band together for mutual assistance. Unlike genes, they can replicate very quickly, and their mutation through the Darwinian process of survival of the fittest, unlike genes, does not require their hosts to die.

As Blackmore conceives of it '*imagine a world full of hosts for memes (i.e. brains) and far more memes than can possibly find homes*. Now ask, which memes are more likely to find a safe home and get passed on again?' Memes that encourage their hosts to keep on mentally rehearsing them (an easy-to-hum tune); that encourage talking; and that encourage their hosts to be friendly and kind are more likely to be successful; i.e. are more likely to be imitated. As with Dawkins' counterintuitive proposition about 'selfish' genes, memes are also 'selfish'; i.e. the Darwinian process of meme evolution does not involve the 'interests' of brains, genes, or host organisms. Survival of memes may not coincide or support survival of host brains or organisms. Meme development may even be detrimental to hosts, as in the case of ideas glorifying patriotism and war, drug use, or suicide.

1.3.2 A MODEL OF STAKEHOLDER DEFINITIONS

Stakeholder definitions generally illuminate the stakeholder concept in two ways. First, they indicate the nature of the connection between organizations and stakeholders. Often this is evident in a verb in the definition. The connecting verb in the Freeman (1984) definition is *affecting*. This is a broad and fairly inactive verb. Other definitions include similarly broad and relatively neutral verbs such as *impact, influence, interact*. However some verbs describe more precisely the nature of the relationship, such as *responsible, support, dependent, provide meaning, risk something of value or invest, harms and benefits, voice* (making stakes known).

Second, the definition may include an adjective or other qualifier or aspect of either the organization or the stakeholder. This can be thought of as leading to a narrowing of the scope of who may be identified as a stakeholder. This narrowing can occur in two ways: strategic or normative.[6] In the Freeman (1984) definition it is the *achievement of the* organization's *objectives* that affects or is affected by stakeholders. This is a strategic narrowing in that the number of stakeholders is limited to those who affect the strategic aims of the organization. Qualifiers such as *legitimate claims* (Calton and Lad 1995) narrow the scope of who may be thought of as a stakeholder using a normative criterion. These aspects of how stakeholder definitions may be distinguished are illustrated in Figure 1.1.

Along the strategic dimension, definitions differ according to a number of factors. We can distinguish definitions with a very high strategic implication that limit stakeholders to those that are critical or affect the very survival or existence of the organization. At the other end are definitions that involve legal or institutional conditions that may force organizations to deal with stakeholders, such as through contracts, explicit or implicit. In the middle are definitions that define stakeholders in terms of their power, influence, or ability to affect the organization.

Along the normative dimension are definitions that differ in their scope either because they embrace everything that one could possibly think of as a stakeholder (including things most people would not think of, such as future generations, rocks, and memes), or because they restrict the scope of stakeholders to reflect societal norms, such as that of legitimacy or validity.[7]

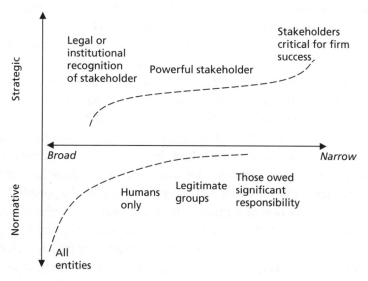

Figure 1.1 Representation of strategic and normative dimensions to the narrowing of stakeholder definitions

The curves are of different shapes.[8] As definitions become narrower in scope, they become more strictly strategic, but less strictly normative. Greater normative claims in a definition imply a wider range of entities included as stakeholders, but in the more specifically strategic definitions, a more limited range of entities are included as stakeholders. The curvature of the strategic curve has a long flat portion reflecting a wide range of the number of stakeholders that can be included in strategic definitions that concentrate on the importance of power for organization attention to stakeholders. Power can be defined in many ways, some include few stakeholder groups, some many (Section 4.6).

The curves are in different positions along the narrow/broad dimension. Strategic definitions occupy a narrower range (right side of the figure) because they tend to be more restrictive in scope both because they are inherently organization-centric and because they involve various ways of specifying those particular stakeholders that can/should be linked to strategic goals. Normative definitions tend to be broader (a range to the left side of the figure) in that they are more likely to be de-centred from the organization and because they aim to draw attention to categories of potential stakeholders that may be overlooked in current organization practice.

There is a third aspect of the definitions that allows them to be distinguished. This is whether the connection proposed between organizations and stakeholders is symmetrical. The first part of the Freeman (1984) definition, *affect and affected by*, is symmetrical. The second part is not. Stakeholders are defined in terms of the achievement of organization objectives. It is not assumed that they determine the organization's objectives, and, furthermore, it is not assumed that the organization–stakeholder relation concerns stakeholder objectives, which might be independent of the connection with the focal organization. Other definitions are more symmetrical.

The Alkhafaji (1989) definition may be thought of as strategically asymmetrical in the opposite direction. It is a relatively narrow definition compared with the Freeman or Gray definitions in that one can imagine a wide range of individuals or groups to which those running the organization do not consider the organization to be accountable or responsible to, but who may be affected or influenced by the organization. This definition introduces a normative element into the very definition of stakeholders. This definition is broader than the Stanford definition in that it leaves it open as to whether it is the organization that decides whether it is accountable or responsible to particular individuals or groups, or if that decision is made by the potential stakeholders themselves, or if the question of legitimacy is determined at a 'higher' level still, at the level of society as a whole. If the latter, it may be that some individuals or groups who think the organization ought to be accountable to them may not be included because this accountability is not accepted widely enough in society. This could work the other way, with some groups not considering themselves as warranting the organization's attention in this manner; but powerful or influential groups in society such as in the

oups, have a general view that the organization owards these groups. For example, members of emselves to be at risk from certain polluting of pollution are not noticeable may be con- vledge of potential damage, due to experiences t agencies may consider these businesses as mation on the risk of pollution occurring to community appreciate the danger.

?

iitions of what are stakeholders and identifica- st common way of classifying stakeholders is to guishable relationship with corporations. The be considered are:

- Shareholders
- Customers
- Suppliers and distributors
- Employees
- Local communities

A key issue is whether stakeholders are confined to those that are crucial for the achievement of corporate objectives or if they are merely any entity affected by corporate actions, especially if the latter includes alternative actions corporations could have taken in order to achieve their objectives, but were not chosen. The latter can lead to a very wide definition of stakeholders. Freeman and Reed (1983) and Freeman (2004) actually label these definitions separately: narrow and wide. Freeman's stakeholder-enabling principle, based on the narrow definition, was stated to apply only to 'stakeholders defined as employees, financiers, customers, and communities'.

Almost all can be considered as affected in some way by many things a corporation might do in order to achieve its objectives. Many types of individuals and groups have been considered to be stakeholders, in addition to those listed above, including:

- Stakeholder representatives such as trade unions or trade associations of suppliers or of distributors
- NGOs or 'activists' that have been considered individually or as stakeholder repre- sentatives

- Competitors
- Government(s), regulators, and other policymakers
- Financiers other than stockholders (creditors, bondholders, debt providers)
- The media
- The public in general
- Non-human aspects of the Earth, the natural environment
- Business partners
- Academics
- Future generations
- Past generations (in particular the memory of founders of organizations)
- Archetypes or 'memes' (Vignette 1.2)

Managers are treated in various ways in the literature. For many they are regarded as stakeholders, but with special access to focal organization resources. For others they are treated as the embodiment of the focal organization's actions and responsibilities. Aoki (1984) saw managers not as stakeholders but as referees between investors and employees.

Much of stakeholder theory is concerned with identifying different ways of segmenting the range of possible stakeholders in order to distinguish different ways corporations ought to deal with stakeholders in each segment, especially primary and secondary stakeholder groups, and groups to whom the organization owes fiduciary and non-fiduciary obligations (section 3.5.1). Donaldson and Preston (1995: 83) argue that it is important to distinguish between influencers and stakeholders. Some actors in the firm may be both (stockholders), some may be recognizable as stakeholders but have no influence (job applicants), while others may have influence but no stake (media).

The number of categories of stakeholder groups identified here is limited by the broad way in which the groups have been defined. The category of employees, for example, can usefully be defined more finely as white-collar and blue-collar, trade unionists and non-trade unionists, permanent or temporary, full-time or part-time, or in terms of which plant or section they work in. Different subcategories of employees may have different interests, identities, claims, and other characteristics. Strategically, organizations may clearly treat different subcategories of employees differently based on differential power. Normatively, the line of legitimacy may run between different employee categories, rather than between the crude category of employees compared with other crude groupings.

An advantage of finer stakeholder categories is that they are likely to embrace more homogeneous groupings of people. A limitation in considering finer categories is that the chances of overlap of interests and actions will be greater (Sections 4.2.6 and 4.5.2).

☐ QUESTIONS/EXERCISES

1 Can you think of other ways of classifying the definitions presented in Table 1.1?

2 Take ten of the definitions from Table 1.1 and plot them on Figure 1.1. Explain why you placed them where you did.

3 Can you think of any examples of different literatures adopting different definitions of the stakeholder concept? What are the implications of these differences?

4 Can you find other examples of a fractured literature or definition confusion holding back fields of study? To what extent do you think this is an inevitable consequence of the popularity of a field of study?

5 Consider the broad category of suppliers. Develop a set of subcategories that could be clearly distinguished by differential power and legitimacy. Consider other criteria for distinguishing subcategories of suppliers in terms of strategic or normative stakeholder definitions.

☐ NOTES

1 We begin with a brief summary of the stakeholder concept in order to introduce the issues dealt with in this book. It is not possible to give a brief categorical summary of the concept that would be universally accepted due to its contested nature. Nevertheless, Freeman's 1984 definition is most often quoted (Table 1.1), even though it has been criticized. Similarly, Evan and Freeman's elaborations of the concept in 1988 and 1993 editions of Beauchamp and Bowie's text *Ethical Theory and Business*, and Freeman's elaborations in later editions of Beauchamp and Bowie, are widely quoted.

2 We did this on 18 July 2005 and 112,000 references were displayed. We also typed in stakeholder theory and 17,400 references were displayed.

3 The British literature refers to stockholders as shareholders. We use the terms interchangeably here.

4 Only the first publication of a definition used by an author is included.

5 Dodd (1932) uses the phrase 'have an interest in' and Dill (1958) uses 'an influence on managerial autonomy' but they do not specifically identify their phrases as a definition of 'stakeholders', rather they are definitions of a concept that later writers have identified with the stakeholder concept.

6 The normative/strategic distinction is not absolute. Several definitions involve verbs that could be interpreted as normative, in the sense of norms rather than moral values. They may also be thought of as strategic in that it is in the interests of organizations to take into account groups that have a claim based on a socially recognized norm.

7 We have dealt with two out of the three attributes of stakeholders in the well-known definition of Mitchell, Agle, and Wood (1997): power and legitimacy (see Section 4.2.5). Their third attribute, urgency, cannot be easily demonstrated in this framework. On one hand, it may reflect a normative definition, i.e. stakeholders are those that show they are in need; however, many would disagree that such agents 'should' be recognized if they are not also legitimate. On the other hand, many organizations indeed deal with agents who demonstrate urgency as a matter of strategy; however, it is arguable that this is an effective strategy.

8 Both relationships are monotonic, but not linear.

Part I

Theory and Theoretical Issues

Theory has been very important in the stakeholder field. The history of the stakeholder concept has been expressed primarily in theoretical terms, usually with a strong normative emphasis. However, the boundaries between different theories and variants of theories are unclear. In Chapter 1 we presented a widely accepted version of the basic stakeholder concept. It is our contention that this represents a very small area of agreement. This proposition is demonstrated by the enormous number of definitions of stakeholders that have been propagated in the literature, as seen in the fifty-five different definitions gleaned from seventy-five different contributions to the literature (see Table 1.1). While there is some agreement on the basic stakeholder concept, just as there is some agreement on one definition (of the seventy-five contributions seventeen adopted one particular definition), there are a multitude of stakeholder theories. In Chapters 2, 3, and 4 we examine and compare over thirty stakeholder theories, as well as several alternative stockholder/shareholder theories and some that are arguably combinations of the two. In order to allow theories to be compared and thereby contribute both to a better understanding of the stakeholder concept and to an understanding of how the stakeholder concept could change management practice, we have organized our exposition of stakeholder theories along several dimensions.

In Chapter 2 we consider stakeholder theory in historical terms, with a focus on the pivotal contribution of Freeman (1984). The chapter ends with a major case study that demonstrates how strongly certain current issues in stakeholder theory have been debated in the past. We also introduce and explain a fundamental distinction that frames much stakeholder theory and discussions of stakeholder theories: between normative, instrumental, and descriptive stakeholder theory. We use this distinction to organize the description of theories presented in Chapters 3 and 4 and we critically evaluate this classification system in Chapter 5. In Chapters 3 and 4 we further distinguish stakeholder theories on dimensions that we believe will help the reader understand the extent to which stakeholder theory has developed, and crucially to gain an insight into directions along which the stakeholder concept may be developed in future. One important set of dimensions we consider is what may be called the nature of 'normativity' along which we distinguish different normative stakeholder theories. In considering normativity we also connect normative stakeholder theories to different basic philosophical traditions. Another critical distinction we pursue is among theories that address responsibilities and strategies managers of organizations should or could take towards stakeholders, those that consider responsibilities and strategies of the stakeholders, and theories that concentrate on the organization–stakeholder relationship itself.

Theories distinguished in Part I are used to guide examination of practice and policy issues in Parts II and III.

2 History and the nature of stakeholder theorizing

2.1 Introduction

Freeman is generally credited with popularizing the stakeholder concept, with his 1984 book *Strategic Management: A Stakeholder Approach*. It is often recognized that the word stakeholder first appeared in management literature via an internal memo at the Stanford Research Institute in 1963. Schilling (2000) argues that the field predates this by over sixty years due to a startling similarity between that stakeholder concept and the work of Follet (1918). Here we consider a concern about the corporation, which emerged along with the origins of the corporation as a legal entity: the soulless corporation. This identifies a moral or normative vacuum that has stimulated ideas of how this could or should be dealt with. The stakeholder concept has emerged as a leading contender to fill this vacuum. We then explore more recent precursors of the stakeholder concept as a way of thinking about how corporations interact with other entities or agents in society. In doing so we distinguish between pre- and post-Freeman (1984), paying particular attention to the concept of corporate social responsibility (CSR). Finally, we explore ideas that may help us understand why the stakeholder concept became so popular during the last two decades of the twentieth century.

2.2 The soulless corporation

Arguably, from the inception of the corporation as an autonomous legal entity, the need for a stakeholder concept has been mooted. As far back as the seventeenth century at least, jurists were concerned about the relationship between the corporation as a separate legal entity and the corporation as an artificial person. According to Lord Edward Coke (1613) corporations 'cannot commit treason, nor be outlawed nor excommunicated, for they have no souls'. The concern that corporations have great power, but no mechanism for identifying responsibility and responsible behaviour, has been expressed many times. In the eighteenth century Lord Thurlow (1731–1806), Lord Chancellor of England, stated: 'Corporations have neither bodies to be punished, nor souls to be condemned, they therefore do as they like' (Stainer 2004: 334). In 1822 Hazlitt stated: 'Corporate bodies are more corrupt and profligate than individuals, because they have more power to do mischief, and are less amenable to disgrace or punishment. They feel neither shame, remorse, gratitude, nor good will' (Hazlitt 1910: 359). Almost a century later Woodrow Wilson, prior to his inauguration as the US President, stated:

If the corporation is doing the things it ought not to do, you really have no voice in the matter and must obey the orders, and you have oftentimes with deep mortification to co-operate in the doing of things which you know are against the public interest. Your individuality is swallowed up in the individuality and purpose of a great organization. . . . The truth is, we are all caught up in a great economic system which is heartless. The modern corporation is not engaged in business as an individual. When we deal with it, we deal with an impersonal element, an immaterial piece of society. (1913: 3–7)

The potential for powerful corporations to do mischief to real people, combined with their lack of inherent moral sense, lack of a soul or 'feelings' for the consequences of their actions on others, such as shame, remorse, or gratitude, has eventually led the representatives of society to impose limits on their power. Three solutions have been suggested.

1. *Market competition.* Adam Smith (1776, 1790) is associated with the view that competitive forces (the invisible hand) can be relied upon to provide a limit to corporate power. This remedy encouraged submergence of these concerns with periodic reinvigoration of liberal ideals during the nineteenth and twentieth centuries, for example, the emergence of neoclassical economics at the end of the nineteenth century (Jevons 1871/ 1970; Walras 1874; Marshall 1890/1910), again after the Second World War through Samuelson (1947), and more recently during the late 1970s and 1980s with the neo-liberal revival of the philosophies of Schumpeter (1934) and Friedman (1962). These ideas underpin the critique of stakeholder theory as expressed more recently by Argenti (1993, 1997) and Sternberg (1997). It is not that these writers do not recognize a danger to society from powerful soulless corporations, rather they contend that corporations do not need souls as long as they are controlled by competition in markets for products, resources, and finance. They can, through competitive financial markets, be kept to their simple mission: to act in the interests of their shareholders. Their power, which might have allowed them to act in ways that would be harmful to society, is limited through competitive markets for products and resources.

2. *Legal sanctions.* The power, scope, or freedom of action of soulless corporations to do 'mischief' can be prohibited through legal sanction. This is necessary if one believes that markets do not 'naturally' tend towards perfect or near-perfect competition. There are two ways legal sanctions can be applied. First, specific abuses may be prohibited. For example, through the law of contract suppliers can be protected from abuses, such as being coerced into accepting unfavourable terms through all conditions of the contract

not being revealed or through intimidation. Second, something like high competition can be imposed by breaking up large firms that could acquire monopoly power, and by removing restrictions on the factors that underlie perfect competition (perfect mobility and perfect information). The problem with this approach is that legal sanctions leading to constraints on the freedom of corporations to act in certain ways must be expressed in very general terms.

3. *Corporate social responsibility*.[1] Society can insist that soulless corporations behave as though they have a soul, or at least that their managers behave as if they are the guardians of a putative soul of the corporation. The concept of CSR was encouraged by the upheaval of the Great Depression and the Second World War and further developed to counter the devastating consequences of imbalance of corporate power such as environmental degradation, unhealthy and even deadly consumer products, inhumane working conditions, and so on (Logsdon and Wood 2002). Despite criticisms, CSR has spotlighted moral issues in business and has raised consciousness. Clarkson (1995) suggests that it is clearly possible for social issues to be widely considered by corporations without it becoming the subject of legislation or regulation, but suggests that this is an unstable situation and that in the long run legislation or regulation will be implemented.

2.3 Early uses of the stakeholder concept (pre-Freeman 1984)

The Stanford Research Institute internal memo of 1963 led to the stakeholder *label* appearing in publications of researchers who were working for Lockheed and who were associated with the Stanford Institute (Rhenman 1964; Ansoff 1965*a*). It is also clear that business leaders were expressing the stakeholder *concept* long before the early 1960s. Dodd (1932) cites GEC as identifying four major groups it needs to deal with during the 1930s (shareholders, employees, customers, and the general public). Similarly, Preston and Sapienza (1990: 362) cite Johnson & Johnson as identifying customers, employees, managers, and the general public in 1947, and Sears listing 'four parties to any business in the order of their importance' as 'customers, employees, community, and stockholders' in 1950.

2.3.1 CORPORATE SOCIAL RESPONSIBILITY

Many of the issues discussed under the label of stakeholder theory were being developed earlier under the label of CSR or corporate social performance (CSP) and have consequently influenced stakeholder theorizing. For Johnson (1971) social responsibility in reference to firms concerns the balancing of a multiplicity of stakeholder interests. For Davis (1973: 313):

Social responsibility begins where the law ends. A firm is not being socially responsible if it merely complies with the minimum requirements of the law, because this is what any good citizen would do.

The roots of modern CSR date back to the 1930s.[2] Carroll (1979: 497) credits the first definitive book on CSR to Bowen (1953). Berle and Means (1932) and Dodd (1932) also made significant early contributions. Berle and Means advocated that corporate property should be considered as public or at least 'quasi-public' property (1932: 6). While they were concerned with shareholder and property rights, there were others who wanted to go further. Berle (1931) claimed that the ability of shareholders to effectively exercise their property rights was being compromised by the growth of passive shareholding and the growth in the power of major corporations. Consequently, he argued that the responsibility of managers to shareholders needed to be shored up. In debate with Berle, Dodd proposed a very early version of normative stakeholder theory (Section 2.7).

Carroll (1979: 500) has been a major contributor to the field of CSR. For him the 'social responsibility of business encompasses the economic, legal, ethical, and discretionary expectations that society has of organizations at a given point in time'. These are ordered in his model in terms of their 'role in the evolution of importance', i.e. early emphasis was on economic concerns, then legal, then ethical, and most recently on discretionary or volitional responsibilities:

1. *Discretionary*—society has no clear-cut message for business, but there are expectations that businesses should assume voluntary social roles such as philanthropic contributions, in-house programmes for drug abusers, day care for working mothers.
2. *Ethical*—expected of business but not codified in law and ill-defined.
3. *Legal*—thought of as partial fulfilment of the social contract.
4. *Economic*—to produce goods and services that society wants and to sell them at a profit.

Carroll's model (1979: 497) was complex and in his view, 'comprehensively described essential aspects of corporate social performance'. It contained three dimensions:

1. Categories of social responsibility
2. Issues for which a social responsibility exists
3. A specification of the philosophy of response to the issues

Carroll (1979: 501) accepted that social issues change and differ by industry, and suggested that this was a reason why the 'issues approach' to business and society gave way to managerial approaches 'that are more concerned with developing or specifying generalized modes of response to all social issues that become significant to the firm'.

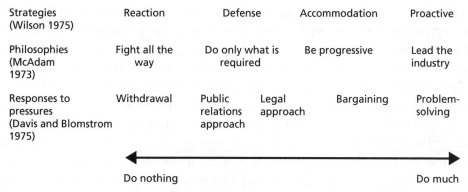

Figure 2.1 Social responsiveness strategies/philosophies/responses
Source: Adapted from Carrol (1979: 502).

Nevertheless Carroll, rather arbitrarily, noted the following social issues: consumerism; the environment; discrimination; product safety; occupational safety, and shareholders.

For his third dimension Carroll took four philosophies and strategies of response from the literature of the mid-1970s, and placed them on to a continuum based on the degree of responsiveness to the issues (Figure 2.1). From the extreme of 'do nothing' to the extreme of 'do much', the four categories ranged from *Reaction* to *Defense* to *Accommodation* to *Proaction*. The labels came from Wilson (1975) who calls them business strategies. Neatly following these are what McAdam (1973) considered to be four social responsibility philosophies, and roughly corresponding to them are what Davis and Blomstrom (1975) called alternative responses to societal pressures. The categories, issues, and response philosophies were then put into a three-dimensional grid. This model was tested by Aupperle, Carroll, and Hatfield (1985) and Clarkson (1995) and developed by Wood (1991).

These ideas have recurred in articles specifically identified as stakeholder literature. Several models discussed in Chapters 3 and 4 owe elements to this model.

2.3.2 MANAGEMENT AND CORPORATE STRATEGY

In the 1970s the stakeholder concept was mainly used in the strategic management literature. Arguably, this was in reaction to upheavals among students, workers, environmentalists, and consumer groups in the 1960s. Freeman (1984) notes that some predicted that shareholder influence would diminish, as companies would also be run for the benefit of other stakeholders (Taylor 1971). Haselhoff (1976) examined the implications of this change on the way management acted within corporations, notably the way organizational goals were formulated, whereas King and Cleland (1978) developed a method for analysing 'clientele groups', 'claimants', or 'stakeholders'.

During the 1970s strategy became closely connected to planning in the literature. The strategy process was conceived as a process whereby organizational capabilities and business environment[3] opportunities and threats were analysed and the results compared with corporate plans and forecasts (Utterback 1979; Porter 1980). One way of thinking about the development of this field is to view the planning process as becoming increasingly sensitive to the business environment and the need for good information about it. At that time the Stanford Research Institute called for information systems to scan and track stakeholder responses to changes in corporate strategy as part of this environment. It developed 'measures of satisfaction' for the stakeholder groups identified. Freeman (1984: 35) noted that a key feature of the use of the stakeholder concept in corporate planning was reactive, i.e. planners did not attempt to influence specific stakeholder behaviour, only to forecast the future environment (which was relatively static and predictable at that time according to Freeman) in order to match it with organizational capabilities.

Freeman concluded that prior to his book, the strategic planning literature only considered stakeholders in exceptional circumstances, and even then, only crudely, as generic groups, and only legitimate or friendly stakeholders. Adversarial groups were not considered at all. Mainstream strategic planning developed simplistic formulae for considering the environment that largely ignored stakeholders, such as strengths, weaknesses, opportunities, and threats (SWOT) analysis (Porter 1980), distinctive competencies (Andrews 1980), and the Boston Consulting Group's classification (stars, question marks/problem children, cash cows, and dogs) based on market growth rates and market share (Rothschild 1976; Henderson 1979).

Ansoff was an interesting exception. He was a key contributor to the strategy literature during the 1960s and 1970s and was part of the Lockheed–Stanford nexus that produced the initial stakeholder definition. Freeman notes that Ansoff (1965a) clearly distanced himself from stakeholder theory by distinguishing between the objectives of the corporation and responsibilities and constraints on it. Top managers accept that corporations have responsibilities, but this was not the same as corporations having an objective to satisfy the needs or desires of those to whom the firm has a responsibility. Ansoff defines *objectives* as 'decision rules which enable management to guide and measure the firm's performance towards its purpose' and *responsibilities* as 'obligations which the firm undertakes to discharge' and not 'part of the firm's internal guidance and control mechanism'. Using the example of the Ford Foundation, which is administered separately from Ford Motor Company, he concluded that such responsibilities are not imposed on the corporation, but are voluntary and arise from the attitudes of the individuals who control the corporation. Ansoff also distinguished *constraints*, defined as 'decision rules which exclude certain options from the corporation's freedom actions' such as a minimum wage level. Only if the corporation chooses to raise this level above what is legally required or above the level negotiated with the union does it become an objective of the corporation (1965*a*: 38). Consequently, he explicitly rejects what he regards as a stakeholder theory of objectives and does not accept that the corporation *must* configure its objectives to meet these responsibilities. This argument appeared twenty-six years later in the stakeholder literature (Goodpaster 1991).

2.4 Freeman (1984): the pivotal contribution to the stakeholder literature

While Freeman (1984) did not invent the term or concept of stakeholders, his contribution was to express it in a forceful and comprehensive manner, arguing that it could/ should be used to revise the entire view of the corporation. Freeman's book is titled *Strategic Management* and only subtitled *A Stakeholder Approach*, indicating that his view of the stakeholder concept was from the perspective of the organization. He argued that a stakeholder approach to strategic management was needed in 1984 because organizations were experiencing turbulence:

Gone are the 'good old days' of worrying only about taking products and services to market, and gone is the usefulness of management theories which concentrate on efficiency and effectiveness within this product–market framework. (1984: 4)

Freeman (1984: 28) acknowledges, in a footnote, that this is a 'tremendous oversimplification of the issues. Business has always dealt with non-marketplace stakeholders...' He presses on in his opening chapter to link the turbulence organizations are 'now facing' with the need for a new management paradigm and new concepts. The calls for increased productivity using methods borrowed from Japan or Europe are 'not the answer, for they only add, subtract or refile some of the issues that need addressing' and he believes that 'business–government–labor cooperation are only part of the solution' (1984: 7). Both internal and external change has meant that the model of the organization as a mere 'resource-conversion entity' is no longer appropriate.

Internal change relates to those entities considered to be part of the prevailing managerial view of the organization: owners, customers, employees, and suppliers. For Freeman internal changes included:

- Both a rise in stockholder activism following a reduction in the amount of stock required to lodge a resolution and the increased likelihood of poor performing managers being ousted through takeover bids based on large-scale share transactions in the 1960s.

- A loss of markets to foreign competition judged by some (Hayes and Abernathy 1980) as a lack of attention to product innovation in the USA.
- A younger labour force with different values requiring authoritarian management styles to be replaced with participative styles and an emphasis on managing culture or shared values, rather than concentrating entirely on strategy and structure (Peters and Waterman 1982).
- Politicization in international supply of raw materials such as the influence of the Organization of Petroleum Exporting Countries (OPEC) from its formation in 1960.

External change for Freeman (1984: 11–13) is:

[T]he emergence of new groups, events and issues which cannot be readily understood within the framework of an existing model or theory. . . . It makes us uncomfortable because it cannot be readily assimilated into the relatively more comfortable relationships with suppliers, owners, customers and employees. . . . It originates in the murky area labelled 'environment' and affects our ability to cope with internal changes.

Examples of external change included:

- Expansion of federal, state, and local government activities that affect business since the Second World War, as well as growth of business area activities through the courts, US government agencies, citizen initiatives, effects of foreign governments, and quasi-agencies such as the World Bank.
- Increase in foreign competition.
- The 1960s consumer movement stimulated by Kennedy's 'Consumer Bill of Rights', which encouraged consumers to pursue what Hirschman (1970) calls voice rather than exit responses to dissatisfaction with products and services.
- The 1960s environmentalist movement associated with the publication of Rachel Carson's *The Silent Spring* (1962) and the formation of the Environmental Protection Acts.
- Growth of groups concerned with special interests such as gun control or abortion became more influential through changes in communication technology and the financing of elections. The media also became more prominent in business life, exposing business practices.

Overall, these changes add up to the need for a new model of the organization. Freeman likens the conceptual shift needed to the one that occurred with the recognition of the separation of ownership from control of corporations stimulated by the work of Berle (1931) and Berle and Means (1932). He illustrates his view of the firm with the now very common hub-and-spokes picture (Figure 2.2). Stakeholder groups are represented by circles at the ends of the spokes emanating from the firm. Managers are not accorded a circle as at least those who act as strategists for the firm are assumed to be within the hub

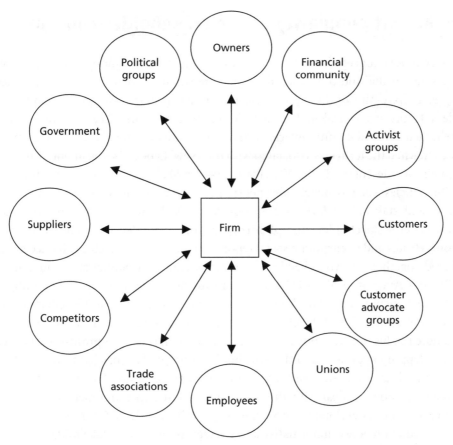

Figure 2.2 Stakeholder map of a very large organization around one major strategic issue
Source: Freeman (1984: 55).

labelled the firm. Freeman notes that the depiction of the stakeholder view of the firm in his diagram is 'enormously oversimplified' in that each of the groups shown can be broken down into more specific categories (See Section 1.4).

Freeman warns management that the consequences of not adopting this approach is to suffer from law suits and damaging regulation, and from loss of markets to foreign competitors who can satisfy a variety of stakeholder needs. Adopting a stakeholder approach requires organizations to develop expertise in the understanding of how stakeholder groups arise, the key issues that they perceive, and their willingness to expend resources either helping or harming corporations on these issues (1984: 26). In addition, he recommends integration of stakeholder relations. We revisit Freeman (1984) in Chapter 4 as part of our discussion of analytic stakeholder models (see Section 4.2.1), and his contributions to normative stakeholder theory are discussed in Sections 3.2.2 and 3.3.2.1.

2.5 **Recent popularity of the stakeholder concept**

The stakeholder concept has achieved widespread popularity among academics, policy-makers, the media, and corporate managers. Enormous academic interest was noted in Chapter 1. Sixty-nine of the seventy-five academic papers that we cite in Chapter 1 (see Table 1.1) proposing stakeholder definitions occurred post-Freeman. References to stakeholders are now commonplace, particularly in the mass media. This was stimulated in the UK when the term was associated with the 'New' Labour Government of Tony Blair and their 'Big Idea' of the Third Way (Blair 1994, 1996) along with their use of the term in specific policies, such as stakeholder pensions. As of 2004, thirty-two states in the USA have passed stakeholder laws (see Section 9.3.1.2). There has also been widespread adoption of the stakeholder concept by corporations, as evidenced by corporate disclosure on websites and in corporate social reports. Recently, considerable evidence has been gathered together in two collections of articles edited by Sutherland-Rahman et al. (2002) and Andriof et al. (2003). These are further supported by widely publicized institutions such as the Dow Jones Sustainability Index and the FTSE4Good index, which emphasize CSP and stakeholder management as well as financial performance.

As noted in Section 1.3, along with this popularity has come a profusion of different and overlapping approaches to the stakeholder concept. This has led to the field being characterized as confused, resulting in the concept becoming 'vague', 'slippery', and 'shallow'. In order to deal with this conceptual confusion a number of classification schemes have been developed (see Section 3.2). We have ordered Chapters 3 and 4 based on the distinction between normative and strategic or analytical stakeholder theory. The prominent contribution to the literature made by Donaldson and Preston (1995) relates to this distinction.

2.6 **Normative, instrumental, and descriptive stakeholder theory: Donaldson and Preston (1995)**

In May 1993 the Center for Corporate Social Performance and Ethics at the University of Toronto ran a small but highly influential conference, 'The Stakeholder Theory of the Corporation and the Management of Ethics in the Workplace'. The conference was extensively reported in *Business and Society* (1994, 33/1). The opening paragraphs of Donaldson and Preston (1995) formed the rubric for the conference. This included the following statement:

[T]he concepts 'stakeholder', 'stakeholder model', 'stakeholder management' and 'stakeholder theory' are explained and used by various authors in very different ways, and supported (or critiqued) with diverse and often contradictory evidence and arguments. Moreover these diversities and their implications are rarely discussed—and possibly not even recognized.

Both the paper and the conference attempted to address these issues. Donaldson and Preston suggested that stakeholder theory had been advanced and justified in the management literature on the basis of its descriptive accuracy, instrumental power, and normative validity. Four theses were presented, viewing stakeholder theory as:

1. *Descriptive.* The corporation is viewed as a constellation of cooperative and competitive interests possessing intrinsic value. The theory is used to describe specific corporate characteristics such as the nature of the firm, the way managers think about managing, how corporations are managed, or how board members think about the interests of constituencies. This is also labelled 'empirical'.

2. *Instrumental.* This approach establishes a framework for examining *ceteris paribus* connections, if any, between the practice of stakeholder management and the achievement of various corporate performance goals (profitability, growth). 'An instrumental approach is essentially hypothetical', it says, in effect, 'If you want to achieve (avoid) results X, Y, Z, then adopt (don't adopt) principles and practices A, B, C' (1995: 71).

3. *Normative.* The identification of moral or philosophical guidelines for the management of corporations. This approach is categorical; it says, in effect, 'Do (Don't do) this because it is the right (wrong) thing to do' (1995: 71). This assumes acceptance that:
   (*a*) Stakeholders are persons or groups with legitimate interests in procedural and/or substantive aspects of corporate activities. Stakeholders are identified by their interests in the corporation, whether (or not) the corporation has any corresponding functional interest in them.
   (*b*) The interests of all stakeholders are of intrinsic value, each group merits consideration for its own sake and not merely because of its ability to further the interests of some other group, such as the shareholders.

4. *Broadly managerial.* It recommends attitudes, structures, and practices that taken together constitute stakeholder management. 'Stakeholder management requires, as its key attribute, simultaneous attention to the legitimate interests of all appropriate stakeholders, both in the establishment of organization structures and general policies and in case-by-case decision making' (1995: 67).

Donaldson and Preston view the confusion associated with the stakeholder concept as arising from descriptive, instrumental, and normative aspects of stakeholder theory often being 'combined without acknowledgement' (1995: 72). Reed (2002: 169–70) notes that these different approaches can allow us to differentiate stakeholder definitions on the following logical basis:

- *Descriptive* stakeholders are defined as to whether they are affected by the firm and/or can potentially affect the firm, the former if the object of investigation is the effect of the firm's activities and the latter if it is the decision-making process of the firm.
- *Instrumental* stakeholders are defined by the need of management to take them into consideration when trying to achieve their goals.
- *Normative* stakeholders have valid normative claims on the firm.

Reed (2002) suggests the terms positive, strategic, and normative instead of Donaldson and Preston's descriptive, instrumental, and normative.

The underlying epistemological issue for Donaldson and Preston (1995: 72) is that of justification: why should stakeholder theory be accepted or preferred over alternative conceptions? Without addressing this question the distinctions between the variants of stakeholder theory are unimportant. To this end they advocate that the normative thesis is the strongest, being the only one able to provide epistemological justification for the stakeholder theory. This does not lead to rejection of instrumental and descriptive variants, but to the recommendation that the three theses be regarded as nested within each other (Figure 2.3). The external shell is the descriptive aspect, which presents and explains practice. Instrumental stakeholder theory forms the next layer, supporting the descriptive thesis through predictive power. At the core is the normative. Descriptive accuracy presumes the truth of the core normative conception in so far as it presumes that managers and other agents act as if all stakeholder interests have intrinsic value. The philosophical justification presented for the normative basis of stakeholder theory is one of property rights, in its modern and pluralistic form.

In Chapter 3 we deal exclusively with normative theories and in Chapter 4 we deal with instrumental and descriptive theories, which we jointly label 'analytic'. The Donaldson and Preston model received considerable attention since its publication with a particularly influential debate in 1999 over the call for convergence among the three strands of stakeholder theory they identify. This debate is discussed in detail in Chapter 5.

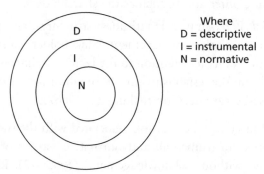

Where
D = descriptive
I = instrumental
N = normative

Figure 2.3 Three aspects of stakeholder theory
Source: Donaldson and Preston (1995: 73).

2.7 **Case 2.1: public use of private property and responsibility to stakeholders: the Berle and Dodd debate**

2.7.1 THE CONTEXT

The debate between A. A. Berle and Merrik Dodd in the early 1930s is often referred to in the stakeholder literature (Hendry 2001). The context of this debate is noteworthy. First, it occurred during the Great Depression in the USA, a time when the very existence of the capitalist system was under question. Second, the debate coincided with the run-up to the 1932 election, which saw Roosevelt sweep to power based on his 'big idea' of the New Deal. Third, economic thinking in the USA was dominated by a group known as the Institutionalists (see Gruchy 1972: 5). While institutionalism was primarily associated with the ideas of the social critic Thorstein Veblen (1904, 1923), Roosevelt was highly influenced by more pragmatic institutionalist thinkers who saw the solution to depression in developing more explicitly managed capitalism through government intervention and regulation. These took their inspiration from John Commons (1924; 1931). He characterized the system as 'reasonable capitalism'.

2.7.2 THE DEBATE

The *Harvard Law Review* of 1931 and 1932 contains three articles, which represent an interesting precursor to the stakeholder–stockholder debate and provide valuable insights into the normative bases for the two positions. The 'debate' began with Berle (1931) arguing for a reiteration of the principle that managerial powers are held in trust for the stockholders as sole beneficiaries of corporate enterprise, based on the view of directors being fiduciaries for the stockholders. Such a reiteration was needed because industrial concentration in the USA had proceeded to such an extent that control of major corporations was now in the hands of executives who were able to divert profit into their own hands without 'passive' stockholders knowing it.

Dodd (1932) accepts the need for stockholders to be protected from self-seeking managers and agrees with many of the specific rules Berle deduces from his trusteeship principle. However, Dodd argues that public opinion is moving towards a view of the business corporation 'as an economic institution which has a social service as well as a profit-making function'. Public opinion ultimately makes law, and Dodd discerns the law as changing towards 'a point of view which will regard all business as affected with a public interest' (1932: 1148). Ultimately, unregulated profits will be allowed only in special cases where competitive conditions are judged as adequate to obviate the necessity for regulation, rather than because owners have a constitutional right to have their property treated as purely private, as in the sense of purely personal use property.

Dodd refers to legal precedent for this view. Several hundred years ago, when conducted by individuals, business was regarded in law to be 'a public profession rather than a purely private matter, and that the businessman, far from being free to obtain all the profits which his skill in bargaining might secure for him, owes a legal duty to give adequate service at reasonable rates' (1932: 1148). Gradually, belief in liberty of contract and the effects of free competition led to this theory being abandoned for business as a whole. *Munn v. Illinois* (1877) was a pivotal case. American judges changed from regarding business enterprise itself in terms of 'the duty of one engaged in business activities toward the public' with all business publicly carried on being 'regarded as public in character'; towards distinguishing 'the public duty of one who has devoted his property to public use' for only those businesses in which property is employed in business 'devoted to public use'. Property employed in other kinds of business remained 'strictly private' (1932: 1149). Business devoted to public use came to refer to public utilities such as interstate railroads, which must 'render adequate service, expand its facilities when called upon by public authority, charge only reasonable rates, and treat all customers alike even though profitable new business might be secured by making concessions to certain patrons' (1932: 1150). Dodd suggests recent acts had intervened in wage negotiation between the railroads and their employees, largely for the purpose of increasing wages. They may have been designed to protect the public from services interruptions due to strikes, but Dodd contends they may also derive from 'a partial recognition of the validity of the claims of labor as an integral part of the enterprise to a fair share of the receipts—fairness to be dependent on criteria which, however vague, are not wholly a matter of bargaining strength' (1932: 1150). At a broader level, Dodd notes that the Transportation Act of 1920 had been construed by the US Supreme Court as treating the railroads as part of a single system and thereby allowing the Interstate Commerce Commission to apportion rate charges in order to give weaker railroads a larger proportional share of the total charge in joint rates between connecting carriers. In addition, these views have affected state laws in 'more advanced states' to regulate other so-called public utilities such as gas, electric, and telephone companies. Dodd also notes that the line separating public utilities from other businesses is not clear-cut though the label emphasizes 'the fact that business is permitted and encouraged by the law primarily because it is of service to the community rather than because it is a source of profit to its owners' (1932: 1149).

Dodd reports that 'business leaders and students of business' suggest that there is a growing feeling 'not only that business has responsibilities to the community but that our corporate managers who control business should voluntarily and without waiting for legal compulsion manage it in such a way as to fulfil those responsibilities' (1932: 1153–4) (of a profession of public service). Owen Young, an executive officer for General Electric (GE), is quoted as saying that there are four groups 'who have an interest' in the institution for which he acts as trustee: stockholders, employees, customers, and the general public. Young lists duties towards each:

- For capital, to provide a 'fair rate of return' through using the capital wisely, safely, and honestly.
- For labour, to provide 'fair wages, continuity of employment and a recognition of their right to their jobs where they have educated themselves to highly skilled and specialized work' (1932: 1154).
- For customers, to get a product that is 'as represented and that the price is such as consistent with the obligation to the people who put their capital and labor in' (1932: 1154).
- For the general public, to be a good citizen.

Dodd (1932: 1155) cites the president of GE who put forward the 'Swope plan' by which capitalism was defended in the time of the Great Depression from government intervention by organized industry taking the lead, 'recognizing its responsibility to its employees, to the public, and to its stockholders'.

In addition, executives sometimes use corporate funds for gifts to local charities, which suggests a social responsibility in spite of 'the orthodox legal attitude' that charitable giving is only allowable by boards of directors if it is in the interest of the giver, such as to increase good will. Dodd uses a parallel between public enterprise for relief funded by taxation and therefore based on the major contribution of wealthy corporations and public enterprise for relief funded by direct voluntary contributions of wealthy corporations as an argument for the legitimacy of a corporate 'right to be charitable'. He also notes that public opinion and a rising number of legal judgments support this. However, this view is hard to justify if corporate executives are thought of purely as trustees of agents for stockholders. 'It is not for a trustee to be public-spirited with his beneficiary's property' (1932: 1160). Corporations should not be viewed as mere aggregates of stockholders. Instead, there is a view with 'distinguished adherents' (Dicey 1914; Laski 1916: 404), which is that any organized group as a factual unit differs from the individuals constituting it.

[If] the unity of the corporate body is real, then there is reality and not simply legal fiction in the proposition that the managers of the unit are fiduciaries for it and not merely for its individual members, that they are in Mr. Young's phrase, trustees for an institution rather than attorneys for the stockholders. (Dodd 1932: 1160)

Dodd considered a version of instrumental stakeholder theory to be beyond doubt: 'that an attempt by business managers to take into consideration the welfare of employees and consumers . . . will in the long run increase the profits of stockholders' (1932: 1156), due to the presumption, widely held in the 1930s, that the depression reflected under-consumption, due to a general lack of feeling of employment security.

Dodd argued that these responsibilities needed renewing and proposed that the law be changed to allow corporations some degree of legal freedom to act on these attitudes without the unanimous consent of the stockholders. They represent a development of business ethics 'beyond the requirements of law and beyond the dictates of enlightened self-interest' (1932: 1161). Recognizing corporations as institutions differing from the individuals that constitute it allows us to think of it as a person affected 'not only by the laws which regulate business but by the attitude of public and business opinion as to the social obligations of business' (1932: 1161).

Business—which is the economic organization of society—is private property only in a qualified sense, and society may properly demand that it be carried on in such a way as to safeguard the interests of those who deal with it either as employees or consumers even if the proprietary rights of its owners are thereby curtailed. (Dodd 1932: 1162)

Dodd explicitly did not want the law changed to impose responsibilities on corporations by legal compulsion.

Berle (1932) countered Dodd by noting that by diluting management responsibility from stockholders, managers would in effect be responsible to no one, to the detriment of all society. He takes the following pragmatic position:

[Y]ou cannot abandon emphasis on 'the view that business corporations exist for the sole purpose of making profits for their stockholders' until such time as you are prepared to offer a clear and reasonably enforceable scheme of responsibilities to someone else. (Berle 1932: 1367)

A major function of securities (largely shares) according to Berle (1932: 1365) 'is to provide safety, security, or means of support for that part of the community which is unable to earn its living in the normal channels of work or trade'. Counting individuals with an interest in corporate securities through life insurance companies and banks, and including the families and dependants of all these people, Berle reckons at least half the US population are directly affected. A society based on the individual, rather than the State, 'can only be carried on by vigorous protection of the property that he [the individual] has' in order particularly to cover the two periods of life, childhood, and old age, when the individual cannot support himself.

According to Berle, Dodd's position is 'theory, not practice', because those in control of industry do not assume responsibilities to the community, nor do those who influence them, their bankers, or their lawyers. 'Nor is there any mechanism now in sight enforcing the accomplishment of his theoretical function' (1932: 1367). Instead, the implication of Dodd's view is that economic power is handed over to the few hundreds or thousands who hold control of major corporations 'with a pious wish that something nice will come out of it all' (1932: 1368). He then warns:

The only thing that can come out of it, in any long view, is the massing of group after group to assert their private claims by force of threat—to take what they can get, just as corporate managements do. The laborer is invited to organize and strike, the security holder is invited either to jettison his corporate securities and demand relief from the state, or to decline to save money at all under a system which grants to someone else power to take his savings at will. The consumer or patron is left nowhere, unless he learns the dubious art of boycott. This is an invitation not to law or orderly government, but to a process of economic civil war. (1932: 1368–9)

This is the basis on which Berle (1932: 1368) states: 'Either you have a system based on individual ownership of property or you do not.' The men from GE are the exception. If present legal checks on the absolute power of corporate administrators based on duties to stockholders are abandoned, and without a new corporate system enforcing a completely new form of economic government satisfying needs of investors, workers, customers, and the aggregated community, then the corporate system will 'involve itself in successive cataclysms perhaps leading to its ultimate downfall' (1932: 1372).

☐ QUESTIONS/EXERCISES

1 Does stakeholder theory suggest a different way of reducing adverse social consequences of the soulless corporation from the three suggested in Section 2.2? How would Berle view this solution?

2 Can you think of any justification for altering Figure 2.3 and drawing the diagram with descriptive stakeholder theory at its core? Or instrumental stakeholder theory at its core? What would this imply for the power of stakeholder theory to influence corporate managers or government policymakers?

3 What would you regard as the moral or ethical basis for Dodd's position compared with Berle?

4 How does each author in the Berle–Dodd debate use evidence to support their position?

☐ NOTES

1 Many authors use the abbreviation CSR to refer to corporate social reporting. In order to differentiate between responsibility and reporting we adopt the abbreviation CESER (corporate environmental, social, and ethical reporting) to refer to the latter.

2 Carroll (1979: 497) notes the actions of Wendell Wilkie in helping to 'educate the businessman to a new sense of social responsibility' in the 1930s.

3 The legal and market context in which organizations operated.

3 Normative stakeholder theorizing

3.1 Introduction

Normative stakeholder theory is popularly considered to be the heart or core of stakeholder theory. However, there are considerable problems with this.[1] The very definition of normative theory is contested. Normative can refer to:

- The norms or standard practices of society as it exists.
- The way one would live in an ideal 'good' society.
- What we ought to do, either in order to achieve a good society or unconnected with any notion of the 'good'.

The latter distinction could relate to two types of rules (Beauchamp and Bowie 2004: 2–4). *Moral rules* are based on values, which should be obeyed because they are 'right'. They either directly express the requirement to contribute to or support the 'good', or are based on a logical connection between actions and consequences, which contribute to the good. *Rules of prudence* are based on self-interest. They make connections between actions and consequences for the actor.

Here we deal with normative theory narrowly based on moral reasoning. However, the division is unclear because the 'should', which makes a theory normative, may be based on fundamental philosophical values, or on historical patterns of behaviour that have become ingrained such that they affect future behaviour in constraining ways. Donaldson and Preston's distinctions (1995) do not help here. If ideas of the good and the right are connected with norms (either generated by norms or in substantial interaction with norms), then they can be presumed to be time- *and* place-dependent. Cultural diversity in behavioural norms is commonly observed. Does this imply ethical relativism, or relativism of 'normativity'? Many of the normative stakeholder theories we examine here seek to establish a foundation for stakeholder theory based on eternal values, rather than observed norms, and are best compared by distinguishing the type of philosophical system adopted or the ultimate view they have of the good. Some take the norm-generated view, often without recognizing the distinction or the relativist consequences of this approach. Others deal with the issue of ethical relativism head on. We propose an ordering of these issues later in this chapter, which allows contributions to be arranged in a manner that helps to illuminate the 'normativity' of normative stakeholder theory. After a discussion of different frameworks for classifying normative stakeholder theories, and presenting our own framework, twenty major contributions to normative stakeholder theory are summarized. Vignettes in this chapter provide a terse rendition of these and other underlying concepts.[2]

3.2 **Classifying normative stakeholder theories**

The foundation of many normative stakeholder models rests on a straightforward application of existing ethical theory to the stakeholder concept. Certain ethical theories have been commonly used and could form the basis of a crude classification. Some writers adopt the universalist approaches of social contract theorists that stem from 'enlightenment' moral philosophy (Rawls, Kant, and Habermas). Others adopt what Lea (2004) calls particularist approaches, which propose that moral or virtuous action should be grasped in terms of culturally and socially specific descriptions (virtue ethics, feminist ethics, and postmodernism). Pragmatism has also been influential, though it is less widely recognized as such.

3.2.1 A FRAMEWORK FOR DISCUSSING NORMATIVE THEORIES: BISHOP (2000)

Bishop (2000) presents a framework and meta-language for comparing and assessing normative theories based on the following seven factors.

1. *Values.* All normative theories are based on either a singular fundamental moral principle (utilitarianism, Kantian, or Rawlsian ethics, rights) or a plurality of values.[3]
2. *Grounds (or basis) of values.* These can be religious or philosophical, or the author may simply make a direct appeal to decency or moral sense.
3. *Decision principle.* Practical guide for actions and policies.
4. *Agents.* Which moral agents ought to use the decision principle? Some theories are aimed at executives, some at all staff; some theories apply to all companies and some only to large corporations.
5. *Scope.* Whose perspective needs to be considered when using the decision principle? Bishop suggests that it is who is *fundamentally* considered that is important. This differentiates instrumental from normative approaches whereby stakeholder interests

are considered, not in their own right, but in consequence of furthering shareholder interests.

6. *Context.* In what circumstances should the decision principle be used?
7. *Structures.* What legal and regulatory structures are assumed, such as company and employment law?

This meta-language is useful in highlighting the differences between approaches. Bishop explores his framework through a comparison of normative stockholder theory, stakeholder theory, and social contract theory. In an attempt to differentiate normative stakeholder theory an assessment of values, grounds, the decision principle, agents, and scope are all pertinent.

3.2.2 LIBERAL PRAGMATISM (PLURALISM): FREEMAN (1994)

Freeman (1994) argues that there is no singular stakeholder theory, rather there is a 'genre' called stakeholder theory. He associates this view with the philosophy of pragmatism (Vignette 3.1). The whole genre is 'one of many ways to blend together the central concepts of business with those of ethics', which can be used 'to create more fine-grained analyses that combine business and ethics: or more simply, we can tell many more, and more interesting stories about business' (1994: 409–10).

Vignette 3.1 PRAGMATISM

Pragmatism is a philosophy, or a tendency[4] in philosophy, that regards practical consequences (action, realization in conduct, possibility of being alive, satisfaction of needs, etc.) to be the test of truth. It is opposed to formalism of 'intellectualist philosophy' as well as all eternally fixed norms of belief and values. It is associated with dynamic values whereby thought and knowledge are biologically and socially evolving means of adaptation and control. It claims that 'all knowledge is a behavioral process evaluative of future experience and thinking is experimentally aimed at organizing, planning, or controlling future experience' (Thayer 1968: 431, cited by Weiner 1973–4: 552). It is associated with the American writers Charles Pierce, credited with inventing it in 1897, William James, and John Dewey. Weiner (1973–4: 553) describes the features of pragmatism as:

1. Piecemeal method of investigation (*pluralistic empiricism*).
2. *Temporalistic* view of reality and knowledge.
3. Traditional ideas of space, time, causation, axiomatic truth, and intrinsic and eternal values are considered relative to psychological, social, historical, or logical contexts.
4. *Probabilistic* view of hypotheses.
5. Secular *democratic* individualism that rejects the sanctions of theology or totalitarian authority.

Theories have different possible 'normative cores' (grounds) (Table 3.1) that must address questions of how corporations ought to be governed and how management ought to act (decision principles), or to explain why these questions are irrelevant.

Table 3.1 A reasonable pluralism

	Corporations ought to be governed	Managers ought to act	The background disciplines of 'value creation' are
Doctrine of fair contracts	In accordance with the six principles	In the interests of stakeholders	• Business theories • Theories that explain stakeholder behaviour
Feminist standpoint theory	In accordance with the principles of caring/ connection and relationships	To maintain and care for relationships and networks of stakeholders	• Business theories • Feminist theories • Social science understanding of networks
Ecological principles	In accordance with the principle of caring for the earth	To care for the earth	• Business theories • Ecology • Others
. . .	. . .	. . .	. . .

Note: . . . Further grounds can be added.
Source: Freeman, (1994a: 414).

This is clearly influenced by postmodern thinking (see Vignette 3.8). Freeman adds 'metaphorical stakeholder theory' to Donaldson and Preston's three-way distinction (1995) although he does not indicate how this relates to normative, descriptive, and instrumental. Freeman does not regard these as different types of theories, but rather different uses for types of stakeholder theories.

3.2.3 A CLASSIFICATION OF NORMATIVE STAKEHOLDER THEORIES: HENDRY (2001)

Hendry (2001) attempts to clarify the field by distinguishing three kinds of normative stakeholder theories and three levels of claims that can be made by such theories (Table 3.2).

Theories of the first kind propose that in a just society businesses should be managed for the benefit of stakeholders. Theories of the second kind require changes in the laws and institutions of society to ensure greater corporate responsibility towards stakeholders. Theories of the third kind maintain that managers should, at the very least, take account of the interest of all the stakeholders in the firm, given the existing legal and institutional environment. Hendry notes that theories of the second kind can appear as consequences to the first kind of theories or they can be derived directly by taking the basic institution of the firm as it is in current society and then applying normative principles to its management. He also distinguishes between the level of claims

Table 3.2 Normative stakeholder theories: varieties of theories and focuses of debates

	Modest theories (claims, e.g. that stakeholders should be treated with respect)	Intermediate theories (incorporating some stakeholder interests in the governance of the corporation)	Demanding theories (claiming participation for all stakeholders in corporate decision processes)
Theories of the first kind (concerned with the characteristics of an ideal just society)			Philosophical literature: Rawlsian type (Freeman and Evan, Bowie, Phillips)
Theories of the second kind (concerned with morally desirable legal and institutional changes)		Public policy debate (e.g. Dodd vs. Berle, Boatright vs. Williamson)	Philosophical literature: pragmatic and feminist (e.g. Freeman and associates, Burton and Dunn)
Theories of the third kind (concerned with morally desirable management behaviour in the context of existing laws and institutions)	Management literature (e.g. Donaldson and Preston; Jones and Wicks)		

Source: Hendry (2001: 167).

in relation to the nature and extent of the firm's responsibility to stakeholders: modest, demanding, and intermediate. Hendry concludes that stakeholder theorists have generally pitched their theories at too narrow a scope with too weak a set of claims, or too broadly with too strong claims to engage effectively in the public policy debate with the rival shareholder theory. He recommends developing theories of the second kind, pitched at intermediate stakeholder claims, in order to inform the public policy debate.

3.2.4 A TAXONOMY OF NORMATIVE STAKEHOLDER THEORIES

We present a classification of normative stakeholder theories (Figure 3.1) to elucidate what may be thought of as the *nature of normativity* of the twenty theories examined. The mixture of different types of normative arguments used by contributors has, in our opinion, contributed to the confused state of normative stakeholder theory.

3.2.4.1 **Normativity: futurity**

Taking Hendry's model as a basic framework, we complement the label 'kinds of theory' with the concept of futurity. By calling them different *kinds* of normative theories,

	Kind of theory		Agency Concerned with the ethical behaviour of:	
			Managers	Stakeholders and managers
Degree of normativity or futurity	First kind: ideal just society	1a Total just society Idealizations	Ecology: • Starik (1994)	
		1b Constrained just society Idealizations	Kantian: • Evan and Freeman (1993) • Bowie (1998) Rawlsian: • Phillips (1997) • Freeman (1994, 2004) Common good: • Argandoña (1998)	Critical theory: • Reed (1999) Social contracts theory: • Donaldson and Dunfee (1999)
	Second kind: modify laws and institutions	2a Reflect growing minority ideals, or reflect the direction in which current society is evolving	Feminist: • Wicks, Gilbert, and Freeman (1994) • Burton and Dunn (1996)	Postmodern: • Calton and Kurland (1995)
		2b Reflect legal/institutions in other societies or past forms	• Dodd (1932) Stakeholders as investors: • Schlossberger (1994) • Etzioni (1996, 1998) • Blair (1998)	
	Third kind: corporate response	3 Identify to whom and for what managers are morally responsible given the contemporary legal and institutional context	• Jones and Wicks (1999a) Fiduciary relationships: • Boatright (1994) • Goodpaster (1991) Property rights: • Donaldson and Preston (1995) Aristotelian: • Wijnberg (2000)	

Figure 3.1 Normative stakeholder theories

Hendry emphasizes differences among them. This suits his purpose, which is to demonstrate incompatibility among them and the lack of theory of the second kind. We note that the three kinds of theories can be viewed as points along a dimension of logical time or futurity, or of idealism or normativity. We think of them as based on the *extent* to which changes must be made to current laws and institutions to achieve what the theories consider to be an adequate relationship between managers and stakeholders.

Theories of the third kind can be thought of as immediately realizable, at least in legal or institutional 'time', as they only require changes in managerial behaviour and/or attitudes. They suggest what and to whom managers are morally responsible given existing laws and institutions. Theories of the second kind are less readily realizable, as they propose how society should modify laws and institutions to reflect a just society or other ethical ideal. Theories of the first kind are idealized and therefore unrealizable in the foreseeable future, requiring widespread societal changes.

3.2.4.2 Normativity: outcomes versus justifications

Two types of normative elements are distinguished in these theoretical contributions: *normativity of outcomes* and *normativity of justifications*. Associated with each type is a scale of normativity. In terms of the normativity of outcomes, some call for great leaps in thinking and behaviour of individuals and society as a whole, others can be accommodated by small changes.

There are two ways in which normativity of justification can be expressed:

1. From an idealized rational stance, specifying logical steps based on some idealized version of what society and individuals are, could be, or should be.
2. From the perspective of norms that exist, but with different degrees of pervasiveness. Different degrees of pervasiveness can be thought of in terms of the size or the distance such communities may be from the target society.

In placing contributions on the framework we view justifications of type 1 to reflect a higher degree of normativity than those of type 2. Some contributions rely entirely on one or other form of justification; others use both arguments, but to varying degrees.

There is a problem in classifying a number of the contributions because the degree of normativity they express appears to be very different when considered from the position of outcomes compared with justification. Some use highly normative justifications but recommend outcomes that are easily achieved or require little change in behaviour (such as Argandoña 1998), while others recommend deep and broad outcomes but justify them in terms of existing practices and ways of thinking (such as Etzioni 1998).

We have chosen to classify each contribution at the highest level that it could be placed according to either outcome or justification. Consequently, theories of the first kind must exhibit either a high normative outcome or a high normative justification, but not necessarily both. We do not automatically consider those contributions that have both high normative justification and call for high normative outcomes to be higher than ones that reach that level on only one criterion. They are not more normative, merely consistently normative.

Contributions are classified on the basis of our judgement as to their primary emphasis. Some contributions straddle different categories. Several use a range of justifications that may even be viewed as contradictory. The framework contextualizes this aspect of normative stakeholder theory. We aim to provide enough information in the contribution summaries below for the reader to understand the arguments put forward and to judge the nature and extent of normativity employed.

3.2.4.3 Elaboration of the first kind of theories

In terms of different degrees of normativity/futurity, further points along the continuum can be distinguished. The first kind of theories are generated by a theoretical view of a just society[5] and are elaborated through logical or rational argument.[6] However, the theoretically just society envisioned can range in scope. Some first kind of theories are based on a just community of stakeholders where stakeholders are limited in some way. Others are based on a notion of a just society, which transcends the particular stakeholder groups associated with any particular focal organizations. Clearly, the narrow definition of stakeholders used by Evan and Freeman (1988) is based on a limited view of a just society. Freeman himself accepts that the vision retains many aspects of current society even though Hendry places this article in the theories of the first kind. In addition most normative stakeholder theories are based on a definition of stakeholders that is implicitly limited to 'legitimate' stakeholders (see Section 1.3). Must other elements of society also be just? Our model distinguishes between broad theories, labelled 1a, and constrained theories of the just society that may underlie normative stakeholder theory, 1b. We regard broad theories as having a 'higher' degree of 'normativity'.

3.2.4.4 Elaboration of the second kind of theories

The second kind of theories can be differentiated according to the degree of change suggested. This can be done in two ways: (*a*) to assess the resources and/or time required to make changes to laws and/or institutions proposed, or (*b*) to consider the way the theories conceive of underlying social movement. Hendry did not explicitly consider this aspect of normativity, but it has been discussed by some of the authors he classified. Theories may be differentiated according to whether they reflect:

(1) Ideas and/or practices of a growing minority in society, growing in terms of some measure of ability to develop new legal/institutional patterns.
(2) The general direction that current society is moving in, due to changes in public opinion concerning the way laws are formulated or the way key institutions are evolving.
(3) Interpretations of existing legal/institutional patterns in a logical but unfamiliar manner.
(4) A legal/institutional pattern that exists in other societies.
(5) A return to past or historic legal/institutional patterns.

Justification of the good, and generation of ideas of the good, may be associated with the processes of right behaviour, i.e. they may provide what Habermas (1993) would call the moral reasoning that complements the ethical reasoning of the theories (see Vignette 3.3). We propose, like Hendry, that awareness of the point along this dimension at which different normative stakeholder theories are pitched helps to understand relations among the theories as well as debates between normative stakeholder theories and alternatives, whether normative theories of business ethics or more broadly ethics of socio-economic and/or political activity.

Another way of thinking about these theories is that they rest on a pragmatic philosophy as proposed by Freeman (1994). That is, they derive 'ought', not from 'is', but from 'becoming' or from 'models of workable systems from elsewhere'. We described the early stakeholder concept as expressed by Dodd (1932) and noted not only what he proposed (that the law be changed to allow non-shareholder interests to be taken into account) but why. This was not based on a deontological or utilitarian principle, but rather on his reading of trends in public opinion buttressed by case law judgements, in addition to recognizing changes in actual practice among managers and changes to the institutional framework (i.e. dispersed and passive shareholding). This would place him mainly in category (2) and possibly (1). He also uses an argument, which harkens to the past, a (5) argument.

The model combines (1) and (2) as both relate to strong recommendations for new (not yet existing) laws and institutions. These are labelled 2a and reflect different paths of social change. The emergence of new laws and institutions requires social movement. Similarly, (3), (4), and (5) are combined as these relate to logical extensions of existing models or models that exist elsewhere or have existed in the past. These are labelled 2b and reflect different combinations of recognized laws and institutions whose emergence is more easily achievable. Adopting an existing framework is assumed to be more straightforward, involving less of a leap from what is to what ought to be than those justifications labelled 2a.

For some contributors, how their ideas 'fit' with directions of laws and institutions are essential normative justifications and are part of the theories themselves. Others appear to consider their pronouncements about the evolution of laws and institutions or their characterizations of current and past laws and institutions as *obiter dicta*, the kind of statements that merely introduce their theories or ethical propositions.

3.2.4.5 Targets of normativity: agency

Most normative stakeholder theories are aimed at altering management behaviour and presume that managers represent and act for focal organizations vis-à-vis stakeholders. Recently some contributors have become less manager-centric. Analytic theories discussed in Chapter 4 also demonstrate a decentring from a strategic management perspective towards focusing on the organization–stakeholder relationship per se. The model in Figure 3.1 highlights this difference in relation to normative stakeholder theories through the second column. Relatively few contributions have been placed in there, and we highlight this as an area for future theoretical work.[7]

3.3 **Normative theories of the first kind**

3.3.1 ECOLOGY AND SPIRITUALITY: STARIK (1994)

Starik's contribution lies in his argument that non-human entities, particularly the natural environment, merit stakeholder status due to the extent of environmental deterioration of the planet caused by humans (Starik 1994, 1995; Drisco and Starik 2004). Starik includes the natural environment (living and non-living) in terms of elements (particular landmarks), categories of elements (trees, rocks, etc.), and systems of elements (like river delta systems on a micro scale and the cosmos on a macro scale). He proposes a very broad stakeholder definition, suggesting that the standard Freeman definition be expanded to include 'any naturally occurring entity which affects or is affected by organizational performance' (1993: 22, 1994: 92). He justifies this on four grounds.

1. The natural environment is a business environment. As nature provides many constraints on business life, it ultimately affects and is affected by organizations.

2. Traditionally, the stakeholder idea has been an exclusively political–economic concept whereby those without the political and economic power to have their voices heard by the organization cannot be regarded as stakeholders. His 'affect and affected by' relationship extends to include 'socio-emotional (spiritual), ethical and legal' foundations. The natural environment 'fits each of these domains, concerning environmental aesthetics, the land ethic and environmental protection laws' (1994: 92). He suggests a similarity between the natural environment and historically disenfranchised groups such as slaves, indigenous people, and political prisoners, who although they have no political voice would nevertheless count as stakeholders on his account. The ethical nature of stakeholder theory combined with the appropriate environmental ethic bolsters the case for the environment to be considered. This may be interpreted as using a 2b argument to justify a 1a outcome.

3. Human stakeholders, acting as proxies for the environment through activist groups and government agencies, are necessary but insufficient given how degraded the natural environment is.

4. People can try to manage their interactions with the natural environment using stakeholder management processes as evidenced by environmental audits and impact statements.

Starik's position is a clear example of an unconstrained first kind of normative stakeholder foundation (1a). Unsurprisingly, he has been heavily criticized. Phillips (2003b: 142) argues that agents cannot be deemed stakeholders simply because they have problems and that stakeholder theory is not intended to be a comprehensive moral theory but simply describes the obligations that result from a special organizational relationship. Those outside these special relations should look elsewhere for relief.

3.3.2 KANTIAN STAKEHOLDER THEORIES

The normative theories proposed by Evan and Freeman (1993) and Bowie (1998) have their foundations in Kantian ethics (Vignette 3.2). These are all classified as 1b theories. Like Starik, they have been criticized due to the wide normative scope or distant futurity of their justifications (Langtry 1994; Hasnas 1998; Wicks 1998; Child and Marcoux 1999).[8]

Vignette 3.2 KANT'S MORAL THEORY

Immanuel Kant (1724–1804) considered moral actions to arise solely from a sense of duty (obligation). Kant believed that a person's motive for action must be recognition of the duty to act. He termed this good will. To act from good will is to act from duty. It is the intention or motive behind the act rather than the consequences that make actions good: one should make the right decision for the right reason. If corporate managers support a charity only because they believe it will bring cheap advertising or enhance corporate reputation, it cheapens the act and cannot be thought of as moral. This emphasis on duty and the associated lack of concern with consequences makes Kant 'the quintessential deontologist' (Bowie 1999: 4). Kant distinguishes two kinds of duties: hypothetical imperatives that take the form 'if you want to do y, do x' and categorical imperatives, which are the duties that are required. The action can only be undertaken if the principle on which it is based passes the test of the categorical imperative. The categorical imperative has been expressed in many ways. The following three are most frequently cited (Bowie 1998).

1. *Act only on maxims (principles) that you can will to be universal laws of nature.*
What would happen if what we want to do would be done always by all people? If the action can be willed universally without contradiction it is morally permissible. This test demonstrates that acceptance of certain (unethical) actions is self-defeating as universal participation in such behaviour undermines the action. If everybody cheated in exams, testing would be futile.
2. *Always treat people as ends and not means.*
As humans have free will and dignity, one human cannot use another simply to satisfy his or her own interests. Failure to respect persons means either ignoring their concerns and needs, rejecting their opinions, or denying them the opportunity to act on their judgements. Kant permits situations whereby people treat others as means to their ends, such as in commercial transactions, if the exchange is voluntary, without coercion and deception, and if both parties benefit. Refraining from coercion and deception alone is insufficient, one must also permit positive freedom: the freedom to develop human, rational, and moral capabilities.
3. *Act as if you were a member of an ideal kingdom of ends in which you were both subject and sovereign at the same time.*

Kant stresses the moral imagination. We must imagine ourselves at the receiving end of the decisions of others. Governing rules should be formulated so that they are applicable to everyone within the organization being governed.

3.3.2.1 Kantian capitalism: Evan and Freeman (1988, 1993)

Evan and Freeman argue that the true purpose of the organization is to pursue the interests of the stakeholders. In so doing management should act as though they do not know which stake is theirs. Management have a fiduciary duty to stakeholders to act as their agents and stakeholder groups have 'a right not to be treated as means to some end, and therefore must participate in determining the future direction of the firm in which they have a stake' (1993: 76). Any theory of corporations must be consistent with the Kantian principles of:

- *Corporate rights*—the corporation and its managers may not violate the legitimate rights of others to determine their own future.
- *Corporate effects*—the corporation and its managers are responsible for the effects of their actions on others.

Evan and Freeman contend that Kant's principle of respect for persons is not so idealistic and can be incorporated in practice. However, corporate law is ambiguous and fails to answer unequivocally the question: 'In whose interest and for whose benefit should the modern corporation be governed?' (1993: 76). They point out that in the nineteenth century the law evolved to constrain the pursuit of shareholder interests by requiring claims of customers, suppliers, local communities, and employees to be taken into account, but in ways that were subordinate to claims of shareholders (a 2b argument). Certain cases have led to the rise of liability for damage caused by products. They cite cases such as the Consumer Product Safety Commission's power to enact product recalls, requirements for companies to provide information about product ingredients, and employee and environmental protections acts. These are strong 2a arguments.

While they note both narrow and wide stakeholders definitions, Evan and Freeman select a narrow definition: 'those groups who are vital to the survival and success of the corporation' to make their model more strategically convincing. Customers/clients, employees, suppliers, local communities, shareholders, and managers are included. They exclude competitors and government, but state that these would be the first to be included in any theory extension. They see the implementation of stakeholder management principles as mitigating against the need for government intervention.

It may seem confusing that companies that need to make profits should not use stakeholders as means to that end. Evan and Freeman (1993: 80) do not exclude this possibility, rather they say, referring here to employees: 'Where they are used as means to an end, they must participate in decisions affecting such use'. They present an instrumental argument to justify their normative position:

The evidence that such policies and values as described here lead to productive company–employee relationships is compelling. It is equally compelling to realize that the opportunities for 'bad faith' on the part of both management and employees are enormous. (1993: 80)

They cite Peters and Waterman (1982) for evidence that being close to the consumer and having a good reputation in the community are distinguishing characteristics of 'excellent' companies. This is the third kind of argument.

Evan and Freeman call for a redefinition of the purpose of the firm to act as a vehicle for coordinating stakeholder interests. They propose two stakeholder management principles (1993: 82):

P1: *Principle of Corporate Legitimacy.* The corporation should be managed for the benefit of its stakeholders. The rights of stakeholders must be ensured, and, further, they must participate, in some sense, in decisions that substantially affect their welfare.

P2: *The Stakeholder Fiduciary Principle.* Management bears a fiduciary relationship to stakeholders and to the corporation as an abstract entity (see Vignette 3.9). They must act in the interests of the stakeholders as their agent in the interests of the corporation to ensure the survival of the firm, safeguarding the long-term stakes of each group.

Management have a stake similar to other employees, but they also have a duty of safeguarding the welfare of the firm. This involves balancing the multiple claims of conflicting stakeholders: a role 'akin to that of King Solomon'. Two structural mechanisms for making stakeholder management 'practicable' are proposed:

1. A stakeholder board of directors comprising representatives of the five stakeholder groups, plus a 'metaphysical director' responsible for the metaphysical entity that is the corporation. Each director would be vested with the duty of caring for all stakeholders: the metaphysical director would be elected unanimously by the others.

2. A redefinition of corporate law to recognize P1 as the legitimate purpose of the corporation.

As a transition mechanism they suggest large corporations could form stakeholder advisory boards to prepare a charter detailing how the organization will deal with stakeholders, advise, and eventually replace the current board. They also suggest legal scholars and practitioners and business groups could get involved in designing ways of changing corporate charters.

Like most normative stakeholder theories Evan and Freeman only address the ethical behaviour of managers. Stakeholders are passive recipients of normative management behaviour.

They make normative claims of the first kind, based on Kantian principles. The radical view that 'the very purpose of the firm is, in our view, to serve as a vehicle for co-ordinating stakeholder interests' (1988: 103) and the associated proposed principles of corporate legitimacy and stakeholder fiduciary are strong departures from current management thinking (Langtry 1994) and institutional arrangements. This theory relates to an ideal just society, though a bounded one, constrained particularly by the narrow definition of stakeholder adopted (1b). Evan and Freeman use arguments of the second and third kind of theories to justify their first kind of outcomes. This has led to confusion about the nature of their contribution.

3.3.2.2 Kantian capitalism: Bowie (1999)

Bowie proposes seven principles for a Kantian approach to business:

1. The interests of all affected stakeholders should be considered on any decision a firm makes.
2. Those affected by the firm's rules and policies should participate in determining those rules and policies before they are implemented.
3. One stakeholder's interests should not automatically take priority for all decisions.
4. When stakeholder group interests conflict, decisions should not be made solely on the grounds of there being a greater number of stakeholders in one group than in another.
5. No business rule or practice can be adopted that is inconsistent with the formulae of the categorical imperative (*universal laws of nature and never treat people as means to an end*).
6. Every profit-making firm has a limited, but genuine, duty of beneficence.
7. All firms must establish procedures designed to ensure relations among stakeholders are governed by rules of justice.

The first principle is a straightforward requirement of any moral theory that takes respect for persons seriously. The Kantian notion of freedom to develop human rational and moral capabilities is linked to autonomy and provides the rationale for the second principle. Kantian ethics demands some form of participation by all stakeholders, but especially shareholders and employees. Respective stakeholder groups should represent all individuals and these groups must consent to the rules and policies that govern the firm. Bowie (1999) provides examples of democratic work practices at Levi Strauss and Singapore Airlines to demonstrate that this is not idealist. In this sense Bowie crosses from the first to the second kind of normative theory (2a). He argues that the third principle provides a kind of organizational legitimacy, ensuring that those involved in the firm receive some minimum benefit from being part of it. The fourth principle rules out utilitarianism[9] as a basis for decision-making. If firms have benefited from society, they have a duty of beneficence to society in return. Corporations receive benefits from society far in excess of corporate taxes returned. These include the provision of legal structures to enforce contracts and the provision of infrastructure (roads, sanitation, police and fire protection, and an educated work force), which allow firms to function.

Bowie acknowledges that purity of motive (actions must arise out of duty in order to be moral) may be too difficult to apply to business. Any action that enhances the bottom line can be interpreted as being motivated out of self-interest. He argues that firms have an obligation to make a profit based on legal obligations to shareholders, the charters of incorporation, and an implied contract with the public. Consequently, the effort to strive for profits can be viewed as a moral one, even in strict Kantian terms. He suggests that instead of focusing on profits as an objective, businesses should view profits as a consequence of good business practice: management should instead focus on respecting the humanity of all stakeholders. In this Bowie seems to mix 1b outcomes with the third kind of policies.

3.3.3 HABERMASIAN DISCOURSE ETHICS: REED (1999, 2002)

Reed takes a 'critical theory approach[10] to normative stakeholder analysis based on the work of Habermas (Vignette 3.3). His approach accords with Donaldson and Preston's view (1995) that normative theory should take precedence over instrumental and descriptive theory (Reed prefers the terms positive and analytical). Reed distinguishes different normative stakeholder theories according to breadth of scope. At one end of the spectrum is narrowly understood professional ethics employing stakeholder analysis. This assumes the basic legitimacy of the profession as well as how it is currently regulated. At the other end is a more broadly understood form of practical ethics, willing to question the legitimacy of the profession and/or how it is currently regulated (2002: 171). This is similar to our third and first kinds of normative theories. Reed places his Habermasian approach firmly in the broad (first kind) end of the spectrum.

Vignette 3.3 HABERMASIAN DISCOURSE ETHICS

Jürgen Habermas' moral theory is grounded in the principle of discourse ethics. His theory is deontological, cognitivist, formalist, and universalist and can be thought of as a scaled-down version of Kant's categorical imperative. Habermas' theory has two central elements, which differentiates it from the moral theories of Rawls (see Vignette 3.5) and Kant.

1. *Practical discourse*. The insistence on participatory 'practical discourse' as a procedure for testing the validity of hypothetical norms, not for producing justified norms. Discourse ethics starts from the assumption that even moral problems are capable of being solved in a rational and cognitive way. Habermas ensures impartiality in the process of making judgements by stipulating that 'only those norms can claim to be valid that meet (or could meet) with the approval of all affected in their capacity as participants in a practical discourse'. (In contrast to Rawls, who seeks to make impartial the orientation of the individual making a moral judgement.)

Vignette 3.3 (*contd.*)

2. *Universalization*. The individual nature of Kant's categorical imperative is transformed into a 'collective imperative' by reformulating it to ensure the expression of a general will. This elevates it to a rule of 'argumentation'. Kant's imperative is extended to include all those affected by a norm or a conflict. Here we are only concerned with the normative content of a *procedure*, not the argument. Habermas is explicit that his theory contains no substantive moral content. The principle of universalization formally determines those conditions that must be met if the claim of legitimacy is really justified:

- *Equal participation* of all who are affected
- *Postulate of unlimitedness*: unboundedness and openness concerning time and persons
- *Postulate of freedom from constraint* from accidental and structural forms of power
- *Postulate of seriousness or authenticity*: the absence of deception in expressing intentions and in performing speech acts.

Habermas (1993) distinguishes three forms of practical reason when addressing the question 'what should I do?'

1. *Pragmatic reasoning* concerns questions of rational choice when the goal of actions is given. The validity claim is effectiveness, which can be contested. Rationality of the claim will depend on the ability to respond to challenges. The 'ought' involves arbitrary choices and is linked to the subject's own interests. Consequently, it involves weak demands. This relates to Kant's 'hypothetical imperatives' and instrumental stakeholder theory.

2. *Ethical reasoning* concerns situations in which the goal of action is being evaluated. The validity claim is goodness. It concerns individuals in relation to their individual identities and life projects, or groups and their collective goals. It does not admit universal judgements. The 'ought' is connected to the interests and identities of relevant parties. This also relates to Kant's 'hypothetical imperatives', though the demands of authenticity take this beyond individual demands of prudence.

3. *Moral reasoning* is concerned with procedures that ought to be implemented for regulating interpersonal affairs and conflicts. The principle of morality is that norms are valid only if everyone could agree to them under 'ideal speech' conditions: truthfulness, absence of coercion, freedom of access, and equal rights to participate. This reflects Kantianism in that the moral force of this discourse is directed to the free will (one that acts autonomously according to self-given laws).

For Reed, an adequate normative stakeholder theory needs to establish:

1. What constitutes a stake? This requires definitions of 'stake' and 'stakeholder'. It must 'establish the type and range of norms that can ground a stake as well as provide some form of justification for these norms' (1999: 467).

2. The extent of management responsibility in the face of stakes and mitigating factors such as others who may share responsibilities (like governments). It requires an elucidation of what extenuating circumstances would diminish or augment management responsibilities.

3. Priority rules to allow conflicts between stakes to be resolved.

Reed distinguishes three types of stake and associated 'normative realms' (Table 3.3) and the associated nature of each type of normative claim, the responsibilities of management, and criteria to evaluate states and management responsibilities.

Table 3.3 The normative basis of stakeholder claims: Habermasian view

Relevant interest of management	Normative claim	Stake	Basic responsibilities	Criteria to evaluate stakes and management responsibilities
Influencing norms and policies of public interaction	Public interaction should be coordinated on the basis of legitimate law	Legitimacy: political equality	Respect legitimate law and conditions necessary for its generation	1. System of rights 2. Principles of the constitutional State
Securing material efficiency needs, pursuing economic management opportunities	Economic structures and practices should reflect a generalizable interest	Morality: fair economic opportunity	Act fairly in a consistent manner	1. Market efficiency 2. Hierarchical 3. Distribution 4. Marginalization 5. Colonization
Developing and sustaining individual and community identity	Community members should live in accord with the norms and values of their chosen communities	Ethics: authenticity	Clarify identity; be authentic	Norms and values consistent with the firm's identity

Source: Adapted from Reed (1999: 471, 478).

The basic responsibilities of management in the normative realm of legitimacy stakes are to respect legitimate law (both the letter and the spirit) and the conditions necessary for its generation. These conditions are the system of rights (for private and public autonomy and welfare rights) and the principles of the constitutional state (popular sovereignty, legal protection, legality of administration, and separation of the state and the society). Management responsibilities concerning private autonomy in relation to employees include issues like drug testing, surveillance, access to personnel information; those concerning public autonomy are to allow employees unpaid leave to run for political office. Separation of State and society refers to lobbying activities and attempts to influence politicians and government officials by threats, bribes, personal relationships, rather than sound arguments.

Management responsibilities in the normative realm of morality concern stakes of fair economic opportunity. Firms producing profits on the basis of efficient allocation of resources, using best available techniques and innovation rather than monopolistic or oligopolistic practices, can evaluate these. A stake is also assumed against the production of negative externalities such as pollution. The management hierarchy condition means 'decision-making should be decentralized and democratized as much as possible (i.e. at least to the point that it does not inhibit efficiency)' (1999: 475). The distributive condition implies that managers should provide wages and benefits that at least match what they are likely to get under the next best alternative system. It also means that firms would be expected to participate in redistribution at the societal level by paying their fair share of taxes. Another criterion is for management to ensure its actions do not deepen marginalization of specific social groups such as racial minorities or women. By colonization Habermas refers to forms of instrumental reason that steer specific systems (money for the economic system; power for the administrative system) spilling over into the lifeworld and displacing communicative reason, i.e. the monetization and bureaucratization of daily life. This relates to treating employees as factors of production and the effects of marketing on creating a consumer culture.

Management responsibilities in the normative realm of ethics concern the stake of authenticity. Ethical judgements involve the validity of ideas of the good and do not make universal claims. 'Not to live according to one's own chosen conception of the good life and the values and norms implicit in it is to be hypocritical, cowardly, inauthentic' (1999: 476). But people and communities can change over time. Reed distinguishes between management responsibility for the firm as a community with an identity, values, and norms and the firm as part of a larger community. He also distinguishes between authenticity of managers as individuals with their own issues, and managers as managers, concerned with the authenticity of the firm and its place in the larger community. He only addresses the latter.

Reed provides some indication of priority rules for competing claims. Between normative claims based on legitimacy and morality there should be little conflict because the basic principles of both derive from the universalizable procedure. However, both claims take precedence over those based upon ethics. Conflict within normative realms will only occur with respect to ethical claims. Reed distinguishes groups internal to the firm (managers, employees, shareholders) and external groups (suppliers, consumers, local communities). He recognizes that his approach is not able to provide priority rules between the groups; the communities themselves must decide how they are to be prioritized. In this sense Reed blends universalist and particularist approaches. However, where there are conflicting views over the identity of the firm between shareholders and other internal stakeholders (managers and employees), Reed judges that shareholder views of how the firm should be run should have priority. This is because the stakes of shareholders are legitimately established property rights and therefore a demand of legitimacy not authenticity. The State, if close to an ideal democracy, can relieve management of some of the above obligations; if not, there will be greater responsibility on all agents, including management.

Strong idealism is represented in Reed's insistence that several different normative claims should all be realized: legal/political, economic, and authenticity of communities. However, this theory is constrained by the recognition that shareholders have property rights over the corporation (1b). Reed's contribution is placed in the 'stakeholders and managers' column of Figure 3.1. He views the firm as a community within itself as well as being part of the larger community and he suggests actions for how communities should behave, placing responsibilities on the stakeholders themselves in identifying how conflicts of interest should be prioritized.

3.3.4 INTEGRATIVE SOCIAL CONTRACTS THEORY: DONALDSON AND DUNFEE (1994, 1999)

Donaldson and Dunfee's Integrative Social Contracts Theory (ISCT) was intended to be a general business ethics theory. It can be regarded as a form of stakeholder theory based on a social contract (Vignette 3.4).

Vignette 3.4 WHAT IS A SOCIAL CONTRACT?

A social contract is a thought experiment designed to ensure fairness in setting its terms. Widely used in traditional philosophy, it is thought of as a contract between the people comprising a State. Socrates argued that a guilty person should accept punishment meted out by the laws of Athens, rather than escape to another city, because that person had implicitly agreed to abide by its laws, through the act of choosing to live there. These laws ensure the Athenian way of life and security of living there (Plato 1981).

The 'State of Nature' or the 'natural' condition specified in the thought experiment prior to the establishment of society is crucial for the social contract and the obligations derived from it. Hobbes (1588–1679) assumed people to be exclusively self-interested in his version of the State of Nature in which resources are limited. Terms like good and bad have no meaning other than to describe our likes and dislikes. People have the rational capacity to pursue their desires as effectively as possible, but not to determine what to desire: rationality is purely instrumental. In this State of Nature life is brutal and short: a perpetual state of war and devoid of trust. Even the strongest fear for their lives as they can be killed in their sleep. In these circumstances people can be expected to construct a Social Contract in which all would agree to establish society by giving up the right they had to deal with each other individually in favour of common laws. They would give a single person or group of people the authority and power to enforce the contract and those laws (Hobbes 1651/1958).

For Locke (1632–1704) the State of Nature is pre-political but not pre-moral. In it people are equally able to discover and be bound by the Law of Nature. All belong equally to God and because we cannot take what is rightfully His, we are prohibited from harming others with regard to their life, health, liberty, or possessions. Private property is created when a person mixes labour with the raw material of nature, but the Law of Nature implies that no one is allowed to take more from nature than they can use. This is a state of complete liberty, to live life free from interference from others. It is also conceived as a set of families or a conjugal society. However, it could devolve into a state of war over property disputes. The Social Contract arises when individual men representing their families agree to give up the power to punish those who transgress the Law of Nature and give it over to a government. They then become subject to the will of the majority. Unlike Hobbes, Locke allows for the Social Contract to be broken if government devolves into tyranny. Furthermore, resistance to the civil government is justified in these circumstances.

According to Rousseau (1712–78) in the State of Nature the population was small and nature easily satisfied people's needs. They lived simple, free, and solitary lives, which were morally pure due to their natural endowment with a capacity for pity. Over time people came to live together in small families and then small communities.

Vignette 3.4 (*contd.*)

With the division of labour, leisure time became available and private property invented. This led to people making comparisons with others and to envy, pride, vanity, greed, competition, inequality, and vice. Eventually, those with property came to create a government to protect it from others who would take it by force; a government that appeared to guarantee equality and protection for all, but in fact maintained existing inequalities.

Rousseau contrasted this 'historical' social contract with a normative one designed to restore freedom in the new circumstances of civilization. In it we are recommended to come together to form a 'people', where individuals transfer individual rights and freedoms from the State of Nature to a collective body, which may be said to possess the general will directed towards the common good. This requires direct democracy whereby each citizen decides collectively how to live and what laws to enact in near unanimity. To achieve this people must assemble regularly. It cannot rely on representative democracy and was intended by Rousseau to apply only to relatively small states where people can identify with one another.

ISCT suggests that management should take into account the *norms* (not interests) of certain stakeholders because society allows corporations to operate in exchange for the promotion of society's interests. This differs from many stakeholder theories in that it distinguishes certain moral restrictions on those stakeholder norms as well as obligations on management. Donaldson and Dunfee frame their theory in part as an answer to criticisms that stakeholder theory:

- is mute with respect to community standards;
- leaves unresolved problems of stakeholders who have conflicting interests and questions of who should be counted as stakeholders;
- lacks a normative foundation for assessing the ethical validity of the interests asserted by particular stakeholders and for identifying and prioritizing rights and duties of affected stakeholders;
- lacks sophistication needed to allow precise moral distinctions in moral dilemmas.

They proposed a two-level normative theory based on two kinds of contracts.

1. A normative hypothetical *macrosocial* contract among economic participants, created 'by including among the contractors *all* persons whose interests are affected and by requiring consensus in the adoption of the terms of the contract' (1994: 260). These contractors are distinguished as those 'who are aware of the strongly bounded nature of moral rationality in economic affairs'. The content of the macrosocial contract would be a set of *hypernorms* that 'entail principles so fundamental to human existence that they serve as a guide in evaluating lower level moral norms' (1994: 265).

2. An existing implicit *microsocial* contract arising from specific communities that are 'a self-defined, self-circumscribed group of people who interact in the context of shared tasks, values, or goals and who are capable of establishing norms of ethical behavior for themselves' (1994: 262). They can be firms, groupings within firms, industries, professional bodies, and national and international economic organizations.

The need for a two-level theory arises due to 'bounded moral rationality'. People have a finite capacity to understand details of the 'facts' of ethical relevance to a specific situation. Also, they are bounded by the limited ability of moral theory to account for the numerous and changing divergence between common sense moral convictions and what moral theory dictates (different moral priorities given, say, to family members and nationals compared with non-family members and foreigners). Finally, there is a particular problem with business ethics in that economic systems are artefacts ('games') made by people and clearly different for different groups of people (such as differing conceptions of the firm in capitalist and communist societies).

Donaldson and Dunfee's model is communitarian in nature, as macrosocial contractors will insist on 'moral free space' in their transactions. This permits a degree of latitude in the establishment of ethical criteria within the bounds of the relevant communities, the details of which are the subject matter for the microsocial contracts. They propose several principles for the macrosocial contract (1994: 262–9) and provide a complex set of priority rules for dealing with situations in which norms conflict, even when they are authentic and legitimate:

1. Local communities, through microsocial contracts, specify ethical norms for their members.
2. Microsocial contracts must be grounded in 'informed consent buttressed by a right of exit' to be regarded as 'authentic'. Consent need not be expressed: engaging in a practice can be sufficient to imply consent.
3. A microsocial contract norm must be compatible with hypernorms to be obligatory.
4. Priority among norms satisfying Principles 1–3 must be based on consistency with the spirit and letter of the macrosocial contract.

Donaldson and Dunfee clearly state that a person is entitled to object or to try and change a norm (voice), leave an economic group (exit), or refuse to obey a norm (civil disobedience). Bishop (2000: 577) argues that the normative decision principle is not simply that 'economic agents should act according to the norms of the relevant groups unless those violate a hypernorm' but that 'they can be exercised if a person thinks the norm is not in her self-interest'. He suggests a reformulated decision principle: 'people should pursue their economic self-interests by creating, entering, changing and/or exiting economic groups with norms that are authentic and legitimate' (2000: 578).

Consent is necessary, though not sufficient, for a transaction to be morally legitimate. Coercion would invalidate consent such as with indentured servitude or commercial slavery. Donaldson and Dunfee state that coercive restraint on the right to exit is uncommon in commerce, but they ask: 'Can poor employees living in areas of extremely high unemployment, with no alternate sources of work or food, be said to have 'consented' to the terms of their employment through their failure to exit?' They leave the issue unresolved, however it is arguably a severe problem for the authenticity of community norms.

ISCT is a theory of the first kind because:

1. The macrosocial contract arises through a hypothetical and rational process in the tradition of social contract theory.
2. The macrosocial contract dominates microsocial contract.

The macrosocial contract is a social contract in the tradition of social contract philosophy while the microsocial contract is an *implicit contract* meaning that it is unspoken and unwritten, but presumed to exist among real people in real situations, as opposed to a thought experiment among idealized participants.

Donaldson and Dunfee emphasize that their theory takes into account real implicit contracts of actual communities. They are 'the ties that bind' (Donaldson and Dunfee 1999) and refer to a general approach to business ethics. ISCT is one of the few normative models that apply equally to all agents, as obvious from where it has been placed in Figure 3.1.

3.3.5 RAWLSIAN STAKEHOLDER THEORY

For Freeman and Phillips, stakeholder theory should reflect the principle of stakeholder fairness based on the concept of fair play as discussed by John Stuart Mill in 1859 and elaborated by John Rawls (Vignette 3.5).

Vignette 3.5 RAWLS'S THEORY OF JUSTICE

John Rawls (1921–2002) believed politics based on justice could not rely on our intuitions about good social outcomes.[11] Rather it should be based on the idea of 'procedural justice': the design of a procedure embodying in its structure the moral ideal of justice. Rawls turns the 'ends justify the means' formula on its head; the means justify the end for his 'Entitlement Theorem' (Rawls 1971). This is based on a thought experiment in which people of roughly equal ability decide to agree on principles of social cooperation (the 'basic structure' of society): a form of social contract. They are presumed to be in 'the original position', i.e. they are able to develop whatever principles they wish. This includes the political constitution, legally recognized forms of property, how the economy is organized, and the nature of the family. These are distinguished from particular organizations such as corporations and other voluntary associations, which will develop 'later' within the basic structure.

In this thought experiment people are assumed to be rational and self-interested, but also cognisant that their needs can be more effectively met by cooperation than non-cooperation. They do this on the basis of the 'veil of ignorance'. In this procedure participants do not know their place in society, family background, talent, intelligence, work ethic, or other distinguishing characteristic. Like the situation of siblings dividing a cake, one can trust the other to divide fairly (equally) if they do not know which piece they will get. Rawls presumes

(contd.)

Vignette 3.5 (*contd.*)

people would arrive at an arrangement of society's benefits and burdens that would be fair to all because they did not know who they will be when the veil is lifted and society goes about its activity.

The thought experiment is assumed to lead to a set of principles arranged in lexical order (the higher principles must be satisfied before lower ones are applied):

1. The *Liberty* principle: Each person should have equal right to the most extensive total system of basic liberty compatible with a similar system of liberty for all.
2. The *Difference* principle: Social and economic inequalities must be arranged to the greatest benefit of the least advantaged and attached to positions open to all under conditions of fair equality of opportunity.
3. *Efficiency*: All social primary goods (liberty, opportunity, income, wealth, and the bases of self-respect) are to be distributed equally unless an unequal distribution, which is more efficient (whereby more can be produced with available resources), is to the advantage of the least favoured.

3.3.5.1 Fair contracts: Freeman (1994, 2004)

Freeman (1994) developed a 'normative core' for stakeholder theory based on the idea that value creation activity is a contractual process among financiers, customers, suppliers, employees, and communities.[12] The normative core adopts the Rawlsian liberal notions of autonomy, solidarity, and fairness. Freeman's intention was to address Goodpaster's 'Separation Thesis' (1991), i.e. business without ethics or ethics without business was a paradox that could not be resolved by existing stakeholder theory (Section 3.5.3). In doing so Freeman invokes a Rawlsian thought experiment. The contract defines the 'rules of the game' of how the corporation will operate (the 'corporate constitution') what is to be decided behind a veil of ignorance. Stakeholder representatives are assumed to be rationally self-interested and to:

- Possess knowledge of current and potential corporate arrangements.
- Possess knowledge of the range of other social institutions that exist.
- Understand the implications of different corporate designs for success or failure.

Under these circumstances the parties would choose the following six ground rules, which Freeman (1994: 416–17) labels the 'Doctrine of Fair Contracts'.

1. *The principle of entry and exit*: The contract has to define processes that clarify entry, exit, and renegotiation conditions for stakeholders to decide when an agreement exists and if it can be fulfilled.
2. *The principle of governance*: Procedures for changing the rules of the game must be agreed by unanimous consent. This would lead to 'each stakeholder never giving up its right to participate in the governance of the corporation' and may lead to stakeholder governing boards. Mechanisms involving stakeholder representatives rather than each individual stakeholder can be invented.

3. *The principle of externalities*: '[I]f a contract between A and B imposes a cost on C, then C has the option to become a party to the contract, and the terms renegotiated.'[13]

4. *The principle of contracting costs*: '[A]ll parties to the contract must share in the cost of contracting'.

5. *The agency principle*: '[A]ny agent must serve the interests of all stakeholders. It must adjudicate conflicts within the bounds of the other principals.'

6. *The principle of limited immortality*: 'The corporation shall be managed as if it can continue to serve the interests of stakeholders through time.' Though stakeholders are uncertain about the future, they know the corporation's continued existence is in their interests and those of the collective. This principle becomes unnecessary if the collective interest is merely the sum of individual interests.

Autonomy is achieved by 'the realization that each stakeholder must be free to enter agreements that create value for themselves' (1994: 416).[14] The liberal ideal of solidarity is realized through recognition of the mutuality of stakeholder interests (principle 6 and partly principles 2 and 5). The liberal ideal of fairness comes from 'a basic equality among stakeholders in terms of their moral rights, as these are realized in the firm, and if it recognizes that inequalities among stakeholders are justified if they raise the level of the least well-off stakeholder' (415–16). The latter condition is not explicitly addressed in the six principles, but is presumed to result from their operation as a whole. The principles represent an ideal to guide actual stakeholders in devising a corporate constitution or charter. Freeman recognizes that laws would have to change to enable this to occur and proposes stakeholder enabling, director responsibility, and stakeholder recourse principles described in Section 1.1.

3.3.5.2 Stakeholder fairness: Phillips (1997, 2003*b*)

Phillips proposes a stakeholder fairness principle in response to criticisms that stakeholder theory lacks the philosophical sophistication of other business ethics models.

Obligations of fairness arise when individuals, or groups of individuals interact for mutual benefit. Such persons and groups engage in voluntary activities that require mutual contribution and restriction of liberty. These voluntary activities provide a normative justification (on par with consent) for the idea of stakeholder management. (1997: 52)

and

Whenever persons or groups of persons voluntarily accept the benefits of a mutually beneficial scheme of co-operation requiring a sacrifice or contribution on the parts of the participants and there exists a possibility of free-riding, obligations of fairness are created among the participants in the co-operative scheme in proportion to the benefits accepted. (2003*b*: 116)

Phillips notes four conditions for a moral system based on *obligation* (as opposed to other moral concepts such as *duty*). He claims that the principles are 'operative in all contexts of commercial interaction' (2003*b*: 96).

1. Principle of organizational ethics. Organizational obligations are generated by a voluntary act,[15] characterized by the possibility of exit. This is a key structural distinction that would not apply to all moral considerations (as participation in the human race is not voluntary) and does not apply in the same way to participation in a particular polity. Emigration is an option for the latter, but for Rawls, justice in a society must not depend on emigration. This is the basis on which Rawls distinguishes justice from fairness: both concern reciprocity, but justice refers to 'a practice in which there is no option whether to engage in it or not, and one must play' and fairness refers to 'a practice in which there is such an option, and one may decline the invitation' (2003*b*: 190).[16] This should exclude innocent bystanders and limit inclusion to genuine parties who either try and succeed in getting the benefit or take the benefit willingly and knowingly (2003*b*: 97).

2. Obligations are owed by a specific individual (obligor) to another specific individual or individuals (obligee(s)), i.e. obligations are not owed to 'all people' as are other duties.

3. '[F]or every obligation generated, a correlative right is simultaneously generated.'

4. The act is obligatory due to the relationship entered into, not the nature of the required act itself. Whether the act is itself a moral act or not is a distinct issue, and it may be that the morality of the act required needs to be weighed against the duty to fulfil an obligation.[17]

Only some previously defined stakeholders would qualify as normative stakeholders entitled to fairness-based stakeholder consideration by managers. Stakeholder fairness allows the Donaldson and Preston (1995: 86) distinction between people who have a stake in an organization and those who can influence the corporation to be clarified. For Phillips, the latter groups are derivatively legitimate stakeholders: 'groups whose actions and claims must be accounted for by managers due to their potential effects upon the normative stakeholders' (2003*b*: 125) such as activists, competitors, and the media. Their legitimacy is not due to any obligations due to themselves directly. This leads to a rather differently structured typical stakeholder map (Figure 3.2).

Phillips admits that his model only allows stakeholders to be identified, it says nothing about how the cooperative scheme should be organized or how obligations should be fulfilled. The content arises from specific stakeholder interactions, and the stakeholders themselves must decide how the scheme should be organized. However, he does suggest that communicative discourse ethics should be used to analyse and judge particular schemes. Following Habermas (1990: 66), to be valid, norms must 'meet (or

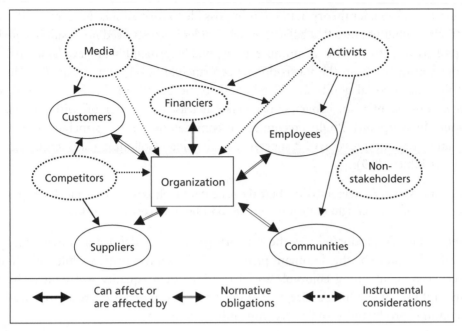

Figure 3.2 Stakeholder map—legitimate, derivative, and non-stakeholders
Source: Phillips (2003*b*: 127)

could meet) with the approval of all affected in their capacity *as participants in a practical discourse*. This is intended to qualify 'communicative action' whereby one seeks to motivate another rationally by relying on the 'illocutionary binding/bonding effect of the offer contained in their speech act' as opposed to 'strategic action' whereby one seeks to influence the behaviour of another via the 'threat of sanctions or the prospect of gratification in order to *cause* the interaction to continue as the first actor desires'. For discourse by which stakeholder norms are tested to be moral, they must adhere to what Habermas calls an 'ideal speech situation' whereby 'all external or internal coercion other than the force of the better argument' is ruled out (1990: 58). The problem with this test is that the ideal is almost impossible to realize in the real world, so it must remain a relative test, leading to the notion that morality is relative. Phillips recognizes this problem to some extent when he states: 'While difficult in practice, the implication is that managing for stakeholders would entail duplicating as far as possible the conditions of the ideal speech situation' (2003*b*: 112).

Phillips recommends particular norms for determining at least which normative stakeholders 'should' receive more attention than others by suggesting the principle of equity (rather than equality or need) should apply. This distances him from the view of many normative stakeholder theorists who suggest that all (legitimate) stakeholders should be treated equally. It distances him from the criticism that this is a weakness of normative stakeholder theory in that it is impossible to treat all stakeholders equally and be efficient. Phillips notes that balancing stakeholder interests need not result in equality of returns and treatment. A number of equitable principles are available such as egalitarianism based on the Rawls difference principle (1971) (any inequalities in the distribution of social goods should rebound to the benefit of the least well off) and pareto-consequentialism (policies that make at least one better off without making anyone else worse off). Phillips recommends consideration of the principle of meritocracy and cites an expression of it suggested by the Sloan Colloquy (Clarkson Center for Business Ethics 1999):

Corporations should attempt to distribute the benefits of their activities as equitably as possible among stakeholders, in light of their respective contributions, costs, and risks.

When economic productivity is the primary goal, equity defined as meritocracy (as above) will tend to be the dominant principle of distributive justice, while if the aim is fostering or maintaining enjoyable social relations then equality will tend to be the dominant principle. Phillips accepts that the primary aim of commercial organizations is economic productivity and so recommends meritocracy.

3.3.6 THE COMMON GOOD: ARGANDOÑA (1998)

The common good (Vignette 3.6) is the only religion-based value used to develop a normative stakeholder model; all other models are based on philosophical values or no foundations are given. The concept is largely associated with Christian theologians like Saint Augustine and Thomas of Aquinas, though it can be traced back to Aristotle.

Vignette 3.6 THE COMMON GOOD

The utilitarian version of the common good is nothing more than the sum of the utilities of each individual. Valasquez (1992) refers to this as the weak definition and associates it with a collective good. The strong version is associated with Catholicism: 'the overall conditions of life in society that allow different groups and their members to achieve their own perfection more fully and more easily' (The Second Vatican Council 1965, cited in Argandoña 1998: 1095). Simply stated, it is everything that is good to more than one person, that is common to all. Valasquez cites Wallace (1977):

> A common good is clearly distinct from a private good, the latter being the good of one person only, to the exclusion of its being possessed by any other. A common good is distinct also from a collective good, which, though possessed by all of a group, is not really participated in by the members of the group; divided up, a collective good becomes respectively the private goods of the members. A true common good is universal, not singular or collective, and is distributive in character, being communicable to many without becoming anyone's private good. Moreover, each person participates in the whole common good, not merely in a part of it, nor can any one person possess it wholly. (1992: 29)

Vignette 3.6 (*contd.*)

This includes all goods that benefit all the members of a society in the sense that they have access to these goods. Common goods are not divisible, and no one can be excluded from enjoying them. It is more than the agglomeration of the interests of the individuals that make up society, because society enables its members to achieve a greater degree of perfection. Therefore it includes, but exceeds, laws and institutions that uphold the law such as the army and institutions that meet general needs for education, health care, or culture. The primacy of the common good does not exclude pursuit of private ends as such, only pursuing those that are to the detriment of the common good. The personal objectives of people are associated with the assertion: 'Man is a social being', which means '(1) that he needs others to satisfy his own needs, and (2) that he improves himself (becomes "more human", exercises and develops his capacities) in his relationships with others' (Argandoña 1998: 1094).

Argandoña (1998) presents the common good as a possible foundation for stakeholder theory, but also suggests that stakeholder theory may help to clarify the meaning of the common good itself. The common good of the company is to create the conditions that will enable its members to achieve their personal goals. The company facilitates achieving these personal goals through achievement of its own goals.

Company obligations to contribute to the common good extend 'from the common good of the company itself to that of the local community, the country and all humankind, including future generations' (1998: 1099). Stakeholders seem to provide a transmission mechanism of different routes whereby company obligations move from the common good of the company itself to that of all humanity. Argandoña proposes that the common good extends to all corporate relationships. This would extend the list of stakeholders 'until it encompasses all men of all times, by virtue of the unity of the human family' (1998: 1099). This is confusing as he talks of the society that he is encompassing including those with whom the company has social relations. He discusses a different type of 'society' and a different common good, comparing the duties of a construction company that occasionally builds a block of flats in a town, with an animal feed factory with premises in the town. If it extends to all of society, it is difficult to see what the concept of stakeholders has to offer that is not covered by the concept of humanity and 'man as a social being'. Further confusion arises when Argandoña states that he is not necessarily suggesting that companies do 'something special'. 'A company that shows a normal ethical concern for the problems of the local community fulfils most of its duties towards that community in the ordinary run of its activities' (1998: 1100). This seems an extraordinary statement: Who is to define what normal ethical concern means? Just as maintaining an army is hard to justify in terms of contributing to the common good of all humanity. In spite of the seemingly clear intention that the common good is an ideal concept to which society should tend leading to a first kind theory in our model, it appears from the above that Argandoña builds into his theory a third kind of argument, that this can be achieved without substantial social change. For Argandoña the common good is there already, embodied within existing social arrangements, or more accurately it is independent of particular social arrangements, inherent in any social arrangements. Rather it is a matter of people expressing what is their God-given potentiality through their inherent sociability.

Argandoña admits that the concept is open to vague and contradictory interpretations and it is not accepted as a concept by many. 'Perfection' and becoming 'more human' are conceptual vessels that can be filled in many ways. Who is to say what is the true purpose of a business enterprise? Who is to decide what are useful products? The market? The market for cigarettes and military hardware?

Even if we were to accept the notion of the common good for society as a whole, there is a particular problem in applying the concept to 'lesser societies'. Some in those societies exclude others from them. Also, the common good may be most associated with the longevity of a company, but some will have an interest in destroying the company. For example, if it is insolvent, creditors will want to bankrupt the company to realize some proportion of the liabilities accrued to them. According to Argandoña: 'to the extent that the company develops its common good, all will have a share in it (although in different ways and in different proportions)' (1998: 1098). What about employees who are dismissed due to needed cost savings when a fall in product demand occurs in order to maintain the common good of remaining stakeholders?

Valasquez (1992) highlights that businesses operating in a competitive international environment do not have any moral obligations to contribute to the international common good, such as the avoidance of greenhouse gases or the avoidance of a global nuclear war, due to an absence of an enforcement agency. He argues that the common good is susceptible to the free rider problem. One function of government is supposedly to solve this problem by forcing all companies within its jurisdiction to contribute to the maintenance of the common good. International companies can be forced to do so through their relations with host governments. However, governments themselves can be free riders and can join forces with corporations to gain a competitive advantage in a global market. Realists such as Thomas Hobbes (1958)[18] argue that morality has no place in international affairs and so multinationals are *not* morally obliged to contribute to global common goods. Argandoña does not address this concern despite aiming his stakeholder model at 'all of humanity'.

3.4 **Normative theories of the second kind**

3.4.1 FEMINIST THEORIES

Traditional economics-based approaches to management have concentrated on the legalistic, contractual (as a surrogate for trust), masculine side of human existence (Burton and Dunn 1996). Managers are presumed to view the corporation as being in competition with others. Managers are presumed to act to protect and further the interests of the corporation alone, or at least it is presumed that incentives will be in place to encourage them to act in the interests of the corporation rather than their own self-interest. Stakeholder theory can be viewed as a feminine counterpart, whereby corporations seek to promote stakeholder satisfaction through a more cooperative, caring relationship. This reinterpretation of stakeholder theory is informed by the feminist ethics of care (Vignette 3.7).

Vignette 3.7 VIRTUE ETHICS AND FEMINIST ETHICS

Virtue ethics has evolved from Aristotlean morality. Moral philosophy is often traced to the Ancient Greeks. For Socrates (469–399 BC) people have a function (real self) and 'real' happiness comes from achieving perfection of this real self. This can be discovered through discussion, debate, and self-reflection. Morality is a journey of self-discovery, which, when and if achieved, will lead people to know what is right. Plato (428–354 BC) viewed moral facts as existing in the universe in coded form, discoverable through rational thought by elite philosophers. Aristotle (384–322 BC) was concerned with ordinary goodness whereby morality is an individual matter, associated with our purpose in life and the self-fulfilment of that purpose, which differs between people.

For MacIntyre (1981) the basis of ethics is the virtues necessary to be a good person: strength, courage, comradeship, legal and distributive justice, temperance, and wisdom. Virtue is a disposition or set of dispositions, based on innate capacities, which can become habitual if honed by exercise: a person becomes just by performing just acts. Our motivation and our desires can be shaped by the particular traditions we follow. We must look to history to identify virtues. People can (and should) be encouraged to exercise those virtues by public praise and encouragement. If people act out of virtuous feelings, one is more likely to find them trustworthy compared with those who act merely out of a sense of obligation or self-interest.[19]

Feminist ethics is related to virtue ethics. It postulates that caring is good and that marginal voices must be heard. The ethics of care focuses on virtues that are associated with close relationships: sympathy, compassion, love, faithfulness, and friendship.

Feminist approaches are characterized by two presumptions: the subordination of women is as wrong as it is common and the experiences of women are worthy of respect and should be taken seriously. They emphasize the way men have denigrated the nature of women as irrational, passive, selfless, sympathetic, and compassionate. 'Feminine' qualities, such as cooperation and caring, are virtues to be celebrated and if incorporated would radically reform business practice (Beauchamp and Bowie 2004).

Feminists criticize Rawlsian, Kantian, and utilitarian ethics for treating humans individualistically: the self cannot be separated from its existence and relationships. Universal principles are inadequate guides to actions because they fail to consider the beliefs, attitudes, feelings, and concerns of individuals involved. For Gilligan (1982) the voice of care and compassion is more prevalent in females (care perspective) and masculine discourse is more prevalent in males (justice perspective). Though often thought of as gender issues, types of discourse are present in varying degrees in both sexes. For Gilligan, women tend to conceptualize moral questions as problems of caring involving empathy and compassion, while men conceptualize them as problems of rights, although this is disputed (Dobson 1996) and believed to be dependent upon individual needs and actions. Moral judgements should be made within the specific context (relationships and emotions) of the problems being addressed. Instead of the relentless and insensitive application of moral systems to moral problems, negotiation is encouraged, perhaps mediated by sympathetic and careful supporters.[20]

Feminist interpretations of stakeholder theory are classified as the second kind of theories. They argue that norms, already existing in certain spheres and among certain people, should be extended to other situations. They call for more cooperative, caring type of relationships in which firms seek to make decisions that satisfy stakeholders, leading to situations where all parties are involved in a relationship gain. The inherent relatedness of the firm should force the firm to examine the effect of its decisions on others. By stressing relationships and not rights, responsibilities are brought to the forefront of all managerial thought. Institutional change is called for if a guiding principle based on feminist ethics is adopted.

3.4.1.1 Feminist reinterpretation: Wicks, Gilbert, and Freeman (1994)

Wicks, Gilbert, and Freeman (1994) call for a reinterpretation of stakeholder theory based on Gilligan's ethics of care and dispute the male gender bias of traditional economics-based approaches to management. They restate five examples of masculine metaphors that have shaped the stakeholder concept and thought about business in general.

1. Corporations should be thought of as autonomous entities, independent from, and separate to, their environment and hence from their stakeholders. From the feminist perspective, individuals are connected through a web of relations, which together with the language and culture experienced, form part of their existence. Individuals retain distinct personal identities, but they are not isolated from connections with others. As the corporation comprises a network of relations, the corporate boundary is extended to incorporate 'external' parties (stakeholders). Wicks, Gilbert, and Freeman embellish the debate to suggest that a failure by managers to reject the concept of 'them and us' with respect to stakeholders will render managers at a disadvantage:

    [C]ompanies and persons cannot ignore the responsibility they bear for all of their actions which affect others, even when there is no legal duty to refrain from such behavior. Replacing the identity of persons as isolated and autonomous with a model which fundamentally ties them together not only makes these sensibilities intelligible, but provides an impetus for acting on them. (1994: 484)

2. Corporations can and should enact or control their external environment. The desire for control partially stems from fear of uncertainty and disorder. This has clear associations with traditional strategic analysis, whereby managers seek to identify and analyse strengths, weaknesses, opportunities, and threats in order to govern these forces and to thrive. For feminists, change would be viewed as a dynamic new experience offering new opportunities. The 'external environment' is captured to some degree through relationship networks. The desire is to achieve equilibrium, harmony, and sustainability rather than control the environment. This suggests it is

best to accept change and work in partnership with others in the network to try to achieve positive inclusive outcomes.

3. The language of competition and conflict best describes managing a firm. Competition is essential to a healthy, efficient corporation and violent terms such as 'kill or be killed', 'outgun the opposition' and 'look out for number one' prevail (1994: 487). Such language damages the network of relationships and undermines trust and the potential for cooperation. Language emphasizing cooperation, effective communication, and caring to resolve conflict can facilitate trust building and enable negotiated discussions that offer win–win solutions.

4. Objective thinking in generating strategy, reliance on 'hard facts', 'scientific' models, or 'scientifically' supported analysis not only contributes to removing the decision-maker from their culture, beliefs and perceptions, but also discourages interpretations of stakeholders as legitimate individuals with rights. Feminists embrace the notion that human perception should be mistrusted. The human capacity to call upon empathy and communication facilitates problem-solving. Feminists reject science on several accounts: it cannot tell us how we live and relationships cannot be easily abstracted. Rather than looking to science, statistics, or facts to create an image of a problem that all can accept, stakeholders must work through the painful process of piecing together their different impressions of the situation, what is at stake, and how it can be best dealt with (Wicks, Gilbert, and Freeman 1994: 489). These views are embraced within postmodernism (Vignette 3.8).

5. Corporations should structure power and authority with strict hierarchies. Hierarchies are in part a consequence of the first four metaphors: they satisfy the desire for order, they simplify the channels in which blame and responsibility are funnelled, and they facilitate quick and effective control. On the other hand, hierarchies stifle creativity and innovation from those occupying lower echelons. Feminism would suggest replacing hierarchies with radical decentralized corporate structures characterized by employee empowerment.

Feminist theory advocates that value should be created for the entire network. For stakeholder management this would be achievable through strategic decision-making that embraces power decentralization, cooperation, and consensus building among stakeholders.

3.4.1.2 Feminist ethics: Burton and Dunn (1996)

Wicks, Gilbert, and Freeman are criticized by Burton and Dunn (1996) for calling for a rule of consensus and understanding, following the ethics of care, as this is only achievable if all parties adopt a caring approach and individuals do not insist on advancing individual rights. Drawing on Noddings (1984) in the field of ethics of care, who recognizes that people naturally privilege family members and friends in decision-making, Burton and Dunn expand on Wicks, Gilbert, and Freeman and derive a guiding principle for managers faced with balancing stakeholder demands: 'I will privilege those with whom I have a close relationship' (1996: 142–3). However, this they argue should be partially rejected. Burton and Dunn illustrate why through the story of managers of a US corporation deciding how to dispose of lead acid batteries. Wishing to act responsibly and recycle the batteries, the managers are concerned with the cost of recycling and with regulations regarding health and safety at work. They send the batteries to Taiwan to be recycled, where health and safety regulations are less stringent. The ethics of care principle is being followed, but by privileging those with whom they have a close relationship (US employees) their actions harm Taiwanese workers. This conflicts with basic moral ethics. Burton and Dunn reformulate the principle to read 'care enough for the least advantaged stakeholders that they not be harmed; insofar as they are not harmed, privilege those stakeholders with whom you have a close relationship' (1996: 144). Not only should those with a stake in a decision be considered, and the associated power of each, but also those most vulnerable to the outcome of the decision.

3.4.2 POSTMODERN NORMATIVE THEORIES

Postmodern ideas have influenced several normative stakeholder theories. Postmodernism contains echoes of pragmatism, virtue ethics, and feminist ethics. As a general movement of late twentieth century thought, postmodernist ideas may be regarded as inspiring or supporting (or a way of labelling) ideas that recognize the need to introduce particularist elements to theories that have previously relied on universalist principles or the search for universalist principles in normative theory (Section 3.5). Postmodernism may be regarded as a way of encouraging us to think about what is left out of taken-for-granted ideas and theories, which may then encourage us to develop more rounded theories. This is one way of interpreting the whole stakeholder debate. Normative stakeholder theory may be interpreted as a call to recognize and take into account interests and relationships that are left out of traditional theories of the purpose of the corporation, the range of managerial responsibilities, and the recognition of who and what should count in making policy about the corporation. However, postmodernism may also be regarded as a particularist way of thinking that ultimately denies universalism and the validity of tools used by others to establish universalist principles. The line of postmodern thinking can lead further to denial of the validity of normative theory per se and to radical relativism (Vignette 3.8).

Vignette 3.8 POSTMODERNISM

Postmodernist philosophy has interesting similarities with pragmatism (Vignette 3.1) though its origins are primarily French rather than American. It is generally associated with Foucault (1972, 1973), Lyotard (1984), Derrida (1978, 1980), and Baudrillard (1981), but has gained many adherents since the early 1980s. It represents a more fundamental critique of Enlightenment thought (or modernism) and is associated with a view of social and cultural change (postmodernity) as well as economic change (post-industrialism), a change in political thought, and a change in critical thought (post-structuralism). The literature on postmodernism is huge and extremely varied (see Best and Kellner 1991).

Most postmodern theorists follow discourse theory on assuming that it is language, signs, images, codes, and signifying systems that organize the psyche, society, and everyday life. Meaning is socially constructed across a number of institutional sites and practices. The purpose of discourse theory is to analyse the institutional basis of discourse, the viewpoints and positions from which people speak, and the power relations these allow and presuppose. Different groups strive for hegemony in the production of meaning and ideology.

Postmodernism can be grasped as a set of features, many of which only make sense as juxtapositions with how postmodern theorists characterize modernity and modernism. Postmodernists explicitly reject the grand narratives of modernist thinking, whether they are in terms of human progress, development of national identities and structures, or dialectical change through the activities of social classes. The Enlightenment project promises liberation, but masks forms of oppression and domination behind a barrier of reason. Such totalizing, or all-encompassing explanations in history, science, and culture are rejected in favour of localizing and contingent theories. More fundamental, the very categories used in such interpretations of history are rejected. Rejected are not only categories such as well-defined classes, nation states, mass culture, and science, but also the way such theories operate and the nature of their claims to truth. These theories lay claim to a reality lying below the surface of appearances, by which the true or essential nature of individual and social life may be discovered using careful methods, building on insights gained by past thinkers and only amenable to being set out clearly and comprehensively by individuals seriously dedicated to such activity. All these presumptions are turned on their head by various postmodern thinkers. For postmodernists our sense experience is so thoroughly mediated by manipulated images, particularly through television, that our experience is of 'hyper-reality' whereby there is no depth below surface experiences to be found. Language cannot help because the idea of language faithfully representing a reality is lost, because what is signified and signifiers are elided.

Given this perspective, a common postmodern method of analysis is 'deconstruction'. All texts are viewed as historically situated and deriving meaning through difference with other tests. Meaning is a shifting field of relations that draws on implied or explicitly stated 'Other' or opposites. However there is no resolution or synthesis in the deconstruction method. It is always seeking prior patterns of difference and traces of the exercise of power in prioritizing certain meanings over their 'Other'.

Our very selves are fragmented. We create for ourselves multiple and often conflicting identities in situations that have no simple logical connection. The sense of order and hierarchy through which we might 'map' our position in the world and our consequent sense of self is subverted. Relationships can develop in many new ways. Lack of a 'right' way to think and act is associated with the aestheticization of activities and values, and a shift of attention towards micro relations and individual identities. The look and feel of life becomes more important. Seeking truth and following ethical codes are replaced by virtuosity in playfulness, irony, and metaphor. Morality is more concerned with the immediate impulse of sympathy, through proximate, face-to-face encounters and the ephemeral spontaneous sociality of the crowd, rather than the establishment of ethical codes for universal timeless, placeless application (Bauman 1993).

3.4.2.1 Stakeholder enabling: Calton and Kurland (1995)[21]

Calton and Kurland's postmodern theory of 'stakeholder enabling' decentres organizational discourse by replacing privileged managerial monologues with multilateral stakeholder dialogues. 'Managing' is the process by which agents of the organization exercise control over stakeholders within an institutionalized hierarchy; while 'enabling' is a process of stakeholders, together with agents, jointly exercising control over shared concerns (1995: 156). They note that other authors assume top managers 'are equivalent to the firm and that managers deal with stakeholders through separate bilateral contractual relationships'. In these circumstances top managers maintain 'privileged' control of separate stakeholder dialogue 'texts' (1995: 160).

Calton and Kurland believe their analysis will 'empower the silent voices of marginal groups by deconstructing the hidden meaning within the predominant organizational context' (1995: 164), thus enabling multiple-stakeholder discourses. They also advocate that 'stakeholders must have capacity to co-determine their own identity and destiny by exercising the right of voice or exit in the process of organization discourse' (1995: 171). Donaldson and Dunfee's ISCT model is criticized because their thought experiment 'lacks a viable voice mechanism at either the macro- or microsocial level' and ignores 'power differences among and between macro- and microsocial contractors' (1995: 162–3). These criticisms seem only partly justified. The microsocial level is clearly based on the voices of communities expressing their own and often divergent ethical principles. Admittedly, these voices have been expressed in the past and are now congealed in the existing norms or culture of these communities. However, they are right in that those norms are likely to have been developed by the more powerful within the community and that Donaldson and Dunfee's principle of authentic microsocial contracts is grounded in 'informed consent buttressed by a right of exit', not by any positive support by community members who may be considered relatively powerless; whether that support be expressed by voice or action.[22] However, that is where the purpose of ISCT differs from that of Calton and Kurland. Donaldson and Dunfee are attempting to meld a normative macrosocial contract with empirical microsocial contracts. The former is generated by a thought experiment. The latter comes from existing community norms (though subject to certain limitations from the macrosocial contract). Calton and Kurland are expanding what they see as normatively desirable seeds of the future in the present by providing a supportive discursive structure for such conversations. Their contribution is therefore placed in the 2a category of the second kind of theories in Figure 3.1.

Calton and Kurland attempt to integrate emerging postmodern epistemological, ontological, and praxis elements of organizational discourse. Postmodern epistemology concerns attempts to decentre the authorship of metanarratives and thereby empower 'silent voices' of marginal groups by deconstructing hidden privileged unitary meanings within the predominant organizational text (Freeman and Gilbert 1992; Rosenau 1992). To avoid criticism that the methodology of textual deconstruction leads to no more than ironic word play, they subscribe to 'affirmative' postmodern epistemology (Rosenau 1992), which specifically preserves for authors a role as interpreter of multiple voices in local community conversations, to give voice to, and to legitimate previously silenced voices. They reprise the five metaphors offered by Wicks, Gilbert, and Freeman (1994) (Section 3.4.1.1) that draw from feminist ethics of care and theories of connected knowing, as what they call alternative ways of expressing and expanding conversations about the meaning and significance of organizational life.

Postmodern ontology (concerning existing forms of organizations) is based on what Calton and Kurland see as the new emerging 'post-bureaucratic' networked organization. They admit their positive interpretation of emerging postmodern community conversations, as seen in flexible networking, and interactive organizing,[23] can be interpreted as new forms of manufacturing consent in only nominally transformed organizations: forms of 'organizational seduction' (Heydebrand 1989; Calton 1991; Deetz 1995).

Calton and Kurland rely heavily on the example of the Saturn Team project at General Motors where a '70 per cent comfortable' rule governs joint decision-making among managers, United Auto Worker representatives, and work group members. Anyone at least 70 per cent comfortable with a decision is expected to fully support the final team decision and anyone dissenting from decisions must offer a positive alternative. They also cite Gray's guide (1989: 11–16) to effective collaboration:

- Stakeholders' concerns must be interdependent.
- Stakeholders must share responsibility for any future direction.
- Decisions must be jointly owned.
- Solutions should emerge by dealing constructively with decision outcomes.
- Collaboration itself must be an evolving process.

Nurturing interpersonal trust is important for these network relations. This requires investment in trusting, non-opportunistic interactions that must build up over time. They cite Lewicki and Bunker's three stages (1994) of trust building.

1. *Calculus-based trust*—a fragile form of trust in which each party continuously assesses costs and benefits associated with continuing or breaking the agreed terms of the relationship. This lasts only as long as the cost of cheating is sufficiently credible to deter each party from opportunistic behaviour.

2. *Knowledge-based trust*—over time parties gain confidence in the other's goodwill (Dore 1983).

3. *Identification-based trust*—long-term personal relations involving 'full internalization of the other's desires and intentions to a point where each can effectively act as the agent for the other' (Lewicki and Bunker 1994: 19).

They suggest stage 3 would occur only in 'normatively ideal agent–stakeholder relationships' (1995: 174). The onus they place on managers is far-reaching. Arguably, Calton and Kurland are still locked into a management-centred approach, even if it is a negative one, i.e. they assume all problems of organization–stakeholder relations arise from an existing management-centric viewpoint reflecting male hierarchical thinking and discourse.[24] The implications they draw for stakeholders are merely that if they have a 'context and rationale for their inclusion as legitimate participants in sense-making, rule-building conversations within and among organizations' (1995: 175–6), all will be well. For managers there is the need to exercise their discretion in a new way, to jointly take credit for what come to be seen as good decisions, as well as take joint responsibility or blame for those that go badly. For academics there is the invitation to participate in organizational conversations.

3.4.3 STAKEHOLDERS AS INVESTORS

Blair (1998), Etzioni (1996, 1998), and Schlossberger (1994) present normative stakeholder theories based on the premise that all stakeholders provide sources of capital to a corporation and consequently they should be viewed as investors to whom management owe a fiduciary duty. These normative stakeholder theories are of the second kind, but are close to the third kind in that they require legal or institutional clarification of existing patterns, rather than substantive changes. They are based on interpretations of concepts of property, investment, and capital that could be read into existing legal/institutional patterns, but are not (yet). Schlossberger recommends that corporate objectives be revised to incorporate this fiduciary duty and that it become part of government obligations to set up a variety of public/private ownership relationships. For Etzioni, with the extension of property rights comes a *right* to participate in the governance of the corporation, alongside shareholders. Both provide the kind of intermediate normative stakeholder theory, which proposes how contemporary society should modify laws and institutions to reflect a just society or other ethical ideals. These public policy-oriented contributions were ignored by Hendry (2001), though he regarded public policy orientation as the major gap in the normative stakeholder field.

3.4.3.1 Whose interests should corporations serve? Blair (1998)

Blair argues that the model of corporations viewing shareholders as earning all the returns and bearing all the risks is a throwback to a time when the typical corporation owned and operated a canal, a rail road, or a big manufacturing plant. Then the initial investors were the only ones with significant assets tied up and at risk in the enterprise. With modern corporations this no longer holds as much of the wealth-generating capacity, Blair argues, is derived from intangible assets such as 'the skills and knowledge of the workforce and the ability of the organization as a whole to put those skills to work for customers and clients' (1998: 64).

3.4.3.2 Dual investor theory: Schlossberger (1994)

Schlossberger (1994) suggests that all businesses have fiduciary duties to stakeholders, not because of implicit social contracts, but because stakeholders are a type of shareholder that has invested capital in the business. Every business venture has two types of investors providing two types of capital.

1. *Specific capital* provided by shareholders, partners, or proprietors, needed to finance operations and investment within the business.
2. *Opportunity capital* provided by society, needed to provide material infrastructure (roads, sewerage, etc.), education systems, monetary systems, policing, as well as an 'infrastructure' of knowledge. These resources are available for any business to draw on even if they are not normally provided specifically to a company.

Therefore 'society is a shareholder in every business venture, though not the same type of shareholder as stockowners' and 'every stakeholder is at the same time a shareholder (of a sort) and every business venture in a capitalist nation is at the same time both privately and publicly owned'(1994: 459). Corporations therefore have 'the same kind of fiduciary obligation to society as to stockholders' (1994: 462). Attending to the interests and needs of non-shareholding stakeholders is not merely a responsibility or constraint on the achievement of corporate objectives; it is part of corporate objectives. This is a multi-fiduciary model: managers have a fiduciary duty to all stakeholders. Stakeholders need not be served out of manager benevolence or out of a general obligation to promote good consequences. No implicit social contract needs to be imagined. Schlossberger (1994: 462–3) argues that the social contract idea is a weak foundation for stakeholder theory: 'To contract is to constrain oneself in certain specific ways. Social contract theory would at most justify sensitivity to stakeholder needs as a constraint on business, not as part of a business objective.'[25]

Schlossberger's dual investment theory may be thought of as quite different from a stakeholder theory in that neither individual stakeholders nor stakeholder groups are directly connected to the business in a fiduciary manner. Rather it is with society as a whole as represented by government or the State that managers have the proposed fiduciary relationship. In fact, the dual investor theory is grounded on a theory of property rights based on a general theory of natural rights as governing the relations between people and government.

The bite of Schlossberger's theory is that it provides a criterion for deciding on what degree of ownership or of 'special usage rights towards things' (1994: 469) is required of government. Schlossberger is clear that this natural right to property is not a right of absolute ownership. It does not give someone the right to poison their neighbours through the use of pesticides on their own land. However, other things that may be owned can be used up or made unavailable for others. Therefore it becomes part of the obligations of government to establish a variety of public/private ownership relationships. The more public the business,[26] the heavier its demands on opportunity capital, the higher are the obligations to opportunity capital investors. Schlossberger treats this public trust as a form of opportunity capital, provided by the public to social institutions like CBS News or IBM, which is not available to a convenience store. Similarly, some businesses receive forms of monopoly and are thereby more public than others. There are several bases on which a blend of public and private ownership of business can be achieved.

3.4.3.3 Communitarian theory: Etzioni (1996, 1998)

For Etzioni all involved in the corporation are potentially members of one community in that they have shared goals and bonds, even if they have divergent interests, needs, and values. The members of this community, the stakeholders, are all *investors* in the company and, consequently, the company may be thought of as their property. Invest-ment is defined as 'the outlay of money, time, or other resources, in something that offers (promises) a profitable return' (1998: 682). This differs from an act of charity in that there is the expectation of a specific return. It differs from a sale of assets in that it entails a 'futuristic element' of a continuing relationship. According to Etzioni, investors 'grant their investment on the condition that they will be able to participate to some extent, and even if indirectly via directors of pension funds and mutual funds, in the decisions that affect what their return may be in future' (1998: 682). The basis of this assumption is that shareholders have a legitimate interest in limiting the risk of their investment. Receiving dividends in the short run should not be considered full compensation for use of assets or a substitute for their right to participate in the governance of the corporation. Share-holders participate in decisions concerning the social usage of the resources they invest, such as taking a view on whether those assets should be used to harm the environment or investing in products or regimes they do not find acceptable. He argues that the same futurity element, the same interest in risk limitation, and the same desire and legitimacy of the right to participate in corporate governance exists for other stakeholders.

Employees invest years of their labour (they do not sell their labour in that the transaction involves futurity) and expect to be employed and paid in future. They are also encouraged to believe that if they work hard and with dedication and loyalty, these benefits will improve. Employees risk benefits if the corporation is managed recklessly or illegally. Etzioni points to court decisions that recognize employee rights to employment based on good faith implied by continuous satisfactory service. He notes employee representation in German corporate governance.

Communities also make specific investments in corporations to the extent that they provide special access roads at public expense, offer free land, loans at less that the going interest rates, and grant exemptions from regulations that generally apply, such as on pollution controls or traffic zoning. These asset transfers should not be regarded as charitable or as complete sales. Communities (legitimately) expect future returns in terms of job creation, taxes, and prestige. They are (understandably) concerned if these resources are used in ways that are against their interests or values.

Creditors may also provide specific resources if they provide capital when it is at high risk or provide capital below market rates. In addition, *clients* may be thought of as investing in corporations when, out of loyalty, they (primarily wholesalers) continue to purchase goods that they could source more cheaply or of better quality elsewhere.

For all these stakeholders, the longer the relationship, the larger the corporate investment, other things being equal. Etzioni argues that the scope of representation should parallel the scope of investment; just as shareholder votes typically reflect the size of shareholding, so worker votes should reflect years at work, community votes the extent of specific investments, creditors the size of capital provided under more favourable terms and clients the time they have transacted with the corporation.

Etzioni suggests the argument that attending to stakeholders other than shareholders will jeopardize corporate survival in a competitive world is based on a simplified model of perfect competition. In the real world, corporations have considerable slack that is allotted to cultural factors (such as giving to charity), political donations, and giving executives large bonuses and golden parachutes. Some of this slack can be used to accommodate stakeholders without compromising the corporation (1998: 688).[27]

With this extension of property rights comes a *right* to participate in the governance of the corporation, alongside shareholders. Etzioni notes that 'the accountable to none since accountable to many' argument ignores the experience of other democratic systems whereby divergent interests are accommodated. Differences can be settled by voting on the corporate board, by dialogue leading to consensus, and by coalition building. He also notes that 'executives more often manage their boards rather than are managed by them' and therefore 'it is at least as likely that the enhanced participation in corporate boards will lead to more accountability of executives than less' (1998: 689). Participation by others than shareholders may also reduce the effect of 'the myopic tendency of shareholders and executives'.

Etzioni admits that many would consider his stakeholder theory to be 'at best a visionary idea, if not outlandish or damaging', but there are 'several important precedents that indicate it is merely a significant extension of developments already in hand' (1998: 679). This is a clear statement of 2a reasoning; however, most of Etzioni's contribution is based on a logical, but unfamiliar interpretation of existing legal/ institutional patterns and therefore we have placed it in the 2b category in Figure 3.1. For example, he notes that with the inclusion of a wide range of stakeholders as representatives in corporate governance, claiming this as a right, if there is no practical way of implementing it 'would seriously undermine the claim' (1998: 686). Indicating that forming a mechanism to implement it is possible in contemporary society is therefore important to Etzioni.

3.5 Normative theories of the third kind

3.5.1 PROPERTY RIGHTS: DONALDSON AND PRESTON (1995)

Donaldson and Preston's model is discussed as some length in Section 2.6. They argue that the normative basis for stakeholder theory can be based on the evolving theory of property. This, they argue, is ironic as the traditional view suggests that corporations should be managed for the exclusive (or at least paramount) benefit of the shareholders because their property rights are superior to all other interests in the corporation.

Referring to Coase (1960), Becker (1978, 1992), Honore (1961), and Munzer (1992) they note that property rights are not exclusively related to the interest of owners. Property is viewed as a bundle of many rights, some of which may be limited. Central to the notion of property is the notion of human rights and the restrictions against harmful uses. This clearly brings the interests of non-owner stakeholders into the equation and does not support the claim that management should act solely in the interest of the shareholders. They argue that unless property rights are regarded as simple self-evident moral conceptions they must be based on more fundamental ideas of distributive justice, such as utilitarianism or social contract theory. They reject the notion that a single theory is universally applicable and consequently advocate a pluralist approach. In doing so the connection between the theory of property and stakeholder theory becomes explicit: all critical underlying principles of the classic theories of distributive justice are present among the stakeholders of the corporation and are conceived and presented in stakeholder theory. It is not necessary to assume that these stakes constitute formal or legal property rights, merely that a moral interest exists in order to recognize whether there is a 'stake' in the corporation.

3.5.2 STAKEHOLDER PARADOX: GOODPASTER (1991)

Goodpaster argues that stakeholder synthesis is naturally either strategic or multi-fiduciary. This, he argues, suggests a paradox whereby the former yields business without ethics and the latter ethics without business.

Strategic stakeholder management is non-moral. Goodpaster formulates a specific rule for it: (*a*) maximize the benefits and minimize the costs to stockholder group, short and long term, and (*b*) pay close attention to the interests of other stakeholder groups that might potentially influence the achievements of (*a*) (1991: 109). He argues that whilst there is nothing wrong with strategic reasoning, the kind of concern exhibited is not moral. Therefore the progress from stakeholder analysis to stakeholder synthesis (see Section 6.8.1) is not necessarily ethical.

Multi-fiduciary stakeholder management treats all stakeholders as having equally important interests and deserving joint maximization. Stakeholders are viewed apart from their instrumental, economic, or legal clout (1991: 112). Critics such as Marcoux (2003) argue that multi-fiduciary stakeholder management is incompatible with widely held convictions about the special moral status of shareholders and the fiduciary duties owed to them by managers. The obligations of agents to principals are stronger, or of a different nature, from those between agents and third parties. Consequently, given the economic mission of the corporation and the legal environment in which it operates, the strategic approach is the only legitimate model.

Goodpaster's paradox (1991: 113) is that there is an ethical problem regardless of the route that managers chose: 'Ethics seems to forbid and demand a strategic profit-maximizing mind set'. He cites Ruder (1965) who argues that multi-fiduciary stakeholder synthesis dilutes the fiduciary obligations to stockholders (by extending it to customers, employees, suppliers, etc.) and he sees this as a threat to the 'privacy' of the private-sector organization (1991: 115). This would effectively make stakeholders quasi-stockholders and would call for a restructuring of corporate governance.

Goodpaster's model attempts to 'develop an account of the moral responsibilities of management that (*a*) avoids surrendering the moral relationship between management and stakeholders as the strategic view does, while (*b*) not transforming stakeholder obligations into fiduciary obligations (thus protecting the uniqueness of the principal–agent relationship between management and stockholder) (1991: 116). For Goodpaster fiduciary duties are owed to shareholders alone. Managers do not have to bear additional fiduciary relationships to third parties in order to take business ethics seriously, but there are substantial non-fiduciary obligations owed to third parties that surround fiduciary relationships, such as the duty not to harm or coerce, or duties not to lie, cheat, or steal. The strategic approach would consider such duties as indirect and managers would only consider them under this model to the extent that they contribute to meeting the goals of the organization. Neither principal nor agent could ever claim moral immunity from the basic obligations that would apply to any human being towards other members of the community (1991: 118). He cites the Latin proverb *nemo dat quod non habet* (no one can give a better title than he has) as a guiding principle to apply to decision-making:

Investors cannot expect of managers (more generally, principals cannot expect of their agents) behavior that would be inconsistent with the reasonable ethical expectations of the community. (1991: 117)

3.5.3 PUBLIC POLICY: BOATRIGHT (1994)

Boatright (1994) asks what is so special about shareholders? What entitles them to the special status afforded to them by theorists such as Goodpaster? Boatright argues that shareholders do not need additional fiduciary duties because they are given rights, such as to elect directors and to receive dividends, and have the ability to sell their shares on the open market if they are disappointed with how the corporation is being run. Furthermore, shareholders are rewarded for the level of risk they take in rights. Boatright argues that in order to show that a fiduciary duty exists one has to show that a contract exists, whether explicit or implied. He suggests that even implied contracts are not relevant here as there is a lack of face-to-face dealings between the two parties and the lack of any specific representation by management to individual shareholders. He further argues that managers are agents for the corporation, not the shareholders. Directors in a sense are the corporation, not agents at all (1994: 399). This is supported by reference to the standard legal definition of an agent, which has three crucial elements: consent to the relation; the power to act on behalf of another; the element of control. Boatright argues all are absent from the shareholder–manager relation and therefore Goodpaster is mistaken about the ethical basis for fiduciary duties. Boatright calls on Berle's argument (1932) that 'corporations' ought to be run for the benefit of shareholders, not because they 'own' the corporation, or because of some contract or agency relation, but because all other constituencies are better off as a result. The underlying assumption is that the fiduciary duties of management are and ought to be determined by considerations of public policy (1994: 402). Boatright suggests that Goodpaster's solution to the stakeholder paradox (that shareholders cannot expect managers, as their agents, to act in ways that are inconsistent with the ethical standards of the community) does not work if managers are not the agents of the shareholders. However, if public policy is accepted as the basis for fiduciary duties, a different solution to the paradox is suggested. This is based on the premise that the obligations of management to shareholders can be differentiated according to whether they are fiduciary or non-fiduciary. Fiduciary duties of management are those for which they are held personally liable (act with due diligence within the scope of their authority and exercise ordinary care and prudence). Non-fiduciary duties are all other obligations for which there is no corresponding personal liability. Boatright reformulates the guiding principle to read:

It is illegitimate to orient corporate decisions that bear fiduciary duties of management by ethical values that go beyond strategic stakeholder considerations to include the interests of other constituencies, but it is essential to orient other corporate decisions by these values. (1994: 404)

3.5.4 ARISTOTELIAN STAKEHOLDER THEORY: WIJNBERG (2000)

Wijnberg (2000) applies Aristotelian ethics (Vignette 3.9) and politics to stakeholder theory. As moral virtue is gained from action, a good person of practical wisdom needs moral dilemmas: to have to act politically and to deal with conflicting interests. The corporation is a political association in which decisions have to be made that affect the interests of different stakeholders and express the values of the decision-makers. Consequently, Wijnberg argues that 'the organization exists to allow the decision maker within the organization, the manager, to be confronted by ethical dilemmas involving different stakeholders, to exercise their deliberative faculties and virtues, and thus to live good lives' (2000: 338). The end is the good life of the individual decision-maker, not the welfare of the corporation or of society (2000: 340).

Vignette 3.9 ARISTOTELIAN ETHICS

Aristotle (384–322 BC) opposed a simple universal concept of the good, such as proposed by Plato. He rejected the claim that all values are commensurable. Reducing virtues to quantities of the same standard means ignoring precisely what makes the different goods good. Values can conflict and man has to make judgements without optimizing rules. It is possible to distinguish the good from the bad in an objective manner 'through the features of humanness that lie beneath all local traditions' (Nussbaum and Hurley 1993: 243). Aristotle divided human life into spheres of experience to which different virtues relate. To impart meaning to the virtues he introduces the doctrine of the mean and suggests that excess and defect should be avoided in every sphere of influence. The mean differs between men and between spheres of influence. It is not the mathematical mean. For justice, the mean is not the mean between being too just and too little just but between acting unjustly and being justly treated. Being too just means acting as if justice was the only value or as if all other values could be reduced to justice or an issue related to justice. An Aristotelian good man is able to express many virtues without destroying their differences and their potentially conflicting demands. For Aristotle man is not born with virtues. Instead, they are acquired through our acts: a just man is one who behaves justly; performing honest acts makes an honest man and so forth. In these terms virtue is a state of character concerned with choice and deliberation. For Aristotle the scope of the law was clear: matters that belong to the sphere of deliberation are obviously ones on which it is not possible to lay down a law.

Wijnberg makes a number of recommendations.

1. Corporate structure must permit sufficient autonomy to allow managers to practice their practical wisdom: sufficient empowerment to confront ethical dilemmas.

2. The systematic identification of stakeholders and their interests is warranted in order to identify significant spheres of influence and thereby specify further the meaning of the virtues the decision-maker should strive to acquire and exercise.

3. Codes of conduct or mission statements *can* be fruitfully used to enforce or encourage virtuous decision-making. Wijnberg offers two examples: rules on how far decision makers should go in investigating the interests of stakeholders before making a

decision, and how much of the process should be made public so that individual decision makers can be held responsible by other stakeholders, if not legally then at least morally (2000: 339).

4. Education is of crucial importance. Only the well-educated man who acts politically out of generosity can become a liberal gentleman.

He concludes with:

Prospective managers should be educated to understand that management means not applying rules but serious deliberations and that deliberations means being liberal with one's self in the sense that one is willing to show, in the practice of making decisions involving the interests of different stakeholders, what kind of person one is. (2000: 341)

It could be argued that Wijnberg's contribution is a theory of the second kind because it calls for the recommendations listed above, which may be interpreted as institutional changes. However, none of his recommendations require substantial alterations to existing institutions, rather they are recommendations concerning detailed elaboration of existing institutions such as codes of conduct and the degree of autonomy offered to managers. It could be argued that Wijnberg's Aristotelian logic offers a justification for not changing existing laws and institutions. Morality must come from the internal virtues of individuals and not from social structures or constructs.

☐ QUESTIONS/EXERCISES

1 Can you classify the normative stakeholder theories according to the Habermasian distinction between pragmatic, moral, and ethical reasoning?

2 Does it matter if there is an inconsistency in the normativity of a theory's propositions in terms of outcomes and justifications?

3 In Figure 3.1 contributions were classified by the highest level they could be placed according to either outcome or justification. Show how the figure would alter if contributions were classified by the lowest level at which they could be placed.

4 Compare Argandoña (1998) and Wijnberg (2000) in terms of the category of theory in which they have been placed in Figure 3.1. Explain why you agree or disagree with our judgement.

☐ NOTES

1 Normative stakeholder theory 'appears to be in a state of disarray and confusion' and 'to have wound up in a thoroughgoing mess' (Hendry 2001: 159, 163).

2 For detailed accounts of these underlying concepts see Beauchamp and Bowie (2004), Robinson and Garratt (1996), and MacIntyre (1967).

3 Bishop notes that many practitioners prefer to use values such as honesty, integrity, wealth creation, loyalty, no harm, freedom, and respect for property.

4 This labelling reflects considerable conflicts among proponents. Lovejoy (1963) summarizes these divisions: Is the nature of knowledge with which action can be associated based on immediate perception or the result of a mediation of ideas which interpret experience? Are ethical and aesthetic judgements validated by the subjective criteria 'the will to believe' (James 1890, 1907) or verifiable social consequences along utilitarian lines (Dewey 1885/1967). Does truth evolve primarily through psychological properties of belief as a disposition to act, or changing characteristics of the objects of belief? While Lovejoy considers this to be a weakness of pragmatism, Schiller (1915), like Freeman (1994), welcomed the profusion.

5 A just society can be deemed as one that is honourable and fair, consistent with what is morally right, whereby members act in accordance with the law.

6 This distinction need not be absolute. The vision of a just society could be connected to current or past-observed society or derived from imagined visions of heaven. We could differentiate theories of the first kind by the degree to which their inspiration (not their justification) is based on aspects of current society or visions of logical extensions of societal trends.

7 Hendry's second dimension, level of claims, is regarded as adding little to the framework. Kind of theory and severity of the claims on managers regarding their obligations to stakeholders or to how stakeholders should be treated are strongly correlated. Rather than using the model to highlight the lack of second kind and intermediate claim theories (Hendry's purpose or result), Figure 3.1 highlights the relative deficiency of ethical concerns for agents other than managers.

8 See Beauchamp and Bowie (2004). Criticisms include, first, that moral rules may conflict, such as keeping a promise and telling the truth; second, that if followed inflexibly it can lead to disastrous consequences, e.g. there are occasions to lie for the greater good such as when being questioned by the Gestapo in Nazi-occupied France.

9 Utilitarianism would state that an action is 'morally right' if and only if it leads to at least as great a balance of pleasure against pain (or utility against disutility) as would be achieved by any other available action.

10 Historically associated with the Frankfurt School of radical theorists, 'critical theory', and especially 'critical management theory', has been adopted by a broad range of theorists, many postmodernist. To avoid confusion, we label Reed's approach Habermasian.

11 Habermas called this ethical reasoning.

12 Freeman is not ultimately committed to this narrow definition.

13 Freeman (1994: 421) responds to criticisms of this principle for failing to recognize that opportunity costs are pervasive: '[W]e should build our understanding of economics on a reasonable moral order, rather than *vice-versa*; or, so much the worse for the idea of "opportunity cost".'

14 This is a critical problem for stakeholder fairness models. Freedom of entry and exit from corporations is affected by factors beyond the design of particular corporate forms, such as the degree of information stakeholders have of external conditions and on the nature of those conditions. This is not a problem under perfect competition, but Freeman explicitly rules this out by recognizing that even in the *ex ante* pre-design state, externalities, transaction costs, and positive costs of contracting exist. These limit the effectiveness of markets including the freedom of entry and exit in that they add costs to them and thereby allow for inequalities to emerge. A continual Rawlsian process of corporate redesign could counter this: it would be difficult to imagine the development of corporations in relation to the ideal if the ideal is clouded from our imagination in the absence of real experiences.

15 This could be a choice not to act if silence indicates consent.

16 Voluntary acceptance removes the principle of stakeholder fairness from Nozick's criticism (1974) that receipt of benefits would not always morally generate an obligation. According to Phillips, Nozick conflates voluntary acceptance and mere receipt of benefits.

17 Murder is ruled out for other reasons, and in terms of this act the duty to other humans as humans takes precedence over obligations to fulfil voluntary pact that may lead to the expectation of such an act.

18 In the absence of an agency powerful enough to guarantee that other agents generally adhere to the tenets of morality, men are in a state of nature within which moral concepts have no meaning (Vignette 3.4).

19 Virtue ethics is criticized for failing to specify the basis on which potentially conflicting virtues (stemming from different traditions or societies) can be judged.

20 Feminist ethics has been criticized for relying on particular feelings of sympathy and negotiating skills of the parties involved, which could lead to unfair results.

21 Calton and Lad (1995) present a similar, more conciliatory framework.

22 Boatright (1994) criticized ISCT for being a doctrine of 'majoritarianism'. Donaldson and Dunfee (2000: 486) point out that 'constructive dissenters' and whistle-blowers can be dealt with through 'priority rules of thumb, making use of an authentic norm belonging to a larger socio-political community'.

23 Examples cited are Japanese keiretsu (Gerlach and Lincoln 1992); total quality management linkages among employees, suppliers, and customers (Schonberger 1992); and cross-functional product development teams and quality circles (Snow, Miles, and Coleman 1992).

24 Calton and Kurland (1995: 163) exhort Donaldson and Dunfee: 'The two authors, sharing relatively similar cultural histories and gender experiences, must break free of their psychic or communal boundaries sufficiently to determine ethical principles acceptable to, and inclusive of, a diverse group of macrosocial contractors.'

25 This is a weak argument. Schlossberger is essentially describing an employment contract. Some forms of infrastructure are provided by contract, such as publicly funded business parks or airports, which form a community of individual businesses that pay rent for the facilities.

26 Public businesses must function as a social institution, with well-understood social and internal roles. The ability to function depends on public trust in conducting those roles according to the associated expectations and norms.

27 If stakeholder representation and management is based on the existence of slack, it is likely that there will be periods when there is less slack available due to the changing competitive environment. Does this mean that stakeholder representation should be reduced, or that their interests curtailed in those times? This is what occurs for non-critical stakeholders (Jawahar and McLaughlin 2001).

4 Analytic stakeholder theorizing

4.1 Introduction

Analytic stakeholder theory is the label we use to cover all stakeholder theory that is not strictly normative. This includes theories Donaldson and Preston (1995) call descriptive and instrumental, and Reed (2002) calls positive[1] and strategic (see Section 2.6).

First, contributions are ordered by whether they are primarily organization-centric, stakeholder-centric, or focus on the organization–stakeholder relation per se. Second, within these categories we order contributions according to whether they are primarily strategic/instrumental or descriptive/positive (Figure 4.1).

Many contributions express an attitude towards stakeholding without elaborating a model that provides a context for either justifying their attitude or allowing predictions about the nature and development of organization–stakeholder relationship. Only those contributions that present more than a restatement or empirical testing of an existing model have been included. Many empirical contributions would occupy the empty category of organization-centric contributions that are descriptive/positive.

Contributions must present either an original stakeholder model, a distinctive theoretical perspective, or a development of the stakeholder principle. This could be an exploration of the rationale for stakeholder consideration, a typology of stakeholders, an investigation of the different circumstances when stakeholder consideration as a whole will be more or less likely, or circumstances when we may expect different types of stakeholders to be considered.

Figure 4.1 includes relatively few contributions under the stakeholder-centric column and under the 'focusing on the organization–stakeholder relation' column. However, we note that these contributions are relatively recent and we would predict/recommend that in future more 'will/should' occupy this space.

		Focus along the organization–stakeholder continuum		
		Organization-centric	Focusing on the organization–stakeholder relation	Stakeholder-centric
Analytic category	Strategic/ instrumental	• Freeman (1984) • Savage et al. (1991) • Clarkson (1995) • Jones (1995) • Mitchell, Agle, and Wood (1997) • Rowley (1997) • Jawahar and McLaughlin (2001)	• Friedman and Miles (2002)	• Frooman (1999) • Rowley and Moldoveanu (2003)
	Descriptive/ positive		• Hill and Jones (1992)	

Figure 4.1 Analytical stakeholder theories

4.2 Strategic/instrumental and organization-centric stakeholder models

4.2.1 STRATEGIC MANAGEMENT: FREEMAN (1984)

There is conceptual confusion in the stakeholder field (see Section 1.3). One reason for this is that Freeman's position has evolved substantially over the years. Here we describe Freeman's original instrumental position, i.e. stakeholders are seen as a means by which the firm can achieve its assumed ends (maximizing profits). However, in his later work (Evan and Freeman 1988; Freeman and Evan 1990; Freeman and Gilbert 1992; Wicks, Gilbert, and Freeman 1994) stakeholders are seen as ends: as individuals with personal projects and interests the firm was constructed to serve. Freeman's later normative work has been dealt with in Chapter 3.

Freeman states:

Any framework which seeks to enhance an organization's stakeholder management capabilities must begin with an application of the basic definition. Who are those groups and individuals who can affect and are affected by the achievements of an organization's purpose? (1984: 54)

This involves mapping the stakeholders, providing a detailed list of the specific groups, organizations, and companies related to each category of stakeholder, and a corresponding list of interests. Freeman (1984) presented what has now become the traditional view of the organization–stakeholder relation, in which the corporation occupies a central position and has direct connections to all stakeholders (see Figure 2.2). Coalitions of stakeholders and intermediaries acting on behalf of stakeholders are ignored in this hub-

and-spokes representation, though Freeman assesses these aspects at a later stage of his model.[2]

Freeman (1984: 242) suggests the following review questions to facilitate stakeholder mapping, which can be applied to specific divisions, operations, or businesses or applied to specific issues:

1. Who are our current and potential stakeholders?
2. What are their interests/rights?
3. How does each stakeholder affect us (challenges and opportunities)?
4. How do we affect each stakeholder?
5. What assumption does our current strategy make about each important stakeholder?
6. What are the current 'environmental variables' that affect us and our stakeholders?
7. How do we measure each of these variables and their impact on us and our stakeholders?
8. How do we keep score with our stakeholders?

The next step is to analyse stakeholder behaviour (Figure 4.2). This should involve an investigation of past and future stakeholder actions that could enhance or hinder corporate goals. According to Freeman, if a manager explores all possible scenarios, strategic surprise is limited and the downside risk associated with dealing with a particular stakeholder is covered. Next he recommends that managers attempt to construct logical explanations of why a stakeholder could act in the manner observed. The overall long-term objectives of each group should be examined as well as the objectives advanced on specific issues. Differences between these need to be highlighted. How these are connected needs to be analysed to assess the external forces acting on that stakeholder, the vulnerabilities of each group, and which issues are most salient. Finally, stakeholder perceptions of the organization should be elicited. This should lead to a logical statement such as 'stakeholder S has exhibited behavior B because S's objectives are O. S's stakeholders are S' and S believes A about us' (Freeman 1984: 134). For Freeman, managers should refrain from explaining stakeholder behaviour merely as 'irrational'.

Stakeholder coalitions should be mapped. Coalitions may develop when lobbyists join forces against a common enemy (Weiss 2003: 37) or less formally around issues or interests that groups have, or seek to have, in common.[3] Managers should scan the environment for instances of similar actions, interests, beliefs, or objectives between stakeholder groups and then examine group stakes according to economic, technological, social, political, and managerial effects. This is because media exposure, politics, economics, legal actions, and public reactions change stakeholder strategies and positions on issues (Weiss 2003). Frederick, Post, and Davis (1988) and Svendsen (1998) also recommend environment scanning.

Effective stakeholder management, like any other form of management, should be informed by theory as well as best practice. Until Freeman's seminal work (1984),

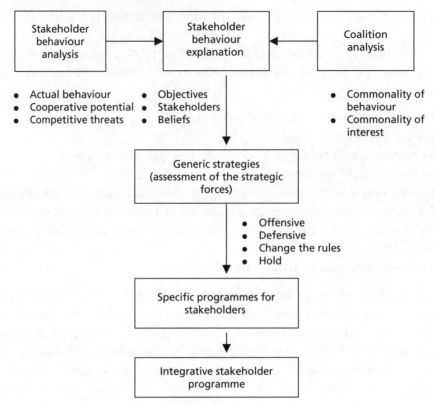

Figure 4.2 Stakeholder strategy formulation process
Source: Freeman (1984: 131)

strategists such as Porter (1980) ignored the impact of stakeholders on the formulation of strategy, advocating that industry structure alone determines appropriate strategy. Freeman takes Porter's five forces analysis model (competitiveness, the relative power of customers and suppliers, and the threat of substitutes and new entrants) and adds a further dimension: the relative power of stakeholders and their potential to cooperate or threaten corporate strategy. The result is a four-way typology of generic stakeholder strategies (Figure 4.3). Freeman suggests that the success of particular strategic programmes can be affected by a stakeholder's potential for change and its relative power. Management can seek strategic guidance by examining the relative competitive threat and relative cooperative potential of each stakeholder, and classifying the stakeholder accordingly.

Four strategies are distinguished:

1. *Offensive strategies* should be adopted if a stakeholder group has relatively high cooperative potential and relatively low competitive threat, in order to try to bring about the stakeholder's cooperative potential. Offensive strategies include attempts

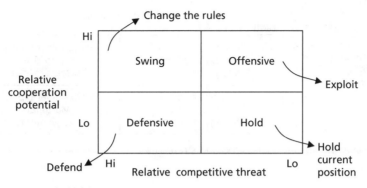

Figure 4.3 Generic stakeholder strategies
Source: Freeman (1984: 143).

to change stakeholder objectives, or perceptions, to adopt the stakeholder's position or to link the programme to others that the stakeholder views more favourably.

2. *Defensive strategies* should be adopted if a stakeholder group has a relatively high competitive threat and relatively low cooperative potential to prevent competitive threat on the part of these stakeholders. Examples include reinforcing current beliefs about the firm, maintaining existing programmes, linking the programmes to others that the stakeholder views more favourably, or letting the stakeholder drive the transaction process.

3. *Swing strategies*, which seek to influence the rules of the game that govern organization–stakeholder relations should be adopted if a stakeholder group has a relatively high cooperative potential and competitive threat. Examples include changing one or more of the following: the rules, the decision forum, the kinds of decisions that are being made, or the transaction process.

4. *Hold strategies* should be adopted if a stakeholder group has a relatively low competitive threat and cooperative potential, in order to continue current strategic programmes and maintain the current stakeholder position. Examples include doing nothing and monitoring existing programmes or reinforcing current beliefs about the firm.

4.2.2 STRATEGIES FOR ASSESSING AND MANAGING STAKEHOLDERS: SAVAGE ET AL. (1991)

Savage et al. (1991) build on Freeman's model using the same constructs: stakeholder capacity and willingness to threaten or cooperate with the corporation (Figure 4.4). Guidance on the measurement of these variables is given. The power of threat is

		Potential for threat	
		High	Low
Potential for cooperation	High	Stakeholder type 4 Mixed blessing Strategy: collaborate	Stakeholder type 1 Supportive Strategy: involve
	Low	Stakeholder type 3 Non-supportive Strategy: defend	Stakeholder type 2 Marginal Strategy: monitor

Figure 4.4 Managing stakeholders: type and strategies
Source: Savage et al. (1991: 65).

determined by resource dependence, the stakeholder's ability to form coalitions, and relevance of the threat to a particular issue. Examining the quality and durability of the organization–stakeholder relationship can help in assessing the potential for threat. The potential to cooperate is partially determined by the stakeholder's capacity to expand its interdependence with the organization: the greater the dependence, the greater the willingness to cooperate. Willingness to cooperate can also be affected by the business environment. Exactly how a factor will affect the potential for threat or cooperation will depend on the specific context and history of the organization–stakeholder relation and other key stakeholders influencing the organization. Managers need to continually assess stakeholder interests, capabilities, and needs, as stakeholder engagement tends to be issue-specific. Consequently, managers cannot expect a previously supportive stakeholder to be cooperative on future issues.

Type 1 stakeholders have a low potential for threat and a high potential for cooperation. This corresponds to Freeman's 'offensive' category and associated strategy of exploitation. Savage et al. consider 'supportive' stakeholders as the 'ideal type' and include the board of trustees, managers, employees, and parent companies. This category can include suppliers, service providers, and non-profit organizations. Both models agree on a strategy of involvement, although Freeman explicitly states 'exploitation', indicating a greater power distribution in favour of the organization. Type 2 stakeholders are marginal: they are unconcerned about their stake in the business as they have a low potential for threat or cooperation. This corresponds to Freeman's 'hold' quadrant. Savage et al. suggest consumer interest groups, professional associations for employees, and shareholders as examples. Both models suggest a monitoring strategy as certain issues could cause these stakeholders to change category, increasing their potential threat. Type 3 stakeholders are non-supportive, with a high potential for threat and a low potential for cooperation. These stakeholders are the most distressing for corporations, such as competitors, unions, the media, and government.

Both models suggest a defensive strategy. The final category is coined 'mixed blessing' as the potential to threat and cooperation are equally high. This includes employees in short supply, clients, and organizations with complimentary products and services. Here, the strategic advice differs. Savage et al. suggest collaboration whereas Freeman suggests changing the rules; however, both approaches have the same end in sight: to enhance the potential for cooperation and reduce the potential for threat.

4.2.3 A STAKEHOLDER FRAMEWORK FOR ANALYSING AND EVALUATING CORPORATE SOCIAL PERFORMANCE: CLARKSON (1995)

A pivotal date marking a step change in the popularity of stakeholder theory seems to have occurred with the publication of Clarkson's article (1995) in which he rather bravely described his own conceptual confusion during the time he and colleagues at the University of Toronto conducted more than seventy field studies of CSP from 1983 to 1993. His position was that a framework based on managing relations with stakeholders would allow more effective analysis and evaluation of CSP than models based on concepts of CSR and responsiveness. Much of Clarkson's work had been guided by Carroll's model of CSP (see Section 2.3.1), which forms the basis of his reactive–accomodative–defensive–proactive (RADP) scale (Table 4.1).

Clarkson noted that Carroll's model was comprehensive and integrative and that it had a strong influence as judged by its 'longevity and progeny' (1995: 94). However, when it came to identifying and measuring the dimensions of the Carroll model, Clarkson concluded that analysing CSP based on categories of social responsibility, social issues, and philosophies or strategies of corporate responsiveness did not lead to satisfactory results. Clarkson noted that he was not alone in his concerns (Votaw 1973;[4] Wood 1991[5]). He states:

The fundamental problem was, and remains, that no definition of social responsiveness provides a framework for the systematic collection, organization, and analysis of corporate data. The term *social responsiveness* carried no clear meaning for managers, students, or academic researchers and scholars. Consequently, much time, energy, and paper have been consumed in attempts to

Table 4.1 The reactive–accommodative–defensive–proactive scale

Rating	Posture or strategy	Performance
Proactive	Anticipate responsibility	Doing more than is required
Accommodative	Accept responsibility	Doing all that is required
Defensive	Admit responsibility but fight it	Doing the least that is required
Reactive	Deny responsibility	Doing less than required

Source: based on Clarkson (1995: 109).

explain the term. But it remains an elusive construct, lacking both logic and rigor, which limits seriously its usefulness in empirical research. . . . The data showed that, in the normal course of conducting their business, corporate managers do not think or act in terms of the concepts of corporate social responsibilities and responsiveness, nor of social issues and performance. . . . [They] are concepts that have been generated outside business. They have normative connotations lacking clarity and specificity and have the disadvantage of sounding like jargon. 'Socially responsible to whom?' 'Socially responsive about what?' 'Social performance judged by whom and by what standards?' (1995: 96–8)

Clarkson found that managers understand accountability, obligations, and responsibilities to *stakeholder* groups, even though they had no training in these issues.[6] Clarkson drew a practical, though not always a valid, distinction.

1. A particular society (municipal, state, or national) determines, usually over an extended period of time, what is a *social* issue, and when it is considered necessary, the relevant polity enacts legislation and regulation.

2. When there is no such legislation or regulation, an issue may be a *stakeholder* issue, but it is not necessarily a *social* issue. A test of whether an issue has become a *social* issue is the presence or absence of legislation or regulation (1995: 103).

Clearly, it is possible for social issues to be considered so by many without them becoming the subject of legislation or regulation, but Clarkson suggests that this is an unstable situation and that in the long run legislation or regulation will be implemented.[7] He notes that doing more or less than required invites the question: 'Required by whom?' Sometimes this will be specified by legislation, sometimes in a code or advertising by the company, and sometimes obligations occur as transactions with stakeholders. Finally, there is what Clarkson considers to be a general requirement to keep the corporation's principal stakeholder groups 'reasonably satisfied so that they continue as part of the corporate stakeholder system' (1995: 109).

4.2.4 INSTRUMENTAL STAKEHOLDER THEORY: JONES (1995)

Jones (1995) develops instrumental stakeholder theory by delving into the reasons why acting ethically should (or at least is likely to) lead to competitive advantage.[8] His arguments are based on the economics literature, which focuses on information imperfections in markets, and in particular on the costs involved in attempts to overcome those imperfections. Jones proposes that a reputation for acting ethically will, to some degree, overcome consequences of those information imperfections in a much less costly, or even costless manner. Therefore visible management actions that accord with such a reputation will be associated with greater market success; actions that indicate the lack of a reputation for acting ethically will be associated with lesser market success.

Jones begins with three assumptions about the firm–stakeholder relationship.

1. Firms have relationships, called contracts, with many stakeholders and can therefore be seen as a 'nexus of contracts' (Jensen and Meckling 1976) or a set of principal–agent relationships, between themselves (as agents), and their stakeholders (as principals) (Vignette 4.1).
2. Firms are run by professional managers who are their contracting agents
3. Firms exist in markets in which competitive pressures do influence behaviour but do not necessarily penalize moderately inefficient behaviour.

Based on these assumptions the basic instrumental stakeholder proposition is formulated as:

If 'firms... contract (through their managers) with their stakeholders on the basis of mutual trust and cooperation', then these firms 'will have a competitive advantage over firms that do not'. (1995: 422)

Vignette 4.1 AGENCY THEORY

Agency relationships occur when principals engage another person, the agent, to perform a service for them involving the delegation of some decision-making authority to the agent (Ross 1973; Jensen and Meckling 1976). Interests of the two are assumed to diverge, but this can be limited if the principal is able to establish appropriate incentives for the agent or if the principal monitors the agent. As an incentive to the principal to take on the agent, the agent can bind himself/herself to either not taking opportunistic actions or insuring the principal against losses due to such acts. These are *ex ante* bonding costs as they are promised before the contract is agreed. However, it is recognized in agency theory that these devices may not work perfectly and so there will still be a residual loss; i.e. a reduction in principal's welfare incurred as part of the agency relation. Agency costs are then the sum of:

1. Monitoring costs borne by principals to reduce agent actions that would harm the interests of principals;
2. Bonding costs borne by agents to guarantee that the agent will not take actions to harm the interests of principals;
3. Residual loss.

A key proposition is that a process of market-like competition ('natural selection') will lead to governance structures (mechanisms that police contracts between principals and agents) that economize on agency costs (Fama and Jensen 1983). Governance mechanisms include laws governing corporate behaviour, corporate governance institutions like boards of directors, and market mechanisms such as capital markets and managerial labour markets. If new institutions lead to a reduction in monitoring and enforcement costs, rational principals will adopt them. If they lead to raising the credibility of agent bonding, thereby reducing bonding costs, agents will adopt them and principals will accept this. The process is predicated on easy exit from existing arrangements and entry into new forms of contractual arrangements.

The rational connection between the 'if' and the 'then' sides of the instrumental proposition is based on costs of solving agency problems (Jensen and Meckling 1976), transaction cost problems (Williamson 1975), and team production problems (Alchian and Demsetz 1972). These problems arise because markets are not perfect (in particular because information is not freely available) and those imperfections allow economic agents, managers in particular, to behave opportunistically, i.e. they are able to pursue their self-interest 'with guile' (Williamson 1975). They can misrepresent their activities or efforts. Costs are then incurred either because opportunism succeeds (and returns to the firm and/or to other stakeholders are less, as opportunistic managers reap the benefit of their guile), or because one or more of the parties to the relationship spend resources to reduce opportunism. Costs incurred due to opportunism or to reduce it are variously identified by the theoretical frameworks to which Jones refers.

1. Agency costs arise due to principals having insufficient information about the quality of managers before the contract is struck (adverse selection) or about the way they perform under contract (moral hazard). Opportunism can be reduced by incurring monitoring and bonding costs.

2. Transaction costs arise due to lack of information about the quality of contracting partners and the resources they have to offer. Costs of transacting include costs of:
   (*a*) searching;
   (*b*) monitoring;
   (*c*) enforcing; and
   (*d*) insuring or diversifying.

3. Monitoring costs associated with team production arise to counteract the 'free rider' problem whereby team members shirk without detection and receive rewards disproportionate to their efforts.

Jones contends that managers who relate to stakeholders on the basis of mutual trust and cooperation, as long as they can be identified as such, will be recognized as efficient potential contracting partners. This will obviate the necessity for contracting parties to incur the costs listed above.

How can managers of this type be identified? Jones cites Frank (1988) who suggests the moral sentiments of others can be judged either by their 'sincere manner' or by reputation. Reputation is a good guide to moral sentiments because, Frank contends, it is difficult for someone who is merely prudent to maintain a reputation for honesty because, on pure self-interest calculations, dishonest actions will often be regarded as coming within acceptable risk. The rewards for opportunism are often immediate compared with those of cooperation, and distant rewards are often discounted excessively. People who are honest for reasons of enlightened self-interest (rather than ethical beliefs or moral sentiments) will eventually succumb to dishonest actions, and are therefore likely to get caught and lose their reputation. It is difficult to acquire and maintain a good reputation. If this is known, people will infer that someone who has not been caught is likely to be more than merely prudent (1988: 88).

Jones contends that a reputation for corporate morality is identifiable, largely through the absence of corporate policies that would indicate lack of moral sentiments such as massive lay-offs to boost profits or no-returns policies on merchandise. These policies are assumed to be readily detectable by current and potential stakeholders. Other policies, such as the system of incentives and sanctions employed within the firm, the language used, and other internal reflections of top management moral sentiments, will lead individuals with incompatible moral sentiments to these to leave, leading to a relatively homogeneous culture with respect to morality (or opportunism). This, Jones suggests, will be visible to stakeholders in their dealings with employees and other representatives of the firm. 'Firm morality, like individual morality, is difficult to fake' (Jones 1995: 420).[9]

Jones develops a number of detailed instances of the instrumental stakeholder proposition. If firms refrain from certain common practices, they will have a competitive advantage over firms that do these things and will outperform them. There are many policies or devices that could achieve this:

1. Mechanisms to deter takeover:
   - Shark repellents—anti-takeover charter amendments
   - Poison pills—'contingent securities that burden an acquiring firm with various obligations after takeovers' (1995: 424)
   - Greenmail—purchases of large blocks of shares from potential takeover raiders
2. High levels of executive compensation.
3. Particular supplier relation patterns:
   - Having many suppliers indicating that some are being kept on line competing for business
   - Changing suppliers often; thus not building long-term contracts on mutual trust
4. Contracting out work normally done by employees.
5. Reliance on external rather than internal labour markets.
6. Monitoring employees closely.

Jones points out that his predictions are subject to the usual empirical caveat of 'all other things being equal'. Inefficient production processes, uninspired marketing plans, and obsolete products can outweigh a reputation for trusting relations with stakeholders. He also suggests that individual propositions may not be verified empirically because the relationships are not independent: 'it may be that a threshold of trusting and cooperative relationships between the firm and its stakeholders must be met before empirically significant differences in performance are found' (1995: 429).

This is the only contribution we have included in this group, which is explicitly an instrumental stakeholder theory. It differs from the others in that it emphasizes what companies should *not* do strategically in order to fulfil the conditions of the instrumental proposition, rather than specifying ways in which they should deal with stakeholders to advance corporate objectives.

4.2.5 STAKEHOLDER IDENTIFICATION AND SALIENCE: MITCHELL, AGLE, AND WOOD (1997)

Mitchell, Agle, and Wood (1997) argue that there is no agreement on what Freeman (1994) calls 'the principle of who or what really counts', i.e. who are the stakeholders of the firm and to whom do managers pay attention. They call for a 'normative theory'[10] of stakeholder identification to explain logically why managers should consider certain classes of entities as stakeholders, to separate stakeholders from non-stakeholders, and to explain how managers prioritize stakeholder relationships. They suggest that stakeholders become salient to managers to the extent that those managers perceive stakeholders as possessing three attributes: the stakeholder's *power* to influence the firm; the *legitimacy* of the stakeholder's relationship with the firm, and the *urgency* of the stakeholder's claim on the firm. The concepts of legitimacy, power, and urgency and permutations of these attributes are used to create seven stakeholder categories and one non-stakeholder category. Figure 4.5 shows how a mixture of attributes can create different types of stakeholders with different expected behavioural patterns with respect to the firm (1997: 287).

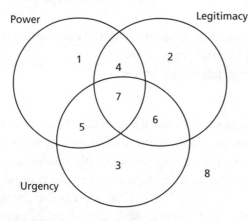

Figure 4.5 Model of stakeholder salience
Source: Mitchell, Agle, and Wood (1997: 298).

Power is the extent an organization can gain access to:

- coercive power, based on physical resources of force, violence, or restraint,
- utilitarian power, based on financial or material resources, or
- normative power, based on symbolic resources such as being able to command the attention of the media.

Power alone is insufficient for classifying a stakeholder as high priority. Legitimacy is required to provide authority. Urgency is necessary for execution, hence the stakeholder must be aware of its power and be willing to exercise it. They accept Suchman's definition of legitimacy as 'a generalized perception or assumption that the actions of an entity are desirable, proper, or appropriate within some socially constructed system of norms, values, beliefs and definitions' (1995: 574). Urgency is based on:

1. *Time sensitivity*—the degree to which managerial delay in attending to the claim or relationship is unacceptable to the stakeholder.
2. *Criticality*—the importance of the claim or the relationship to the stakeholder.

All attributes are transitory; they can be gained as well as lost. A party must be perceived by management to possess at least one attribute to be recognized as a stakeholder. If only one attribute is recognized the stakeholder is viewed as low priority and few, if any, resources will be devoted to managing that stakeholder relation. Stakeholders become moderate priority if two attributes are held and high priority if all three are perceived (Figure 4.6).

Narrow stakeholder definitions often emphasize legitimacy via contract, exchange, legal title, legal right, moral right, at-risk status, or moral interest in the harms and benefits generated by corporate actions (1997: 287). Legitimacy captures only one attribute of salience. Legitimate stakeholders may not have their claims addressed by an organization if, at a certain point in time, they lack power and/or urgency. Such stakeholders are most likely to be recipients of discretionary CSR. Alternatively, a stakeholder may not have a legitimate claim but may be able to affect the organization and thus the interest of those who do have legitimate claims. Consequently, managers have an interest in managing the claims of such powerful, yet non-legitimate, stakeholders. Power and legitimacy are independent dimensions; they can be overlapping but each can exist without the other. In addition, the degree to which stakeholder claims call for immediate attention adds a catalytic component: urgency demands attention.

Presence of each attribute is a matter of multiple perceptions and is socially constructed in effect. An individual or entity may not be conscious of possessing an attribute, or may not choose to enact any implied behaviour. Groups can be reliably identified as stakeholders based on their possession of power, legitimacy, and/or urgency, but it is the managers who determine which stakeholders are salient and therefore

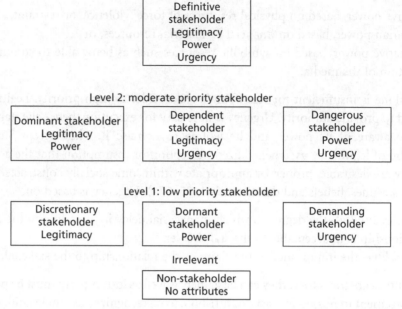

Figure 4.6 Model of stakeholder priority for managers, stakeholder type, and associated attributes

Source: Adapted from Page (2002: 78).

which will receive attention. So a stakeholder can be identified by its attributes, but a manager could incorrectly perceive the field. Mitchell, Agle, and Wood recognize that each attribute is treated in their model as absent or present for simplicity: in reality each operates on a continuum.

Dynamism is briefly addressed. Latent stakeholders can increase their salience to managers and move into the expected stakeholder category by acquiring a further attribute via coalition building, political action, or social construction of reality. The African National Congress is used as an example. As a stakeholder of multinational companies located in South Africa it originally only possessed urgency. Legitimacy was achieved via media support, and power came through the divestment movement supported by shareholders.

Agle, Mitchell, and Sonnenfeld (1999) empirically tested the model on CEOs in eighty US firms. The selection of the stakeholder attributes was further justified in relation to social cognition theory, organizational theory, and institutional theory.[11] The results suggest that as the stakeholder attributes gather in the mind of the manager, selectivity is enhanced, intensity is increased, and salience is heightened. Urgency was found to be the best predictor of salience.

4.2.6 A NETWORK THEORY OF STAKEHOLDER INFLUENCES: ROWLEY (1997)

Rowley (1997) considers multiple and interdependent interactions that simultaneously exist in stakeholder environments, leading to a more complex field than that mapped by Freeman (see Figure 2.2). Figure 4.7 shows the organization in a network of stakeholders, each possessing its own stakeholders and without the focal organization necessarily occupying the hub.

How stakeholders affect the firm and how firms respond to these influences will depend on the network of stakeholders surrounding the relationship. The existence of dense ties between and within stakeholder groups enables better communication and facilitates the transfer of norms and expectations. Networks also act as a governance mechanism, encouraging joint action and deterring individual opportunism such as free riding. Density (interconnectedness between stakeholders) and centrality (position in the network relative to others) are key factors for analysis. As density increases, coordination and communication between participants grows and the promotion of shared behaviours and behavioural expectations increases, increasing the chance of stakeholders forming coalitions and increasing their ability to constrain the focal organization. Focal organization strategies aimed at playing one group off against another, or finding a sympathetic group with whom it can form an alliance, will falter. Position will confer power: the higher the degree of centrality, the greater the power obtained through the network's structure. This is distinct from power gained from individual attributes. Power is afforded through the number of direct ties an actor has (centrality), the extent of independent access to others (closeness), and control over others (betweenness). As an organization's centrality increases, its ability to resist stakeholder pressures increases. A four-way typology is presented (Figure 4.8).

1. *Compromiser.* When a centrally located organization operates within a densely connected set of stakeholders all parties have a degree of power to influence each

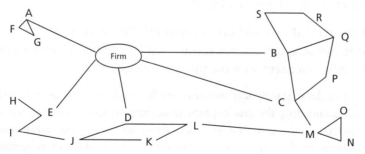

Figure 4.7 Mapping stakeholder networks
Source: Rowley (1997: 891).

Centrality of the focal organization

	High	Low
High Density of the stakeholder network	Compromiser	Subordinate
Low	Commander	Solitarian

Figure 4.8 A structural classification of stakeholder influences: organizational responses to stakeholder pressures
Source: Rowley (1997: 901).

other. High network density facilitates stakeholder communication and coordination to create a more influential collective force, but the central position occupied by the organization indicates that it can influence the formation of expectations. The proposed strategy is to compromise: to balance, pacify, and negotiate with stakeholders to appease expectations and to reduce the likelihood of collective action and achieve a predictable environment.

2. *Commander.* If an organization enjoys a central position among uncoordinated stakeholders, it will achieve high levels of discretion, face few constraints, and be able to adopt a commander role in which stakeholders are co-opted through the manipulation of information flows and expectations.

3. *Subordinate.* If an organization is positioned at the edges of a high-density stakeholder network it will have a power disadvantage, with limited access to information flows. It will have no option but to subordinate authority, acceding to stakeholder expectation.

4. *Solitarian.* If the organization is positioned on the edges of a low-density network, the power differential will be inconsequential. Although it lacks influence, so do its stakeholders. In a sparsely connected network, information flow is impeded and consequently the focal organization will adopt a withdrawal strategy, of concealment and buffering, to avoid stakeholder attention.

Rowley (2000) tested this model on one network constructed for the semiconductor manufacturing industry and another constructed for the steel producing industry. His results are broadly consistent with the suggested model:

Firms operating in dense stakeholder networks are less likely to manage their stakeholders by controlling and dominating the relationships than firms in sparsely connected networks.... Centrality negatively affects compromiser and subordinate behaviour. Thus firms occupying peripheral positions in their stakeholder networks are more likely to cooperate with their stakeholder—negotiate with, and acquiesce to, their stakeholders—than firms situated in central positions. (2000: 32–3)

4.2.7 AN ORGANIZATIONAL LIFE CYCLE APPROACH: JAWAHAR AND MCLAUGHLIN (2001)

Jawahar and McLaughlin propose a stakeholder theory built on a combination of resource dependence theory and prospect theory. From resource dependence theory (Pfeffer and Salancik 1978) they take the idea that organizations must attend to those who provide resources needed for the organization's survival and, given limited time and money, the organization will attend more to those who control critical resources (Pfeffer 1982) (Section 4.5.1). From prospect theory they take the idea that people (managers) will be risk-seeking when contemplating losses and risk-averse when considering gains. Thus, citing Tversky and Kahneman (1981), in a loss situation or one framed in terms of losses, a risky prospect, which is of equal expected value to a certain prospect, will be selected.[12] When the issue is framed in terms of gains, the certain outcome will be selected.[13] They suggest that threat and opportunity situations, which are used to characterize environmental events in the strategic literature, can be used to identify how issues to be decided upon will be framed: in a loss or a gain frame.

Using the Carroll/Clarkson RADP categories (Table 4.1), Jawahar and McLaughlin reason that the equivalent of the certain prospect that would be preferred in a risk-averse or gain frame would be for corporations to address all primary stakeholder interests and issues proactively or at least accommodatively. Managers, it is assumed, would be most likely to satisfy stakeholders and thereby avoid unfavourable actions on their part that could impede the flow of resources coming into the organization. The highest risk strategy would be to ignore the interests and issues of all stakeholders. They consider this untenable. However, they predict that organizations will adopt the risky option of a defence or reaction strategy towards less critical stakeholders.

The final element of the model is to map these risk strategies to stages in the organization life cycle (Table 4.2). The presumption is that all organizations go through a life cycle composed of roughly the same four stages: start-up, emerging growth, maturity, and decline/transition. They cite considerable evidence for the four-stage model (e.g. Miller and Friesen 1980), though they note that there is no unanimity in the literature. In addition, they cite literature in support of claims that external and internal threats and opportunities vary systematically in different stages (Dodge and Robbins 1992) and that organization behaviour can be predicted using a life cycle model (Smith, Mitchell, and Summer 1985).

In start-up and decline/transition stages, the reference point for managerial postures towards stakeholders is the threat of organizational failure. They will pursue a risky strategy of actively addressing only the interests of stakeholders that are viewed as critical for avoiding failure. For non-critical stakeholders they will pursue strategies of

Table 4.2 Management stakeholder strategies and the organizational life cycle

Stage	Typical frame/risk strategy	Strategic posture	Stakeholder group
1. Start-up	Loss/risk seeking	Proaction	Stockholders, creditors, customers
		Accommodation	Employees, suppliers
		Reaction	Trade associations, environmental groups
		Defence	Government, community
2. Emerging growth	Gains/risk adverse	Proaction	Creditors, employees, suppliers, trade unions
		Accommodation	Stockholders, customers, governments, communities, environmental groups
3. Mature	Gains/risk adverse	Proaction	All except creditors
		Accommodation	Creditors
4. Decline/ transition	Losses/risk seeking	Proaction	Stockholders, creditors, customers
		Accommodation	Employees, suppliers
		Reaction	Trade associations, environmental groups
		Defence	Government, community

Source: Adapted from Jawahar and McLaughlin (2001: 406–10).

defending against, ignoring interests or denying responsibility for issues.[14] In part this occurs because the resources required to deal with critical stakeholders leave little surplus to deal with others, in part it is due to a calculated risk strategy. For example, in the start-up stage firms will actively pursue suppliers of capital, but will defer tax remittances as much as possible.

During the emerging growth stage the firm is engaged in expansion opportunities and during the mature stage it rests on past success with a strong cash flow. In both situations managers make resource allocation decisions framed from a gain domain, and a risk-averse strategy will be pursued. This involves dealing with all stakeholders in a proactive or accommodative manner. The particular strategies applied to different stakeholders will partly depend on contingent factors, such as whether the company expands through equity or debt financial instruments. Stakeholders relevant to the favoured instrument will receive proactive treatment while the others are only accommodated. During the expansionary stage demand will usually outstrip supply so firms will be less concerned with customers than with suppliers. During the mature stage strong cash flow will mean creditors only have to be accommodated. Slack resources will be available to allow all other stakeholders to be treated proactively, thereby reducing risk from any dissatisfied group.

As with Rowley (1997) (Section 4.2.6), Jawahar and McLaughlin analyse focal organization dealings with stakeholders through the prism of simultaneous demands of multiple stakeholders. Their theory is falsifiable with many testable hypotheses, which they suggest can be tested using Clarkson's methodology (1988, 1991, 1995).

4.3 Strategic/instrumental and relationship-focused stakeholder models

4.3.1 CRITICAL REALIST STAKEHOLDER THEORY: FRIEDMAN AND MILES (2002)

Friedman and Miles (2002) present a stakeholder model based on a critical realist theory of social change and differentiation (Vignette 4.2). Unlike some social construction of reality theories, rules, structures, and cultural systems are to be treated as analytically distinct from perceptions of them, or actions taken through them. They argue that social structures (itinerary of interests, roles, opportunities, power differentials) and cultural systems (sets of ideas about what is true or false subject to presumed universal laws of logic) shape actions, perceptions of ideas, and people's attempts to influence the ideas and actions of others. These in turn lead to further development of those social structures and cultural systems. Material structures and systems of ideas endow sections of society with different vested interests. These different vested interests lead to particular and diverse opportunity costs, which are associated with different responses to those structures and systems. These do not force actions; rather they put prices and premiums on different interpretations of situations as well as associated activities. Acting or changing perceptions then result in further elaboration of the material structures and systems of ideas. In critical realist theory the stratified nature of social reality is emphasized, with each stratum having different emergent powers and properties.

Vignette 4.2   CRITICAL REALISM

According to realists, the world exists independent of our knowledge and experience of it. This leads to two dimensions of knowledge. The intransitive dimension concerns the objects of science, physical processes, and social phenomena. The transitive dimension concerns theories and discourses of physical and social science (Bhaskar 1975). Critical realists distinguish the real from the actual. Things are real if they have an effect, if they make a difference. This applies to material or physical things as well as to discourses, ideas, theories, and beliefs, as well as social structures like bureaucracies.

Making a difference applies to the capacity real things have to behave in certain ways (their performative potential) and their causal powers (capacity to produce effects in other entities). This should not be thought of in the active sense only, real things have passive causal powers in that the way they are structured leads them to be susceptible to certain kinds of changes, and not to others. A crucial aspect of critical realist endeavour is to identify and distinguish between necessary connections among things and connections, which are possible or potential. For example, the grammar of a language specifies that certain types of word combinations must go together, while others are possible, but not necessary.

The actual refers to what happens when those causal powers are activated: not only what they do, but also eventual outcomes of the activation of those powers. Speech is the activation of language; though once

(*contd.*)

> **Vignette 4.2** (*contd.*)
>
> spoken, a speech is real in that whatever it conveys has structure and generative powers and can affect ideas and actions.
>
> The empirical concerns what is experienced. This is clearly different from what is real for critical realists. Experiencing something may increase our confidence that something exists, but it is no guarantee. More important, things can be real without it being possible to experience or to observe them directly. 'Unexperienced' entities can have effects, which are experienced. However, the causal powers of real entities may not be actualized or experienced. What is experienced does not exhaust the possibilities of what could happen.
>
> Two implications are worth mentioning (Bhaskar 1975; Archer 1995; Sayer 2000; Fleetwood and Ackroyd 2004):
>
> 1. Entities are structured; they are made up of constituents that are related in such a way that the causal powers of those elements emerge from their combination. This applies to physical entities and social structures as well as theoretical or belief constructs.
> 2. Structures are not created independent of human agency. Social interaction occurs in the context of existing structures, which have been created by prior activities of people, most of whom are long dead. Social interaction changes social structures, but in limited ways, constrained by the nature of pre-existing social structures. In terms of the structure–agency debate, critical realists allow both for agents to make a difference through their interactions and for structures to affect their actions.

Friedman and Miles (2002) view the organization–stakeholder relation as a combination out of which a further elaboration of ideas, material interests, and institutional supports emerge. Their typology of organization–stakeholder relations is based on two distinctions.

1. Whether the relationships are compatible or incompatible in terms of sets of ideas and material interests.
2. Whether the relationships between groups are necessary or contingent. Necessary relationships are internal to a social structure (such as an organization, but not exclusively so) or to a set of logically connected ideas. Contingent relations are external or not integrally connected.

Four institutional configurations for understanding relationships between social groups are distinguished. Each is associated with a particular situational logic and encourages certain strategic action. Friedman and Miles propose different contractual organization–stakeholder forms associated with each configuration (explicit recognized contracts, implicit recognized contracts, implicit unrecognized contracts, and no contract).

The model focuses at the meso level in that it covers relations between, as well as within, organizations. This is due to their recognition that individuals will play different roles with respect to different institutions and sets of ideas, for example, an employee also being a shareholder. Consequently, there will be groupings of vested interests and opportunities associated with different types of resources, leading to different situational logics operating at the same time. Figure 4.9 associates different stakeholder types with different situational logics and contractual forms. However, this only indi-

	Necessary	Contingent
Compatible	**A** **Explicit/implicit recognized** *Protectionist/defensive* Shareholders Top management Partners	**B** **Implicit unrecognized** *Opportunism/opportunistic* The general public Companies connected through common trade associations/ initiatives
Incompatible	**D** **Explicit/implicit recognized** *Concessionary/compromise* Trade unions Low-level employees Government and their agencies Customers Creditors Some NGOs	**C** **No contract** *competition/elimination* Aggrieved or criminal members of the public Some NGOs

Figure 4.9 Stakeholder configurations, **associated contractual forms** and *strategic actions*, and associated stakeholder types
Source: Adapted from Friedman and Miles (2002: 7–8).

cates *usual* positions for different stakeholder types: different stakeholder types can be in different categories of the model depending on circumstances surrounding the particular organization–stakeholder relation.

Necessary compatible (A) relationships are created whereby all parties have something to lose by disruption to the relationships. The associated situational logic is protectionist; all interests are served by the continuation of the relationship. The shareholder–corporate relationship is an example. The capital market for shares provides powerful institutional support for ensuring that these contracts are fulfilled de facto as well as de jure. All parties have an interest in building further institutions to monitor and enforce individual contracts and in defending and strengthening existing institutional supports, thus enabling general enforcement and monitoring of the whole web of contracts that make up the market. This type of strategic action does not rely on the form of contract, providing the contracts are recognized as valid by the parties involved.

At the opposite extreme are *contingent incompatible* (C) institutional arrangements. Here the stakeholder and the corporation have separate, opposed, and unconnected sets of ideas, which only come into conflict if someone insists on counterpoising them. The incompatibility is made competitive by groups taking sides and by trying to mobilize others for support. Defence of interests consists in inflicting maximum damage on the opposing party by seeking to eliminate it or by discrediting oppositional views. A key feature of this model is that it does not presume that all organization–stakeholder issues can be resolved through an appropriate (social) contract. In this structural configuration there is no contractual relationship; normal social rules will be suspended. The relationship between companies and certain NGOs is given as an illustration. The combination of antagonism and total independence will result in an interest in eliminating or completely discrediting each other. This is only feasible if the NGO remains immaterial to the company and relatively unknown or treated as eccentric in the media. In such circumstances, the company can choose to ignore them (or fight them using illegal or unethical tactics) with little consequence. Likewise, as long as the activists have few resources to lose, they too can use illegal or extreme tactics.

Necessary incompatible (D) relations occur when material interests or sets of ideas are necessarily related to each other, but their operations will lead to the relationship itself being threatened. The situational logic is concession leading to compromise because if the vested interests of one party are advanced, this intensifies diminution of interests of the other. The relationship itself is threatened. Organizations are encouraged to answer stakeholder claims, in spite of incompatible interests, because there is recognition by both parties that a contract exists, whether implicit or explicit. Adverse publicity and the possibility of attracting unwelcome attention from champions or intermediaries who represent stakeholders encourage organizations to respond to stakeholder challenges. The interests behind these organization–stakeholder relations are antagonistic, but the parties still have an interest in continuing the relationship. It is a condition of being in this quadrant that opportunity costs of leaving the relationship are considered to be higher than the value of what is being fought over. Struggles over resources will characterize many organization–stakeholder relations. Explicit long-term contracts that cover relations such as the employment relation and long-term financing or supplier relations are given as examples.

The fourth category is *contingent compatible* (B) institutional arrangements. The situational logic associated is of opportunities or opportunism in that those who adhere to one view or derive material interest from one institution are free to approach, or avoid, people associated with other institutions or ideas. This covers relations where there is no formal contract and no direct relationship between the parties. Forming other relationships or recognizing implicit contracts may further compatible interests. Organizations connected through common trade associations or joined by national initiatives are examples.

The model allows changes in organization–stakeholder relations to be analysed. Four processes are distinguished:

1. Changes in material interests of either side.
2. Changes in ideas held by either side.
3. Changes in institutional supports.
4. Emerging contingent factors (both internal to the relationship and external to it).

All four are demonstrated with the organization–stakeholder relationship via the history of Greenpeace, an environmental NGO. Phase 1 refers to the era in which Greenpeace

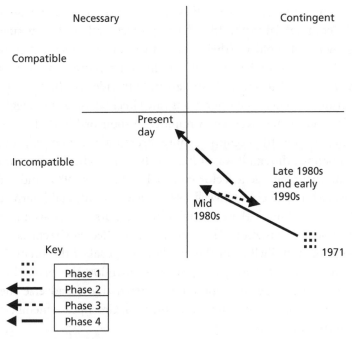

Figure 4.10 The changing nature of Greenpeace–corporation relationships
Source: Friedman and Miles (2002: 12).

was founded in 1971(Figure 4.10). The founders were environmentalists with a 'deep ecology' set of beliefs who regarded large corporations as the 'enemy': immoral, wasteful, and harmful to the planet. According to environmentalists, large corporations (and most of the media) were infused with 'the dominant worldview' that environmental issues were at best subsidiary to the main concern of corporations (O'Riordan 1981). They regarded Greenpeace as cranks or radicals. Greenpeace famously attempted to disrupt corporate activities, while corporations either tried to ignore them or used the courts to get injunctions or to sue them for damages. Each tried to inflict maximum damage to the other. They typified contingent incompatible relationships where no social contract can be said to exist among the parties.

The external contingent factors that affected their relationship included the series of environmental disasters that received wide media coverage in the 1980s (Bhopal, Chernobyl, Exxon Valdez (see Section 9.3.2)). An internal emergent situation arising from the relationship was the bombing of the Greenpeace yacht *The Rainbow Warrior*, in which a Greenpeace member was killed. This, combined with the environmental disasters, led to a huge increase in media attention and sympathy for Greenpeace. This led to a change in the material condition of Greenpeace. The great rise in sympathy for Greenpeace boosted membership and funding. This in turn led to more substantial projects being attempted. To carry out these projects people with managerial skills were hired from the commercial sector. In order to protect a relatively new significant set of Greenpeace's own stakeholders (their non-active new members) they became more concerned with the risk of being sued. At this time more radical members of the organization were asked to leave. Attitudes on both sides of the Greenpeace–corporations relationship softened as corporations saw Greenpeace as more legitimate due to its growing size and media presence. A number of sponsorship deals were signed. The relationship moved towards becoming more structurally connected, more necessary, and more compatible, though it was still in the bottom right-hand quadrant.

A further internal contingent factor emerged in the late 1980s and early 1990s: an anti-green backlash in the USA (Rowell 1996). New institutional intermediaries (Wise Use and Alliance for America) were established to pursue this agenda and to lobby against environmental legislation. This retrenchment affected Greenpeace as evidenced by its campaign to stop Shell from the off-shore disposal of the Brent-Spar oil rig in 1995. While they succeeded in getting Shell to abandon the plan, through a well-organized boycott, Greenpeace's reputation suffered due to adverse media reaction when the rationale behind their claim was challenged. Greenpeace membership declined significantly in the late 1990s.

Finally, a significant change in ideas on both sides of the relationship was also emerging in the 1990s that restructured the Greenpeace–corporation relation. Sustainable development emerged as a concept to bridge the gap between the deep ecology and traditional dominant worldview of environmental issues. The new 'solutions-based' approach has led to partnerships and alliances between Greenpeace and different corporations to promote environmentally friendly products, packaging, and energy sources (see Section 6.6.8).

4.4 Descriptive/positive and relationship-focused stakeholder models

4.4.1 STAKEHOLDER–AGENCY THEORY: HILL AND JONES (1992)

Hill and Jones (1992) view the firm as a 'nexus' of implicit and explicit contracts, among all stakeholders, including managers. They consider it to be a more general theory of agency than is normally considered (Vignette 4.1): first, because they include more than explicit contractual relations between shareholders and managers and, second, because they reject the assumption that markets are efficient and adjust instantly or even quickly to new circumstances. This allows power differentials to be introduced.

In perfectly efficient markets, principals and agents are free to enter and exit contracts: there are assumed to be an infinite number of potential contractors and all are assumed to have perfect information about all possible contractual conditions (Barney and Ouchi 1986). Inefficient markets surround firms because agents cannot exit contractual relations without taking substantial losses (because better alternatives are either not available or not known). This leads to power differentials between principals and agents, because of unequal dependence between parties to an exchange (Emerson 1962). If there is an oversupply of agents, power shifts towards principals. If there is a shortage of agents or if principals cannot easily exit the contractual relations, power shifts towards agents.

Hill and Jones consider markets to be so slow to adjust that there will be prolonged periods of disequilibrium (there will be shortages or gluts of resources and people in different markets and adjustments will be taking place in response to those situations). These adjustments are prolonged by 'friction' in the system due to the following reasons:

- Structural barriers to entry and exit such as legal restrictions or geographical limitations.
- Strategic barriers constructed by advantaged parties in contracts attempting to reduce competition, such as managers increasing entry barriers by collusion or predatory pricing.
- Organizational inertia: in disequilibrium situations disadvantaged parties may need to develop new incentive structures or monitoring and enforcement mechanisms. Such innovations may not emerge due to 'sunk costs, political coalitions, the tendency to regard precedents as standards', or merely due to a lack of imagination (1992: 136).

Hill and Jones consider only 'legitimate' stakeholders and this legitimacy is established through an exchange relationship with the corporation. Managers are at the centre of a 'nexus of contracts'. They enter into contracts with all other stakeholders and they are the only ones with '*direct* control over the decision-making apparatus of the firm' (1992: 134). Managers are regarded as agents of all other stakeholders. Though most stakeholders do not hire managers (as in the principal–agent relationship), there are implicit or explicit contracts between them. Even if there is a degree of convergence of interests in the claims of managers and stakeholders (e.g. if raising employee wages leads to higher productivity thereby providing managers with more resources), beyond a certain point this convergence gives way to divergent interests.

Hill and Jones define utility loss as 'the difference between the utility that stakeholders could achieve if management acted in stakeholders' best interests and the utility that is achieved if management acts in its own best interest' (1992: 138).[15] The stakeholder utility loss can be reduced through the following techniques or procedures; however, they involve costs, which (eventually) fall on stakeholders. Costs are borne by different stakeholder groups in varying proportions depending on the technique or procedure:

1. *Interest alignment (incentive) structures*:
   - Stock option plans
   - Tax breaks for investment in pollution containment equipment
   - Stakeholder insistence on managers absorbing *ex ante* bonding costs via credible commitments to taking losses upon deviant behaviour, e.g. customer warranties, supplier 'lock in' investments from large customer firms, reciprocal trade agreements, inflexible prices, posted prices, exclusive territories, most-favoured-buyer clauses, franchise-specific investments, patent pools, and union shop agreements.

2. *Monitoring procedures.* Managers are in a powerful situation compared with stakeholders in terms of the imbalance of information concerning how the contracts are being executed. It is difficult and expensive for stakeholders to monitor managers directly. Institutional structures have evolved to economize on information-gathering and analysis efforts:
   - Legislation: requirement of public companies to publish consolidated annual accounts.
   - Intermediaries that profit from gathering, analysing, and selling information to stakeholders: stock analysts, consumer reports.
   - Non-profit organizations that monitor managers to see if they act in stakeholder interests.

3. *Enforcement mechanisms* act as a deterrent to the extent that they are credible (Schelling 1956). This means both commanding widespread support in the society and being communicated to management before contracts are put in place. Examples include:
   - Laws such as those against insider trading, antitrust, and anti-pollution. Much of business law reflects critical points of conflict in stakeholder–agent relations.
   - Exit supporting institutions that make up for stakeholder coordination problems and the availability of alternative resource supplies to management, such as labour unions, consumer unions, and special interest groups that support and coordinate collective action.
   - Voice mechanisms, which are least costly; publicity can damage the human capital of managers.

4. *Residual utility loss.* As with agency costs, there is a residual loss because the above three mechanisms will not work perfectly.

Hill and Jones define an efficient equilibrium situation as one where,

Specifically, stakeholders would increase the complexity of institutional structures up to that point where the marginal benefits of doing so (in terms of a reduction in utility loss) were equivalent to the marginal costs of maintaining those structures (in terms of the utility that has to be sacrificed to support them). (1992: 143)

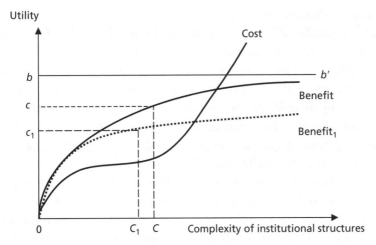

Figure 4.11 Benefit–cost relationship to stakeholders with increasing institutional complexity
Source: Adapted from Hill and Jones (1992: 144).

This is illustrated in Figure 4.11. On the vertical axis is utility of stakeholders. The horizontal axis represents degrees of complexity of existing institutional structures. The market mechanism is assumed to be the simplest. Increasing complexity in institutions to align manager interests with stakeholders and to monitor and enforce stakeholder interests are presumed to 'work', i.e. to reduce stakeholder utility loss, but with decreasing returns as complexity rises (the Benefit curve).[16] On the costs side, they assume economies of scale to the money and emotion that have to be invested by stakeholders in increasingly complex institutions 'due to the benefits of specialization' so costs will rise with increasingly complex institutions, but at a decreasing rate, until some point where diminishing returns to specialization are likely to set in. At point C the gradients of the Benefit and the Cost curves are the same, the marginal benefit (increase in benefit due to a 'very small' increase in complexity) and the marginal cost (increase in cost due to a 'very small' increase in complexity) are equal. Up to that level of complexity marginal benefits exceed marginal costs, so a further step along the horizontal axis is worthwhile. After that point the opposite is true and the extra benefit will be less than the extra cost in terms of stakeholder utility.

Stakeholders differ by the size of the stake they have in the firm, which is 'a function of the extent to which that actor's exchange relationship with the firm is supported by investments in firm specific assets' (1992: 133). Specific assets are defined as those that cannot be redeployed to alternative uses without a loss of value (Williamson 1975). The extent of this loss of value represents the stake that the stakeholders have 'tied up' in the contract with the firm or with the management of the firm.

Though markets are slow to adjust, Hill and Jones believe markets work in the long run: they eliminate the most inefficient organizational forms. Though market forces work towards equilibrium, they note that the market system generates innovations, which may continually shift the equilibrium to which market forces are tending (Schumpeter 1942). In addition, managers or stakeholders may act to restrain equilibrating forces; they may take actions to exploit and to extend power differentials through encouraging friction in the system. For example, managers may attempt to reduce customer power by diversifying the customer base and reduce community power by geographic diversification. They may directly try to increase their power by horizontal and vertical mergers and acquisitions as well as establishing cooperative agreements with managers in different firms (Pfeffer and Salancik 1978). Managers may be limited in their ability to pursue these strategies due to stakeholder actions, such as the establishment of boards of directors and the institutions described above. However, in turn, managers may take advantage of power differentials to reverse credible commitments made to stakeholders such as warranties, reciprocal purchasing agreements, and union shops.

Figure 4.11 may be regarded as depicting a particular (static) situation to which stakeholders react. If the parameters of the situation change, say, by managers using their power to alter the situation in which stakeholders operate (making it more difficult), this would change the position of the benefits curve, making it rise less steeply (Benefit$_1$ curve), and thereby change the equilibrium level of institutional structure complexity to C_1. Any institutions introduced by stakeholders will have less effect on reducing stakeholder utility loss. Hill and Jones note that the distance between the ultimate level of utility possible and the equilibrium level represents 'an incentive to stakeholders to find new ways of economizing on contracting costs (to develop new institutional structures)' (1992: 150). The more the benefits curve is moved lower (through management's anti-stakeholder power strategies), the greater will be the potential benefit to innovation, as measured by the size of the distance between the ultimate level of utility possible and the equilibrium level. Hill and Jones point to the development of the factory system in nineteenth-century England as leading to the declining of the craft guilds, which in turn led to the development of labour unions in order to re-establish mutual dependency between employers and employees.

4.5 Strategic/instrumental and stakeholder-centric stakeholder models

4.5.1 STAKEHOLDER INFLUENCING STRATEGIES: FROOMAN (1999)

Frooman (1999) makes a significant contribution to stakeholder theory by modelling stakeholder influencing strategies to help management understand and manage stakeholder relations. He also introduced the idea that stakeholders may influence focal organizations indirectly, through intermediaries. He argues that Mitchell, Agle, and Wood (1997) fail to distinguish the *relative importance* of the attributes of power, legitimacy and urgency they use in their model of stakeholder salience (Section 4.2.5). For Frooman, power is the dominant attribute. It is most likely to decide the outcome of organization–stakeholder conflict, particularly in cases where the organization is unwilling to compromise. Power is not a straightforward attribute to assess. It can be described as the potential to influence, which can take the form of either dependence or punitive capability (Lawler and Bacharach 1987). Various taxonomies of power have been suggested including formal, economic, and political (Freeman and Reed 1983) and coercive, utilitarian, and normative (Etzioni 1964; Mitchell, Agle, and Wood 1997). Rowley (1997) identifies power in terms of network structures and Carroll (1989) suggests concentration of resources is tantamount to power. Resource dependence theory (Pfeffer 1972; Salancik 1979) suggests that the degree of dependence on external stakeholders for resources will determine the extent such stakeholders can exert power over an organization in forcing their claims to be addressed. Resource dependence (a state in which one actor relies on the actions of another to achieve particular outcomes) is said to exist when one actor is supplying another with a resource (anything that an actor perceives as valuable) that is marked by:

1. Concentration (suppliers are few in number)
2. Controllability
3. Non-mobility
4. Non-substitutability
5. Essentiality, being a function of two factors: relative magnitude of exchange and criticality

Pfeffer and Leong (1977) test the power dependence formula, providing empirical support that power is structurally determined by the relationship. Frooman's typology is heavily informed by resource dependency. Figure 4.12 depicts the four-way model that identifies stakeholder-influencing strategies with the degree of interdependence between stakeholder and organization.

		Is the stakeholder dependent on the firm?	
		No	Yes
Is the firm dependent on the stakeholder?	No	Low interdependence Indirect/withholding	Firm power Indirect/usage
	Yes	Stakeholder power Direct/withholding	High interdependence Direct/usage

Figure 4.12 Typology of resource relationships and influencing strategies
Source: Adapted from Frooman (1999: 199–200).

Strategies are classified as withholding or usage, which can be executed directly or indirectly. Withholding strategies depend upon a credible threat of withdrawal. They include employee strikes, consumer boycotts, or the withdrawal of funds by share-holders or creditors. Threat efficacy depends on the credulity of the stakeholder's commitment to undertake an act that the corporation would prefer not to see executed. A stakeholder may need to bluff that the costs of withholding resources to themselves are immaterial, or that the enjoyment of revenge would outweigh any potential self-damage. To maximize impact, discretion in carrying out the threat must be minimized. This can be achieved by staking reputation on fulfilment and declaring that if bonds are broken there will be no renegotiation (Schelling 1956). Frooman suggests that this will rarely exist if the welfare of the stakeholder and corporation are intrinsically linked, as they will only succeed by attending to the needs of each other. Usage strategies occur when a stakeholder continues to provide a resource, but with conditions attached that if behaviour is not altered, resources will ultimately be withdrawn. Suppliers and progres-sive socially responsible funds commonly employ usage strategies.

Indirect strategies involve stakeholders acting through agents or intermediaries. When dependence of the firm on a stakeholder is low, indirect strategies are more effective. Firms do not have to be responsive to direct stakeholder pressure. The stakeholder then acts through agents on whom the firm is more dependent and therefore more responsive.

4.5.2 AN INTEREST- AND IDENTITY-BASED MODEL OF STAKEHOLDER GROUP MOBILIZATION: ROWLEY AND MOLDOVEANU (2003)

Rowley and Moldoveanu (2003) question the assumption that interest intensity or urgency is the primary condition driving stakeholders to take action. They propose an identity-based perspective to challenge the interest-based perspective. The interest-based view does not explain why some stakeholders pursue lost causes, knowing that their actions will have an immaterial impact on corporate behaviour and why some stakeholders with a high degree of discontent and access to necessary resources prefer not to mobilize. Interest intensity, by itself, is insufficient for mobilization of action, because resources are required to organize collective action (McCarthy and Zald 1977). There are two types of critical resources for mobilization identified in the social movement literature (della Porta and Mario 1999):

- Material resources such as money, labour, telephones, computers.
- Non-material resources such as leadership, consensus, and moral engagement that are necessary to motivate participation and facilitate coordination.

They suggest that collective identity can act as an alternative basis for mobilization through the creation of individual commitment and group solidarity (Ashforth and Kreiner 1999). This proposition has support from social psychology (Peteraf and Shanley 1997). Social identity theory suggests that individual identities are socially constructed and embedded: one's identity is created through interactions with, and reference to, similar others. Individuals will associate themselves with the social identity of groups to which they belong and those characteristics that distinguish them from non-members, thereby generating a shared identity. Through a desire to defend and preserve the group, individuals may participate in collective action even when there are limited prospects of success. Groups with a history of collective action are more likely to engage in action in the future, due to established mechanisms created by the inter-actions and experiences from the past actions, which work to build trust, norms, and roles. This also reduces the costs of subsequent action. The social relationship structure is influential in producing group action: the stronger the social ties, the lower the costs associated with the identification of individuals to group issues and agreement of the desired course of action (Section 4.2.6). Dense ties are a form of social capital that enhance the possibilities for mobilization. Action is taken to affirm the group's collective identity, not necessarily to fulfil individual rational interests. In this sense the act of acting is the main objective.

For Rowley and Moldeveanu (2003) the degree to which a stakeholder group will mobilize is dependent upon both interest overlap and identity overlap. Interest overlap relates to the level of interest similarity across stakeholders that belong to multiple stakeholder groups, which is a common phenomenon (Carroll and Ratner 1996). Even if a stakeholder group has an urgent claim, the individual members may have diverse and conflicting interests, stemming from membership of a range of stakeholder groups. This dilutes the level of urgency individuals feel. Consequently, such a group may not act despite being in possession of sufficient resources for mobilization. Identity overlap draws on social research that suggests group members who define themselves in terms of their uniqueness are likely to feel greater animosity towards groups with similar identities than towards dissimilar identity groups. Rowley and Moldeveanu (2003) suggest that taking action when a rival group has already mobilized on a similar issue, or targeted the same industry, will impede identity building, thereby decreasing the value of mobilization for that particular group. This proposition contradicts an interest-based explanation of mobilization. We represent their ideas via a four-way model of stakeholder mobilization (Figure 4.13).

Figure 4.13 suggests that group mobilization is most likely if interest overlap is high, but identity overlap between groups is low. Under situations of high interest and high identity overlap, the likelihood of mobilization will diminish, as the distinctiveness of identity will be eroded through joint action. When interest overlap and identity overlap are both low, any action will embellish the identity of the group but the motivation to

Identity overlap		Interest overlap	
		High	Low
	High	Low probability of mobilization	Unlikely probability of mobilization
	Low	High probability of mobilization	Low probability of mobilization

Figure 4.13 Stakeholder mobilization model

act will be hampered by the presence of conflicts of interest stemming from external group membership. Finally, mobilization is deemed unlikely if interest overlap is low and identity overlap is high as neither provides an impetus for action. Relating this model to the work of Frooman (1999), who suggests that powerful stakeholders are likely to employ direct influencing strategies, Rowley and Moldeveanu (2003) state that identity-based groups will have a special interest in using media channels to express their uniqueness and therefore may employ indirect strategies, despite resource dependence.

4.6 Comparison of strategic stakeholder models

In Figure 4.1 a crude classification of analytic models was presented in which most contributions were identified as organization-centric and strategic/instrumental. Here we develop a finer distinction (Figure 4.14) based on Freeman's recommendation (1984) to identify and map stakeholders and his subsequent outline of the stakeholder strategy formulation process (Figure 4.2). This specifies a series of steps that are listed on the left-hand side of Figure 4.14 in descending order as Freeman suggested would occur in 'logical time'. This distinction permits an alternative view of all those contributions classified in Figure 4.1 as strategic/instrumental, but does not reclassify descriptive contributions.

Different segments of the strategy formulation process can be undertaken by stakeholders as well as organizations. Figure 4.14 shows which segments are included in each model, irrespective of whether it is the stakeholders or the organizations to which the strategic recommendations are aimed. We have added two segments in the strategy formulation process not explicitly identified by Freeman (1984): (*a*) issue identification and (*b*) stakeholder salience. These are assumed to occur before stakeholder identification and are placed above Freeman's list in the figure. The former has been dealt with in

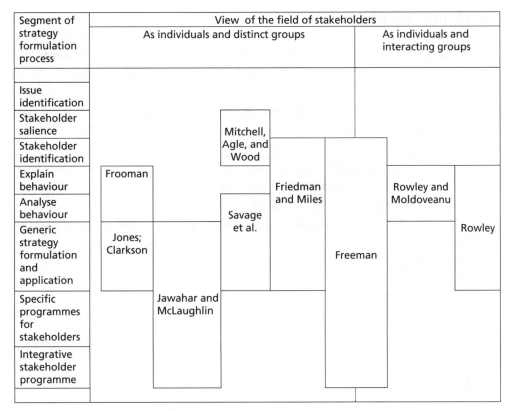

Figure 4.14 Strategic stakeholder models and the strategy formulation process

earlier theories that focus on CSR (Carroll 1979; see Section 2.3.1). The latter was highlighted by Mitchell, Agle, and Wood (1997). Freeman also identified the need to analyse coalitions of stakeholders, particularly the commonality of behaviour and interest among stakeholder groups. This has been taken up by Rowley (1997) and Rowley and Moldoveanu (2003). Instead of specifying coalition analysis as a separate segment in the strategy formulation process, we consider analysis of interactions among stakeholder groups to be a broad type of strategic analysis, which can contain all the segments Freeman identified for individual stakeholder strategy formulation.

Many of the contributions are easy to place within Figure 4.14. Others are debatable. Freeman (1984) identifies the range of segments to be analysed, and stimulates others to follow up with more focused contributions. We note that most contributions focus on analysing and explaining stakeholder behaviour and recommending formulation and application of generic strategies. Issue identification is an area that may be developed in future when more case studies become available.

☐ QUESTIONS/EXERCISES

1 Goodpaster (1991) and Boatright (1994) are shown in Figure 3.1 as normative stakeholder theories. Present an argument for including these contributions as analytical. Would you use the same arguments for Donaldson and Preston (1995)?

2 Clarkson (1995) credits the stakeholder concept as a distinct improvement over corporate social responsibility on two grounds: management recognition of the concept and conceptual confusion. Assess the extent of this improvement.

3 Jones (1995) and Clarkson (1995) propose very different models; however, they both occupy the 'generic strategy formulation and application' box in Figure 4.14. Compare their different approaches to this segment of the strategy formulation process.

4 What issues do the following authors consider to be fundamental in explaining stakeholder behaviour?
   (a) Frooman
   (b) Freeman
   (c) Friedman and Miles
   (d) Rowley
   (e) Rowley and Moldoveanu

☐ NOTES

1 Reed uses the term positive in a similar sense as it appears in economics textbooks, which distinguish positive economics from normative economics. In such textbooks strategic theories are usually included under the broad category of positive economics (Lipsey and Chrystal 2003).

2 Freeman (1984) has become the bible of stakeholder theory. Like the Bible, many refer to it without reading it carefully. The hub-and-spokes representation has been used uncritically by many practitioners and academics (see Figure 6.3).

3 See Rowley (1997) and Rowley and Moldoveanu (2003) (Sections 4.2.6 and 4.5.2).

4 Votaw (1973: 11) in criticizing CSP states: 'The term is a brilliant one; it means something, but not always the same thing, to everybody. To some it conveys the idea of legal responsibility or liability; to others it means socially responsible behavior in an ethical sense; to still others, the meaning transmitted is that of "responsible for", in a causal mode; many simply equate it with a charitable contribution.'

5 She noted that the inclusive and vague meaning of the word 'social' logically had allowed Milton Friedman to connect social issues and responsibilities to non-business issues and responsibilities, and to socialism.

6 This has clearly changed in the past decade with the growth of ethics courses on MBA programmes.

7 Hill and Jones (1992) provide an argument for why this may not occur in the long run. The social cost of such legislation or regulation may outweigh the utility benefit to stakeholders (Section 4.4.1).

8 This proposition has been tested empirically, e.g. Berman (2000).

9 Though Jones allows that some firms may have different moral stances towards different stakeholders and there may be subcultures within corporations of different moral hues (1995: 420).

10 Note their use of the term normative refers to observed norms, rather than eternal social values (see Section 3.1).

11 Social cognition theory suggests salience depends upon attentional tasks ('domination' of the visual field), prior knowledge or expectation, immediate context (Fiske and Taylor 1984), and the extent of mental effort devoted to the focus of attention. Resource dependency theory suggests that domination of the visual field is associated with access to critical resources (Pfeffer and Salancik 1978: 258). Institutional theory and population ecology theory suggests that prior knowledge is used in selection processes in determining legitimacy as cultural norms and behaviour-bound legitimacy. Cyert and March observed that most organizational objectives take the form of an aspiration level on the part of the coalition-participant stakeholders (1963: 27–8). The actions of high-aspiration stakeholders will, in the immediate context, figure prominently in the selectivity and intensity judgements (perceptions) of managers (Agle, Mitchell, and Sonnenfeld 1999: 509–10).

12 For example, in a disease situation, a one-third chance of losing no lives plus a two-thirds chance of losing all lives will be chosen over the mathematically equivalent option of a certain loss of two-thirds of lives.

13 For example, a certain option of saving one-third of lives will be chosen over the mathematically equivalent one-third chance of saving all lives plus a two-thirds chance of saving no lives.

14 Jawahar and McLaughlin note that this is recognized in the literature (Meznar, Chrisman, and Carroll 1991).

15 Following Marris (1964), Hill and Jones (1992: 137) assume that managers' interests are best served by maximizing corporate growth: the larger the firm, the greater the remuneration, power, job security, and status of managers.

16 It is unclear why this should be so. There appears to be an underlying assumption that more complex mechanisms are created by adding extra features to more simple ones. However, a more complex mechanism may work better to reduce stakeholder utility loss by getting managers to abandon aspects of their self interest that lead to behaviour that is against stakeholder interests, compared with a simpler one, if there are synergies to combining different mechanisms in terms of pushing managers over some trigger point in the development of a more trusting or positive attitude to their work.

5 General theoretical stakeholder issues

5.1 Introduction

The stakeholder concept has not gone unchallenged. Many have reiterated the alternative stockholder position. Others have challenged implications of the stakeholder concept for certain groups and its broader implications for social institutions (Section 5.2). In Chapter 2 we noted Donaldson and Preston's claim (1995) that the core of stakeholder theory should be normative as it was the strongest basis capable of providing a convincing justification for stakeholder theory. Jones and Wicks (1999*a*) repeated this claim in stronger terms and sparked an important discussion (the 'convergence' debate) over the future direction that stakeholder theory should take. This debate is reviewed in detail in Section 5.3. We argue that the call for convergence has been premature and encourage future development of analytic stakeholder theory and particularly 'value-attuned' (Swanson 1999) analytic stakeholder theory as well as analytic stakeholder theory that takes into account identities and belief systems of the players involved (Friedman and Miles 2002; Rowley and Moldoveanu 2003). Many critical issues in analytical stakeholder theory are yet to be explored. In Sections 5.4 and 5.5 we deal with the following underexplored issues: stakeholder decision-making; complex managerial structures; ways of categorizing intermediaries; stakeholder legitimacy; and dynamic organization–stakeholder relations. The outcome of such analyses can influence, and may strengthen, normative stakeholder theorizing. Some implications of considering these issues, along with arguments against the convergence thesis based on normative theory, are presented in Section 5.6. Finally, in Section 5.7 we consider a range of classification schemes for distinguishing different contributions to the stakeholder concept as proposed by Stoney and Winstanley (2001).

5.2 **Critiques of the stakeholder concept**

The fundamental alternative to the stakeholder concept is that corporations should serve stockholders exclusively because stockholders own the corporation. The interests of stockholders are for the corporation to maximize stockholder value expressed either as maximizing long-run profits, growth, or dividends (though how long 'long run' should be is debatable). Friedman (1962: 74) argued that this is the 'one and only social responsibility of business' as long as companies keep to the rules of the capitalist game, i.e. 'engage in open and free competition without deception or fraud'. This position has been reiterated to criticize *normative* stakeholder theory by Argenti (1993, 1997), Marcoux (2000, 2003), and Sternberg (1996, 1997, 2000). Their concerns can be grouped in the following way to emphasize different negative consequences if the stakeholder concept replaced the stockholder concept as the accepted theory of the firm:

1. Weakening or vitiating the fiduciary duty owed by managers to stockholders.
2. Weakening the power of certain stakeholder groups.
3. Weakening the corporation as a whole.
4. Altering the long-term characteristics of the capitalist system.

5.2.1 WEAKENING THE FIDUCIARY DUTY OWED BY MANAGERS TO STOCKHOLDERS

The clearest criticism of the stakeholder concept is that it violates the nature of the stockholder–manager relation, which is based on the fiduciary duties owed by managers (agents) to stockholders (principals) who own the corporation (see Vignette 1.1). This was clearly expressed by Berle and Means in the context of concern about the restraints on unlimited management power and discretion in running large-scale corporations:

Whenever one man or a group of men entrusted another man or group with the management of property, the second group became fiduciaries. As such they were obliged to act conscionably, which meant in fidelity to the interests of the persons whose wealth they had undertaken to handle. (1932: 336)

This is a deontological argument (see Vignette 3.2) for the stockholder theory of corporate responsibility as noted by Hasnas:

[S]tockholders advance their money to business managers on the condition that it be used in accordance with their wishes. If managers accept the money on this condition and then proceed to spend it to accomplish social goals not authorized by the stockholders, they would be violating their agreement and spending other people's money without their consent, which is wrong. (1998: 23)

Or more generally:

[O]ne who breaches an agreement that induced another to deal with him or her is treating the other merely as a means to his or her own ends, and is thus violating the Kantian principle of respect for persons. (Hasnas 1998: 37)

The moral basis for this fiduciary relation can be thought of as one of trust and the stricture against violation of trust. It can be based on property rights, or on contract, or at least implied contract associated with an agency relationship (see Vignette 4.1). It can be claimed that the property rights of stockholders can only be protected by strict duties of managers to act in their interests as implied by the notion of fiduciary duties. Behind this argument could be either of the following arguments.

> *Argument 1* Property rights are the moral backbone to capitalist society and ought to be protected above other economic claims. If managers are attending to stockholders and other stakeholders, the interests of stockholders must suffer.
>
> *Argument 2* Stockholder investment is particularly vulnerable and deserves to be protected more than other 'investments' in the corporation. The whole investment is at risk. Stockholders only have a residual claim on the corporation and can only have their investments protected by corporate survival. They have no preferential claims or claims on particular assets, and cannot be partially compensated. Further-more, stockholders are 'the only voluntary constituency whose relation with the corporation does not come up for periodic renewal' (Williamson 1985: 304–5).

The contractual argument for the unique position of stockholders, based on agency theory, is particularly common. According to Goodpaster:

It can be argued that multi-fiduciary stakeholder analysis is simply incompatible with widely held moral convictions about the special fiduciary obligations owed by management to stock-holders. At the center of the objection is the belief that the obligations of agents to principals are stronger or different in kind from those of agents to third parties. (1991: 63)

The agency relation is in effect a promise that management gives exclusively to stock-holders that they will be provided a 'return on investment'. The obligations that managers have to other stakeholders is based, for Goodpaster, on an understanding that:

[T]he conscience of the corporation is a logical and moral extension of the consciences of its principals. It is *not* an expansion of the list of principals, but a gloss on the principal–agent relationship itself. Whatever the structure of the principal–agent relationship, neither principal nor agent can ever claim that an agent has 'moral immunity' from the basic obligations that would apply to any human being toward other members of the community. (1991: 68)

Though the principal–agent relationship is not based on an expressed contract (based on verbal or written agreement), Goodpaster suggests there is an implicit contract, such as that recognized in law. Managers owe obligations to other stakeholders: of abiding with the law, of respect, and of honest dealing. However, for Goodpaster these are not fiduciary duties. He considers this position to bridge the gap between the standard right-wing critical approach to stakeholder theory and the theory that has been attributed to 'mainstream' theorists. In his view the first takes a purely instrumental approach to stakeholder interests; strategically, managers should only take into account stakeholder interests if it will contribute to achieving the goal of maximizing stockholder value. They have a fiduciary duty towards stockholders alone. The second regards the managers as having a multi-fiduciary responsibility towards all stakeholders (equally). Goodpaster proposes a fiduciary duty towards stockholders, but different non-fiduciary responsibilities towards other stakeholders[1] (see Section 3.5.2).

Boatright (1994) counters Argument 1 by noting that stockholders have certain rights of protection: to elect boards of directors and to vote on stockholder resolutions. Argument 2 is weakened by the existence of a market for shares allowing stockholders to dispose of a poorly performing share with little cost. Arguably, the stock market is well known to involve risk and to some degree that risk is mitigated by the level of information available through the market. In addition, firm-specific risk can be diversified through obtaining a portfolio holding. It is also easier to divest shares than to divest other investments that are characterized by less developed markets.

5.2.2 WEAKENING THE POWER OF CERTAIN STAKEHOLDER GROUPS

Not all stakeholders will benefit from a stakeholder approach. Some stakeholders have a special relationship with management that could be prejudiced by a stakeholder approach. Left-wing writers point to the existence of collective representation of employee interests that have emerged from employee self-organizing or from other working class institutions. Employee interests and values are furthered through negotiations with management undertaken by these organizations. A new strategy of treating all stakeholders equally, or similarly, and where the initiatives for the relationship are generated by management, may be seen as a way of avoiding, or even destroying, independent labour organizations. In this way stakeholder management can be seen as one of a long line of management attempts to circumvent independent labour organizations such as through company unions or calls for employee empowerment (Braverman 1974; Edwards 1979; Froud et al. 1996; Monks 1996).

5.2.3 WEAKENING THE CORPORATION AS A WHOLE

If corporations try to serve the interests of all stakeholders they will be at a competitive disadvantage in terms of their ability to maximize stockholder value, which is unsustainable. Serving stakeholder interests 'would sacrifice not only property rights and accountability, but also the wealth-creating capabilities of business' (Sternberg 1997: 7). This would be reflected in greater difficulty for those corporations acting in the interests of all stakeholders to achieve stock market and bank financing.

5.2.4 ALTERING THE LONG-TERM CHARACTERISTICS OF THE CAPITALIST SYSTEM

Neoliberal and left-wing arguments have been levelled against the stakeholder challenge at two levels. First, the traditional argument states that it is not necessary for corporations to have any further ethical obligation beyond those to stockholders that are not covered by the law, because of the disciplining power of market forces. This is based on the invisible hand put forward by Adam Smith. By pursuing self-interest an individual 'frequently promotes that of the society more effectually than when he really intends to promote it' (Smith 1776: bk. IV, ch. 2).

Second, there is concern with the lack of managerial accountability in general. Marcoux (2000: 97) notes that opportunistic managers will find it easier to justify self-serving behaviour by claiming that their actions 'serve the interests of *some* stakeholder constituencies' even if it works 'against the interests of others'. Argenti (1993: 37) goes further to say that it would lead to corporations becoming 'literally unmanageable'. These arguments are based on the idea that the stakeholder concept is incompatible with the modern corporation and modern corporate governance. Sternberg (2000: 51) summed up the position clearly: 'a business that is accountable to all is actually accountable to none'.

Left-wing writers criticize the pluralist basis of the stakeholder concept. Coming from a framework that sees the fundamental power imbalance in capitalist society between capital and labour and their respective representatives, they see the presumption that all can benefit within a stakeholder regime as utopian in that it ignores the 'realities' of the fundamental structure of capitalist society (Froud et al. 1996). At best they view those proposing the stakeholder concept as unsophisticated do-gooders and at worst as proposing a new method of disguising the stark reality of capital–labour relations along with previous ideas and practices such as 'participation', 'empowerment', and 'realizing human potential' (Monks 1996).

5.3 The 1999 convergence debate: normative/instrumental/descriptive distinction revisited

In the April 1999 issue of the *Academy of Management Review*, an article by Jones and Wicks entitled 'Convergent Stakeholder Theory' was published along with responses by Donaldson, Freeman, Gioia, and Treviño and Weaver. The debate continued in the journal in the 'Dialogue' pages of the October 1999 issue. In terms of academic respectability, stakeholder theory seemed to have 'made it' with this level of attention in an eminent management journal.

5.3.1 CONVERGENCE THAT IS EXPLICITLY NORMATIVE: JONES AND WICKS

Jones and Wicks noted that the term *stakeholder concept* is 'relatively vague and thus, gives little direction to either the study or the practice of management' (1999*a*: 206). Starting from the Donaldson and Preston (1995) taxonomy as a way of considering the stakeholder concept as theory, they discern a growing divergence of perspective between normative theories, and instrumental and descriptive/empirical theory as to what stakeholder theory should be. For the former it is 'an umbrella term describing a class of narrative accounts, each based on its own moral principles' and for the latter a 'potential foundation for social science-based research' (1999*a*: 206). Jones and Wicks argue that each perspective is incomplete without the other. They dismiss descriptive stakeholder theory, at least as currently developed, as not sufficiently promising to comprise a component of convergent stakeholder theory. What Jones and Wicks argue for is an explicitly normative theory that is both moral and workable: a combination of normative and instrumental stakeholder theories. By being explicitly normative they claim their convergent theory is 'fundamentally transformational' (Bacharach 1989).

Convergent stakeholder theory is defined as a class of theories with certain characteristics (Jones and Wicks 1999*a*: 213):

1. It has *Boundary conditions*:
   - Publicly held firm in a market economy.
   - Under professional management.
   - The normative behaviour referred to in the instrumental proposition is adhered to.

2. It has *Limited behavioural assumptions*. Human behaviour is:
   - varied and variable (can be self-interested as well as altruistic, trusting or cooperative);
   - malleable (context-dependent and influenced by organizational structures and cultures).

3. It is of *relationships* (broader than contracts or transactions).

4. It contains both *normative* standards of behaviour and *instrumental* arguments that posit adherence to standards, resulting in morally and practically acceptable outcomes:
   - The normative core is moral (not merely prudential) and defended in moral terms: instrumental means are not applied to immoral behavioural standards or used to pursue immoral ends.

- An instrumental proposition is argued for (not merely debated) and demonstrates the *practicality* of the behaviour called for in the normative core.

5. It is *managerial in focus*, offering instruction on:
   - how relationships with stakeholders should be structured (means to corporate ends),
   - the moral foundation for the recommended structuring,
   - outcomes (corporate ends) expected and reasons for the expectation of the link between means and ends,
   - the moral defence of ends, if unconventional.

Following Weaver and Treviño (1994), Jones and Wicks characterize their theory as a *symbiotic joining of normative and instrumental stakeholder theory*; the two modes of inquiry take insights from each other while remaining 'essentially distinct in their theoretical principles, methodologies and metatheoretical assumptions' (Weaver and Treviño 1994: 133). In addition, they claim their convergent stakeholder theory meets some, but not all, of the demands required of Weaver and Treviño's closest form of connection: theoretical integration, which involves progressively conceptual importation, theoretical reciprocity, and ultimately theoretical unity.

5.3.2 RESPONSES TO THE CALL FOR CONVERGENCE

5.3.2.1 Divergence: Freeman

Freeman (1999) responded to Jones and Wicks with 'Divergent Stakeholder Theory'. He argued that more narratives 'that show us different but useful ways to understand organizations in stakeholder terms' (1999: 233) are needed rather than more theory that converges. He criticized Donaldson and Preston's typology as a form of the separation thesis (see Section 3.3.5.1): 'The very idea of a purely descriptive, value-free, or value-neutral stakeholder theory is a contradiction in terms' (1999: 234). He associates descriptive stakeholder theory with the idea of a value-free (social) science that is a holdover of out-of-date positivism and the view that language can represent the world as it really is. 'Likewise the existence of a "normative world" in isolation from actual human values and conventions is a fiction that has long outlived its usefulness' (1999: 233).[2]

> By choosing to call groups 'stakeholders', rather than 'interest group', 'constituencies', or 'publics', we have already mixed up 'fact' and 'value'. *Stakeholder* is an obvious literary device meant to call into question the emphasis on 'stockholders' (Freeman 1999: 234).

However, the term stakeholder is not inherently moral. While it may call into question the emphasis on stockholders, it does, for some, clarify those towards whom corporations do not have a fiduciary duty (non-stockholder stakeholders) (Friedman 1970; Goodpaster 1991). Freeman's definition (1984) of stakeholders is widely considered in the descriptive stakeholder literature as having no inherently normative (in the moral sense) connotation.

Freeman criticizes Jones and Wicks for their claim that an instrumental theory of the structure 'if A, then B' must accept 'only fully moral A's and B's' and that the morality of these propositions must be evaluated by 'some independent moral realm'. This defeats the purpose of instrumental stakeholder theory, as it

is not value free precisely because it claims that consequences count. . . . Instrumental theses need backup and justification, but not exclusively moral backup and justification, precisely because they are instrumental: only consequences count. (Freeman 1999: 235)

Freeman presumes concern for consequences of actions is inherently moral. He suggests the normative thesis of stakeholder theory is of the form 'managers ought to pay attention to key stakeholder relationships'. However, this clearly mixes two notions of normative discussed in Section 3.1 and Jones and Wicks are right to distinguish instrumental stakeholder theory that is moral from that which is merely prudential. To say that managers ought to pay attention to key stakeholder relationships could simply be interpreted as managers ought to figure out how to keep key stakeholders from prejudicing profit maximization by lying to them about what they are doing and pretending to act on their concerns. There is evidence from the accounting literature (see Vignette 10.2) that this is precisely how some companies have acted.

Freeman is in favour of instrumental stakeholder theory, which he believes occupies space that is not either purely normative or purely descriptive, or purely deontological or purely consequentialist. This Freeman (1999: 236) associates with 'a kind of philosophical pragmatism laid out by Wicks and Freeman (1998)' (see Vignette 3.1).

5.3.2.2 Stronger 'glue': Donaldson

Donaldson (1999) responded positively to Jones and Wicks, but judged the 'glue' they use to bind the normative and the instrumental to be insufficient, as their linkage depends on the views of theorists, which may converge accidentally. Donaldson (1999: 237) asks: 'What happens if, in the future, normative theorists fail to hold their current instrumental beliefs?' Underlying this is the view that the instrumental component must be based on an empirical methodology, which may well diverge from the normative view.

Donaldson redefines normative and instrumental stakeholder theories to be glued together. He defines instrumental stakeholder theory:

[A]ny theory asserting that, all other things being equal, if managers view the interests of stakeholders as having intrinsic worth and pursue the interests of multiple stakeholders, then the corporation they manage will achieve higher traditional performance measures, such as return on investment, than had they denied such intrinsic worth and pursued only the interests of a single group. (1999: 238)

Donaldson notes that this is more restrictive than the Jones and Wicks definition that encompasses many versions of the 'if/then' statements.

He defines normative stakeholder theory:

[A]ny theory asserting some form of claim that managers *ought* to view the interest of stakeholders as having intrinsic worth and should pursue the interests of multiple stakeholders. (1999: 238)

Donaldson then proposes that, in line with Donaldson and Preston (1995), stakeholder theory is managerial in nature and the normative/instrumental glue needs to be based on propositions concerning connections between managers' (psychological) beliefs. Explicitly, the connection he proposes is between the belief by managers that the definitions stated above are true. If a rational person holds one of these views, should he or she also hold the other? He concludes that there is a logical connection between the propositions,[3] which is of the form:

(a) B-Instrumental ∩ (as-if) B-Normative;
(b) B-Normative ∩ (as-if) B-Instrumental.

The symbol ∩ signifies an if-then relationship. Donaldson defines the prefix B- to mean 'believe in'. The two propositions suggested read as follows:

(a) If managers believe in the instrumental proposition; then they will behave *as if* they believe in the normative proposition;
(b) If managers believe in the normative proposition; then they will behave *as if* they believe in the instrumental proposition.

The arguments for these two connecting propositions are different.

> Concerning (a) *If* a manager believes that treating the interests of stakeholders as having intrinsic worth and pursuing the interests of multiple stakeholders will lead to achieving higher traditional performance measures for the corporation,
> *then* assuming the manager wants to achieve higher traditional performance measures,
> *then* that manager should pursue the interests of multiple stakeholders and should treat those interests as if they have intrinsic worth.

Donaldson presents this as an evident truth without further argument. However, the options of B-Instrumental or not B-Instrumental are not the only ones that make sense. A manager might believe that the B-Instrumental proposition is true only in the long term, once the risks involved in this strategy have time to accumulate, or once damage to reputation has been sufficiently widely communicated to make a difference to the bottom line. Alternatively, managers may hold B-Instrumental only in certain circumstances, such as under stable conditions or when its survival is not threatened. There is considerable evidence to show that managerial behaviour and beliefs in instrumental propositions are variable and systematically affected by the market circumstances of the corporation (*re* phases). Here we see a connection between instrumental, normative, and descriptive stakeholder theory that is a weakness of not taking into account descriptive stakeholder theory. Donaldson shows he is aware of the likelihood of the range of belief in the instrumental proposition in practice being more complex than a simple 'believe in' or 'not believe in' when he states 'to the extent that the manager accepts the content of B-Instrumental, he or she should act *as if* the content of B-Normative were true' (1999: 239).

> *Concerning (b)*, Donaldson considers the hypothetical situation of a person who believes he or she has an ethical duty to attempt to rescue a child who has fallen down a well. This person must act as if it is possible to rescue the child, even if other onlookers do not believe the rescue is possible. He refers to 'the well-accepted ethical doctrine that "ought implies can", or in other words it cannot be true that one *ought* to do something that one *cannot* do' (1999: 240). However, this presumes a symmetry between 'ought' and 'can' that is not as strong as Donaldson's proposition. To say that one ought not be obligated to do something that is impossible is not the same as saying one ought to believe whatever you may think you are obligated to do is possible. You may believe you ought to attempt to rescue the child (even if you believe it is hopeless) for the sake of the onlooking mother. It is probably true that you will act more effectively if you did believe the rescue was possible, but then the proposition becomes a prudential or consequential one, rather than a logical connection referring to what one 'ought to believe' in a moral or deontological sense. Also, we must consider what one should do in the context of other actions one could take, rather than merely the option of doing nothing. It may be better to make the child as comfortable as possible in her/his last moments of life, rather than suffer the pain and distress of attempting to pull her/him out of the well (which say has partially collapsed) with what all onlookers regard to be no prospect of success.

Donaldson notes that proposition (b) seems to apply only to the consequent B-Instrumental referring to firm survival, i.e. the practicability notion that Jones and Wicks use refers to the idea that managers must believe the link between stakeholder attention and profitability of the firm is 'good enough' to permit firm survival. Other approaches that do not follow the normative proposition could be more profitable. However, Donaldson adds two arguments to support proposition (b).

1. Under competitive market conditions, in the long run, inferior competitive policies will be driven out of the market. Managers may be able to do what they ought to do

temporarily, but in the long run they must believe they will be out of business if they pursue the normative proposition and do not believe the instrumental proposition.

2. Granting that managers have a fiduciary obligation to stockholders, how is it possible to satisfy this and simultaneously satisfy the normative proposition to pursue the interests of multiple stakeholders? It can only be so if the instrumental proposition were true. Again Donaldson notes that this does not make the instrumental proposition true, only that it provides a reason why managers B-Normative, should behave as if B-Instrumental were true.

Donaldson claims these arguments are reasons for managers who hold B-Normative to act as if the content of B-Instrumental were true, 'even in instances where he or she is uncertain about the facts' (1999: 241). Given the lack of clear conclusions on the instrumental proposition from empirical research, managers are most likely to be uncertain as to the veracity of the content of B-Instrumental. However, Donaldson believes his arguments will supersede wishful thinking or instinctive pessimism and help explain 'why the often-heard refrain from corporate managers that "doing well and doing good go hand-in-hand" reflects more than naïveté'.[4]

5.3.2.3 Lack of a research tradition: Treviño and Weaver

Treviño and Weaver (1999a) responded to Jones and Wicks with four key points.

1. There is no plausible empirical stakeholder theory (either normative or descriptive) to integrate with normative stakeholder theory. Empirical stakeholder theory is at too early a stage of development. It lacks 'explicitly delineated and empirically testable and tested constructs, variables and explanatory relationships' (1999a: 222). If descriptive stakeholder theory claims that in general managers actually act as if all legitimate stakeholders have intrinsic value, the theory seems 'implausible'. If it is not true then instrumental stakeholder loses relevance. For example, Mitchell, Agle, and Wood (1997) predict that managers will give low salience to stakeholders with high legitimacy, but low power and urgency. This would be consistent with an instrumental theory that states that corporate performance will be enhanced if managers respond to stakeholders according to their salience as defined by Mitchell, Agle, and Wood, but not with normative stakeholder theory as defined by Jones and Wicks.

2. They accuse Jones and Wicks of arguing that integration occurs because empirical concerns provide limits on normative claims. Rather than the critical aspect of normative theory limiting allowable behaviour, here it is 'practicability' that limits normativity. This they label 'normative surrender—not integration' (1999a: 225).

3. Jones and Wicks failed to develop a convergent theory that takes empirical/normative integration any further than it already exists.

4. Shared commitments among theorists should be labelled as the *stakeholder research tradition*, rather than an integrated theory. They note that Jones and Wicks confusingly refer to convergent stakeholder theory as both a theory and a class of theories. Research traditions 'incorporate multiple, varied theories that are focused on the same domain of observed or postulated phenomena or related sets of questions or problems...research traditions...also may implicitly delineate important questions, basic concepts, and taken-for-granted assumptions' (referring to Laudan 1977, 1981).

Treviño and Weaver make another point, which bears on the way we have presented descriptive/analytical stakeholder theory:

As researchers elaborate empirical stakeholder theories to make them more precise and plausible, these theories look less like distinctively stakeholder theories and more like special case applications of the existing organizational science theories of resource dependence, power, conflict and negotiation, legitimacy, and so on. (1999*a*: 223)

Treviño and Weaver believe that the contributions of Mitchell, Agle, and Wood (1997) and Rowley (1997)

have advanced our understanding of organization–stakeholder relationships, [but] 'stakeholder theory' has added little to the theoretical analysis beyond an umbrella concept and useful heuristic. (1999*a*: 223)

It is interesting that Treviño and Weaver state at the outset that scientific theories in their early stages of development lack the conceptual precision and explanatory power of long-studied theories: What is a theory? Or rather what is a paradigm or scientific research programme? It seems to us that Treviño and Weaver are correct to argue that shared commitments among theorists should be labelled as something other than a theory, however, it is more than a research tradition. There is theory, and theory is, after all, generated through and reflecting of a heuristic and a shared understanding of certain umbrella terms. The weakness of Jones and Wicks is that they fudge certain umbrella terms, the strength is that they propose certain distinctions that have stimulated thoughtful debate around the terms and that can lead to greater shared understanding of terms. In Section 5.4 more distinctions, which we believe will further analytic stakeholder theory, are considered.

5.3.2.4 Credibility of normative stakeholder theory: Gioia

Gioia (1999*a*), like Treviño and Weaver, believe that Jones and Wicks have not achieved a convergent stakeholder theory that is more integrated than already exists. Gioia also thinks it may be better to think of stakeholder theory itself as a research tradition, though he is doubtful of the accuracy of the word 'research' in view of the lack of work based on data. Managers do not find normative stakeholder theory to be credible according to Gioia (1999a: 228): 'The normative approach too often has seemed to bereprepresented by articulate voices shouting from the sidelines that organizational decision makers should do the right thing.' In this Gioia repeats an accusation against normative stakeholder theory that is an exaggeration: the proposition that no set of legitimate stakeholder interests should dominate the others is taken to mean that legitimate stakeholder interests should be weighted equally when making corporate decisions.

5.3.3 RESPONSE AND COUNTERARGUMENTS: JONES AND WICKS

Jones and Wicks (1999b) responded to Treviño and Weaver and Gioia. They question Treviño and Weaver's presumed connection between evidence suggesting that stakeholder theory is descriptively false and that instrumental stakeholder theory becomes irrelevant. They ask if Treviño and Weaver consider the establishment of the instrumental proposition as impossible. Their argument rests on a restricted view of descriptive stakeholder theory, i.e. that it applies only to the simple statement that managers act as normative stakeholder theory presumes they ought to act.

Jones and Wicks (1999b) accept Treviño and Weaver's proposal that stakeholder research tradition be used to describe the field rather than stakeholder theory. In the pragmatic vein of Freeman (1994), they advocate the generation of a multitude of instrumentally sound 'normative cores'. They do not agree that they are 'selling out' normative stakeholder theory in that practicability is indeed a 'presumptive standard for stakeholder theory', because stakeholders will have an interest in corporate survival in addition to their own individual interests, though they acknowledge there may be instances where a firm ought to go out of business for normative reasons. This is a problematic argument because there may be normative and instrumental arguments favouring bankruptcy for some stakeholders, but not for others.

Treviño and Weaver reply that all a research tradition implies is 'shared concepts and a common normative concern ... thus allowing stakeholder research to continue without necessarily expecting convergence or integration among the diverse theories' (1999b: 623). However, they point out that Jones and Wicks' reciprocity standard risks normative surrender because they rely on the rarity of stakeholders having interests in corporate collapse. We would point out that not only can such situations occur, but also their likelihood will depend on aspects of actual features of modern society. For example, if companies are exploiting or poorly treating employees, their interest in firm viability will depend on welfare provisions.

Jones and Wicks (1999b: 623) consider Gioia's 'extension' of one of the normative premises of stakeholder theory: the interests of all legitimate stakeholders have intrinsic value is taken 'to mean that the interests of all stakeholders should be weighted *equally*'. They deny an intention not to acknowledge that 'some interests are more important or more sensitive than others'.[5]

Gioia (1999*b*) retorts that if you say 'the interests of *all* (legitimate) stakeholders have intrinsic value, and no set of interests is assumed to dominate the others' as in Jones and Wicks (1999: 207), the second part of this statement 'seems to imply no recognition that some interests are pragmatically more dominant than others, which would compromise the practical relevance of the theory' (1999*b*: 625). Gioia complains that Jones and Wicks' view that their statement of the normative proposition does not imply no recognition that some interests are pragmatically more dominant than others is to play with language in a way that is not understandable: 'Is there some arcane code concerning the meaning of words here?' (1999*b*: 625). This misunderstanding is interesting. It is a reason why theory is important and elaborations of concepts and distinctions are useful in order to aid understanding.

Gioia fails to understand the concept of the consideration of one stakeholder *not* dominating over others, without implying equality. On the other hand, Jones and Wicks do not comprehend that in considering some interests more than others, those interests may dominate the interests of others. Both lack a category that distinguishes the idea that some stakeholders may be primary and others secondary and that some stakeholders (not necessarily stockholders) can dominate others in a way that is not merely a primary–secondary relation but also a domination relation. For example, government can be part of the primary group that could dominate interests of employees or the local community when what is at stake is the location of a dumping site for toxic wastes or a halfway house for recently released prisoners. There are instances when the interests of some stakeholders conflict with others in such a way as to preclude straightforward compromise or 'balancing of interests'. Some may suffer (be dominated) by the interests of others, even if it is not domination by manager self-interests or the interests of stockholders.

Jones and Wicks (1999*a*: 207) also presented what they regarded to be the *essential premises* of stakeholder theory in four points:[6]

1. The corporation has relationships with many stakeholders that affect and are affected by its decisions.
2. The theory is concerned with the nature of these relationships in terms of both processes and outcomes for the firm and its stakeholders.
3. Interests of all (legitimate) stakeholders have intrinsic value and no set of interests is assumed to dominate the others.
4. The theory focuses on managerial decision-making.

We note that these essential premises are not currently widely adhered to, particularly in the more recent contributions to descriptive/analytical theory (see Chapter 4).

Organizations rather than just corporations are considered. Interests of non-legitimate stakeholders are considered as well as those of legitimate ones. The presumption of intrinsic value and that no set of interests dominates the others are assumptions limited to normative stakeholder theory. The latter proposition is somewhat mitigated in some normative theories by the distinction between primary or direct stakeholders and other stakeholders. Finally, some recent stakeholder theorists no longer focus exclusively on managerial decision-making. Stakeholders and those who mediate between direct stakeholders and managers of focal organizations are increasingly considered as active, decision-making agents with strategies that affect the organization–stakeholder relation.

5.4 Critical issues for analytical stakeholder theory: finer ontological distinctions

The four essential premises put forward by Jones and Wicks (1999*a*) are highly restrictive. We agree with Treviño and Weaver that it is too early in the development of stakeholder theory to set such strict boundaries around the concept. Rather the boundary conditions, as well as other ways of qualifying the actors involved in the stakeholder concept, and their relevant characteristics need to be explored. The first two premises are general and relatively uncontroversial, though the first premise implies a particular (popular) stakeholder definition, of which there are many (see Section 1.3.1). Here we consider the third and fourth premises: legitimate stakeholders and the confinement to managerial decision-making focus. Stakeholder theory should not be bounded by managerial decision-making. It also needs to take account of stakeholder decision-making. We consider the organization–stakeholder relationship to involve a complex set of intermediate decision-makers and influencers of outcomes and of decision processes on both sides of the relationship. Managerial decisions in organizations are not made by a single mind and stakeholder decisions and actions are not made by individuals or even by specific well-defined groups.

Legitimacy is also an issue that should not define a boundary of stakeholder theory. Illegitimate stakeholders should be considered. Furthermore, the legitimacy of managers and focal organizations is an issue that needs to be explored in order to understand the organization–stakeholder relationship. Legitimacy is at heart a matter of perception and belief. The perceptions of different members of a management team may well differ considerably, particularly when top managers are not the managers dealing directly with stakeholder groups. Also, legitimacy, by its very nature, will involve actors outside the direct organization–stakeholder relationship.

5.4.1 FOCUS ON MANAGERIAL DECISION-MAKING

5.4.1.1 Stakeholder decision-making

As emphasized by many writings in the descriptive stakeholder theory field (Frooman 1999; Friedman and Miles 2002; Rowley and Moldoveanu 2003), stakeholders and stakeholder groups also make decisions. They are not merely the environment of organizations. They affect outcomes, and managers in focal organizations can make their decisions in response to, and in anticipation of, responses by specific stakeholders or stakeholder groups. In order to understand the nature and development of stakeholder relations, stakeholder interests, values, beliefs, and identities underlying their own decision-making, processes and outcomes need to be analysed, not only by managers in focal organizations, but also by stakeholders, stakeholder group strategists, and academic analysts of the stakeholder concept. In particular, the compatibility or incompatibility of values, identities, and belief systems between managers in focal organizations and stakeholder decision-makers, and between different stakeholder groups, need to be explored in order to understand and predict outcomes of organization–stakeholder encounters and to support decision-making and actions on both sides of the relationship.

5.4.1.2 Complex managerial structures

Managerial decision-making processes are complex. Furthermore, actions may not directly link to a decision-making process. The organization behaviour and strategic management literatures are replete with evidence of this: see in particular the garbage can model, Cohen, March, and Olsen (1972) and the emergent strategy position of Mintzberg (1994). Analysing different managerial functions within organizations leads to a consideration of a range of mixes of interests, values, identities, and moral positions. The fiduciary nature of the relation between managers and stockholders or other stakeholders is one between the board of directors and these stakeholders, not lower-level managers. Lower-level managers fulfil particular functions and may systematically be influenced in particular ways as to their regard for the interests and values of certain stakeholders. For example, those involved in the development of environmental reports are likely to regard local communities and environmental NGOs as more salient and have a more positive attitude towards taking their interests into account than those involved in public relations (PR) or corporate finance. Investor relations and PR executives are also likely to regard different stakeholders to be more salient than top managers or managers of other functions. These issues are yet to be explored in the stakeholder literature (see Miles and Friedman 2004).

5.4.2 CATEGORIZING INTERMEDIARIES

There are a number of ways of categorizing intermediaries, for example, distinguishing between those that exist to support stakeholder relations compared with those that exist for other reasons but become embroiled in stakeholder relations (see Chapter 8). Other dimensions could be:

- Are intermediaries concerned with dealing with short-term problems between corporations and stakeholders, or do they exist to build long-term frameworks?
- Are they interested in the interests of the parties, or are they interested in the relationship itself? If the former, whose perspective are they coming from?

Hill and Jones (1992) developed a model of how institutions develop as intermediaries between focal organizations and stakeholders to govern the relationship in order that stakeholders would reduce their utility loss due to managerial opportunism (Section 4.4.1). Another way of looking at intermediary institutions is to see how they affect the 'glue' between focal organizations and stakeholders, i.e. trust rather than utility loss reduction.

5.4.3 STAKEHOLDER LEGITIMACY

According to Frooman, legitimacy is not so important:

From a firm's strategic planning standpoint, does it matter whether society deems appropriate a stakeholder's claim? The appropriateness of the stakeholder's claim may not matter nearly as much as the ability of the stakeholder to affect the direction of the firm. (1999: 193)

This is a valid point. However, gaining legitimacy is an important way to achieve influence over the direction of the firm, though it is likely that building legitimacy must be a long-run strategy of stakeholders. It is also likely to involve activities with or through intermediaries such as the media or a PR organization. Legitimacy is not everything, but it can be important, which is why it should not be considered a boundary condition of essential stakeholder theory.

Fineman and Clark (1996: 727) suggest legitimacy comprises:

- The language the stakeholder uses (the more like the industry's the more it is accepted).
- Its image (not too radical preferred).
- Its style of interaction (not too confrontational).
- The perceived competence of the stakeholder's officers.

These issues are also important for focal organizations. Corporations dedicate resources to legitimizing their actions and contesting their opponents. Legitimacy can be gained from knowledge and research, alliances and networks, or seeking to influence policy. Legitimacy theory suggests that companies can only continue to exist if they are perceived by society to be operating within a value system commensurate to that of society. Corporations seeking legitimation can use stakeholder management for such purposes (Adams, Hill, and Roberts 1998). Lindblom (1994) suggests this will be particularly so if corporations wish to help close a legitimacy gap, for example, in seeking to:

1. educate its stakeholders about the organization's intentions to improve that performance;
2. change the perceptions of stakeholders, but not behaviour;
3. manipulate perception by deflecting attention; and
4. change external expectations of its performance.

Although legitimacy theory may have value as ideals for claims on organizations that stakeholders or 'enlightened' management consultants may pursue, it is essentially a firm-dominant, not a social responsibility, approach.

5.5 **Dynamic organization–stakeholder relations**

The stakeholder concept has grown tremendously in popularity with academics and in the media over the past two decades. This is in part due to:

- A rise in the importance attributed to stakeholder relations by major corporations.
- More visible strategies of prominent stakeholder groups and intermediaries claiming to represent stakeholder group.

This is a field where static analysis seems particularly inadequate. Little stakeholder theory has been devoted to the study of organization–stakeholder relations as they develop over time. Exceptions include Jawahar and McLaughlin (2001), who examine differences in strategic postures towards different stakeholder groups throughout the organization life cycle (see Section 4.2.7) and Friedman and Miles (2002) who trace a particular stakeholder's relations with different organizations over thirty years and develop some hypotheses about how the organization–stakeholder relation will be affected by certain structural configurations that may change over time (see Section 4.3.1). More research is required.

Three issues need to be addressed to develop an adequate dynamic theory of stakeholder relations:

1. How are stakeholder relations affected by *changes in external factors* that affect the material interests and cultures of thought of focal organizations and stakeholders and stakeholder groups? Such changes can then affect both the integration of interests and ideas between firms and stakeholders, their resource dependency, relative power, and compatibility.

2. Stakeholder relations may be affected by *strategic choices* made by those on either side of the stakeholder relation (Berman et al. 1999). Particularly relevant here are the involvement of intermediaries on the part of stakeholders, involvement of the law and the media, and the choice of stakeholder influencing strategy pursued (see Chapter 7).

3. The process of the relationship *affects* stakeholder relations. Issues here include personalities (Agle, Mitchell, and Sonnenfeld 1999) and how they interact, ways that parties discover tactics to pursue, reactions to initial tactics of one side or other, the development of new tactics, or new variations of established tactics. There is a wide literature on this subject in relation to employer–trade union–employee negotiations and some in relation to negotiations among environmental groups, local communities, and focal organizations (Chapter 7).

In Part II we present some empirical evidence and cases bearing on these issues. They are yet to be adequately incorporated into analytical or descriptive stakeholder theory.

5.6 Revisiting the core of stakeholder theory

We disagree with Donaldson and Preston (1995) and Jones and Wicks (1999*a*) and conclude that it is premature to consider normative theory to be the core of stakeholder theory. This judgement is based on the following observations arising from previous chapters and sections of this chapter.

1. *Lack of consistency in normative stakeholder theory.* Though there has been considerable work done on normative stakeholder theory since Evan and Freeman's influential work in 1988, the overall picture painted in Chapter 3 is of ambiguity and contestation; however, there has been some building on normative work, particularly around the concept of fairness as marked by Phillips' contributions (1997, 2003*b*).

2. *Descriptive stakeholder theory is at too early a stage of development.* There is much work to do on descriptive/analytical stakeholder theory. Even if normative stakeholder theory should prove to become robust enough to form the foundation for stakeholder theory in future, there are too many critical issues that need to be explored in analytic stakeholder theory that may support the overall argument for preferring stakeholder

theory to the alternative stockholder theory, including the possibility of stakeholder theory itself developing to such an extent that it transforms into some sort of hybrid. Since the mid-1990s there has been a quickening of what may be regarded as an inevitable process of researchers applying concepts from other literatures to the stakeholder concept and to organization–stakeholder relations. As a form of business and managerial behaviour, ideas from those literatures (such as the issue of managerial control; the strategy debate between business planning models and models of emergent strategy; and influences of new technology) are likely to be applied. As a form of social relations involving a mix of cooperation and conflict, concepts developed in sociology and politics literatures (such as trust, legitimacy, democracy) are clearly applicable. In Section 5.4 only a few such concepts that could be further explored from the perspective of stakeholders and the organization–stakeholder relationship were outlined. Concepts such as trust and legitimacy can potentially straddle the normative/analytic divide, at least in the sense that theories and evidence from one sphere can inform the other. Descriptive/analytical stakeholder theory needs to become what Swanson (1999) calls 'value-attuned' theory. We interpret this as a need for descriptive/analytical stakeholder theory that is sensitive to values and norms, through explicit consideration of ideas, belief systems, and identities. Once more is known of these issues, more interesting normative stakeholder theories are also likely to emerge.

3. *The descriptive basis of much normative stakeholder theory needs to be recognized and developed.* The normativity of many normative stakeholder theories rests on empirical grounds, i.e. what Donaldson and Preston would label descriptive theory. Justification for the normative stakeholder concept may be as an interpretation of actual social trends. They rely on an analysis of what people increasingly do, and combine this with reasons why it is 'good' or 'ethically right' that such things be done, and why the doing of such things should be supported by developments in laws and institutions. Others consider the practice of a minority in society or point towards practice in other societies as a justification based on what people (in this case only some people) actually do, which can be combined with ethical and moral reasons in order to get to recommendations for support and development of laws and institutions in a certain direction. Rather than deriving 'is' from 'ought', all these normative stakeholder theories use 'is' as a basis for justifying 'ought'. Clearly, they do not proceed in an analytical fashion first and a normative fashion second. These are normative stakeholder theories. Nevertheless, they do rely on a descriptive analysis to justify the normative principles they propose. At their core are normative propositions. But these are propositions that are based both on normativity, meaning (observed) norms, *and* normativity meaning ethical and moral principles. They are what we have called normative theories of the second kind, justified because they reflect an interpretation of social trends or laws and institutions from the past or existing in other societies, or as practiced by a significant (growing) minority at present (see Figure 3.1).

As discussed in Section 3.2, some normative stakeholder theories rely purely on an ethical or moral principle to justify a departure from current practice: theories of the first kind. Only normativity of the first kind can claim to be a core independent of prior justification by descriptive or analytical means. Even here the ideas may be expressed as ultimately reflecting some experience source. Finally, some normative stakeholder theories identify to whom and for what managers are morally responsible given the contemporary legal and institutional context: the third kind of theories.

We showed in Chapter 3 that a substantial number of normative stakeholder theories are based on the second kind of interpretation of normativity for justification. Not only that but also many theories of the first kind use some second kind of arguments.[7] The validity of these theories rests not merely on the persuasiveness or logic of the ethical principles proposed, but also on the validity of claims that society either did in fact have laws and institutions like those proposed, or that current society is really moving in the direction claimed, or that the minority really do adhere to the principles claimed and that they really are a growing force in the society. In effect, normative theories of the second kind rest on a kind of dynamic analytical stakeholder theory, not of the dynamics of particular organization–stakeholder relations (such as Greenpeace's history, Section 4.3.1), but rather the dynamics of the whole population of organization–stakeholder relationships, i.e. an ecological model of changing stakeholder relations.

An adequate theory of the ecology of the population of organization–stakeholder relationships may require building blocks made of trajectories of particular organization–stakeholder relationships. The life cycle of organizations and of human populations are well known (Jawahar and McLaughlin 2001). Can there also be a life cycle for organization–stakeholder relations? Changes in length and nature of large numbers of individual organization–stakeholder relations would be expected to affect the overall development of the stakeholder field, as the human life cycle affects human population characteristics over time. The overall field would also be affected by changes in 'birth' and 'death' rates of organization–stakeholder relations. Arguably, many second kind normative stakeholder theories are based on propositions concerning birth rates, but few examine stages of 'life' or likelihood of 'death'. Arguably, descriptive theory addressing these issues could be used to provide stronger justification to normative stakeholder theories of the second kind.

4. *Descriptive stakeholder theory can lead to changes in normative stakeholder theory*, particularly if it is value-attuned. For example, Donaldson and Preston (1995) and Jones and Wicks (1999*a*) are clear that stakeholder theory is focused on management. This is derived from the normative focus on managerial behaviour. However, from an analytical perspective, stakeholder theory concerns relationships *between* management and stakeholders (intervened by other indirect players: intermediaries, secondary stakeholders). These relations involve, like other relations between groups of people, social, economic and political dimensions. They involve actions based on interests, values,

beliefs, and identities, which sometimes differ, sometimes converge, and which therefore cannot be comprehended by only viewing them from the perspective of one side of these relationships. Decentring stakeholder theory, by noting the active role of stakeholder groups in forming outcomes, leads to viewing moral obligations in a broader context than the duties owed by managers to stakeholders. Stakeholders and indirect players also reason in ethical and moral terms leading to a sense of obligation, as well as strategic aims. Society also imposes obligations on these players. By developing analytical stakeholder theory, which considers the values of stakeholders and intermediaries as well as managers, a more embracive, and possibly a more convincing normative stakeholder theory can be developed. This may go some way to answering Gioia's critique (1999*a*) that managers do not consider normative stakeholder theory to be credible. The degree to which managers regard normative stakeholder theory to be exaggerated rests on the view that it puts burdens on managers of large corporations, which are beyond the obligations of other economic agents. A normative stakeholder theory that includes consideration of the moral obligations of stakeholders themselves is likely to be more credible with managers.

5.7 Further ways of distinguishing contributions to the stakeholder literature: Stoney and Winstanley (2001)

Stoney and Winstanley (2001) note that the bewildering array of analytical positions on stakeholder theory is underpinned by wildly different philosophical traditions and theories. As with Donaldson and Preston (1995), Stoney and Winstanley attempt to reduce the conceptual confusion that has developed around the term stakeholding. It is with this in mind that expositional frameworks have been developed in this book. Here we consider the five dimensions that Stoney and Winstanley use to distinguish different stakeholder contributions and note how we have attempted to develop their insights further through related classification schemes.

5.7.1 POLITICAL PERSPECTIVES

This is a straightforward political dimension with left wing (Marxist) and right wing (neoliberal) at the two extremes and a pluralist position in the middle. The interesting aspect of this dimension is that it emphasizes that the concept of stakeholding is, by and large, opposed by the two extreme political positions, though for different reasons.

The left-wing position considers the fundamental division in society as between working class and capitalist class or between working class and the capitalist system as a whole. At best the stakeholding concept loses the sharpness of this distinction by considering a plurality of interests (including employees) that are affected by organizations. By presuming that stakeholder management can yield practical reforms through which all stakeholders are accommodated and will benefit by such activities, the stakeholder concept actively and categorically disguises the class-based nature of corporate policies towards labour and attempts to co-opt workers and their representatives into participating in corporate methods of achieving control over themselves. As such it represents another attempt (along with techniques like 'empowerment', 'participation', and total quality management) to weaken the resolve of workers to support trade unions, their own collective forms of resistance to management control. Ackers and Payne (1998), Froud et al. (1996), Gamble and Kelly (1996), and Stoney and Aylott (1994) all represent this anti-stakeholding position.

The right-wing position considers the fundamental characteristic of private corporations to be that stockholders own them and according to the laws and primacy of private property, they should be run in the interests of stockholders. Attending to the interests of other stakeholders will at best weaken the ability of the corporation to serve the interests of stockholders and will weaken corporate governance. At worst organizations that try to be all things to all people will be at a competitive disadvantage and will become literally unmanageable (Argenti 1993). This position follows the strong classic neoliberal line espoused by Friedman (1962), which has been explicitly used against the idea of stakeholding by Argenti (1993, 1997) and Sternberg (1994, 1997). Wealth creation and the underpinning concept of private property overrides any benefit from a 'spurious expectation of achieving vaguely "nicer" business behavior' (Sternberg 1997: 9).

The pluralist position is that manageable relations can be achieved among a plurality of interest groups. Industrial relations writers argued this position, particularly in the 1960s (Kerr et al. 1964; Fox 1966, 1974). It is through this route, rather than the strategic management route that something like a stakeholder position was reached long before Freeman's work. According to the Donovan Commission on Industrial Relations (1965–8) in the UK:

While in the long term shareholders, employees and customers all stand to benefit if a concern flourishes, the immediate interests of these groups often conflict. Directors and managers have to balance these conflicting interests, and in practice they generally seek to strike for whatever balance will best promote the welfare of the enterprise as such. (1968: 8)

In Section 5.2 we dealt with right- and left-wing critiques of stakeholder theory in terms of the types of negative consequences they predict if the stakeholder concept is widely accepted.

5.7.2 PURPOSE OF STAKEHOLDING

The second dimension distinguishes between analysis and reform as purposes of stakeholding. Analysis serves as a tool to map different interests and shifting power relations among stakeholder groups. According to Stoney and Winstanley, prescriptive work needs to be specific about the nature and scope of the social changes desired. In particular they believe the wide range of voices for advancing stakeholding need to develop a more coordinated and coherent agenda for change. This dimension, while interesting, needs to be clarified. Is this merely the distinction between descriptive and normative stakeholder theory proposed by Donaldson and Preston (1995)? It is difficult to see why some should be 'more analytical' if their purpose is purely analysis or 'more reform' if their purpose is prescription. For example, should we judge a contribution as more analytical if it is unsympathetic to reform, or if it is abstract? Stoney and Winstanley notably place Donaldson and Preston (1995) near the most extreme position along the analysis dimension, though as we have noted above, they propose that normative stakeholder theory should be at the core of stakeholder theory. Though clearly they do not propose reforms of practice, only that theory should be developed in some ways rather than others. On the other hand, should the suggested reforms be further classified by the magnitude, difficulty, time required, or resources involved? We regard Figure 3.1 as a development of this dimension along these lines. What we have not done is to develop the other half of the dimension, the analytic half, by further classifying analytical contributions according to degree of 'analyticalness'. Instead, in Chapter 4 we classified analytical theories in terms of:

- Whether they took a strategic/instrumental or a descriptive/positive approach and whether their focus was organization-centric, stakeholder-centric, or whether they focused on the organization–stakeholder relationship itself (see Figure 4.1).
- Segments of the strategy formulation process they touch on and whether they regard stakeholders as distinct entities or interacting entities (see Figure 4.14).

5.7.3 ONTOLOGY OF STAKEHOLDING

This dimension is between those who believe that stakeholder interests should be pursued as an end in itself so that it is of intrinsic worth, and those who take an instrumental view and see serving stakeholder interests as a means to an end, primarily profit maximization. The former view would be driven by moral views of ethics and workplace rights. The latter need not even be sympathetic to stakeholding and support for stakeholding may be contingent on particular circumstances. This distinction is less important if the instrumental position turns out to be empirically correct, but if it does not then this dimension would map a clear difference in position on stakeholding. This is reminiscent of Donaldson and Preston's distinction between normative and instrumental approaches. A problem with this dimension is that it is not complete in that there are plenty of analyses, those Donaldson and Preston labelled descriptive, that would take neither an intrinsic worth nor an instrumental view of stakeholding, and that would not necessarily be properly placed midway between the intrinsic and instrumental poles. Rather, the ontology of stakeholding underlying a descriptive analysis would be that stakeholding shares the ontological status of other phenomena being described. It is likely that those presenting the descriptive analysis hold their own realist or interpretivist view of the social phenomena they describe, and are likely to include stakeholding as ontologically similar to those other social phenomena.

5.7.4 LEVEL OF STAKEHOLDER INTERVENTIONS

The four reference points along this dimension are:

1. Micro-level interventions, establishing stakeholder principles at the level of individual rights
2. Corporate governance
3. National public policy institutions
4. Macro level of reformation of developing international institutions for the regulation of stakeholding.

Stoney and Winstanley describe this dimension as the level at which stakeholding principles are established *in order to be effective.* This is a particularly interesting dimension. However, it loses some of its value if it has to be formulated purely in normative terms or in terms of efficacy. Putting these limitations on this dimension in part reflects the relative novelty of analyses of interventions; that we should presume that only proponents of stakeholding, or campaigners for particular methods of stakeholding, would write about interventions. This dimension is useful for clarifying the level of analysis writers are using due to the confusion in the field and the underlying philosophical debates that are relevant to different points along this continuum. At the extreme indicating individual rights, the Kantian notion of human rights or debates about industrial democracy may be relevant. At the level of corporate governance are various reforms concerning accountability. National public policy and international levels of regulation require:

• Explicit consideration of existing national and international institutions and relevant forms of social evaluation.
• Political and philosophical supports.
• Particular mechanisms for formulating national and international policies.

It is clear that arguments in favour of particular stakeholder interventions need to be sensitive to the background and constraints that are specific to particular levels of intervention.

5.7.5 DEGREE OF STAKEHOLDER ENFORCEMENT

The final dimension relates to the degree of coercion required to implement stakeholding. The six reference points along this continuum are:

1. Voluntarism, which refers to a completely non-coercive stance to create a state of mind or ethos to encourage stakeholding.
2. Exhortation.
3. Best practice.
4. Codes of conduct.
5. Specific directives.
6. Legal entrenchment of stakeholder rights, presumably with clear punishments for non-compliance that may increase the range at the coercion end with more and more harsh punishments.

We regard these dimensions as a useful starting point for the classification of stakeholder positions. However, there are problems with some of them. Stoney and Winstanley recognize overlaps between the dimensions, but do not explore them systematically. In particular we note issues of overlap between the third and fourth dimensions (Sections 5.7.3 and 5.7.4). We have dealt with these dimensions as indicated above.

The last two dimensions (Sections 5.7.4 and 5.7.5) may be regarded as orthogonal to each other, each describing issues that may be regarded as contributing independently to the effectiveness of policies relating to the stakeholder concept. In Chapter 9 on stakeholder policy we combine and develop these dimensions and map both the nature of enforcement and the level at which stakeholder intervention occurs (see Figures 9.1 and 9.2). These dimensions are combined to explore the effectiveness of policy.

Both Donaldson and Preston (1995) and Stoney and Winstanley (2001) advance the stakeholder concept through the provision of what is, in effect, a language for assessing and comparing stakeholder contributions. As noted above, we push this agenda on by further developing discourses that link contributions to the stakeholder concept, which will, we hope, further the development of the concept of stakeholding and in addition improve the chances of certain policies and practices advocated by supporters of the stakeholder concept being implemented. We next turn to practice and policy issues.

☐ QUESTIONS/EXERCISES

1 Compare the moral arguments for the stakeholder theory with those for the stockholder theory. On what grounds could you choose between them?

2 Critically evaluate the convergent stakeholder theory proposition.

3 Jones and Wicks' argument (1999*a*) rests on a restricted view of descriptive stakeholder theory, i.e. that it applies only to the simple statement that managers act as normative stakeholder theory presumes they ought to act. Critically discuss.

4 Consider a life cycle model of particular organization–stakeholder relations.
    (a) Would it mirror organization life cycle models?
    (b) How would it be affected by life cycles of both the focal organization involved and of the stakeholder groups considered?

5 What would affect the 'death rate' in the population of relations in an ecological model of the population of organization–stakeholder relation?

6 We have interpreted Donaldson and Preston (1995) and Stoney and Winstanley (2001) as providing a language that supports the development and acceptance of the stakeholder concept. Compare Donaldson and Preston, Stoney and Winstanley's second and third dimensions, and the models presented in Chapters 3 and 4 in terms of the ability of these 'languages' to support the development and acceptance of the stakeholder concept.

☐ NOTES

1 A similar argument was presented when the term stakeholder first appeared in the management literature. Ansoff (1965*b*) distinguishes between responsibilities and objectives. He criticizes stakeholder theory for balancing conflicting stakeholder claims as part of corporate economic objectives. Instead, such claims should be considered a social responsibility, and a secondary modifying and constraining influence alone.

2 Freeman (1999: 233) notes: 'Wicks himself (Wicks and Freeman 1998) argues that such a positivism contrasted with relativism needs to be replaced by modern pragmatism.'

3 Donaldson notes that the connection is not so strong as to imply material equivalence. That it would be true in all worlds that either of these propositions is true, if and only if the other were true. In this sense the connection is tautological (true by definition): if a proposition is true the null of the proposition (its opposite by definition) is untrue.

4 Perhaps it rather gives a rational observer's explanation for the *naïveté* of managers for whom B-Normative holds.

5 An example could be 'composite groups' of certain traditionally distinguished stakeholders.

6 They refer to Freeman (1984) for point 1. They recognize the distinction between legitimate and non-legitimate stakeholders, referring to Donaldson and Preston (1995) and Mitchell, Agle, and Wood (1997),

but then ignore this in point 2. They refer to Clarkson (1995) and Donaldson and Preston (1995) for point 3 and Donaldson and Preston (1995) for point 4.

7 We note that many normative stakeholder theories use a range of justifications that mix degrees and kinds of normativity. Contributions are classified (see Figure 3.1) according to the highest level that they could be placed.

Part II
Practice: Management, Stakeholders, and Intermediaries

In Part I we introduced the distinction between organization- and stakeholder-centric models. In Part II we use this distinction to arrange our exposition of stakeholder practice. Chapter 6 begins with the practice of stakeholder management from the organization perspective. Examples of practice are organized along a 'ladder' of stakeholder management and engagement. In addition to this, we examine surveys of stakeholder practice and particular issues that affect stakeholder management such as balancing different stakeholder interests and the impacts of cultures and societies.

In parallel with the way stakeholder theory has developed, we move on in Chapter 7, to examining stakeholder relations from the viewpoint of the stakeholders themselves. This approach is more recent and is still very much in the minority. Nevertheless, several authors have come to see it as important, as a contribution to better descriptive theory, in that only considering stakeholder relations from the viewpoint of 'focal' organizations is incomplete, and also for improving the effectiveness of policymakers and managers in focal organizations themselves. Focal organizations are the target of stakeholder claims and the source of impact on stakeholders. They are those organizations that would be represented as the hub of a traditional stakeholder map (see Figure 2.2). We use the adjective focal to distinguish such organizations from other organizations involved in organization–stakeholder relations. Some categories of other organizations are discussed in Chapter 8.

In Chapter 8 stakeholder relations are viewed from a perspective that is rather new. We consider intermediaries in the relationship between traditional stakeholders and focal organizations. We also consider the structure of stakeholder groups as intermediary to this relationship. We note that 'intermediary' organizations claim to represent stakeholders and stakeholder groups and that there are similar representative organizations or claimants to represent focal organizations. Ultimately, the media itself is considered as an intermediary in organization–stakeholder relations and a preliminary general theory of the media as an intermediary agency is offered. Many cases of stakeholder mismanagement are considered in relation to the operation of intermediaries in several vignettes. The chapter ends with a major case study of supplier mismanagement. It is our contention that the role of intermediaries will increasingly have to be examined in future for stakeholder theory to flourish.

6 Stakeholder management from the perspective of the organization

6.1 Introduction

In this chapter we deal with the practice of stakeholder management from the perspective of the organization. Stakeholder management is essentially stakeholder relationship management as it is the relationship and not the actual stakeholder groups that are managed. Attending to particular stakeholder relations (especially when they have gone wrong or when they have threatened to go wrong) is not a recent phenomenon. Specialist personnel or industrial relations staff have dealt with employees for years and many of them take an attitude towards employees as stakeholders and not just costs. It is the explicit recognition of these specialities as connected by a common purpose under the label of stakeholder relations that has emerged in recent times. A longitudinal study of British 'managerial mindsets' between 1980 and 2000 (Poole, Mansfield, and Mendes 2001) indicates a sharp increase (20 per cent on average) in the managerial emphasis on stakeholder interests and a drop (10 per cent) in emphasis on shareholder value in 2000 compared with 1980. A majority of managers (80 per cent) attached importance to stakeholders in 2000 compared with only 50 per cent in 1980. According to Vinten (2001) 75 per cent of US managers are now familiar with the term stakeholder. In some organizations a specific new management function has been created with labels such as 'social responsibility manager', 'community manager', 'environmental manager', or even 'stakeholder manager' (Miles, Hammond, and Friedman 2002). Some of these positions indicate a more strategic and proactive role towards stakeholders in general. Some represent reactive and symbolic attempts to deal with what are perceived to be new pressures, largely connected to media attention and PR.

This leads to a problem in assessing the extent and quality of stakeholder management in practice. For many companies aspects of stakeholder management have become almost synonymous with twenty-first century corporate PR. Corporate relations with stakeholders must be seen to be managed seriously and proactively. However, in practice this PR activity may be unconnected to practice. In order to assess the extent of stakeholder management practice we must develop some criteria that would reveal the quality and extent of stakeholder management. This is a theme that runs through this chapter and is treated both through a formal model for assessing quality of individual practice and through specific examples.

There are many reasons corporations devote resources to stakeholder management. Business case motives are most frequently linked to the attainment of maximizing long-term profits through strategies either to forestall government regulation or for risk management. Effective risk management can lead to damage limitation and reduction of financial penalties for acting unethically, whether directly through lawsuits or clean-up costs or indirectly through the deterioration of relationships. Employee relations are most commonly highlighted, as poor relations can result in declining productivity, creativity, and loyalty as well as recruitment and staff retention problems. The development of a close stakeholder network can provide corporations with valuable information about external events, market conditions, technological advances, or consumer trends, which can help corporations anticipate, understand, and respond to external changes more efficiently and effectively (Svendsen 1998: 51). Where stakeholders feel they are being ignored, or that their claims are not being met, dissatisfaction is often expressed through protest. Stakeholder engagement cannot only diffuse protest but is also credited with leading to more effective solutions (Neligan 2003). A business case also exists for being outstandingly socially responsible, as evidenced by the success of corporations such as Starbucks, Ben & Jerry's, and the Body Shop. Some corporations may view this as a niche position, attainable for only a few pioneers, and not strategically viable if operating under high competition and judged by stock markets that focus on short-term results.[1]

A satisfactory descriptive stakeholder theory still appears to be a long way off because of the complexities and dynamics of practice. In addition, each of the different ethical stances among organizations faces a unique set of stakeholders, with varying interests, power, mechanisms for action, degrees of interconnectedness, and so forth, which influence the manner in which it will engage. Ambler and Wilson (1995) and Gibson (2000) argue that corporations do not respond to stakeholders individually but react to them as identifiable groups. One individual can belong to several groups, each with different claims and needs. In practice these multiple interests can conflict, leading to a further problem of how to balance stakeholder group interests.

This chapter begins by examining the 'Clarkson Principles', a list of principles that summarize the key features of stakeholder management, which are intended as a general managerial aid (Section 6.2). We then discuss paradigms of stakeholder management that have been adopted in practice (Section 6.3). In Section 6.4 we present criteria for assessing the quality of engagement and in Section 6.5 a comprehensive model identifying levels of stakeholder engagement 'quality' is presented. This model is used in Section 6.6 to order a wide range of stakeholder management practice. These are illustrated by a series of vignettes and surveys of practice. In Section 6.7 some empirical contributions to the literature on stakeholder engagement are discussed. Finally four practical issues are discussed in Section 6.8: the process of stakeholder management, balancing stakeholder interests, culture, and issue management.

6.2 **The principles of stakeholder management**

The Clarkson Center for Business Ethics (1999) developed a list of principles that summarize the key features of stakeholder management (Table 6.1).

The first principle arises from a need to recognize the existence of multiple and diverse stakeholder interests. Only legitimate interests are considered, as defined by those stakeholders that have explicit or implied contracts with the firm and those whose well being has been impacted by the firm (1999: 5). Two-way dialogue, the second principle, is a prerequisite for good stakeholder management. The Clarkson Center note that a commitment to dialogue does not constitute a commitment to collective decision-making and there are practical limits to the amount of information a company may wish to divulge. However, it is likely that transparency will reduce serious

Table 6.1 Principles of stakeholder management

Principle 1	Managers should **acknowledge** and actively **monitor** the concerns of all legitimate stakeholders, and should take their interests appropriately into account in decision-making and operations.
Principle 2	Managers should **listen** to and openly **communicate** with stakeholders about their respective concerns and contributions, and about the risks that they assume because of the involvement with the corporation.
Principle 3	Managers should **adopt** processes and modes of behaviour that are sensitive to the concerns and capabilities of each stakeholder constituency.
Principle 4	Managers should **recognize the interdependence** of efforts and rewards among stakeholders, and should attempt to achieve a fair distribution of the benefits and burdens of corporate activity among them, taking into account their respective risks and vulnerabilities.
Principle 5	Managers should **work cooperatively** with other entities, both public and private, to ensure that risks and harms arising from corporate activities are minimized and, where they cannot be avoided, appropriately compensated.
Principle 6	Managers should **avoid altogether** activities that might jeopardize inalienable human rights (e.g. the right to life) or give rise to risks that, if clearly understood, would be patently unacceptable to relevant stakeholders.
Principle 7	Managers should **acknowledge the potential conflicts** between (a) their own role as corporate stakeholders; and (b) their legal and moral responsibilities for the interests of stakeholders, and should address such conflicts through open communication, appropriate reporting, and incentive systems, and, where necessary, third party review.

Source: The Clarkson Center for Business Ethics (1999: 4).

stakeholder conflict. Stakeholder engagement is defined as the process of effectively eliciting stakeholder views on their relationship with the organization. The third principle attempts to raise managers' awareness that stakeholders differ with respect to their involvement with the organization. Governance mechanisms have created official arenas for some stakeholders to engage through formal processes, such as annual general meetings (AGMs) and union representation. Others require an unofficial approach, such as through direct contact, advertising, or press releases. Two points are raised: regardless of the means of engagement a consistent message should be delivered; and extreme caution should be taken when dealing with stakeholders that have a limited capacity to interpret complex situations and options (1999: 6). The fourth principle highlights the need to balance risk and rewards between different stakeholders and to make the distribution of benefits apparent to all parties. The fifth principle seeks to promote cooperation and joint corporate action in order to reduce harmful externalities on the premise that individual action is inadequate. The sixth principle relates to the need to avoid activities that endanger basic rights. Companies should be honest and open about potential risks and if future risks emerge that are unacceptable, activities should be restructured. The seventh principle asks managers to recognize their own conflicts of interest and to encourage practices intended to regulate this. This should lead to increased credibility and hence increased trust in the organization.

6.3 Stakeholder management paradigms

The Clarkson Principles are highly respected in the literature as a model of best practice. Although the principles are essentially normative they are presented in a manner that is intended to aid adoption rather than to preach from 'on high'. For example, by recognizing that a commitment to dialogue does not constitute a commitment to collective decision-making and that there are practical limits to the amount of information a company may wish to divulge. In terms of Figure 3.1, the Clarkson Principles may be regarded as reflecting a normative stakeholder theory of the third kind. They do not propose moving beyond the existing legal and institutional framework. However, they do advocate a change in management practice that involves principles of respect, good communication, cooperative working, and care towards stakeholders.

In this section a number of cases are presented in what we regard as descending order of stakeholder management quality. The 'true' stakeholder organization would exist as part of a stakeholder network linked by mutually dependent relationships. As representatives of the organization form part of the relation itself, they participate in the relation rather than actively managing it. The moral or social obligations towards stakeholders can be driven by the philosophy of the founders, the top management team, or the chief executive officer (CEO), and/or may arise from strategy. Stakeholders are not viewed in a negative or defensive manner. Only in its purest form will this involve full collaboration and high levels of integration, risk, and trust, such as joint ventures and stakeholder representation at the board level. Few corporations adopt best practice. An example that has been frequently cited in the stakeholder literature is the Saturn project at General Motors (Vignette 6.1). Evidence of the significance of the Saturn project for its employees can be found on the very active Saturn website (www.saturn.com).

Vignette 6.1 STAKEHOLDER MANAGEMENT: THE SATURN PROJECT

Saturn is a wholly owned subsidiary of General Motors. It was created in 1985 following a declining market share and threat of job losses due to highly competitive imports, particularly from Korea and Japan. General Motors formed a joint venture with Toyota to import cars. The success of Toyota's business strategy was evident and convinced some that a business model based on the beliefs and values of trust in the workforce, teamwork, continual improvement, and customer satisfaction was the future. General Motors wished to transfer this 'new' philosophy to car building in the USA and to transfer knowledge, technology, and experience throughout General Motors. The proposed structure called for co-management by representatives of United Automobile Workers union and General Motors. This was highly controversial. Voluntary recognition of a union is extremely rare in the USA, which is typified by 'union avoidance' strategies (Kochan and Rubinstein 2000: 375). Kochan and Rubinstein (2000: 375) state that a stakeholder model would not have evolved without the influence of the union. Employee commitment was also a prerequisite. General Motors could not compete on price. Consequently, the new operating system needed to achieve higher quality and productivity. Employees receive, on average 148 hours of training per year, they are organized in teams with 'decision-rings', which support consultation and joint decision-making, and receive performance-related pay. The risk/reward compensation system designed by management at Saturn made individual employees face substantial economic losses if Saturn failed. If Saturn failed, workers were required to quit General Motors, and forgo any rights to transfer to another site. Other stakeholders are treated with respect. Single-source suppliers are engaged on long-term contracts and Saturn focus on maintaining high levels of customer satisfaction and loyalty and operate a fixed price, no haggle sales practice.

Saturn is a small subsidiary of General Motors, which has clearly been treated differently from the other parts of the organization. Kochan and Rubinstein (2000) question whether the rate of return on investment would be comparable to other parts of General Motors if the full cost of the capital investment were taken into account. A substantial number of General Motors employees were transferred to Saturn from other plants. These employees were aware of the unique risk/reward compensation system and therefore at least a major proportion of Saturn employee 'stakeholders' were a self-selected subset of General Motors employees who favoured the Saturn style of management and were willing to accept the risks.

Pure stakeholder corporations are rare and most examples of good stakeholder management do not go as far as to give voices and decision-making power to all stakeholders. Vignette 6.2 examines stakeholder management at Starbucks, which has a reputation as being a stakeholder-focused firm.

Vignette 6.2 STAKEHOLDER MANAGEMENT AT STARBUCKS

Starbucks was established in the USA in 1971 as a single coffee shop. By 2004 it operated out of 8,569 stores employing 100,000 staff. The company is listed on a number of socially responsible stock market indices. The following stakeholder management practices are evident from a reading of the independently verified 2004 social report. Starbucks list its stakeholders as employees, customers, coffee farmers, suppliers, community members, environmental groups, activists, and shareholders.

Coffee farmers: Since 2002 Starbucks claims it has paid premium prices (74 per cent higher) to help farmers make profit and support their families. Starbucks operate a responsible coffee purchasing policy covering the social, environmental, economic, and quality aspects of growing, processing, and selling coffee, which it calls the coffee and farmer equity (CAFÉ) practices. In 2004, of the total coffee purchased 14.5 per cent was CAFÉ coffee. Following stakeholder engagement to refine CAFÉ principles, it is to be rolled out to the global procurement team in 2005. Of the coffee purchased during 2004 1.6 per cent came from recognized 'Fair Trade' suppliers. Further stakeholder support is evident. Starbucks provide farmers access to affordable credit. In 2004 $6 million was advanced at an average interest rate of 2.5 per cent, benefiting over 25,000 small-scale farmers. In Costa Rica there is a farmer support centre to provide farmers with technical support and training needed to ensure 'sustainable production of high-quality coffee'.

Suppliers must meet minimum standards and demonstrate best practice, as determined by Starbucks and subject to independent verification. Twenty-eight indicators are specified under the following areas: product quality (required), economic accountability (required), social responsibility (covering employment policies such as paying the minimum wage and worker conditions such as access to housing, health care, and education), and environmental leadership (protecting and conserving water resources, conserving biodiversity, waste management, energy use). High-scoring suppliers receive preferential buying status, higher prices, and better contract terms. Starbucks engaged with dairy and bakery suppliers in 2004 to encourage them to adopt more stringent measures to produce sustainable products.

Local communities: In 2004 $1.8 million was donated for social projects to improve conditions in coffee-farming regions, which often lack basic necessities such as adequate housing, health clinics, schools, good roads, and fresh drinking water. Recent projects include the provision of housing in Columbia (benefiting 2,300 individuals since its inception in 1999) and a health clinic and kindergarten in Guatemala. In the USA local communities have been hostile to Starbucks. It is accused of hurting independent coffee houses and eroding the unique character of local neighbourhoods. In some cities, such as San Francisco, activists have successfully lobbied for a ban that restricts particular chain stores from locating in certain neighbourhoods. This has increased Starbuck's awareness of their potential impact on local communities and has increased the level of engagement prior to the launch of new stores.

Customers: Satisfaction surveys are regularly conducted. There is a dedicated phone line if customers feel their grievance is not adequately dealt with at the store level. Comprehensive food labelling and nutrition information is provided.

Environment: Starbucks has been a major contributor to the sustainable packaging coalition. It was the first company to gain approval from the Food and Drug Administration to incorporate 10 per cent post-consumer waste fibre into paper cups. Other schemes include offering recycled coffee grounds as soil improver to

Vignette 6.2 (*contd.*)

customers free of charge. Starbucks offer 10 per cent discount to commuters who use their own mugs. In 2004 commuter mugs were used 15.1 million times eliminating 655,000 lb of paper waste from reaching landfill. Despite sounding impressive this only accounted for 1.6 per cent of customers. Environmental reporting is crude as there is a lack of company-wide metrics and data collection systems to permit full performance measurement. Starbucks are transparent about this, stating it is partially due to the number of licensed stores and the number of international stores that are not measured.

Employees: The corporate philosophy is to make 'partners' feel valued and to treat them with respect and dignity. In 2004 Starbucks was ranked thirty-fourth in the Fortune magazine top 100 companies to work for. This was Starbucks' sixth listing. Benefits include health care for eligible staff and dependants and a policy of awarding the same per cent stock option grants to all staff, regardless of seniority. Two-way communication channels are encouraged including a mission review where staff can inform senior management of situations where on-job experiences are inconsistent with guiding principles.

While much of Vignette 6.2 sounds impressive, and Starbucks certainly do more than most companies, many of their initiatives may be criticized as partial and only involving stakeholders as reactive recipients of their programmes. This leaves little room for stakeholder empowerment. Also, Starbucks generates the criteria for 'ethical' farming and purchasing practices (albeit influenced by stakeholder reactions) rather than the criteria being set by stakeholders or by an independent agency.

At a level below pioneer companies like General Motors' Saturn and Starbucks, progressive companies are also beginning to publish their stakeholder management policies in corporate annual or social report or via websites. One example is British Telecom (BT) (Vignette 6.3). BT has a long history of convened environmental panels with members from stakeholder groups representing the company, community, environmentalists, government, NGOs, and academics. BT analyses the feedback from a range of stakeholder consultation. This information is presented to the board executive committee, with hot topics actioned via steering committees chaired by the director of corporate relations.

Vignette 6.3 STAKEHOLDER ENGAGEMENT AT BRITISH TELECOM

Stakeholder dialogue

We have important relationships with a range of stakeholders. While no formal process has been used to identify stakeholders, over time it has become clear that six groups are particularly crucial to the success of our business:

- Customers
- Employees

(*contd.*)

Vignette 6.3 (*contd.*)

- Suppliers
- Shareholders
- Partners
- Community

Our *Statement of Business Practice*, The Way We Work, sets out the aspirations and commitments which apply in our relationship with each stakeholder group.

The more positive and mutually beneficial these relationships are, the more successful our business will be. Here we discuss:

- The various ways we engage with the different stakeholder groups
- Our Leadership Panel
- Stakeholder influence
- Online debates

You can also provide feedback on our social and environmental performance by e-mailing us at yourviews@bt.com.

Stakeholder engagement

We engage with our stakeholders in different ways. Here are some examples.

Customers

- Consumer Liaison Panels
- Surveys of customers on quality of service and future expectations
- Telecommunications Advisory Committees.

Employees

- Our annual employee survey
- Relationships with trade unions
- European Consultative Works Council.

Suppliers

- Our annual supplier satisfaction survey
- Ethical trading forums with key suppliers and industry colleagues.

Shareholders

The *Investors* section of our report was developed following close consultation with analysts specifically interested in the social and environmental performance of companies.

BT always values feedback from shareholders and aims to inform investors of the issues we face. More details can be found in *Services for Shareholders*.

Partners

A description of our relationship with joint ventures and wholly owned subsidiaries on social and environmental issues is given in the *Statement of Business Practice* section.

Leadership Panel

The Leadership Panel is an external advisory group of experts renowned for excelling in their field. The panel has six members:

- Jonathon Porritt, Chair of the Panel and Director of Forum for the Future, a UK sustainable development think-tank
- Mark Goyder, Director, Centre for Tomorrow's Company, a UK think-tank

Vignette 6.3 (*contd.*)

- Rob Lake, Head of SRI Engagement and Corporate Governance, Henderson Global Investors
- Elizabeth Laville, Director of Utopies, a Paris-based sustainability consultancy
- Yve Newbold, independent advisor
- Jorgen Randers, Professor, the Norwegian School of Management, Oslo.

The purpose of the panel is to encourage innovation and leadership on sustainable development and corporate social responsibility in BT. It meets four times a year and provides independent guidance and expert advice.

Its responsibility covers key areas of CSR strategy and performance, including policy, performance measures, targets, future objectives, governance, stakeholder relationships and external communications.

The panel provides an annual *independent comment* for inclusion on this report.

Stakeholder influence

It is important to be clear about what BT is trying to achieve with each stakeholder group and to deepen our understanding of what they expect from us.

This is why our *Statement of Business Practice* sets out the specific aspirations and commitments that apply in our relations with our customers, employees, shareholders, partners, suppliers and communities.

BT's performance against these specific principles, aspirations and commitments can be found via our *site index* based on the *Statement of Business Practice*.

It is difficult to make direct links between a specific consultation exercise and a particular company decision.

But we try to show, in the various sections of this site, how specific stakeholder groups do influence BT's policy, strategy and practice. For example, we show:

- How our Consumer Liaison Panels have helped shape our Next Generation Contact Centre strategy for call centres
- How BT managers work with their teams to analyse the results of the annual employee survey and carry out action plans
- How ethical trading forums set up with our suppliers are leading to an industry-wide approach to promote human rights through the supply chain
- How regular communication with socially responsible investment analysts led to further disclosure about the links between CSR and the BT strategy
- How stakeholder dialogue was used in the selection of non-financial key performance indicators
- How stakeholder dialogue led to us to choose education and better communications as key themes of our social investment programmes.

Information and data on this page has been verified by Lloyd's Register Quality Assurance Limited

Source: http://www.btplc.com/Societyandenvironment/Socialandenvironmentreport/Stakeholderdialogue/Stakeholderdialogue.htm

A number of features of this statement are worth noting. The quality assurance stamp at the end and the section on how stakeholders influence policy and the membership of their leadership panel represent independent and well-known sources of quality assurance. However, there is little specific reference to actual effects of stakeholder engagement. Most of the items under stakeholder influence refer to communication and dialogue. There is no reference to targets, or to shortcomings, or instances of stakeholder mismanagement. Certain issues are not dealt with at all, such as the sitings of mobile phone reception masts, which have been linked to cancer.

Many corporations undertake explicit stakeholder management associated with official procedures, policies, and allocated lines of responsibility, without adopting a comprehensive approach founded on the principles of participation, empowerment, and inclusion. The explicit nature of this approach can also afford greater corporate legitimacy. Some organizations have created 'community relations' or CSR positions or even departments in order to highlight their commitment to stakeholder management. However, such practices do not necessarily reflect a high level of stakeholder synthesis. The focus of stakeholder management may be as a strategic tool for competitive advantage, which is not deeply embedded and could be abandoned with changed competitive environments. Stakeholders are looked upon as a selective source of opportunity and potential, such as to embark on a collaborative venture, to facilitate enhanced management techniques (such as total quality management), or to aid in the development of a specific competitive advantage.

Many organizations are unbalanced in their approach to stakeholders. Primary stakeholders (employees or customers) are often dedicated greater resources to the management of their relations. For example, John Lewis, a UK department store, has a strong reputation for being a responsible employer. For many years John Lewis placed employee interests ahead of other stakeholders by closing their stores on Sundays and Wednesdays in order to maintain a regular, predictable and limited working week. The most common organization structure in the UK and the USA assigns respective stakeholder responsibility to specific corporate functions. For example, human resource management (HRM) is assigned responsibility for employees; the marketing department concerns itself with managing consumer relations; procurement oversees supplier relations; investor relations deals with shareholder affairs; and corporate affairs deals with the media and political stakeholders such as regulators. This model suppresses stakeholder conflicts through limiting interaction among parties through hierarchy or functional specialization (Kochan and Rubinstein 2000: 377).

Many organizations have no commitment to stakeholder management. Fiduciary duties to shareholders and legal, not moral, obligations are the driving factors and so stakeholder management exists only to resolve conflict, such as boycotts, protests, and strikes, which can negatively impact short-term shareholder value. The organization is viewed as a system of inputs and outputs. Suppliers, investors, and employees provide inputs, which are transformed into outputs for consumers. Here stakeholder management is considered in defensive terms on an ad hoc, reactionary basis. The associated management style is non-participatory, seeking to pacify stakeholders. Interest groups are not necessarily referred to as stakeholders or recognized in a stakeholder context (as having a claim on the firm) and stakeholder-specific policies may not exist.

6.4 **Assessing the quality of engagement**

In the previous examples we have used certain implicit criteria for distinguishing levels of quality in stakeholder management. We present a more formal model in Section 6.5. Here we examine some lists and categories of stakeholder management quality that have been suggested.

Strong, Ringer, and Taylor (2001) suggest three critical factors for stakeholder satisfaction: timeliness of communication, honesty and completeness of information, and empathy and equity of treatment by managers. There are some common sense aspects to effective dialogue, such as a willingness to learn for each other and the flexibility to ensure the implementation of good ideas. Zöller (1999) suggests that effective dialogues require:

- Symmetrical communication
- Transparency of the benefits and risks
- Unbiased facilitation
- Inclusivity
- An early start to facilitate change if needed.

Zadek and Raynard (2002: 11–12) suggest three dimensions of quality: procedural quality, responsiveness quality, and the quality of outcomes. *Procedural quality* encapsulates how the engagement was undertaken and whether it was consistent with the declared purpose. The terms of engagement, the parameters for discussion, and the areas that are negotiable or not relevant should all be clearly understood and shared by all parties. Most engagement is restricted to operational issues and therefore precludes stakeholders from having a say in terms of the broader structures and policies that impact them. This risks depoliticizing participation whereby stakeholder choices are framed within the options and on the terms given to them by those in power. Quality characteristics include the existence of formalized procedures, the facility for stakeholders to initiate engagement, and the assurance that stakeholders are empowered to raise the issues of most concern to them. It is important that stakeholders feel happy that they have had their say. Information, including feedback, should be accurate, timely, and widely disseminated. The legitimacy of engagement is also important in assessing quality. Stakeholders should be selected in an unbiased and comprehensive fashion, with some verification process included to ensure that all relevant parties are represented and that participants represent the interests of those they claim to speak on behalf of. Neligan (2003) also discusses the issue of whether mechanisms exist for stakeholders who have a grievance regarding the engagement process, such as an ombudsman, complaints panels, or tribunals. Neligan identifies four dimensions of procedural quality: access to timely and accurate information; terms of engagement; legitimacy of engagement; and procedures for redress. It should be noted that a poor stakeholder management process may deliver outstanding outcomes.

Responsiveness quality relates to whether an organization responded in a coherent and responsible manner and the way stakeholder views were dealt with. Were recommendations forwarded to the relevant decision-makers? Did the organization have the competencies to understand stakeholder concerns? How might they be addressed in practice? Was there evidence of organizational learning through the engagement and of putting such learning into practice in policies and decisions? Were corporate responses consistent with general policy statements such as represented in budgets and staff performance reviews?

Tangible evidence of the extent that the organization adjusted its policies and practices in line with stakeholder engagements or evidence of stakeholder satisfaction would indicate a level of *quality of outcomes*. Quality stakeholder engagement must involve mechanisms that link engagement with decision-making. A key question is whether stakeholders have been able to actively and meaningfully participate in the process.

Ethics is a central concern for assessing the quality of stakeholder management. Weiss (2003) suggests constructing a matrix of stakeholder moral responsibilities, distinguishing between legal, economic, ethical, and voluntary corporate responsibilities for each stakeholder group. It is possible for managers to implement stakeholder management and to be proponents of best practice, engaging in good stakeholder activities, such as effective constructive dialogue, but ignoring ethics when generating policy.

6.5 A ladder of stakeholder engagement

In this section we present a model of stakeholder engagement that is intended to illustrate degrees of the quality of stakeholder management from the perspective of the stakeholders. We also present a series of cases and other evidence of practice, which coincides with the levels of quality distinguished in the model.

The model is based on Arnstein (1969), who developed a ladder of public involvement in policy creation, ranging from a paternalistic to a more participatory system.

Her ladder comprises eight categories (Figure 6.1). On the lower rungs of non-partici-pation lie manipulation and therapy. The middle section of the ladder is identified as degrees of tokenism (informing, consultation, and placation) and the higher rungs are degrees of citizen power (partnership, delegated power, and citizen control).

Arnstein admits that the model is a simplification of reality, that 'there might be 150 rungs with less sharp and "pure" distinctions among them' and that neither the powerful nor the powerless are homogenous groups but 'encompasses a host of diver-gent points of view, significant cleavages, competing vested interests, and splintered subgroups' (1969: 217). Arnstein only distinguishes groups as 'powerful' or 'non-powerful', while in stakeholder analysis we are concerned with the degree of power that different groups might have. Nevertheless, the Arnstein model usefully highlights the progression to citizen control and, although it was intended for application within

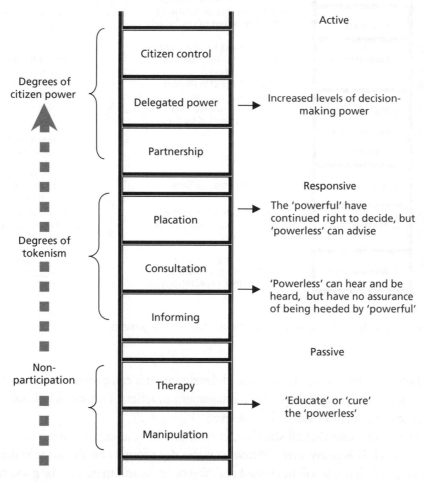

Figure 6.1 Arnstein's ladder of participation (annotated) (1969)

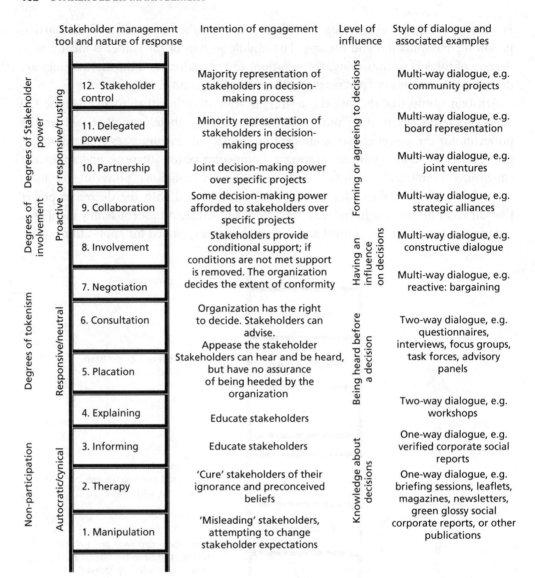

Figure 6.2 A Ladder of stakeholder management and engagement

public policy, with some modification and development it can provide a clear and useful framework for analysing stakeholder management practices. Our model of stakeholder management comprises twelve distinct levels (Figure 6.2).

We do not advocate that all stakeholder relations be conducted at level 12, or at any particular level. It is likely that different stakeholder groups and the same stakeholder groups at different times will be treated at different levels and there may be good reasons for this to be so. In Chapter 4 a number of analytic models were presented which specifically predict differential strategic responses to stakeholders based on stakeholder characteristics (Mitchell, Agle, and Wood 1997; Friedman and Miles 2002), different stages in organization life cycles (Jawahar and McLaughlin 2001), different strategies pursued by stakeholders (Freeman 1984; Savage et al. 1991; Frooman 1999). However, it is clear from the way that they have been described that levels 1 and 2 represent bad practice, if done in isolation. Our reasoning reflects a weak form of the instrumental theory proposition, i.e. if organizations are seen to either neglect important stakeholders or treat them with contempt, this will hurt the organization in the long run in terms of its reputation and ultimately its sustainability.

The lower levels (manipulation, therapy, and informing) relate to situations in which the organization is merely informing stakeholders about decisions that have already taken place. This style of stakeholder management is autocratic and does not involve any form of participation between the organization and its stakeholders. The lower two rungs are distinguished from the third in that they are cynical; attempts are contrived to appear to be indicative of true participation but are mere PR attempts at changing stakeholder expectations along the lines suggested by Lindblom (1994) (see Section 5.4.3).

At middle levels stakeholder management involves token gestures of participation: direct actions in response to stakeholder concerns. Here stakeholders have the opportunity to voice their concerns prior to the decision being made, but no assurance that concerns will impact the end result. Level 4 is that of 'explaining' whereby organizations continue to educate and inform stakeholders but do so through a two-way process, such as in a workshop situation. Consequently stakeholders have the opportunity to raise issues of concern or to question material delivered, but are not assured any impact on the outcome. The fifth level is placation. This is a direct response to stakeholder unrest, which requires some form of appeasement in order to contain the situation. However, if the response is not heartfelt the degree of resulting stakeholder influence is likely to be low.[2] Consultation through stakeholder surveys is the sixth level of engagement. There are two reasons why consultation is not ranked more highly:

1. Organizations solicit stakeholder opinion over issues determined beforehand by the organization and consequently, the issues of real concern to the stakeholder may be ignored in the survey;
2. The results of the survey will not necessarily filter into the decision-making process, although it could be argued that organizations would not waste resources unnecessarily.

The final category of tokenism is negotiation. Here organizations respond defensively to stakeholder demands through multi-way dialogue such as bargaining due to the threat that the stakeholder may withdraw its support. This is the first category of engagement in which the stakeholder group has a tangible possibility of influencing the decision-making process. However, this is not classified on higher levels of stakeholder power because the organization may chose to call the stakeholder's bluff or to force the stakeholder's hand. It would be possible to adopt such strategies if the organization holds the balance of power, i.e. the organization is less dependent on the stakeholder for survival than the stakeholder is on the organization. For example, employees may threaten to strike over low pay rises, but if the labour market is buoyant and the workers are easily replaced, the organization may limit the extent of negotiations very early on in the process.

The highest levels of engagement are characterized by active or responsive attempts at empowering stakeholders in corporate decision-making. This involves trust. Level 8 is involvement. Here the organization willingly engages with stakeholders over common issues. This can be in response to negative or positive stakeholder actions (reactive) or organization actions (active). Examples include the involvement of special interest groups in the development process for products (active) in order to gain expert opinion, or in responding positively to an ethical investment manager over socially responsible screens that a corporation has failed to pass (reactive). The ability to form or agree to decisions is not guaranteed but there is a real ability to influence corporate decisions. Organizations may also collaborate with stakeholders for specific projects. Stakeholders have a degree of power over the outcome but ultimate control still lies with the organization. Strategic alliances are clear examples. Partnerships are similar to collaborations, but imply joint decision-making between the organization and the stakeholder, as evident in a joint venture. However, the extent of stakeholder control is restricted to the remit of particular projects. Organization-wide control is only evident in situations of delegated power or stakeholder control. This is rare in the UK and the USA, though examples of corporations electing stakeholders to the board of directors do exist. The final, and most influential form of stakeholder engagement, is through the renouncement of power to stakeholder groups so that top-level management have only a minority say in decisions. This form of engagement is also exceedingly rare but some examples can be found in community projects. Each of the twelve levels of stakeholder management is considered in more detail with examples in Section 6.6.

6.6 Stakeholder management tools

6.6.1 LEVELS 1 AND 2 MANIPULATION AND THERAPY

The most basic form of stakeholder management is via information releases such as those disseminated via the Internet, briefing sessions, leaflets, magazines, newsletters, corporate social and environmental reports, or other publications. The Internet is gaining in popularity due to the large number of stakeholders who can freely access it, the low marginal cost of publication, and the interactive nature of this form of media (Unerman and Bennett 2004). Information releases occur after a decision has been made to inform stakeholders of the outcome. The power is firmly on the side of the organization and stakeholders are unable to influence practice. There is no dialogue, merely a one-way communication process. The semantics are important here. Manipulation refers to the control, skilful management, or manoeuvring of opinion. This is all about PR management and exists to 'enable power-holders to educate or cure, not to enable participants in planning or conducting programmes' (Arnstein 1969: 218). Therapy relates to any situation in which treatment is aimed at curing a physical or mental disorder. For stakeholder management this means brainwashing stakeholders through the intensive bombardment of self-laudatory corporate information until they are indoctrinated with the same principles as the organization or until they believe that the culture or ideology gap has been reduced to an acceptable level. If successful, stakeholders are 'cured' of their 'mental ailment', i.e. their misperceptions of what they want to change or claim to need. Arnstein (1969: 218) argues that masking group therapy as participation is both dishonest and arrogant. Here we do not assume this is successful in that stakeholders are actually brainwashed, merely that this is the intention behind the use of the tools.

Corporate environmental, social, and ethical reporting (CESER) is widely used as a stakeholder management tool to show stakeholders interested in these issues what the corporation position, policies, and resulting impact is (Gray, Kouhy, and Lavers 1995; Gray, Owen, and Adams 1996). However, care must be taken in positioning CESER on the ladder of stakeholder management as the motivation behind reporting and the subsequent quality of reporting vary considerably (see Section 9.5). For most countries outside of Scandinavia, CESER is a voluntary, unregulated field and reporting is largely ad hoc, self-laudatory, and partial. This is particularly so with respect to social and ethical reporting, a more recent phenomenon than environmental reporting that is characterized by selective and imprecise disclosure. In instances of asymmetric reporting, where corporations portray their activities in a positive light and fail to report meaningfully the nature, extent, and implications of activities, the classification of CESER would be the lowest rung relating to 'manipulation'. CESER has been used as a legitimating tool to change the expectations of stakeholders (Campbell 2003), although this has been found to be ineffective (O'Dwyer 2002). Vignette 6.4 presents an excerpt from the accounts of easyJet, the low-cost airline, as an illustration of this.

Vignette 6.4 CORPORATE SOCIAL, AND ENVIRONMENTAL REPORTING AT EASYJET

Social, environmental and ethical report

Environment
The nature of the easyJet business model reduces the impact of the airline's activities on the environment.

easyJet's stated aim is to operate a fleet of young aircraft. These have lower noise emissions and use less fuel than earlier models. easyJet is implementing a fleet replacement plan that will result in a fleet entirely composed of Boeing 737 New Generation and Airbus A320 family aircraft, which will have all been purchased new by

(contd.)

Vignette 6.4 (*contd.*)

easyJet. The average fleet age at 30 September 2003 is currently six years and this is projected to reduce to four and a half years by September 2004.

Compared with most full-fare airlines, easyJet has high passenger load factors. This, coupled with a young modern fleet, means that noise emissions and fuel burn per passenger are significantly lower than many airlines. Also, easyJet actively manages and investigates incidences of fuel spillages related to our flights.

easyJet aids the reduction of demand for private car transport to and from the main airports from which it operates. easyJet provides support for the regular bus link between London Luton Airport and Luton Airport Parkway railway station, and has commercial arrangements with the Stansted and Gatwick Express rail services. easyJet offers its customers incentives (in the form of cost subsidies) to use public transport to travel to both Luton and Stansted.

Waste production is reduced through our business model. Unlike most of our full-service competitors, we do not have printed tickets and we do not offer free newspapers or free meals on board. easyJet believes that this results in lower usage of packaging and paper and therefore less waste.

We operate an almost paperless administration office, with almost all filing, copying, and faxing based upon the use of electronic images. Although some waste paper is produced, procedures are in place for collecting it for recycling.

Social

easyJet seeks to provide a unique and rewarding work environment for employees. The organization has a relatively flat management structure and it does not have the trappings of hierarchy that many businesses have. For example, the main administration office does not have individual offices or secretaries.

Most of easyJet's corporate information is shared across the general population of staff. Individual employees are able to search and retrieve information electronically.

There is a dedicated director responsible for people development and cultural issues. In addition, there is a consultative council of elected staff that considers cultural issues and makes recommendations to the Chief Executive Officer. This ensures that people issues are given a high profile and are considered at the highest levels within the airline.

A network of Works Councils exists, which ensures that there is formal representation of views from all areas of the business.

easyJet recognizes that it is beneficial for employees to participate in the business alongside investors. Consequently, many staff employed have received either share options or share gifts.

Most staff have some form of incentive-related pay. All administration staff are entitled to a substantial annual bonus, which is partly dependent on Company performance.

easyJet is committed to being an equal opportunities employer as we wish to encourage all our employees to make the best use of their skills and experience. Our policy aims to ensure that no job applicant or employee receives less favourable treatment on the basis of their age, colour, creed, disability, full- or part-time status, gender, marital status, nationality or ethnic origin, race, religion, or sexual orientation. easyJet is building a workforce that has a balanced age profile and intends to maintain opportunities for younger and older people alike. easyJet does not tolerate harassment or bullying in any form.

easyJet provides support to charities in the form of free easyJet flights. The Board has a policy of supporting a single chosen charity, rather than trying to support many good causes.

Ethical

easyJet insists that every employee must:

- Keep all dealings open and legitimate. Ensure that these are always consistent with good business practices;
- Keep full and accurate records of all business dealings;

Vignette 6.4 (*contd.*)

- Avoid any suspicion of a conflict of interest; and
- Refuse any gifts or gratuities, which may be considered to be bribes from any organization with which they have, or might have, business dealings concerned with easyJet's affairs.

easyJet prides itself on the efficient and friendly service that it offers to its customers. Each employee contributes to this and easyJet requires that they must perform their duties with efficiency and diligence and behave towards fellow employees and customers with courtesy and decorum. They must not misuse, damage, or misappropriate easyJet's property nor cause offence to customers or potential customers.

easyJet does not tolerate the verbal or physical assault of its customers or employees. An employee's actions when dealing with easyJet's customers, agents and suppliers should always be those of a competent ambassador.

Source: http://www.easyjet.co.uk/common/img/FY2003EZJAnnualReportandAcconts.pdf

The strategy and business model of easyJet expresses a commitment to safety and customer service, but is fundamentally driven by the desire to enhance shareholder wealth through cost cutting, dense point-to-point networks, increased load factor, and scalability. The vignette indicates little stakeholder management beyond legal compliance and where stakeholder and shareholder interests are congruent. Where conflict exists the low-cost option is followed. For example, the non-provision of free newspapers and meals to customers is justified on environmental grounds. Increased load factor, thereby reducing pollution per passenger, is cited as an environmental benefit despite being a by-product of maximizing returns. From the normative perspective, it could be argued that the alternative to high aircraft loads is more likely to be (should be) more fuel-efficient means of transport for short-haul journeys, rather than lightly loaded aircraft from traditional carriers. The operation of a young fleet of aircraft is professed to lower noise pollution and emission but easyJet fails to make any reference to the environmental implication of operating such a short economic life and consequential impact of disposal. Social disclosure relates almost entirely to employees reflecting a very narrow stakeholder focus. Charitable donations are in the form of free flights as opposed to monetary donations, minimizing the cost of giving for shareholders. Similarly, ethical disclosure states little beyond reproving bribes. Finally, we note that this whole section of easyJet's annual report contains no targets, no measures against performance, and no information that is other than self-laudatory.

6.6.2 LEVEL 3 INFORMING

Corporations may release information to stakeholders in order to be open and transparent. The techniques described above as tools of manipulation or therapy are also used here, but there is no intent to control or manipulate opinion or to deceive stakeholders. In practice it is difficult to distinguish between genuine and contrived attempts at transparency. A differentiating characteristic could be whether the information release is only self-laudatory or whether negative information is included (Deegan and Gordon 1996). This does not preclude cases in which corporations disclose bad news, which is already in the public domain, to detract attention from other operations or in attempts to build unwarranted credibility and trust.

Environmental reporting has developed considerably over the past decade. UNEP/SustainAbility have conducted a number of longitudinal benchmark surveys that highlight examples of best practice. Corporations such as Ben & Jerry's (USA) and Norsk Hydro (Norway) have clearly demonstrated a commitment to transparency and accountability. They are characterized by the annual reporting of quantitative and monetary data, reporting bad as well as good and neutral news, assessing performance against targets, presenting normalized data, comprehensive coverage of all sites and activities, reporting on social, ethical, and environmental issues, and subjecting their reporting process to independent third-party verification. Stakeholders should be able to assess with reasonable accuracy actual corporate performance. Consequently, such reporting would be positioned higher on the ladder, at the third level: informing. If corporations survey stakeholders as part of the CESER process to establish stakeholder concerns, level 6 (consultation) is reached but the report would still be classified as level 3. The report, no matter how comprehensive and accurate, is still only a form of one-way communication. Vignette 6.5 illustrates the CESER process at the Co-operative Financial Services (CFS) (UK). CFS survey stakeholders to establish the issues that should be reported on, and the focus of screens for the ethical policy adopted. This level of stakeholder engagement informing the CESER process is the exception rather than the norm and caution should be used when assessing practice. Swift (2001) suggests that some corporations solicit stakeholder views through the CESER process and then self-report on their trustworthiness as a means of reputation building, thereby attempting to manipulate perception rather than making true attempts at transparency or participation.

Vignette 6.5 STAKEHOLDER REPORTING: CFS (UK)

CFS is a UK financial services company formed in 2002 through the merger of the Co-operative Bank and the Co-operative Insurance Society. The pedigree of reporting by this group is exceedingly high, being recognized externally as a pioneer in sustainability reporting. The bank received the 2003 and 2004 Association of Chartered Certified Accountants (ACCA) award for sustainability and was ranked first, with a score of 61 per cent, by the UNEP Global survey of corporate sustainability reporting in 2002.

CFS direct their sustainability report to six stakeholder 'partners', upon whom their continued success is dependent to varying degrees: shareholders, customers, staff, suppliers, society, and the co-operative movement. The environment is not defined as a separate 'partner' as this relationship is viewed as 'non-negotiable', in contrast to relations held with other stakeholders. Instead, the extent to which value is delivered to each partner is assessed in an ecologically sustainable manner. For 2003, eighty-seven indicators were reported on, covering the areas of ecological sustainability, delivering value, and social responsibility, each in relation to the

Vignette 6.5 (*contd.*)

identified partners. Of these, forty-three were fully achieved, acceptable progress was made against twenty-seven, and sixteen were not yet achieved. This comprehensive range of indicators and associated targets were established through consultation with stakeholders, where appropriate company activities are linked to wider environmental/social issues and global priorities, such as the reduction of carbon dioxide emissions. Disclosure incorporates both qualitative and quantitative data, with comprehensive use of graphs, tables, and case studies to illustrate the data and a 'warts and all' approach is adopted, reflecting good as well as bad news.

The banking arm of the group operates ethical screening formulated in consultation with customers. The ethical policy stipulates who the bank will and will not finance as customers, thereby restricting the provisions of financial services to certain sectors and activities. The ethical policy also extends to screening suppliers. Ethical and ecological cost–benefit accounts were initiated in 2001. For 2003, 30 per cent of profits (£37.53 million) were attributed to customers who cite ethics as an important reason for banking with the group. Estimated income forgone due to exclusion screens included £746,000 for human rights, £558,500 for animal rights, £1,410,500 for ecological impact of fossil fuels, chemicals, and biodiversity and waste management and £152,500 for miscellaneous breaches, totalling £2.88 million. CFS follow Department for the Environment and Rural Affairs (DEFRA) reporting guidelines. Each of the three reporting areas is independently verified using the AA1000 Assurance Standard, which requires opinion on the materiality, completeness, and responsiveness of reporting. 'Delivering value', which covers financial performance, customer, staff, and supplier satisfaction and social inclusion, was verified by CTC. 'Social responsibility', which incorporates ethical policy implementation and customer/supplier screening together with active corporate governance engagement was verified by BiC. The third area, 'ecological sustainability', which relates to emissions to air and water, energy and water use and waste management, was verified by Jonathon Porritt, Chairman of The Natural Step (TNS) and director of Forum for the Future.

6.6.3 LEVEL 4 EXPLAINING

The next category of levels is *tokenism*. Token engagement allows the powerless to have a voice, but they lack the power to ensure their voices are heeded. Holding workshops would be an example of 'explaining', the lowest level of tokenism. Although workshops by their nature involve two-way dialogue, generally the overall objective is to inform stakeholders of decisions already taken, prior to their public announcement. At this level there is little room for stakeholder opinion to influence corporate policies as there is 'no followthrough, no "muscle", hence no assurance of changing the status quo' (Arnstein 1969: 217). If stakeholders feel powerless to influence the situation, the process may be viewed as unproductive and they may not be willing to participate. Organizations may wish to encourage participation to reduce conflict. Stakeholders are more likely to be committed to an initiative if they participate in the process and have some ownership of ideas. As ownership cannot arise from one-way dialogue such as producing a brochure or leaflet, one-to-one interaction is required. To facilitate participation there must be trust and the stakeholder must perceive the matter to be relevant. Unless the issue impacts the stakeholder directly it is difficult for organizations to conjure up support for a workshop. The image of industry is often tarnished with the view of myopic corporations only interested in profit maximization, violating voluntary codes and bending the law to its limits with regards to minimal or non-compliance of regulations. Dialogue can only be effective if there is a degree of mutual respect among participants, and some stakeholders may view any engagement as a matter of compromising their principles. Such barriers may be insurmountable. Alternatively, some stakeholder groups may reconsider if there is tangible evidence of genuine long-term commitment to engage and work towards mutual goals. These problems become more evident as one progresses up the ladder of stakeholder management and are relevant for all levels of actual participation (tokenism and degrees of stakeholder power).

6.6.4 LEVEL 5 PLACATION

Advisory panels, task forces, and focus groups involve two-way dialogue prior to a decision being made, and provide an opportunity for stakeholders to influence the eventual outcome. They afford a channel for organizations to obtain expert opinion, to keep abreast of developments, and to assess stakeholder opinion and can generate innovative approaches. Stakeholder representatives from interest groups who disagree on a proposed action meet with a neutral facilitator to search for solutions that are acceptable to all. The facilitator structures the process, determines the agenda in consultation with the participants, and ensures compliance with the ground rules (Zöller 1999). Although the stakeholders can advise and inform decisions, they do not generate proposals and the organization has the continued right to decide upon its action.

Such methods of stakeholder management can be used for political purposes as task forces or advisory panels supporting organization policy, and can offer a degree of legitimacy and independence to the strategic outcome. As with most stakeholder management tools, there are potential problems associated with task forces, focus groups, roundtables, and advisory panels. It should be noted that some organizations would only pay lip service to such engagement, hence this level of engagement falls under the broad category of tokenism. The issue of representation is important. How are the stakeholders selected? Are there any mechanisms to ensure those that should be heard have a voice? Is the representation biased? Who sets the agenda? For acceptance, it is important that all groups are represented and that participants be authorized to speak on behalf of the stakeholder groups they represent and provide feedback on the results to the group. Habermas (1984, 1987, 1993, 1996) argues that the validity of negotiations increases to the extent that a politically neutral space is achieved. For Habermas this is facilitated through an ideal process formalized in procedures, rules, laws, politics, and constitution. There are barriers to achieving such a process in practice. Edmunds and Wollenberg (2001) suggest that multistakeholder negotiations may not be the best solution for disadvantaged groups due to hidden abuses of power that tend to exaggerate the level of consensus reached, and expose disadvantaged groups to greater manipulation and control by more powerful stakeholders. In addition to inequalities in status and power among participants, a culture of freedom may also be absent due to fundamental differences in ideologies, beliefs, tradition, culture, or religion.

6.6.5 LEVEL 6 CONSULTATION

Focus groups and advisory panels can be highly effective and involve real consultation. Shell (UK) Group (Vignette 6.6) provides one example. Following international concern that Shell was intending to use the sea as a dumping ground, the group conducted workshops and advisory panels in an attempt to devise a decommissioning plan for the Brent Spar oil rig that was acceptable by all stakeholders including the UK government.

Vignette 6.6 WORKSHOPS AND ADVISORY PANELS: SHELL (UK) AND GREENPEACE

In 1995 direct action from Greenpeace over concerns that Shell (UK) Group was intending to sink the Brent Spar oil rig in the North Sea provoked international concern, widespread media attention, and subsequent public boycotts and demonstrations. Shell eventually responded by rescinding its decision and turning to stakeholder engagement to find a solution. The Environment Council independently oversaw this process. The stakeholders surveyed included central and local governments, NGOs and pressure groups, ethics specialists, academics, technical experts, contractors, and staff at Shell. The public were involved indirectly through the creation of a website, the provision of a CD-ROM, the creation of school packs, and through a competition for the best decommissioning idea. The information was widely disseminated due to the high level of press coverage received.

Shell funded a number of workshops and focus groups in the UK, Denmark, the Netherlands, and Germany, costing £450,000. All representatives at the workshops had to represent and report back to a stakeholder constituency. The representative list was determined via telephone calls to interested parties. Shell and the Environmental Council set the agenda for each meeting. The objective of the meeting was to inform Shell of the stakeholder needs and to inform stakeholders of the corporation's needs and the constraints in which it was operating. Part of this process involved putting various dilemmas to participants and asking their opinion. For transparency, the minutes of the meetings were published on the Web. The final decision reached was to place the Brent Spar in a Norwegian fjord as an extension to a pier. The UK government had the last say but was unlikely to reject a consensus decision arrived at in such a transparent manner.

Greenpeace commented that it was to Shell's credit that they worked towards finding an acceptable solution for all. The case can be seen as a defining moment in the relationships between environmental groups, the general public, and a multinational powerful corporation in that it facilitated a more open dialogue for campaigning groups and was a move towards solutions orientated campaigning.

Many companies use stakeholder surveys for assessing stakeholder needs and for use in CESER (Jackson and Bundgård 2002). Corporations have historically used stakeholder surveys with employee and consumer research. This could be conducted in-house, or commissioned to an independent research agency. Surveys can solicit views that would otherwise go unheard and are considered more democratic than other methods of engagement (MacRae and Whittington 1997). Stakeholder interviews can provide detailed information about individual's perceptions. Interviews also allow for a two-way communication and can reduce/avoid misunderstanding. If stakeholders are informed of and participate in the decision-making process, they are more likely to agree with the outcome, and hence the public perception of the decision may be enhanced, leading to a greater degree of public trust (Darnall and Jolley 2004). Consequently, stakeholder surveys can be used for purely political reasons.

Stakeholder surveys represent more serious levels of engagement as the organization is actively soliciting stakeholder feedback. Arguably, organizations would not waste precious resources in conducting such activities if the results were not actively incorporated into future strategic actions. However, the organization has the right to decide what it does with the feedback.

6.6.6 LEVEL 7 NEGOTIATION

Negotiation, by definition, must occur prior to reaching a final decision. A number of corporate activities aimed at stakeholder appeasement fall within this category. These are characterized by situations where the stakeholder continues to provide support for an organization but that support is conditional. If the conditions are not met within a reasonable timeframe, the support is removed through the withdrawal of the resources that the stakeholder has invested. Negotiations may be direct (the terms of trade with a supplier) or indirectly conducted through an intermediary (e.g. employee concerns being voiced through a trade union, or industry concerns being raised through a professional association). Stakeholders have some power to influence the decision through the control of resources. If those resources are unique or highly valued by the organization, the balance of power will rest with the stakeholder (Frooman 1999). In the previous two examples the stakeholder resource relates to the human capital of employees and the social capital (reputation, credibility, legitimacy, etc.) associated with being affiliated to an industrial body. Shrewd negotiators may refuse to reveal all their cards or may bluff about their intentions (Donaldson and Dunfee 1994).

6.6.7 LEVEL 8 INVOLVEMENT

Stakeholder involvement is positioned above negotiation because the balance of power is less extreme, usually because the goals are less divergent. Stakeholder roundtables, for example, are resource-intensive and tend only to be used for major policy matters. A degree of decision-making power is afforded to the roundtable at the onset as the members are expected to draft proposals, rather than just provide advice or recommendations, as is the case with a focus group or advisory panel. The procedures for establishing and monitoring a roundtable require a lot of deliberation, as it is important for credibility and legitimacy that representation be unbiased and comprehensive.

One example is the purchase of company shares by stakeholders in order to voice concerns at AGMs or to lodge resolutions. Another example is 'constructive dialogue'. This occurs when stakeholders actively and positively engage with corporations in order to change or influence corporate behaviour. The corporation is more likely to engage in multi-way discussions if the goals of the stakeholder converge with, or are not excessively different from, those of the corporation. Constructive dialogue is commonly employed by socially responsible investment (SRI) and pension fund managers, and to a lesser degree by individual corporations. Proactive SRI fund managers adopt constructive dialogue because it is considered a more effective way of facilitating change than negative screening (Mackenzie 1998; Friedman and Miles 2001). The funds engage with corporations that fail SRI screens but have shown progressive practice in other areas, with a view to encouraging the corporations to meet the minimal requirement laid down by the fund. If the corporation fails to change practice, the fund divests. Corporations are becoming keener to engage with SRI funds, which were historically viewed as marginal, for a number of reasons:

- Reputation benefits of being approved by an SRI fund
- Obtaining a prestigious listing on a social index
- Pension fund influence (see Section 7.5.2)

SRI fund managers engage on issues such as encouraging CESER; moving towards reducing, reusing, and recycling; and increased female representation on corporate boards. The banking arm of CFS (UK) applies SRI style screening to both investments and potential clients (Vignette 6.7).

Vignette 6.7 CONSTRUCTIVE DIALOGUE AT CFS (UK)

The stakeholder management process at the banking arm of CFS is essentially the management and implementation of the ethical policy. In turn, the action of implementing policy generates wider engagement. The bank has a clearly defined set of stakeholders in its seven 'equal partners'. The views of partners are taken very seriously and often actions are taken as a direct result of feedback. The ethical policy is kept up to date through regular surveys, e.g. by monitoring customer concerns. Examples of consultation include dialogue on human rights, animal welfare, ecological issues, and social issues such as 'fair trade'.

Ethical screening is applied to investments and to potential clients. The bank determines and carries out its own screening procedures according to its ethical policy. Screening is also informed by Ethical Investment Research Information Services (EIRIS). The bank also actively engages with clients, attempting to improve client social, ethical, or environmental performance, e.g. by engaging with clients over the use of unsustainable forestry products and suggesting alternative sustainable forestry suppliers. The bank also engages successfully with clients and other organizations such as peers to promote fair trade coffee provision in the workplace. This is an ongoing engagement process embedded within the corporation.

6.6.8 LEVEL 9 COLLABORATION

Strategic alliances are collaborative 'marriages' between organizations and stakeholders to pursue mutually beneficial goals. Each partner brings a particular (complementary) skill or resource and through joint engagement both parties are expected to benefit. The most common alliances are between corporations and environmental groups (Murphy and Bendell 1997) and with supply chain partners. Strategic alliances can take many forms including loose marketing-driven alliances, product endorsements, corporate sponsorships, and formal agreements such as product development and licensing. Product endorsements involve a high degree of stakeholder influencing power as endorsement is generally only granted once the agency has ensured the product meets established procedures. This often involves a life cycle assessment of the product and annual review, with a formal contract and payment of a fee and a clause that allows either party to end the alliance should the other party breach the conditions (Mendleson and Polonsky 1995). Corporate sponsorships involve situations in which the corporation is directly involved with a stakeholder, either financially or through benefits in kind (allowing staff time off for such work or providing use of corporate premises), in order to enhance reputation. Product licensing agreements result in stakeholder-branded products. If a product is branded by a high-profile environmental group consumer credibility and reliability will increase.

Successful alliances can bring a number of benefits including access to expert opinion, increased markets, positive publicity, and decreased public criticism. Mendleson and Polonsky (1995) cite an Australian National Opinion Poll from 1992, showing that consumers perceive claims made by environmental groups as four times more credible than those of a manufacturer and twice as credible as those from government. A frequently cited successful strategic alliance is McDonald's and the US Environmental Defense Fund (EDF) (Vignette 6.8). Alliances can fail, bringing negative publicity, and can damage corporate reputation. The Loblaws/Pollution Probe association in Canada in the late 1980s (see Vignette 8.6) is a landmark example (Stafford and Hartman 1996). Balancing economic and wider stakeholder goals is not easy. Alliances can jeopardize the strategic positions of the parties and require 'great patience and management savvy to skirt differences in values, organizational structures, and decision-making styles for success' (Stafford and Hartman 1996). In creating strategic alliances Mendleson and Polonsky (1995) offer sensible advice from a marketing perspective: corporations must look for partners that focus on issues of importance to the corporation's consumers and are readily recognizable as such by them. Consumer opinion regarding potential partner image is important, because the image of one partner may affect the other once an alliance is established. The alliance should be structured, with established objectives that are compatible with those of the partner. Partner skills need to be in line with the objectives (expert knowledge, a high media profile, ability to cooperate). Even if a suitable partner is identified, it may not wish to engage with the corporation, particularly if the corporation has a chequered history.

Vignette 6.8 STRATEGIC ALLIANCES: MCDONALD'S AND EDF (USA)

In 1988 environmentalists campaigning against fast food waste targeted McDonald's. The polystyrene packages used by McDonald's were not biodegradable, did not easily compress for landfill disposal, emitted chlorofluorocarbons (CFCs) when produced, emitted toxic by-products when burnt, and were not economically viable for recyclers (who are typically paid by weight) (Stafford and Hartman 1996). McDonald's initial response was that the use of polystyrene minimized the destruction of the world's forests and that foam could be recycled. Facing further negative publicity, the corporation decided to discontinue CFC-blown polystyrene packages and to implement a recycling policy. However, the recycling policy was limited by the fact that takeaway sales account for almost 70 per cent of total turnover, leaving the disposal of waste products up to the consumers. EDF approached McDonald's requesting a non-combative discussion with executives over solid waste disposal. Following several meetings a joint task force was created to look into the problem. For McDonald's the task force provided independent expert opinion. For EDF it provided the opportunity to test its innovations and acted as an impetus for other pressure groups to seek solution-based approaches through direct engagement. The outcome was a forty-two-step waste reduction plan (Stafford and Hartman 1996). The first move was the abandonment of on-site incineration of polystyrene. This was followed by programmes to decrease the amount of packaging used such as: reducing the size of serviettes, reusing resources, encouraging suppliers to use more durable pallets, increasing recycling, composting food waste, and encouraging suppliers to increase the recycled material content of packaging. The corporate culture changed as a result of the alliance. There have also been knock-on effects as competitors introduced similar packaging.

This alliance was successful, in part because both parties maintained their independence. No money exchanged hands. Both parties agreed to the right to disagree with one another and agreed that there should be complete transparency surrounding the process, with relevant documentation made available to the public. The level of transparency and cooperation offered by both parties to the media significantly increased the credibility of the process.

This certainly did not change the general public attitude towards McDonald's as a socially responsible company, as evidenced by the popularity of the award-winning 2004 film *Supersize Me* (supersizeme.com), which examines McDonald's role in contributing to the soaring levels of obesity in the USA.

6.6.9 LEVEL 10 PARTNERSHIPS

Organizations engage in joint ventures, social partnerships, and joint committees with a range of stakeholders. Organizations may join forces with competitors to lobby at the industry level, or with customers, suppliers, or an environmental group for product development. The difference between partnerships and collaborations or alliances is a matter of degree, with the former involving more substantial joint activities and taking on greater risk. Collaborations (involving endorsements, sponsorships, and licensing agreements) are more focused on *joint outcomes*, while partnerships also involve *joint processes* leading up to joint outcomes. Organizations proactively enter into partnerships when environments are more complex, and uncertain webs of interdependence are created among its stakeholders. In such circumstances collaborative, not competitive, strategies are critical in order to build on interdependences rather than buffering them. Such techniques are known as bridging or boundary spanning. Bridging reduces uncertainties that arise from unpredictable demands and pressures that come from high levels of interdependences among stakeholders, by increasing the level of control each party has over the other's activities. Bridging can also increase organizational flexibility. This style of stakeholder management requires high levels of trust between parties. Social capital must be created, values and norms should be shared, and there should be agreement about rules for cooperation. Such activities can positively result in increased levels of decision-making power being transferred to the stakeholder.

6.6.10 LEVEL 11 DELEGATED POWER

Delegated power relates more to incidents whereby stakeholders are empowered via recourse to law or collective stakeholder support. For example, the German Codetermination Law (*Mitbestimmung*) gives employees and shareholders an equal voice on the supervisory committee, which is part of the two-tiered board structure for listed corporations (see Vignette 9.2). This style of corporate governance is restricted to Continental European and some Asian countries and contrasts sharply with Anglo-American practice, where stakeholder management at this level is mainly confined to the not-for-profit sector (Wood 1992; Shiochet 1998; Friedman and Phillips 2005).

6.6.11 LEVEL 12 STAKEHOLDER CONTROL

In principle stakeholder control would occur if they obtain the majority of decision-making seats or full managerial power in an organization. This is extremely rare. There are isolated examples of community or neighbourhood organizations in which the stakeholders are afforded the right to govern, manage, and negotiate on behalf of the community programmes and institutions that they represent (Vignette 6.9). Such programmes provide a social benefit as well as offer political and bureaucratic advantages (Murphy and Bendell 1997). Control is determined from the outset and it is unlikely that stakeholders not involved in the creation of the community organization will gain control at a later date. Metcalfe (1998) argues that the fairness to all stakeholders held out by the stakeholder concept can only be achieved at a societal level and that it is unfair to demand more of corporations than society demands of itself. Once a stakeholder society is achieved the concept of the stakeholder organization will become implicit. Arnstein (1969) stressed that the notion of absolute control is unrealistic in a capitalist society.

Vignette 6.9 COMMUNITY PROJECTS AND THE CANADIAN FOREST CONCEPT

The Canadian Model Forest Concept combines the interests, mandates, and objectives of government agencies, aboriginal peoples, communities, and other stakeholders to create a comprehensive vision and programme of work aimed at achieving sustainable forest management. Tasks delegated to the forest partnerships are established within the process and through such partnerships participants are empowered to work together towards mutually acceptable solutions. While the need for forest resource assessment is often initiated by outsiders rather than the local community, it is important that the collection and use of information is obtained and understood locally. Outside experts are employed as advisers to provide suggestions to the local communities but the final decision-making is left to the local people themselves (Carter et al. 1995).

6.7 Surveys of stakeholder engagement

UNEP/SustainAbility (1999) present empirical evidence showing unprecedented levels of stakeholder dialogue, but they question the sincerity of these practices. Cummings (2001) examined stakeholder management in relation to CESER and assessed this according to Arnstein's ladder. She examined both stakeholder and corporate perspectives. The results suggested that the thirteen national (UK) and multinational organizations surveyed were on the lower rungs of the ladder with respect to stakeholder engagement over CESER, most notably levels associated with tokenism. Respondents stated that the objectives of the process were to identify issues and to measure the extent to which the organization delivers on stakeholder expectations. Although it was clear that corporations had little intention of relinquishing decision-making powers, Cummings did find a willingness to change views and to surrender previous entrenched positions, if confrontation could be avoided. Methods of stakeholder engagement identified depended on the stakeholder groups concerned. Examples of practice included small group techniques, questionnaire surveys (postal, telephone, and Internet), consultation practices (face-to-face interviews, paired interviews, free telephone hotline), and expert or advisory panels. Swift (2001) drew up a similar list of activities. Miles, Hammond, and Friedman (2002) interviewed thirty-eight individuals with responsibility for stakeholder management in twenty-eight Financial Times Stock Exchange (FTSE)-listed companies in the UK. They too found that the majority of activity occurs in the lower rungs of 'non-participation' and 'degrees of tokenism' and that typical engagement tools included focus groups, interviews, surveys, meetings, and the publication of corporate social reports. Robbins (2003) also found few cases of non-participation and many examples of tokenism, but did identify isolated examples of active participation.

Luoma and Goodstein (1999) examined 224 US companies to assess the degree of stakeholder representation. They considered the presence of stakeholders on corporate boards or representation on board committees, such as the audit, compensation, executive, or nominating committees, to be the key direct means through which firms can reflect stakeholder interests in corporate governance and policymaking. Their results indicated a modest stakeholder representation on corporate boards of 14.6 per cent, with similar figures for compensation (14.1 per cent), nomination (15.2 per cent), and audit (19.2 per cent). Evidence was presented that this is a growing trend. The number of corporations with stakeholder representation increased over the period 1984–94 from thirty-one to forty-four. Large corporations and those subject to a high degree of regulation were more likely to have stakeholders on their boards. In a survey of 254 US executives, Weaver, Treviño, and Cochran (1999) found that only corporations with top management commitment to ethics exhibited well-integrated practices, such as ethics-oriented performance appraisals in which staff were held accountable to it, took note of it, and saw it as having a valued role in corporate activities. In cases where ethics codes and supporting structures such as ethics-dedicated telephone lines and ethic officers exist there is no guarantee that they will regularly interact with the organizational policies and functions or that employees will be accountable to them. Weaver, Treviño, and Cochran suggested that programmes resulting from external pressures could be easily decoupled, marginalized, or disconnected from everyday workings. Ethics communication via memos, reminders, and policy documents are particularly likely to be decoupled, as these are often personally irrelevant and are unlikely to trigger employee attention, being skimmed, filed, and forgotten. Such programmes enhance corporate legitimacy by suggesting conformity whilst affording protection against adverse opinion or public expectations, but do little towards true stakeholder engagement.

Kochan and Rubinstein (2000: 383) suggest that the values and leadership styles of top management are important, but alone are insufficient to explain why other stakeholder interests become influential. In addition, they suggest three conditions need to be met:

1. Potential stakeholders will need to supply critical resources or assets to the organization.
2. The value of the assets supplied must be affected by the fate of the organization so that resource providers can legitimately claim a property right for putting their assets at risk.
3. Stakeholders need to amass sufficient power to challenge the position investors have achieved in the organization.

Current research is at best patchy and is almost entirely constructed from the corporate perspective. Stakeholder surveys should also be undertaken. In addition, other related areas could be assessed. For example, Brenner (1995) attempted to assess how embedded stakeholder management is within business, through an examination of the consistency between widely used management techniques adopted by organizations and stakeholder theory. He examined a number of techniques to establish the extent each

1. recognized the relevance of a diverse set of stakeholders;
2. incorporated stakeholder value, interest, or need;
3. drew upon economic, legal, or moral criteria;
4. balanced stakeholder interests.

Brenner found that total quality management's customer focus is far more stakeholder-focused than capital budgeting analysis. However, this was not an empirical study and hence no connection can be made between the management accounting methods adopted and the stakeholder management processes employed.

6.8 **Stakeholder management issues**

Stakeholder management is complicated by a number of issues in practice. Some are conceptual, such as how to deal with cultural differences. Others are procedural, such as:

- how to approach and proceed with stakeholder management;
- the need to balance conflicting stakeholder interest effectively;
- how to map stakeholders when the boundaries between groups are unclear, when multiple group membership exists, or when strong coalitions between groups are apparent.

6.8.1 THE PROCESS OF STAKEHOLDER MANAGEMENT

Several models suggest ways organizations should approach stakeholder management. Freeman, in his seminal work (see Section 4.2.1), recommended that managers map all possible relationships with current and potential stakeholders and then decide how to devote resources and concentrate effort, in order to cover risks and take account of potential opportunities. Frederick, Post, and Davis (1988) proposed six stages in conducting a stakeholder analysis:

1. Map stakeholder relations.
2. Map stakeholder coalitions.

3. Assess the nature of each stakeholder's interest.
4. Assess the nature of each stakeholder's power.
5. Construct a matrix of stakeholder priorities.
6. Monitor shifting coalitions.

Carroll (1989) suggested stakeholder analysis should be approached by finding answers to questions such as: Who are the stakeholders? What are their interests or claims? What opportunities and threats do they present? What responsibility does the corporation have to each group, whether economic, legal, ethical, or philanthropic? What strategies and/or actions are best designed to accommodate or cope with these challenges or opportunities, i.e. direct or indirect dealing, reactive or proactive response, offensive or defensive posturing? What response should be made: accommodating, negotiating, manipulating, resistance, or a combination?

The identification of stakeholders is not new. GEC identified four stakeholder groups in the 1930s: shareholders, employees, customers, and the general public. Johnson & Johnson recognized four 'strictly business stakeholders' in the 1940s: customers, employees, managers, and shareholders. Recognition of third parties as stakeholders is growing in popularity and the number of stakeholders being explicitly recognized is increasing. Miles and Friedman (2004) recorded an average of six stakeholders for thirty-seven UK corporations surveyed, although this varied according to corporate size (the larger the corporation, the higher the number of stakeholders), sensitivity of sector (higher polluters recognize more stakeholders than moderate polluters), and whether the company was recognized by ethical investment listing indices (listed companies recognized more stakeholders).

Figure 6.3 shows Allied Domecq's stakeholder map as presented on their website in November 2004. This UK brewer and hospitality corporation presents a traditional model based on the early work of Freeman in which the corporation occupies the central hub of the wheel with stakeholders in peripheral positions on the circumference. What is really interesting about this diagram is the sheer number of stakeholders identified: thirty-seven arranged over eight broad categories. Included are several that traditionally would not have been recognized, such as NGOs and pressure groups, categorized under civil society, and the media. This style of stakeholder mapping is the most popular form published by corporations on their Internet sites and corporate social reports. It indicates that theoretical developments such as the recognition that coalitions, the intensity of ties among stakeholder groups, and centrality of the position of certain key stakeholder groups can have significant impacts for stakeholder management (Rowley and Moldoveanu 2003) have yet to impact corporate representations of their stakeholders.

Freeman (1984) acknowledged that the construction of a rational stakeholder map is not an easy task. There is a tendency to oversimplify matters, such as failing to recognize that

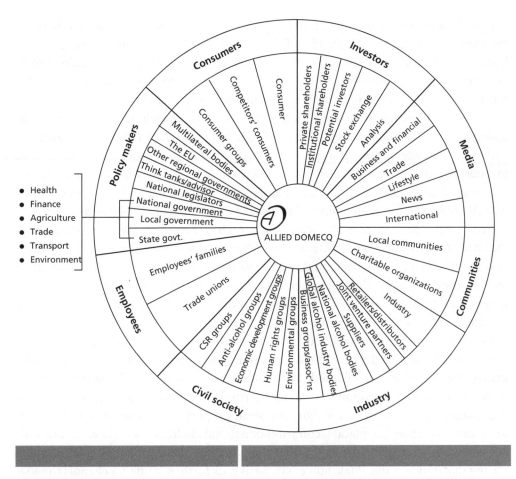

Figure 6.3 Allied Domecq stakeholder map

Source: http://www.allieddomecqplc.com/social-responsibility/report2004/alongside_and_worldwide/stakeholder_map/index.html.

- a stakeholder's stake in the corporation changes over time and with issues;
- some stakeholders may belong to multiple stakeholder groups;
- stakeholder groups are not homogeneous and that each stakeholder has its own agenda, which may come into conflict with group beliefs;
- stakeholder groups can be interconnected via direct coalitions or via independent intermediaries.

The third aspect of stakeholder management, as suggested by Frederick, Post, and Davis (1988) is to assess the nature of each stakeholder's interest. This is a complex matter and encapsulates the compatibility of interests (sets of ideas and material interests) between the corporation and the stakeholder (Friedman and Miles 2002) and hence the likelihood of cooperation (Savage et al. 1991) as well as the legitimacy of the claim and its associated urgency (Mitchell, Agle, and Wood 1997). The higher the potential for business returns, the higher the business impact on stakeholder groups, the more important it is to maintain constructive dialogue with stakeholders. The easier the dialogue becomes, the greater will be the alignment of values between the company and the stakeholder group (Harrison and St John 1996). In practice it may be difficult to assess the nature of the stakeholder's interest due to the dynamics of the relation, the array of issues stakeholders may be interested in pursuing, and the diverse nature of stakeholder groups, with many stakeholders forming multiple stakeholder positions.

Prior to the construction of a stakeholder matrix, Frederick (1998) recommended that the nature of each stakeholder's power should be assessed. This is problematic as power can be evident or latent and direct or indirect. Consulting stakeholders directly is recommended, through direct engagement or survey practices, in order to establish an idea of their priorities and needs. Likewise, it is difficult to monitor changes in shifting coalitions effectively without some form of engagement.

Goodpaster (1991) distinguished between stakeholder analysis and stakeholder synthesis. Stakeholder analysis is morally neutral. The initial stages of the stakeholder management process are followed: stakeholders are identified and analysed but this information does not feed into the strategy formulation process. He suggests it is likely that managers engage in this activity for strategic purposes: to be seen to be doing something in order to placate confrontational stakeholders. Stakeholders are only considered in strategy to the extent that they threaten the overarching goal of maximizing shareholder value. Stakeholder synthesis goes further. It offers a channel to move from stakeholder identification to a practical response. The move from analysis to synthesis is not necessarily ethically driven. It may result from operating under pressure in an imperfect legal environment where antisocial behaviour cannot be avoided, such as for multinational corporations. Stakeholder synthesis represents better practice and is more likely to be associated with higher quality stakeholder management.

6.8.2 BALANCING STAKEHOLDER INTERESTS

Given the number of contractual relations that exist in business, both explicit and implicit, it is likely that all corporations will face a number of mutually exclusive social, ethical, or environmental responsibilities (Unerman and Bennett 2004). In practice this can be problematic because a win-win strategy for one group may force a win-lose or even a lose-lose situation elsewhere (Vignette 6.10).

> **Vignette 6.10** BALANCING STAKEHOLDER INTERESTS AT RAILTRACK (UK)
>
> Railtrack, a privatized railway infrastructure company operating in the UK, came under a lot of scrutiny in the media following a number of fatal train collisions and derailments (Godward 1998). Following the thirty-one fatalities at Ladbroke Grove (5.10.1999), an official report from the regulators criticized Railtrack for inadequate management (ORR 1999). It stated that although there had been considerable investment in the network, there was a decline in the underlying quality of the assets and as a consequence the network was probably in poorer condition than when it was run by the State. Public opinion, fuelled by the media, was that the corporation gave preference to maximizing short-term shareholder value and executive pay over customer and employee safety. Following a further fatal crash at Hatfield (17.10.2000), Railtrack's chairman publicly admitted that there was a conflict between profit and safety: between shareholder value and stakeholder interest (Murray 2001; Wolmar 2001).
>
> The company was liquidated shortly afterwards and replaced with Network Rail, a private company limited by guarantee, without shareholders and hence without dividends. The fundamental change in corporate structure is interesting because it indicates that the regulators did not believe that a satisfactory balancing of stakeholder interests could be achieved under a traditional shareholder, profit-orientated corporate model.

Jensen (2002) and Sternberg (1997) contended that advising management to balance the interests of stakeholders is no advice at all and renders stakeholder theory impractical. Jensen argued that managers who embrace broad, normative strategies to stakeholder management will face irreconcilable conflicts between stakeholder interests in practice. For stakeholder theory to be relevant to business there needs to be guidance about how to achieve equilibrium. For Freeman (1984) the starting point appears to be to examine corporate strategy: to ensure there is congruence between individual stakeholder programmes and the desired strategic direction. There is limited evidence that if strategic focus is not maintained, attempting to accommodate multiple interests can give licence to these groups to substitute their own goals in place of official organizational objectives. In doing so stakeholder managers are both sanctioning and encouraging goal differentiation (Low 1991).

Freeman suggested searching for similarities of actions, interests, and objectives between stakeholder groups or for common elements between strategic programmes in order to integrate them. This is good advice, but he failed to provide any mechanism for deciding which interests to ignore and which to address. Unerman and Bennett (2004) recommended that legal fulfilments be addressed first as there are penalties for failing to do so. Remote stakeholders may be ignored. They concluded that corporations will seek to advance capital hegemony by prioritizing the interests of those stakeholders who exert the greatest economic power and influence over the business (2004: 687). Burton and Dunn (1996: 144) proposed that corporations should 'care enough for the least advantaged stakeholders that they not be harmed; insofar as they are not harmed, privilege those stakeholders with whom you have a close relationship'. Corporations should acknowledge both critical stakeholders as well as those who are most vulnerable to the outcome of the decision when dealing with conflicts of interests.

An economics-based approach may be recommended in which stakeholders are viewed as making contributions to corporate operations and expecting to receive benefits from the corporation as due payment. As corporate survival can only be achieved through satisfaction of its stakeholders, the corporation should identify the extent of the contribution and match this with the necessary inducements. For 'voluntary' stakeholders the basic principle should be mutual benefit. For 'involuntary' stakeholders, who may be affected adversely by pollution or congestion, the core principle should be reduction or avoidance of harm and/or the creation of offsetting benefits. Hosseini and Brenner (1992) also attempted some practical guidance through their construction of a 'stakeholder value and influence matrix'. This consists of a list of stakeholders, their relative influence weights, their value concerns, and the weights that the stakeholder places on them. They proposed that managers derive the relative weights directly from stakeholder surveys. Resources should then be deployed respectively.

Limited research has explored whether conflicting stakeholder interests can be balanced in practice. Ogden and Watson (1999) focused on a UK water company's attempts to balance shareholder and customer interests. Some alignment of apparently conflicting concerns of different stakeholder groups was achieved, but they found little evidence of managers acknowledging the validity of diverse stakeholder interests and attempting to respond to them within a mutually supportive framework. Greenley and Foxall (1997) provided further UK evidence to suggest that the number of companies achieving an effective multiple-stakeholder orientation for impacting performance is low (17 per cent of their sample). The impact of multiple-stakeholder orientation is seemingly moderated by external environment (competitive hostility, ease of market entrance, market turbulence, market growth, and technological change). These 'moderator effects' should be addressed when planning strategies for addressing stakeholders' interests. As companies face greater difficulty in understanding the diversity and complexity of their stakeholders' interests, they need formal approaches. This is an area that would benefit from further research.

For many organizations the development of stakeholder management has been gradual. Consequently, functional departments are assigned responsibility for different stakeholder groups. This may lead to internal inconsistencies and conflict as the organization–stakeholder relation will be a product of the social construction of the individual managers dealing with the relationships and may not explicitly represent the organization values and goals (Miles and Friedman 2004). This is a further issue that should be addressed when attempting to formulate policies or guidelines for managing stakeholder interests in practice.

6.8.3 THE IMPACT OF CULTURES OR SOCIETIES

One would expect different approaches to stakeholder management in different cultures or societies. This chapter has so far focused on Anglo-American profit-seeking organizations, for which stakeholder management is largely voluntary. Other cultures may place less importance on maximizing returns for shareholders. For example, the Japanese notion of trust may lead to the retention of unproductive labour and the German and French social market economies encompass cooperations and social solidarity resulting in worker councils (Barry 1998). The Continental European/Japanese corporation is viewed as an institution with a personality and aspirations. Its objectives encompass a wide range of stakeholders but cannot be equated with any of them. It is perceived as a social institution, with public responsibilities and a proper public interest in defining the way in which it is governed and managed. In contrast the Anglo-American corporation is viewed as a private, rather than a public body, defined by the principal–agent relationship in which busy and numerous shareholders hire executives to run it (Metcalfe 1998). There is scope for stakeholder representation, such as through non-executive directors, but they are still appointed by management. Arguably, for the Anglo-American corporation the only way for stakeholder views to be considered is for them to represent themselves. These differences are discussed in Section 9.4.

The second issue relating to culture is that of cultural relativism. Donaldson and Dunfee addressed this through their ISCT (see Section 3.3.4). They attempted to provide guiding principles for corporations operating in multicultural markets that are faced with conflicting ethical norms. They asked whether it is appropriate to pay employees the average wage rate in developing countries when that rate is lower than the wages paid for similar work in developed countries. Conflicts are easy to deal with in practice if the norm that conflicts with one's community norm also conflicts with the hypernorm. In such circumstances the hypernorm principle should be followed. Problems arise when two legitimate norms emanating from two different communities conflict. They suggested that the creation of priority rules for arbitrating such conflicts must reflect and be consistent with the terms of the macrosocial contract. Where norms have an impact solely within their communities and have no impact on outsiders, they should be allowed to stand, even if they are inconsistent with the norms of other communities.

6.8.4 ISSUE MANAGEMENT

Many corporate controversies revolve around a specific issue that is caused, affected, and managed by stakeholders. Consequently, issue management theory can be fruitful for the stakeholder manager. Marx (1986) suggested that issues develop through four distinct stages (Figure 6.4) with public awareness peaking at the stage of legislative

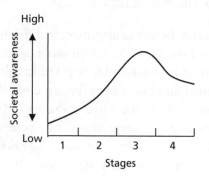

1. Social expectations and awareness
   - Social discussion and debate
   - Interest group attention

2. Political awareness
   - Media attention
   - Legislation initiated
   - Hearings held

3. Legislative engagement
   - Law passed
   - Legal involvement
   - Regulations enacted

4. Social control and litigation
   - Compliance issues
   - Legal conflict
   - Court rulings

Figure 6.4 The four stages of issue development
Source: Marx (1986: 145).

engagement. Weiss (2003) recommended that issue management involves environmental scanning and issue identification, issue analysis, issue ranking and prioritization, issue resolution and strategizing, issue response and implementation, and issue evaluation and monitoring. Which stakeholders are affected by the issue? Who has an interest in the issue? Who is in a position of influence on the issue? Who has expressed an opinion on the issue? Johnson-Cramer et al., writing in Weiss (2003), argued that the critical moment in issue development arises when stakeholders move from latent conflict to manifest conflict. This moment is marked by adoption of external communication channels, such as the legal system or the media, to resolve conflict. The more channels a company provides for mediation, the more likely it will see signs of conflict, but the less likely that conflict will escalate (2003: 154).

Many cases of stakeholder mismanagement have been given substantial press coverage (see Chapter 8). Organizations may publicly protest, sometimes in court, that they had acted responsibly and that the media or pressure groups were ill-informed. The adoption of such tactics can exonerate blame in the eyes of the law, but may lead to an impregnation of half-truths in the minds of the public. The damage to reputation is done and it is incredibly difficult to rebuild. Weiss (2003) recommended that issue management should be tackled by a strategy of reaction through accommodation. The first action following a crisis should be an official response. Great consideration should be given to the nature of this response as it is often the first time that stakeholders gauge how seriously the organization perceives the crisis. This is difficult. Management often lack the information and the time required to analyse the event thoroughly. If mismanaged at this stage, media attention can escalate and an extended period of defence will follow as the organization struggles to protect its reputation. Once the situation has been thoroughly investigated the organization can confirm the extent to which it is responsible for the event. The organization should then refute the claims if it is not responsible, or accept responsibility and address the issue through direct action. It is at this 'accommodation' stage that public pressure and anxiety is addressed. In cases of refutation, organizations should not adopt a high-handed approach, but should take the concerns of the stakeholders seriously, if they are legitimate. Finally organizations should try to fully understand the issue and instigate employee training or an education programme for the public.

□ QUESTIONS/EXERCISES

1 What are the problems involved in assessing the quality of stakeholder management? Consider the annual reports of any two listed companies. How could you decide which one:
  (a) Took stakeholder management more seriously in terms of resources?
  (b) Is more effective?

2 Relate the steps in the ladder of stakeholder engagement concerning the labels given to stakeholder management strategies to the following theoretical models presented in Chapter 4:
  (a) Freeman (1984)
  (b) Friedman and Miles (2002)
  (c) Clarkson (1995).

3 Can you think of additional steps on the ladder of stakeholder engagement?

4 Consider the development of specific functional roles within large organizations. Can you detect a change in emphasis influenced by stakeholder management thinking?
  (a) Can you interpret the change from personnel management to human resource management in these terms?
  (b) Can you interpret the change from purchasing to supply chain management in these terms?

□ NOTES

1 The creation of indices such as Dow Jones Sustainability Index, FTSE4Good Index, KLD's Domini Social Indices, and Calvert Social Index indicate that stock markets are concerned with wider stakeholder issues.

2 Organizations that genuinely engage following unrest with the intention to incorporate stakeholders in earnest in the decision-making process would be categorized as 'involvement', the eighth rung on the ladder.

7 Stakeholder strategies and actions

7.1 Introduction

The literature on stakeholder actions is vast and covers numerous subjects within law (shareholder resolutions and divestitures), marketing (boycotts and strategic alliances), ecology (direct activism and strategic alliances), finance (SRI, constructive dialogue, and screening), and industrial relations (labour strikes). Actions and the literature on those actions long predate the construction of them as *stakeholder* types of actions or strategies. Groups of employees, consumers, or suppliers would rarely have thought of themselves as acting to influence organizations as one group among others, except as against managers and possibly shareholders or the government. These targets of influence would not be seen as other stakeholders, rather as the owners and their representatives of the private corporation, or they would view public-sector bodies as part of the state per se, or as an expression of the will of the political party in power. Consideration of the actions of these groups and their conceptualization as expressions of stakeholder strategies has arisen from the management or the organization side of the organization–stakeholder relation. Traditionally, stakeholder theory has been conceived as a theory of managerial decision-making or of managerial strategy. This is no longer the exclusive view (see Section 5.4.1), but it is still widespread in the literature. As illustrated in Chapters 6 and 9, respectively, the stakeholder concept has affected managerial actions, government policy, and judicial views of the responsibilities of organizations and their managers, though to a lesser degree than recommended in the normative stakeholder literature. Arguably, these factors have influenced stakeholder groups themselves to conceive of their relations with focal organizations in terms of the obligations organizations owe to them, or to the categories of people (and objects) they claim to represent, as part of the general obligations owed by organizations to their stakeholders, or as part of the general health and sustainability of the organization itself. We do not contend that there was a sudden change of view among stakeholder groups, stimulated entirely by how managerial strategy has been changing, but it has clearly been a factor. Nevertheless, as will be seen, particularly in Section 7.5.3 on strategic alliances, recently certain stakeholder groups and their representatives have come to see their actions in terms of broad organization–stakeholder relations in which, as stakeholders, they have common interests with others with whom they traditionally would not have made common cause.

Stakeholders wishing to influence organization behaviour have a wide array of strategies to choose from. Two contributions in particular have informed this area: Frooman (1999) (see Section 4.5.1) considered the form stakeholder action is likely to take and the strategic influences on such action; Rowley and Moldoveanu (2003) (see Section 4.5.2) considered factors that influence whether or not action will be mobilized. Stakeholder mobilization is examined in Section 7.2. Stakeholder strategies to influence organizations are discussed in general terms in Section 7.3. There we take Frooman's two resource-dependent strategies, withholding and usage, and add two further strategies that are not based on resource dependency. We label these voice and damaging strategies. In Sections 7.4–7.7 stakeholder actions are discussed according to these four strategic types. It is impossible in this chapter to present a comprehensive account of stakeholder strategies to influence organizations because of their long history and current complex and elaborate expressions. In Sections 7.4–7.7 we include reference to expressions of stakeholder group actions towards organizations that predate the view of such actions as *stakeholder* actions or expressions of *stakeholder* strategies. We also distinguish indirect from direct strategies. Where evidence exists, the degree of success of various strategies is indicated.

7.2 **Stakeholder mobilization**

Three ways in which mobilization of stakeholders can be important for the effectiveness of stakeholder strategies to influence organizations:

1. Most categories of stakeholders need to be mobilized into groups to take effective action. This may occur as an occasion arises, as in cases of consumer boycotts or neighbourhood campaigns against a proposal for what locals consider inappropriate corporate development in their vicinity. However, mobilization is usually based on prior organizing, and in some cases the establishment of a prior organization is a matter for stakeholder mobilization itself, most clearly in the case of trade unions.

2. Existing groups of stakeholders can be more effective if they are able to mobilize the support of other stakeholder groups, either groups of the same category of stakeholders or different categories.

3. Stakeholder groups can benefit from mobilizing the support of intermediary organizations such as the media, activist groups, and government. On some definitions these are stakeholders themselves, on some they are not.

Many stakeholders that are highly dissatisfied with the manner in which an organization manages relations with them will do nothing about it or will remove themselves from the relation; a few will actively seek to change corporate behaviour. Hirschman (1970) labelled these different strategies loyalty, exit, and voice.[1] Stakeholders can act individually, e.g. by seeking employment elsewhere, selling shares, or embarking on a letter-writing campaign. However, individuals usually lack the ability (power) to change corporate behaviour. They need, therefore, to mobilize others.

In what circumstances may we expect mobilization to occur? Mobilization depends on:

- Identification of an issue.
- Identification of interested parties.
- Technology: availability of techniques of mobilization (telephones, computers, Internet).
- Resources: money, labour, time, access to technology.
- Leadership and organization and emotional commitment.

Mobilization is facilitated by:

- Support intermediaries, such as trade unions, ombudsman, professional associations, and the media.
- Institutional supports, such as AGMs, law courts, and industrial tribunals.
- Dense networks. Dense ties are a form of social capital that enhance mobilization by reducing the costs of identification of individual parties and consensus.
- A history of action. Past actions create mechanisms, which work to build trust, norms, and roles and reduce the costs of subsequent action.

Little has been written about this area of organization–stakeholder relations, with the exception of Rowley and Moldoveanu (2003).[2] Prior to their contribution, the urgency of the issue under consideration felt by stakeholders was considered to be the primary condition driving stakeholders to take action (Mitchell, Agle, and Wood 1997). Rowley and Moldoveanu (2003) argued that urgency fails to explain why some stakeholders pursue lost causes, while others, with an urgent cause and the ability to mobilize, fail to act. For them mobilization is dependent on:

- Interest overlap: the level of interest similarity across stakeholders that belong to multiple stakeholder groups.
- Identity overlap: members who define themselves in terms of their uniqueness are likely to feel greater animosity towards groups with similar identities than towards dissimilar identity groups.

They concluded that mobilization is most likely if interest overlap is high but identity overlap is low, and that the converse is unlikely to provide an impetus for action. Stakeholder mobilization is an underdeveloped area in the literature. We touch on this issue below when discussing types of stakeholder strategies to influence organizations.

7.3 **Stakeholder strategies to influence organizations**

There are numerous strategies that may be employed by stakeholder groups or individuals to attempt to change corporate behaviour. An extensive literature exists. However, Frooman (1999: 194) noted that no one had gone beyond listing and discussing particular strategies or actions in a case study format. The contribution he makes is to construct a strategic model.[3] Stakeholders adopt either usage or withholding strategies, each of which can be executed directly or indirectly, depending on the resource relationship held with the firm. Withholding strategies are 'those where the stakeholder discontinues providing a resource to a firm with the intention of making the firm change certain behavior' (1999: 196). These include consumer boycotts, labour strikes, and other forms of labour actions such as sabotage and 'work to rule', screening and exclusion by investors, and the non-renewal of loans by finance providers. Usage strategies 'are those in which the stakeholder continues to supply a resource, but with strings attached' (1999: 197). These include shareholder and proxy resolutions, strategic alliances, and constructive dialogue. According to Frooman strategies will be adopted indirectly through other agents, when dependence of the organization on stakeholder resources is low.

Many stakeholder actions cannot be classified as either withholding or usage strategies because they do not depend on the direction or degree of resource dependency between organizations and stakeholders. What has been labelled 'modified vendettas', demonstrations, petitions, research, and letter-writing campaigns are actions frequently adopted by agents, such as NGOs or activists, who do not have a resource relationship with the organization to use as leverage. They rarely control any material resources of importance to the organization to withhold or use. On some definitions activists are not stakeholders at all, because they are regarded as lacking legitimacy and/or because they do not have a claim on organization resources (see Table 1.1). However, activists do have the ability to 'affect' the activities of the organization and would therefore count as stakeholders according to the most popular definition from Freeman (1984). Indeed, for some organizations such forms of non-resource-dependent actions can seriously interrupt activities in the short run, and inflict long-term damage. Consequently, these relations need to be managed and a comprehensive model of stakeholder strategies to influence organizations should incorporate them.

We augment Frooman's two strategy types with two further ones: voice and damage. Following Frooman, we note that these strategies can be pursued indirectly or directly. Voice strategies include aiming to inform, educate, or persuade the organization to change. Damage strategies can be pursued through litigation, reputation defamation, demonstrations/events and sabotage. These need have nothing to do with the resource dependency between the organization and the particular stakeholder or stakeholder group undertaking the action.[4]

Voice actions are aimed at convincing managers in focal organizations to change their practices. The forms of argument used can distinguish voice actions. For example, a coordinated letter-writing programme by consumers may appeal to a 'rational' instrumental stakeholder argument, based on a business case. By doing what the stakeholders want, the organization will more easily achieve its aims in terms of sustainability or shareholder value. For example, shoddy goods will ultimately reduce demand for the organization's products; therefore the organization should improve product quality or desist from certain product lines. A second form of argument, a kind of 'moral suasion', may be applied based on normative stakeholder propositions: that it is *right* for the organization to accede to stakeholder request. For example, it is right not to produce goods with misleading labels, even if this is likely to have little effect on sales. A third type of voice argument is one that carries with it the threat of other kinds of action. These can be damage, withholding, or usage types of actions.

Voice actions can also be distinguished by the technologies used and by the degree of threat involved. Different communication channels can be used: publication of research, shareholder resolutions, or personal representations to customer complaints departments. Some of these channels involve more gentle persuasion than others. Research may be directed to general issues, not pointing to particularly bad practices of any one organization. Other actions involve stronger forms of persuasion, such as the Japanese practice of coming to work wearing black armbands to express disapproval of management practices.

The effectiveness of these activities could depend on the direction and degree of resource dependency, but the effectiveness of a letter-writing campaign, customer complaint, or shareholder resolution may have more to do with other factors, such as interest and identity overlap with other stakeholder groups (Rowley and Moldoveanu 2003). Other factors can influence effectiveness:

- How convenient it is for the organization to carry out the request or resolution.
- The likely impact of having acceded to the request on the reputation of the organization.
- The perceived legitimacy of the request or resolution in terms of its connection with existing laws and social institutions, i.e. how likely it is that managers and others in society would agree with the expressed notion of what is 'right'.

It may be that the organization was going to improve the product anyway, or that product design or labelling are technically easy to change. The organization may consider it to be useful for its reputation to admit to problems with product design and to recall the product (as car manufacturers seem to have discovered), or to become a pioneer and niche leader in labelling. But, individuals in the organization may be sympathetic towards the moral argument in favour of labelling. This in itself could sway higher-level management to change their policy. A change in policy may also emerge from recognition of the importance of keeping key staff on board, and using the issue as a way of inspiring staff to get behind the organization's product.

Damaging actions may be interpreted as expressions of frustration and desperation due to the presumption that there are no other ways of getting the organization to change its practices. They may also be the expression of different values, or they may be the extension or development of past conflict. Most would associate this with activists such as environmental NGOs. It is also applicable to employees. According to Hobsbawm (1968) the most famous examples of sabotage in history, Luddism or machine breaking of the early nineteenth century, represented a form of negotiation between farm labourers and employers in the absence of collective means to negotiate during a period when it was illegal to form trade unions (Combination Acts 1799–1824). Brown (1975) provides examples of sabotage. He draws a parallel between organization–employee relations and national warfare in which sabotage is to formal strikes as guerrilla warfare is to set piece battles. Throwing a spanner into the works, or the threat of doing so, can be as effective in getting a foreman to reduce line speeds as formal negotiations or the threat of a strike. Throwing a spanner in the works, like guerrilla warfare, is the choice of those with few resources.

Voice and damage actions in the absence of resource dependency requires imagination, determination, and a willingness at times to flout the law or to carry out activities against the odds. The effectiveness of such actions is influenced by technological factors. A disaffected ex-employee who is able to poison products at a supermarket does not have a resource dependency relation with the organization, nor does he or she need to carry out the strategy indirectly. An individual need not claim harm to himself or herself to initiate a lawsuit against a corporation for flouting the law, say, on tax irregularities, trading with an enemy of the State, or employing under-age children. Greenpeace activists sailing between whalers and whales in full view of the world media can halt a whaling operation more effectively than a strike at the suppliers of harpoons or a boycott of whale meat by consumers in the USA or Europe. It was the novelty, daring, and the high media compatibility of this action that made it effective. It also became an inspiration for other activists.

7.4 Stakeholder withholding strategies

7.4.1 BOYCOTTS

Pressure groups are besieging American companies, politicizing business, and often presenting executives with impossible choices. Consumer boycotts are becoming an epidemic for one simple reason: they work (*The Economist* 1990: 69, cited in Klein, Smith, and John 2002).

Boycotting refers to the act of withholding economic, social, or political participation, as a way of protesting against policies or practices deemed unjust or unfair by the boycotter. However, boycotts are increasingly being used as a form of social control and a mechanism for promoting CSR, rather that a protest on traditional economic grounds such as price rises. A boycott should be differentiated from an individual's decision to refrain from consumption as it involves an organized, collective, non-mandatory refusal to consume (Sen, Gürhan-Canli, and Morwitz 2001). Boycotts can refer to a range of stakeholder withholding strategies, such as the refusal to supply labour (strike) or to finance shares (divestment) but is commonly associated with the refusal to purchase goods or services. Traditionally, consumers that lack power and influence within the political system and therefore cannot use voice or usage strategies carry out boycotts.

Boycotts are more successful when outside support is secured, particularly from the media. The target is seldom the worst offender, but rather a highly visible organization, usually the industry's largest, most profitable company. The 2001 Boycott Bush campaign, for example, objected to the US President Bush's rejection of the Kyoto agreement and the subsequent 'illegal' invasion of Iraq. However, the boycott was targeted at the top 25 Republican Party donors (www.boycottbush.net). Alternatively a progressive company may be targeted on the premise that it might be more easily convinced to reform practices and realign the industrial benchmark compared with a more serious offender.

The past twenty-five years has seen an increase in the number of consumer boycotts globally. In the USA numbers have risen from twenty per annum in 1980 to several hundred by 2004. In the UK there were forty-nine current boycotts in August 2005 (www.ethicalconsumer.org). As Davidson states (1995: 80): '[V]irtually every writer on the subject of boycotts, whether academician or practicing manager, agrees that the use of boycotts by various aggrieved parties or advocacy groups will increase in future years.' This trend has been further accelerated by widespread use of the Internet as a cheap, quick, and effective way of informing millions of consumers of the agenda of boycotting groups.

Boycotts rely on the participation of the general public and are more effective when targets are clear and the public can relate to the issue. The boycott of Barclays Bank over its involvement in South Africa led to Barclays' share of the student market dropping from 27 per cent to 15 per cent (www.ethicalconsumer.org). NGOs are highly skilled in manipulating symbols and gaining media attention in order to move issues up the political agenda. Some issues are more amenable to media attention than others. The effectiveness of the boycotts identified in Vignettes 7.1 and 7.2 illustrates this.

Vignette 7.1 CONSUMER BOYCOTT: HEINZ, RALSTONS PURLINA, AND PILLSBURY

Heinz, Ralstons Purlina, and Pillsbury were subjected to widespread boycotts during 1988–1990 over the production of tinned tuna caught with purse seine or drift nets that simultaneously captured and killed thousands of dolphins. The international boycott of these products resulted in the voluntary acceptance by all three companies to accept only tuna caught by dolphin-friendly methods. This was followed by a US ban on chasing, capturing, and the setting of nets on dolphins leading to a decline in annual deaths by over 90 per cent.

Vignette 7.2 STAKEHOLDER BOYCOTT: NESTLÉ AND THE INTERNATIONAL BABY MILK ACTION NETWORK

Since 1977, Nestlé has been accused of promoting infant formula in developing countries in violation of the World Health Organization's International Code of Marketing of Breast Milk Substitutes. The UN attributes approximately 1.5 million infant deaths per year to the decline in breastfeeding (www.babymilkaction.org). Children die from diarrhoea if the formula is reconstituted with water unfit for drinking and from malnutrition if the formula is excessively diluted due to high poverty levels. The decision to replace breast milk with infant formula can rarely be reversed, so for the price of free samples Nestlé have a captured market. As a result of the boycott, some blatant malpractices have been stopped, such as dressing sales representatives in nurses' uniforms, but Nestlé continues to violate the marketing code. This issue led to Nestlé's exclusion from the FTSE4Good listing in March 2004.

The scale of the Heinz boycott was enormous due to the general public's perception of dolphins as charismatic, appealing, intelligent, and gentle creatures. This issue has been addressed to the extent that practices changed, products are now labelled as 'dolphin friendly', and the boycott lasted a relatively short time. The Nestlé boycott concerned an issue that the media could not regard in a simplistic manner. It has lasted almost three decades, and is still not satisfactorily resolved.

Garrett (1987) identified six factors intrinsic in boycott effectiveness and success:

1. The awareness of consumers.
2. The values of potential consumer participants.
3. The consistency of boycott goals with participant attitudes.
4. The cost of participation.
5. Social pressure.
6. The credibility of the boycott leadership.

Sen, Gürhan-Canli, and Morwitz (2001) also suggested the following:

- Expectation of overall participation;
- Perceived efficacy of individual influence positively contributing to the overall goals of boycott;
- Persuasive pro-boycott communication;
- Product preference and non-substitutability.

Sen, Gürhan-Canli, and Morwitz used reference group theory and argued that consumers are more likely to participate in a boycott if the identity of the boycotters and the nature of their cause are in line with what they perceive to be acceptable social norms. Mobilization is also enhanced if people believe that widespread cooperation by others will occur and that this will make it more likely that the problem will be solved.

Davidson (1995) recognized the importance of understanding boycotts from a stakeholder perspective: How should boycotter claims on the organization be ranked relative to more traditional stakeholders, given that most boycotts stem from activists trying to influence consumers? In trying to understand potential and current boycotting action, it is important to recognize that many boycotters have a sub-agenda, e.g. to educate the public about the boycott issue; to empower and activate individuals; and to provide immediate direct and effective ways to express opinion. The media can provide a valuable service to the boycotters in bringing that message to the public. Friedman (1991) made a distinction between media-orientated boycotts, where a group with limited resources obtain media coverage and merely embarrass its target, and a full-scale boycott aiming to change corporate behaviour and requiring substantial resources.

7.4.2 LABOUR STRIKES AND OTHER FORMS OF LABOUR ACTIONS

Economists have tended to view strikes as irrational because strikes harm both parties and because the outcome is almost invariably a compromise that could have been anticipated and negotiated without the mutual costs of the strike (Hicks 1932: 144–6). However, economists have traditionally assumed information is widely available (if not perfect) and that people are perfectly rational. But power is not easy to assess and the degree of control that each party has over its own resources may only be appraised in its actual exercise (Coser 1956). If we view strikes as a way of bringing employers to the bargaining table by means of mounting a credible threat to their interests (weighed against the costs to the strikers of the action) then we can see that strikes have been an important and very visible strategy for influencing organizations. If we also recognize that strikes are very costly to employees, then we can see that an understanding of the difficulties of acting rationally due to imperfect information and the emotional factors that arise as part of the interaction between parties must both be appreciated in order to understand and learn from this stakeholder influencing activity. These issues are clearly brought out in the analysis by Savage et al. (1991) of stakeholder (mis)management in Vignette 7.3.

Vignette 7.3 LABOUR STRIKES: 1989 EASTERN AIRLINES

Eastern Airlines was in financial trouble and in order to turn it around Frank Lorenzo (chairman of Texas Air Corporation, which acquired Eastern Airlines in 1986) chose to retrench by requiring wage concessions from all employees (around a 28 per cent reduction). The mechanics, baggage handlers, and other ground workers represented by the International Association of Machinists (IAM) union did not agree to this, though unionized pilots and flight attendants had agreed. With the passing of the deadline the IAM went on strike. Eastern planned to use management and other workers to cover for striking IAM members and keep the airline going. However, three days into the strike the Airline Pilots Association (ALPA) voted to support the IAM with a sympathy strike. This led to a virtual close-down of the airline with passengers stranded and travel agencies and tour companies left in the lurch. According to Savage et al. this defection of the pilots and flight attendants was prompted by another aspect of Lorenzo's retrenchment strategy: to sell off assets 'to ensure that a downsized Eastern could survive bankruptcy and reduce the likelihood that striking employees would be able to force concessions from Eastern' (1991: 69). This united unions against the company. More than this, a strong emotional element entered into the process. 'Lorenzo became the villain and striking employees were willing to abandon careers rather than concede to him' (Savage et al. 1991: 70). Savage et al. interpreted Lorenzo's retrenchment policies as misjudgement. They led stakeholders, who had been in the supportive or mixed blessing categories of their model, towards becoming non-supportive stakeholders. In particular they reflected (with the acknowledged benefit of hindsight) that Eastern should have done all in its power to keep pilots and flight attendants from joining the strike. They could have offered a gain-sharing programme in return for wage and work rule concessions to the pilots in particular.

Hicks noted (1932: 146): '[W]eapons grow rusty, and a Union which never strikes may lose the ability to organize a formidable strike, so that its threats become less effective.' Each party to a bargaining process will be at a disadvantage if the other side learns the minimum it is willing to accept. This encourages the kind of process one sees in markets where haggling is common. Thus the normal indeterminacy of power is often compounded by purposeful deception as to power resources by each side. In addition there is a further factor that must be considered in relation to strikes: 'irrational emotion'.[5] The process of grievance, which is likely to characterize the build-up to a strike, and the process of negotiation, which immediately precedes the strike and which continues during a strike, involve emotional elements that do indeed appear to be irrational, or at least errors of judgement with the benefit of hindsight.

There are different types of strikes. The best-known strikes are clearly those that involve a lot of employees and last for a long time. These were coined 'trial of strength' strikes by Hyman (1972: 19–20), who regarded them as the industrial equivalent of war between nations. They involve serious hardship for both sides of the dispute. As these strikes progress, willingness to come to an agreement increases on both sides, as each experiences the costs of the strike, and as the strikes come to demonstrate to each side that the other is not 'bluffing'. Also, as time goes on divisions are likely to appear amongst both sides as those who are more ambivalent about going on strike (the 'doves') become more prominent. In the UK until the 1980s most strikes were spontaneous 'demonstrations in force' (Knowles 1952), where the dispute reflected long-standing grievances and where other means of settling the dispute failed to remedy the grievance. The primary purpose of a demonstration strike is to call attention to the urgency of employee feelings of grievance, and strikers are usually willing to return to work after only a short time for negotiations to be resumed. Such strikes were more frequent in the UK prior to the establishment of legislation during the 1980s requiring formal ballots for strikes to take place (Blyton and Turnbull 1994). Such strikes and other demonstrations of feelings among employees have been common in Japan. Where a strong legal framework exists the distinction between official strikes, sanctioned by law and by official procedures, and unofficial or 'wildcat' strikes (Gouldner 1955) becomes more prominent. Such a situation has long held in the US and more recently has marked the situation in the UK.

In the UK strikes have certainly declined. During the late 1940s and early 1950s the average annual number of working days lost was just under 2 million days. This increased steadily, culminating in a decade of very high strike proneness between 1969 and 1979 when the annual rate of working days lost was on average 12.3 million. Since then the rate has not exceeded 1 million. This may be attributed to the 1988 Employment Act that required unions to hold separate ballots for industrial action if those who are likely to take part in such action have different places of work. The ballot papers must ask whether the member is prepared to take part in action short of a strike as well as a strike. In effect the spontaneous strike has been replaced by the spontaneous threat of a ballot. Most ballots lead to a positive vote for a strike, but few strikes actually occur because the ballot serves the purpose of the strike itself in demonstrating that the employees are not bluffing (Blyton and Turnbull 1994: 280).

Vignette 7.3 demonstrates another aspect of strikes as a stakeholder strategy to influence organizations. Strikes can lead to a situation whereby rational calculation of strategic gain can become clouded by a sense of injustice or by a transgression of other deeply held values. This can lead stakeholders to act in a manner that harms them in order to influence organizations. In this case the IAM and the ALPA decided that they would only settle for a change in ownership of Eastern and they acted to recruit buyers for the airline.

Strikes are the most clearly visible form of action that employees may take to support their bargaining position or to express their dissatisfaction with organization policies and actions. Strikes are not the only form of employee withholding actions and do not form the majority of such acts. Other forms include absenteeism, working to rule, industrial 'accidents', and overtime bans. Some forms of employee action may also be interpreted as damage strategies, such as pilfering and sabotage. Furthermore, strikes may be a relatively inefficient strategy. Strikes are very expensive. An unsuccessful strike can bankrupt a union.

Alternative forms of industrial conflict, such as absenteeism, sabotage, and pilfering (Mars 1982) can be part of an organized, collective, calculative strategy, requiring mobilization. Absenteeism is extremely widespread and may have nothing to do with influencing corporations. People often take a day off without being ill or incapacitated because of fine weather, a birthday, or something else they especially want to do. In organizations there is an 'absence norm' defined by shared understandings about absence legitimacy that is custom and practice by employees and its control by managers. But absence can be highly organized, for example the 'blue flu', when all the offices of the New York Police Department reported sick on the same day. Cook (1990, cited in Blyton and Turnbull 1994: 289) called it the 'silent strike'. In the late 1980s, 5 to 7 per cent of available working time for manual employees in the UK was lost due to absence compared with less than 1 per cent due to strikes.

7.4.3 NEGATIVE INVESTMENT SCREENING AND EXCLUSION

Screening of companies prior to stock market investment according to a list of ethical, environmental, or social criteria is commonly associated with the ethical investment or the SRI market, although not exclusively so. A number of mainstream investment funds now employ SRI style screens, including Prudential Portfolio Managers, one of the UK's largest investment managers (Canham 2001). In addition, SRI style screens have been directed towards customers in a bid to change corporate practice. Pioneer companies such as the CFS (UK) have screened potential customers against their ethical policy since 1992, turning down millions of pounds of potential income per year (£4.39 million in 2002 and £2.88 million in 2003). This is distinct from socially directed investment, also coined ethical banking, which involves targeting community development and social projects for investment whilst waiving most of the interest due. The latter is a debt-based activity, whereas SRI is equity-based.

The most significant increase in screening has resulted from the launch of stock market indices such as the Dow Jones Sustainability Index (USA) and FTSE4Good (UK). These aim to list only companies acting in a socially responsible manner, by assessing them on environmental performance, human rights, social issues, and relations with stakeholders. Companies excluded from an index may feel uncomfortable with the prospect of being branded non-ethical. This is intended to force the investment community to focus more clearly on what constitutes social responsibility, and in turn, put pressure on companies to conform. Such indices have been hailed as a catalyst for change (Dickson 2001). However, it should be noted that this is purely a classification stock market listing and not a withholding strategy per se, unlike direct SRI.

The criteria for screens vary between SRI funds, giving rise to labels such as 'deep green' and 'light green' funds. Typical screens include animal testing, gambling, greenhouse gases, human rights, nature of involvement with the military, nuclear power, ozone-depleting chemicals, political donations, pollution, pornography, Third World issues, tobacco, and the use of tropical hardwood. The SRI sector has historically used screens that are predominantly exclusionist in nature (Lewis and Mackenzie 2000), for example, 'all companies should be excluded from investments that derive any turnover from gambling' (EIRIS 1996). Screening is the predominant SRI tool in the UK, where shareholder activism is restricted by legislation. The manner of the screen selection differs between 'market-led' funds (whereby consumer surveys identify important ethical issues) and deliberative funds (which go to greater lengths to decide what is ethically acceptable or not). Deliberative funds tend to have stricter, more normative, screens as corporate practice is judged using ethical reasoning, not public perception (Mackenzie 1998).

If the primary objective of SRI funds is to promote better CSR, this passive approach to investment lacks urgency and is thought to have minimal impact (Gray, Owen, and Adams 1996: 250). This is particularly so if one considers how small the global SRI sector is in relation to financial markets, despite its recent exponential growth (Friedman and Miles 2001). Many funds select rather loose criteria in order to maintain a large, diverse portfolio from which to select investments. Consequently, poor environmental or social performers may be selected because the practices they employ are marginally better than their peers, possibly signalling that such practice is ethically acceptable. It is interesting to note that one US fund, as a backlash to the SRI movement, uses opposite screens, investing only in unethical companies (Schlegelmilch 1997).

7.5 Stakeholder usage strategies

7.5.1 POSITIVE INVESTMENT SCREENING

Some SRI funds use positive screens, aiming to invest in companies that provide products or services that contribute to social and environmental improvements and/or make sustained efforts to reduce the level of impact of their operations, in addition to using negative screens. Examples of positive screens include beneficial products or services (public transport, health care products) and beneficial practices (implementation of health and safety or labour codes, publication of corporate environmental reports, and the use of a fully integrated environmental management system). This is a usage strategy in that funds specifically indicate their approval for certain corporate practices by publicly including companies that pass their positive screens.

7.5.2 SHAREHOLDER ACTIVISM AND PROXY RESOLUTIONS

Historically, shareholders have adopted a passive stance to investment, relying on stock market mechanisms to evaluate and monitor corporate performance efficiently. Consequently, shareholders did not concern themselves with monitoring managerial actions and generally voted in support of resolutions generated by the corporation except in cases of takeover offers. Shareholder-generated resolutions are becoming an increasingly popular and effective way of raising issues to influence corporate behaviour (Gillan and Starks 2000). A shareholder resolution is a proposal submitted for inclusion in the proxy statement for the AGM for the consideration, via votes, of all ordinary shareholders. Some resolutions are satisfactorily negotiated with management before the AGM and withdrawn from the proxy statement (Lewis and MacKenzie 2000). Popular concerns for resolutions involve corporate governance issues such as board composition and director's pay (Vignette 7.4).

Vignette 7.4 SHAREHOLDER ACTIVISM: DIRECTORS' PAY AT GLAXOSMITHKLINE

GlaxoSmithKline (GSK) is an Anglo-American pharmaceuticals giant. In May 2003 GSK shareholders voted 50.72 per cent against the recommendations of the remuneration committee at the AGM. This was the first time in UK history that a majority shareholder vote had gone against a remuneration committee recommendation at a blue chip company's AGM. Institutional shareholders were opposed to several aspects of the directors' remuneration arrangements, in particular the 'golden parachute' pay package for the CEO, Jean-Pierre Garnier. This severance package, payable even if Garnier was required to resign from poor performance, was estimated to be £22 million. 'Garnier isn't a fat cat . . . he is a cat burglar robbing us blind' (Foley 2003). A revised packaged was approved by 89.49 per cent of the two-thirds of shareholders that voted. If GSK achieved the best share price in the sector for 3 years this would result in a maximum, but unlikely, £18 million remuneration.

The process for lodging a resolution is not standardized globally. Friedman and Miles (2001: 527) noted that in the UK the current legislative framework requires 100 requisitions or a combined shareholding exceeding 5 per cent to lodge a resolution and consequently, the number of resolutions filed is minor. In the USA a $1,000 or 1 per cent shareholding, held for at least one year (Rule 14 (a)(8) of the Securities and Exchange Act 1934), is all that is required and consequently, resolutions are more widely used.

Van Buren and Paul (2000) noted that shareholder activism emerged in the USA in the 1930s. Early resolutions in the USA were predominantly concerned with corporate governance and dividend payout policies. According to the Securities and Exchange Commission (SEC), which regulates proxy voting, social, environmental, or political issues were not legitimate for resolutions. The US Court of Appeal for the District of Columbia Circuit overturned this in 1970. A further boost occurred in the mid-1980s following the revolt of institutional investors against their status as outsiders in corporate governance. They lobbied corporations, government legislators, and the SEC for reform. Thompson and Davis (1997) note that as a direct result, several intermediaries were formed including the United Shareholders Association, the Council of Institutional Investors (CII), Interfaith Centre for Corporate Responsibility (ICCR), and Institutional Shareholder Services. The rise of the Internet has certainly contributed to the increase in resolutions, particularly on bio-engineered foods, global warming, toxic leaks and land use issues, human rights, workplace practices, and political contributions.

Graves, Rehbein, and Waddock (2001) examined US shareholder resolutions for the period 1988–98. They advocated that resolution issues are subject to time and societal context. The most recurrent issue noted related to anti-apartheid (542 resolutions lodged). These peaked in 1990 and faded by 1996 due to the end of the apartheid system in South Africa in 1995. In all twenty-seven categories were captured, the most common ones are listed in Table 7.1 along with those companies that have attracted most resolutions. The average number of resolutions per year was 268. Eighty-two companies were subjected to ten or more resolutions whilst 432 companies received at least one resolution. ICCR's religious and institutional members file over half of these resolutions. Other activists include religious shareholders, labour unions, SRI funds, public pension funds, and unaffiliated individuals.

UK environmental or ethics based resolutions are rare. The first environmental resolution did not occur until 1998 (Vignette 7.5). Other resolutions include:

Table 7.1 US stockholder resolutions: 1988–98

Categories targeted	Number of resolutions	Companies targeted	Number of resolutions
The environment	483	General Electric	80
Human rights	289	General Motors	62
Diversity	253	Philip Morris	55
Tobacco	209	Exxon	43
Labour	198	Chevron	41
Military	173	Dupont De Nemours	40
Governance	101	Pepsico	38
Political action	101	Texaco	38
Energy	100	IBM	36
Abortion/contraception	69	Johnson & Johnson	29
Animal rights	55		
Infant formula	16		

- Oxfam, Friends Ivory Sime, and the Universities Superannuation Scheme's resolution at GSK to lodge dissent over GSK's court action against the South African government over patent rights, which would ultimately restrict access to medicines.
- Greenpeace and Hendersons Global Investors joined forces to attempt to influence British Petroleum (BP) over climate change (McLaren 2004).

Vignette 7.5 SHAREHOLDER RESOLUTIONS: ENVIRONMENTAL RESOLUTION AT SHELL (UK)

In 1998 the first UK environmental resolution was lodged at the AGM of Shell (UK). It questioned Shell's track record on environmental and human rights. The resolution was initiated by Amnesty International (AI) and the World Wide Fund for Nature (WWF) and coordinated by Pensions Investment Research Consultants (PIRC). The resolution received 17 per cent of votes, equivalent to 64.8 million shares (PIRC 1999), with support from 18 pension funds, 5 religious institutional funds, and 1 academic fund (Marinetto 1998). This was insufficient to pass the resolution but Shell did address the issues raised as a direct consequence of events.

Voting is increasing in the UK as industry organizations such as the Institutional Shareholder's Committee, the UK Social Investment Forum (UKSIF), and PIRC lobby members and the financial community to exercise voting rights. Gribben and Faruk's survey (2004) indicated that current voting levels for environmental and social resolutions are promising, with 39 per cent of the 130 UK funds surveyed exercising voting rights regularly and an additional 31 per cent occasionally voting. In addition, 56 per cent of funds stated they would exercise voting rights more in the future.

Friedman and Miles (2001) suggested that the rise in UK shareholder activism is a result of a wider social movement. Following the Pensions Review of the late 1990s rules were issued requiring pension schemes to declare the extent to which ethical, environmental, and social issues are taken into account in their investment decisions. The preferred approach that emerged was one of active engagement: to use ownership to exercise influence over corporate behaviour (Vignette 7.6). Mathieu (2000) surveyed UK pension funds to determine the impact of the pension review and found that funds representing 6 per cent of the all-share index specifically incorporate SRI policies into their investment strategies, either by giving specific requests to their fund managers (81 per cent) or via direct corporate engagement (19 per cent). There was a clear distinction between company and local authority pension funds, with the former generally delegating SRI screening to their fund manager and the latter favouring direct engagement. Targett (2000) predicted that those funds that had failed to act were likely to come under increasing pressure from activist groups. One thing is evident, both in the UK and the USA: the mobilization of activity has been crucially assisted by the creation, development, and expansion of shareholder activist organizations.

Vignette 7.6 SHAREHOLDER VOTING: MORLEY INVESTMENTS, THE ASSOCIATION OF BRITISH INSURERS, AND CALIFORNIA PUBLIC EMPLOYEES' RETIREMENT SYSTEM

Morley Investments controls over £100 billion of assets (2.5 per cent of the UK all-share index). In April 2001 Morley declared that it would vote against the approval of the AR&A of any FTSE-100 company not including a 'comprehensive environmental report' and it would abstain from investing in all FTSE-250 high-risk sector companies (oil and gas, electricity, chemicals, automobiles, construction, health care, and pharmaceuticals) that failed to report (Skorecki 2001).

The Association of British Insurers (ABI) published disclosure guidelines in 2001 in an attempt to persuade companies to increase transparency. The guidelines were modelled on SRI principles. The ABI monitor compliance and encourage investors to use their votes at AGMs if disclosure standards are not met. ABI's members control £1,000 billion of assets, representing 25 per cent of the UK all-share index.

In the USA, the California Public Employees' Retirement System (CalPERS) has played a leading role in promoting better corporate governance and higher proxy votes for shareholder resolutions (Van Buren and Paul 2000).

Thompson (1988) suggests that resolutions are important mechanisms in that:

1. They provide an opportunity for 'outsiders' to voice concerns directly to the board of directors, providing an arena for discussion that may otherwise not exist. We note that this use of shareholder resolution is clearly a voice, not a usage strategy, e.g. an NGO may purchase a single share in order to gain 'legitimate' access to the AGM.

2. The process lends legitimacy to the particular social and political issues at stake.

3. Resolutions help promote corporate accountability by providing a means for shareholders to affect the corporate decision-making process.

4. The submission of a resolution is often an easy way for proponents to gain access to the media and public attention.

Legitimacy is also afforded to stakeholders raising the resolution, as they are engaging with the corporation as shareholders and not, for example, as an NGO, activist, or member of the local community. Resolutions are inexpensive relative to alternative strategies, as the corporation bears the cost of including the shareholder resolution in the annual proxy statement, distributing this to all shareholders and providing the venue for the AGM. However, this depends on the legislative framework in place. For example, resolutions in the UK are expensive to coordinate due to the high thresholds required for submission.

There are limitations to shareholder activism as an influencing strategy:

1. The legislative framework may limit the content of resolutions. In the USA resolutions are restricted to the 'ordinary business' of a company.

2. Even if a resolution is passed by a majority vote, it will only become corporate policy with management approval.

3. Shareholder activism operates on an incremental level, chipping away at step changes, rather than as a radical overhaul of policy. This is partially due to legal restrictions governing resubmissions of failed resolutions, which restrict the number of resolutions submitted per activist group to one per year.

Success of shareholder activism at changing corporate behaviour is mixed. On the downside, there has been a lack of technical wins (Karpoff, Malatesta, and Walking, 1996; Wahal 1996). Voting has historically been poor (albeit increasing) as it is notoriously difficult to mobilize shareholders, particularly institutional funds, behind social and political campaigns (Marinetto 1998). Thompson and Davis (1997) report an average vote of 24 per cent for US resolutions. The Social Investment Forum (1997) makes an important point, which is often missed in the literature: if a shareholder fails to vote at an AGM, the proxy vote defaults to management. Therefore, even relatively low levels of voting will indicate real interest among shareholders. One could argue that withdrawal of resolutions signals the biggest success for shareholder activists as negotiation has culminated in satisfaction for both parties. With increased numbers of resolutions per annum, shareholders become more willing to approach companies directly with their concerns. The process becomes embedded. Thompson and Davis (1997: 155) argued that shareholders have been credited by the media for shake-ups at companies such as IBM, American Express, Kodak, and General Motors. In addition limited empirical support is purported by Strickland, Wiles, and Zenner (1996) and Bizjak and Marquette (1998). Gillan and Starks (2000) concluded that non-coordinated activism and proposals sponsored by gadflies (individual investors) are relatively ineffective, attracting few votes, whereas coordinated or sponsored proposals received higher votes, on average 35 per cent, which although not a majority does afford leverage for stakeholder dialogue.

7.5.3 STAKEHOLDER–ORGANIZATION ALLIANCES

Strategic alliances between organizations and suppliers, distributors, or competitors are certainly not a new phenomenon and the practice long predates the stakeholder literature. They occur when independent organizations come together to develop a common project of mutual benefit. Organizations could be direct competitors, be in a supplier relationship, or have no relationship prior to the alliance. For Frooman (1999) alliances are direct usage strategies and would be expected where a strong mutual resource dependency exists. For Savage et al. (1991) alliances are expected to result from stakeholders with a high potential for threat along with high potential for cooperation.

An unexpected form of strategic alliance has arisen since the late 1980s between companies and environmental NGOs. Traditionally, environmental groups have pursued direct action strategies. Friedman and Miles (2002) suggested marginal NGOs historically had contingent relationships with corporations marked by incompatible material interests and ideological views. Such strategies may be associated with 'second wave environmentalism', which emerged in the 1960s as part of the counterculture and anti-Vietnam war movements, stimulated by Rachel Carson's book *The Silent Spring* (1962) (which criticized the effects of widespread use of pesticides). Second-wave environmentalism was particularly aimed at lobbying for legislation and regulation to control environmental effects of corporate activities. From the mid-1980s a new 'third wave environmentalism' emerged, which was based on a solutions ethic and which embraced socio-economic concerns as well as environmental ones. Corporate–environmental NGO partnerships are the strategic expression of third-wave environmentalism according to Murphy and Bendell (1997).

The causes of third-wave environmentalism follow from changes to both the interests and ideas of environmental groups on the one hand and of certain businesses on the other. We may trace these changes by considering the factors listed in Tables 7.2 and 7.3 which have influenced both sides of the organization–stakeholder relationship.

One way of seeing the causes of the growing number of direct partnerships between large private-sector corporations and environmental NGOs is that environmental groups have become disappointed in governments as intermediaries in support of their claims for corporations to desist from activities linked to environmental degradation. Second-wave environmentalism focused on direct action to bring corporate deviants to the attention of the general public and to use this to support lobbying for legislation or regulation that would curb corporate activity. However, as noted in

Table 7.2 Factors influencing environment and business groups

Influencing environmental groups	Influencing business groups
Affecting material interests	Affecting material interests
• Increased financial resources	• Resource depletion • Savings opportunities • Consumer concerns
Affecting ideas	Affecting ideas
• Greater credibility, power, and responsibility • Cry-wolf fatigue • Increased global networking and knowledge	• New product development opportunities • Threat of legislation
Affecting the negotiation process	Affecting the negotiation process
• Internal demographics of environmental groups • Backlash against environmental protection legislation	• Staff values and concerns

Table 7.3 Factors facilitating international, regional, and grass-roots campaigns

Level	What is particularly helpful?
International	• Existence of international codes, legislation, and conventions • Active international campaign • Consumer activism • Independent monitoring
National or regional	• Progressive legislation upholding rights • Legal pressure points • History of social activism and NGO activity • Aware population • Labelling system • Independent monitoring
Grassroots	• Active civil society organizations • Aware population • Active individuals

Source: Adapted from Chapman and Fisher (2000: 157).

Table 7.2, one problem with this strategy has been a fatigue on the part of the public with claims of imminent environmental disaster. Another is the development of a green backlash, which has been particularly active in developing an anti-environmental legislation lobby (Rowell 1996; Vaughan Switzer 1997). In addition, the tremendous fillip that well-publicized environmental disasters of the 1980s gave to certain environmental NGOs both led to a perceived fiduciary responsibility to show how money donated to them has led to environmental improvements and allowed them to hire the kind of people who not only are able to support those fiduciary responsibilities, but also are familiar with (and in some cases sympathetic to) the language and concerns of major corporations. These factors have contributed to more openness on the part of some key NGOs (WWF and Greenpeace in particular) towards a 'solutions' agenda and towards NGOs working directly with major corporations on solutions. On the other hand, major corporations have been both pushed and pulled in the same direction. They have been pushed by the power of negative publicity on their customers and by rising resource prices. They have been pulled by the new market opportunities green consumption can provide, both in terms of a competitive advantage to having their products endorsed by respectable environmental groups and by developing new green products or green versions of standard products.

Murphy and Bendell (1997) provided many examples of corporate–environmental NGO partnerships. They classified alliances according to three overlapping criteria:

1. Which part of the business is affected.
2. The primary role played by the NGO, whether merely endorsement or more involvement in the development and implementation of products.

3. The number of environmental, ethical, and social issues addressed, whether single or multiple, or total quality analysis. With respect to the part of the business that is affected, alliances can be subcategorized according to whether this relates to management processes, strategic projects, or product performance.

Management processes such as environmental management systems, supply chain management, or environmental auditing have been affected. Examples include the Oregon Growth Management Initiative (US) (MEB 1995), Hoover plc and Groundwork (UK) (Murphy and Bendell 1997:161), Dow Europe and European Partners for the Environment (EPE 1997), and the WWF-UK Timber Group (Vignette 7.7).

Vignette 7.7 STRATEGIC ALLIANCE: WWF-UK TIMBER GROUP

The WWF-UK and the UK do-it-yourself retailing company B&Q set up a management process-oriented partnership in mid-1991 aimed at creating a sustainable world tropical timber market. Other companies, such as pulp and paper buyers, joined together with community forestry groups and forest product certification organizations to create the Forest Stewardship Council in 1993. This concerns itself more broadly to all aspects of the world timber trade, rather than merely tropical rainforest supplies. Much of the bite of the initiative has been for timber retailers to force their suppliers to change towards using sustainable sources. The leverage applied was the promise of secured orders and a long-term relation with the suppliers (see Murphy and Bendell 1997: ch. 4).

Strategic projects such as the development of new mechanisms to assist towards sustainability have emerged. Such partnerships do not involve internal management processes of corporations. Examples include the 1996 partnership of WWF-International and Unilever to establish the Marine Stewardship Council (WWF-International 1996) and the 1986 Timber/Fish/Wildlife Agreement for Washington State (USA) (Vignette 7.8).

Vignette 7.8 STRATEGIC ALLIANCE: TIMBER/FISH/WILDLIFE AGREEMENT FOR WASHINGTON STATE (USA)

This strategic alliance brought together natural resource management agencies, American Indian groups, timber companies, and environmentalists who had been in conflict for many years. Their main concern related to logging and its effect on the local environment, particularly salmon fisheries. Through a mediation company the many organizations involved, which had only interacted through the courts up to then, were brought together to hammer out the agreement (Lee 1993).

Product performance alliances have been formed involving either the development of new products or the endorsement of existing products by an environmental agency or group. These alliances focus on delivering product improvements or higher sales. Examples include the unsuccessful Pollution Probe endorsement of Loblaws 'green' products (see Vignette 8.6) and the Greenpeace investment to develop the environmentally efficient 'Renault Twingo Smiley' car (Murphy and Bendell 1997: 180–1).

Even partnerships that are more transparent than the Pollution Probe/Loblaws case, have been criticized because they can lead to loss of independence on the part of environmental groups and so limit their ability to criticize their partners for activities outside the specific partnership agreement. Also it is difficult to evaluate the actual impact of these initiatives on the environment and to judge the opportunity costs involved for environmental groups, which could be using their limited resources in other ways. In addition, there is a general concern that market-based solutions to environmental and social problems lead to commodification of nature and a skewing of the kinds of projects that get developed to ones for which there is a market, thereby reflecting the value of products and processes to society as consumers only. For example, only those wildernesses that can pay their way get preserved (Murphy and Bendell 1997: 228–35). These concerns have led to splits among and within environmental groups.

7.5.4 DIVESTITURES

Divestiture refers to the forced sale by antitrust authorities of shareholdings in one company that are owned by another, and the forced break-up of a single firm. The divestiture of AT&T, the US Telecoms giant, is cited as the 'most sweeping divestiture case in history' (O'Brien 1986). According to O'Brien there are two grounds for divestiture: to break up an unsatisfactory corporate structure that has disproportionate market concentration, usually defined by size or profitability; and to control anti-competitive conduct, such as price fixing, which, it is judged, cannot be dealt with by regulation (1986: 167). In the UK the powers to order divestitures stem from the 1965 Monopolies and Mergers Act and the 1973 Fair Trading Act and require approval at both houses of parliament. In the USA antitrust laws have a longer history, being first introduced by the Sherman Antitrust Act of 1890. Divestitures are deemed to be in the interest of a number of stakeholders, notably consumers, suppliers, and employees. However, they can be detrimental to shareholders in that the ability to generate superprofits is essentially removed. Also, the administration of a divestiture can be extremely costly. Frooman put this forward as an example of an indirect usage strategy, associated with 'firm power', due to the monopolistic position that divestiture targets are in. Divestiture is a highly restricted stakeholder strategy to influence corporate behaviour. It focuses explicitly on anti-competitive behaviour and is only available indirectly, through lobbying government, and is only applicable to a handful of corporations.

7.6 **Voice strategies**

7.6.1 CONSTRUCTIVE DIALOGUE

Progressive SRI funds and a number of institutional investors, such as pension funds, employ constructive dialogue. The fund purchases shares in the target corporation and uses the power and legitimacy gained from investment to actively lobby from within. This is a voice strategy. If enough shares are purchased the threat of divestment if practice is not changed turns it into a withholding strategy, or at least a threatened withholding strategy. This strategy is most effectively aimed at mid-cap companies where a significant shareholding can be secured.

Miles, Hammond, and Friedman (2002: 43) state that UK SRI funds engage over a range of issues including environmental impact and policy, corporate environmental and ethical reporting, and ethical policy. They argue that this predominantly takes the form of information requests via letters, questionnaires, and telephone conversations, although there is some evidence of shareholder activism and face-to-face meetings.

Engagement by UK SRI funds is evolving, following the Pensions Review's ethical disclosure policy for all UK pension funds. As a direct response from the SRI sector, a number of 'best of sector' engagement funds have emerged designed to seek out companies that are making headway on environmental or social issues compared with their peers, e.g. NPI's social index and Friends Provident's 'Responsible Engagement Overlap'. These funds enable SRI fund managers to invest in a standard portfolio with a commitment to engage on environmental and social issues. A number of mainstream funds have introduced policies of active engagement with companies on social, ethical, and environmental issues. In addition, new institutional supports have emerged, such as PIRC's Corporate Responsibility Service and EIRIS' Ethical Portfolio Manager, which provide information and support to clients pursuing practical and effective SRI policies. Constructive dialogue is potentially a more effective influencing strategy than passive approaches such as screening. This is predominantly concerned with first-step changes in corporate behaviour, i.e. making small adjustments to existing practice without fundamentally questioning underlying values (Levy and Merry 1986).

7.6.2 LETTER-WRITING CAMPAIGNS

Arguably, letter-writing campaigns are the most basic technique that a stakeholder can adopt in attempts to influence corporate behaviour. These may relate to other strategies, such as an SRI fund manager writing to a corporation about the environmental impact of certain practices, with a view that if the corporation is willing to engage, the SRI fund would be willing to invest. They may form stand-alone strategies. In situations where the stakeholder has no other access to the corporation a letter-writing campaign may be employed. There is no guarantee that the corporation will respond, never mind engage over the matter of concern. The chances of gaining a response increase if:

1. the letter is personally addressed to the appropriate corporate officer.
2. the letter is written in business language and raises concerns that are of interest to the corporation.

A campaigner may passionately want to save the environment, but if the agenda is couched in a highly political, exceedingly technical, or radical fashion, the letter is likely to be dismissed on the grounds of irrelevance or illegitimacy. There is little written about letter-writing campaigns (Frooman 1999 cites Smith and Cooper-Martin 1997) and the authors are aware of no research that explores either the extent to which this strategy is employed or its effectiveness. Vignette 7.9 demonstrates (with humour) the lengths to which a company may engage with an individual stakeholder over issues that may be regarded as trivial and possibly illegitimate.

Vignette 7.9 LETTER WRITING AS A VOICE STRATEGY: DEBENHAMS (UK) AND ROBIN COOPER

In the book *The Timewaster Letters* (Cooper 2004) the following letter appears along with the eventual response from the large retail company.

Original letter

Dear Sir/Madam,

I am writing to you for help.

I visited your store last Saturday 28th February. Whilst in the linen department, browsing at duvet covers, I appear to have lost the lace to my right shoe (brogue).

I wonder if anyone handed it in? It's black, about two years old and roughly 25 centimetres long.

Perhaps you have it on close circuit camera? My wife has told me not to hold out too much hope for my missing lace and even suggested buying another one, but it's just not the same is it?

I would be most grateful if you could write back to me ASAP and tell me one way or the other if you have it or not. That way you can put me out of my misery and I can begin to carry on with my life.

I look forward to your reply.

Yours faithfully

. . .

Eventual response

Dear Mr Cooper,

Thank you once again for your correspondence regarding your lost shoe lace.

(contd.)

Vignette 7.9 (*contd.*)

I understand that the loss is causing you great concern and therefore of course I would like to do all that is possible to assist you in bringing this matter to a close.

I have rechecked the linen department this morning unfortunately without success. Due to our high cleaning standards I am very confident that your shoe lace is not anywhere in our store.

However if you would like to come in and look of course you are welcome to do so. Regrettably I cannot close the department for half an hour while the store is open however if you would like to search without interruption I would be happy to assist you when the store is closed. If you would like to let me know a date we can meet at the information desk on the ground floor shortly before we close at 8.00 PM. When we have cleared the store myself or a member of the team will be happy to escort you around. Unfortunately we will not be able to let any dogs except registered guide dogs into the store. May I suggest that the sooner you are able to come in the higher the chance of success.

I look forward to hearing from you if this offer is acceptable.

Yours sincerely

. . . .

7.6.3 OTHER VOICE STRATEGIES

Many organizations have dedicated complaints departments, or at least telephone lines dedicated to recording customer complaints. Suggestion boxes, quality circles, and other procedures are commonly available for employees to express their opinions on organization practices. Many of these procedures were instituted by management, but in response to informal stakeholder pressure.

7.7 **Damage strategies**

7.7.1 INTRODUCTION

Certain activists, particularly environmental activists, carry out confrontational actions aimed directly at preventing organizations from continuing to operate. These actions need not rely on withholding resources the activists own or control on which the organization depends. Rather they rely on the ability to act in such a way that leads to the operation of the organization being disrupted or damaged. In a sense these actions rely on resource dependency, but not resource dependency between activists and the organization. Rather, they exploit the vulnerability of the resource and, more accurately, vulnerability of the methods used to transport or transform resources that are inherent in the operation of the focal organization. We classify these actions as damage strategies.

Damage strategies are usually regarded by outside observers as wasteful. In game theory they may be described as playing strictly negative-sum games whereby the pay-offs to the players in any outcome add up to a negative amount. What one player gains, the other loses, but also both lose in that there are costs to playing the game.[6] This is the situation described above in relation to strikes (Section 7.4.2) which are often considered to be irrational in the sense of the result being one where it is likely that both parties will lose.

Damage actions pursued by individuals, which may be part of a grudge against an organization for past actions, such as firing the individual or perceived neglect in relation to health or safety issues, may be only loosely regarded as reflecting a strategy. Such actions are discussed in Section 7.7.4. Sometimes actions originally part of a campaign based on a withholding or usage strategy may spill over into a damage strategy if withholding or usage proves ineffective. Such a situation is described in Section 7.7.2. However, some damaging actions are part of a long-term strategy, as in the case of organized groups of activists such as Greenpeace.

In the short run such NGOs appear to be playing a strictly negative-sum game. They inflict a cost on a focal organization that also costs the NGO resources. Ideally, the NGO would want to inflict maximum damage, or at least draw maximum attention from those running the organization, with as little cost to the NGO as possible. Here is where the techniques employed in the action undertaken and particularly the impact of the action on the media and general public that may have a strong resource relation with the organization (such as consumers or shareholders or governments) are important influences on the effectiveness of the action. In the long run the aim is to change the behaviour of all similar organizations, not just the targeted one. The aim may be a complete cessation of certain focal organization activities, and in some cases a cessation of all existing focal organization activities and those of all similar organizations. This positive pay-off to the NGO comes from the satisfaction of ethical aims of the activists and from the growth in membership of the NGO predicated on the publicity achieved for particular actions and for the success of the overall campaign.

Damage strategies are not well understood in the literature or among managers of focal organizations. Public Relations theory advocates compatible ground rules for play and symmetric two-way communication, and the resolution of conflict through negotiation and compromise (Pearson 1989). In the absence of power, NGOs are driven to use asymmetrical communication to try to dominate the communication environment. At the base of these confrontations are fundamental value conflicts. Hainsworth (1990) and Grunig and Grunig (1989) stated that this is a function of organizational type and culture, dictated by the worldview of constituents. Sturdivant (1979) and Fineman and Clark (1996) suggested there is a deep ideological divide between business and environmental campaigners. Business executives view NGOs as 'too emotional', characterized by 'lack of balance' and possessing 'commercial naivety'. They find it strange that campaigners use 'moral language' (Fineman and Clark 1996: 719).

7.7.2 BOYCOTTS AS A DAMAGE STRATEGY

If the media is used to mobilize stakeholder participation in a boycott, this may be interpreted as enhancing the boycott as a withholding strategy. However, if the media is called upon to get an organization to change its behaviour by discrediting its behaviour or through tarnishing its overall corporate image, then we would interpret this as turning the boycott into a damage strategy.

The cost of boycott to corporations can be substantial. This not only includes lost sales but also diverted management time to deal with the issues, increased advertising expenditure, and hiring PR experts for brand enhancement. Wah (1998) calculated that the US boycott of PepsiCo instigated due to its operations in Burma (a country with poor human rights practices) cost PepsiCo more than it earned from Burmese operations. PepsiCo eventually pulled out of Burma. There are also intangible costs of boycotts associated with low employee morale during and after the boycott period and perceived difficulties in employing top employees at a company with a reputation for being targeted by boycotters.

7.7.3 DIRECT ACTIVISM

For lack of a better metaphor, I would compare us to fleas. As NGOs, we are minuscule political animals, sometimes difficult to locate, but who bite and irritate. In other words, we annoy the established elephantine system. As we annoy it, we make it walk or move itself, even if it is to fight us.... We are there where we are least expected, and we attack without warning. (Grzybowski 2000: 441)

Direct activism is largely associated with pressure groups. The image of the pressure groups and NGOs range from grass-roots coalitions of eco-warriors to scientific societies and established multinationals that employ technical experts. Taking the diversity of structure, expertise, and function of NGOs, one would also expect them to deploy a variety of influencing strategies. These can be arranged along a continuum ranging from research, community education, conservative persuasion, lobbying, moral exhortation, litigation, and direct confrontation to the most extreme, sabotage (Fineman and Clark 1996; Jasanoff 1997). We would classify the first five of these as voice actions and only the last three as damage strategies.

The NGO–organization relation has predominantly been characterized as one of acrimony and dissent, resulting in impasse and frustration. The effectiveness of NGO action rarely depends on a single action. Chapman and Fisher (2000) stated that campaigns are complex, dynamic, and cannot be grasped at any one time in their entirety: they cannot be thought of as linear, methodical, or logical sequences. Campaigns often have unclear foundations. They can be the result of a major disaster, a personal experience, or commitment, or evolve from other campaigns. In turn campaigns may evolve into new campaigns. The emphasis of the campaign may change and the focus and scope may grow, narrow, or widen throughout the campaign. Campaigns do not always focus on industry, but may do so at a particular point in time to deliver a message.

Post (1978) found a discernible life cycle pattern of issue evolution comprising four stages:

1. Issues arise because of a hiatus between public expectation and corporate performance.
2. This is followed by a period of political controversy as the issue is politicized.
3. The next stage involves legislative action.
4. This is followed by litigation.

Bigelow, Fahey, and Mahon (1991, 1993) proposed stages of issue emergence, interpretation, positioning, and resolution. Graves, Rehbein, and Waddock (2001) suggested several evolution patterns (normal, unidirectional, recursive) of issues.

The increased scale and frequency of direct actions has been attributed to wider social movements such as those involving civil rights, consumerism, antiwar, and ecology, which 'unleashed a spirit of changing expectations and a willingness to engage in confrontation tactics to produce change' (Sturdivant 1979: 53). There are clear examples of NGO victories, such as Greenpeace's action against Shell over the Brent Spar oil rig, yet the majority of assaults on corporations merely lead to the arrest of activists, often for trespassing, and resultant fines for NGOs (Vignette 7.10).

Vignette 7.10 DIRECT ACTIVISM: GREENPEACE AND DU PONT

Between 1988 and 1990 Greenpeace targeted Du Pont, the world's largest manufacturer of CFCs. CFCs react with the Sun's ultraviolet radiation and release chlorine into the atmosphere, depleting the ozone layer. Greenpeace appeared to pursue a zero-sum or a negative-sum strategy dictated by the nature of its members as 'high-involvement, information-seeking publics'; the support of whom Greenpeace is dependent upon for maintaining its reputation as an organization that will not concede and the need to attract a passive public's attention. The strategy involved extreme actions, unilateral demands, intolerance of compromise, biased manipulation of issues, use of flamboyant symbols, and highly visible actions to draw media attention. Greenpeace appeared to be playing incompatible games that rule out mutual cooperation and undermined all opportunities for conflict resolution.

Du Pont appeared to follow a positive-sum model. On one hand it punished non-compliant behaviour, such as charging activists with trespass following demonstrations. Simultaneously, it released pacifying signals indirectly through the media to Greenpeace that the company was working on environmental solutions. In doing this it made Greenpeace an outsider to its own audience, it aligned itself to mainstream environmentalism and portrayed Greenpeace as radicals who were out of step with the mainstream. Consequently, the public identified with Du Pont.

(contd.)

Vignette 7.10 (*contd.*)

The campaign resulted in an impasse. Du Pont, with superior power and local support, refused to change policies. Although Greenpeace was successful in grabbing media attention, the coverage was neither extensive nor sympathetic. Disjunction occurred as each party was driven by different constituencies with incompatible needs and motives. Murphy and Dee (1992) suggested that the game was not concerned with resolving conflict but was about mobilizing attention from particular audiences, a goal that made prolonged conflict a central strategy. They argued that Greenpeace probably misjudged how Du Pont would react, expecting a similar zero-sum approach, which would likely result in extreme conflict that could only be resolved by an outside arbitrator, such as a legislator: an outcome that would have been detrimental to Du Pont.

Why are some strategies more successful than others? Based on game theory, Axelrod (1984) stated that vindictive strategies do well against other vindictive strategies at the start of conflict. As conflict matures, cooperative or 'tit for tat' strategies are more successful. Tit-for-tat strategists follow these rules. They cooperate at the first encounter (or 'play' of a game) and then duplicate their opponent/partner's previous moves in all subsequent encounters. Tit-for-tat strategists are therefore characterized by initial trust, provocability, and forgiveness. Using computer simulations, Axelrod found that tit-for-tat strategists produce higher pay-offs than all others. They tend to induce a regime of mutual cooperation after a short number of encounters. Jones (1995) provided a range of reasons why mutual cooperation should produce higher returns for firms in market situations (see Section 4.2.4).

An effective campaign relies heavily on public participation and the mobilization of value-based action. Exchange theorists recognize that power is gained through the control of valuable resources and that the capacity and capability to form coalitions is a prerequisite for power. For Tilly (1978), there are four factors that determine effective action. First, it relates to the stability of the political structure: the more stable the system the harder it is to challenge the status. Second, it is easier to gain public support if interests are homogeneous, easily recognizable, and small in number. Third, it is easier to transform individual concerns into collective action if the social infrastructure has established social ties and existing networks. Fourth, mobilization is a prerequisite to success. Mobilization can be enhanced by adopting a narrow focus on issues and identifying a clear opponent, as this enhances communication. However, it should be noted that adopting a narrow focus can oversimplify the campaign and distract from the wider issues and can make involvement of grass roots harder. Individual champions play an important role in motivating others. 'Heroes and heroines are created whose actions and exploits become mythologized, and so serve to motivate supporters' (Chapman and Fisher 2000). This is enhanced by the skill of many NGOs in manipulating symbols and grabbing media attention to extend the availability of symbolic forms to a wider audience. The use of symbols can reduce the perceived legitimacy of the NGO in the eyes of the organization as it can be viewed as replacing reason with emotion (Jasanoff

1997). Chapman and Fisher (2000) list factors facilitating campaigns at the international, national, or grass-roots levels (Table 7.2).

It is unlikely that a single organization can effectively campaign at grass-roots, regional, national, and international levels. Each level has different arenas for action and requires different attitudes, strategies, and different skills. Although there can be conflict arising from different approaches, collaborations with other organizations are often necessary to move the agenda forward.

7.7.4 MODIFIED VENDETTAS

Direct activism has been labelled as 'modified vendettas' by Shipp (1987) and Corlett (1989). A vendetta is a family blood feud, usually of hereditary character. Feud is defined in the *Oxford English Dictionary* as:

A state of bitter and lasting hostility; especially such a state existing between two families, tribes, or individuals, marked by murderous assaults in revenge for some previous insult or wrong.

The idea behind the term *modified* vendetta is that certain direct action appears to be motivated by values or emotions (like revenge) by stakeholders adversely affected by organizational actions in the past, even if those actions have ceased.

This can be a useful term, but not as a synonym for direct action. It was meant to indicate that *certain* direct actions can be characterized as a strictly negative-sum game, i.e. they are intended to inflict damage on the target/opponent and they will be pursued even if the initiator is not likely to achieve a positive result. For most economists this would be regarded as a contradictory or inconsistent strategy in that it would work against self-interest. However, if we observe pay-offs in material terms only (including time and effort expended), but motivation in terms of values and ideas as well as material interests, then such an endeavour need not be irrational in the sense of inconsistent. Some people sometimes do pursue what even they regard as a lost cause. Normative stakeholder theory, predicated on deontological ethical premises, not only contemplates such actions, but also recommends them.

7.8 **Conclusion**

Strategies are not the same as actions and actions are not necessarily effective actions. It may be that actions taken are not conceived as strategies as we have labelled them. The effectiveness of actions will depend in part on what the aims of the strategy are. Some stakeholder strategies are aimed at very limited influence over the organization. The aim may be merely to get the organization to provide more information in the annual report on a particular subject, or to get an apology for organizational actions regarded as damaging or unfair. On the other hand many stakeholder groups, particularly those that do not conceive of themselves purely in terms of being the stakeholders of a single focal organization, aim to change the way a class of organizations, or how all organizations, deal with certain other stakeholders, such as the environment or child labourers. Here the strategic aims are very broad and success of particular actions, at getting a single organization to make a small change to its behaviour, may be regarded as ineffective in terms of the wide strategic aims. These are issues that are likely to be explored further in future. These longer-term strategic issues are closely connected with the role of the media and other intermediaries (see Chapter 8).

☐ QUESTIONS/EXERCISES

1 Compare the problems of mobilization in relation to any two of the following types of stakeholder strategies:
  (a) Usage
  (b) Withholding
  (c) Voice
  (d) Damage

2 Relate the four types of stakeholder strategies distinguished in Section 7.3 to the different aspects of power noted by Mitchell, Agle, and Wood (1997) (Section 4.2.5):
  (a) Normative power, based on symbolic resources such as being able to command the attention of the media.
  (b) Coercive power, based on physical resources of force, violence, or restraint.
  (c) Utilitarian power, based on financial or material resources.

How well are each of the strategies covered by a single aspect of power?

3 Ten vignettes demonstrating stakeholder action to influence organizations have been presented in this chapter. Choose any three of them and investigate them on the Internet. Answer the following questions.
  (a) How successful was the primary action in the short run?
  (b) How successful was the primary action and any secondary actions by the stakeholder group in the long run?
  (c) Which of the four types of strategies best describes the primary action? Why?
  (d) Consider whether the primary action and secondary actions together can be classified under other strategies than the one identified in (c).
  (e) Could the set of actions taken have been more effective? If so, how could this have been achieved?

☐ NOTES

1 Loyalty may be a misnomer. Those that do nothing may be viewed as influenced by inertia rather than by a strategy. Inertia may result from any combination of a lack of perceived opportunities to change organizations; a belief that voice will have no effect; or a lack of vision of what voice might achieve.

2 A substantial literature exists on 'new social movements', which can clearly coincide with mobilization and stakeholder–organization relations (e.g. see Kriesi et al. 1995; the UK journal *Social Movement Studies*, or the American Sociological Association website on Collective Behavior and Social Movements (http://www.asanet.org/sections/collect.html)).

3 Frooman used the label 'stakeholder influencing strategies'. This may be interpreted as strategies to influence stakeholders as easily as strategies to influence organizations. We prefer the label stakeholder strategies to influence organizations.

4 The effectiveness of voice strategies may be enhanced by a strong resource dependency of the organization on the stakeholder or stakeholder group. However, this will largely be due to attachment of usage or withholding strategies to the voice.

5 Care is needed when using the term irrational. Irrational can be used by one side to delegitimize the position of the other side, either in the eyes of their or their opponent's constituencies, for media consumption, or in order to signal to the other side that they are not willing to consider certain issues or positions.

6 Both parties need not lose in a negative-sum game. Negative sum can be achieved by one side gaining, but their gain is accompanied by a larger loss to the other side. We label a negative-sum game in which both parties do lose as a strictly negative-sum game.

8 Intermediaries, the media, and stakeholder mismanagement

8.1 Introduction

Contributors to the stakeholder literature have typically considered the stakeholder–organization relation as dyadic: a direct, linear relationship. This simplifies reality and ignores the impact of interdependent stakeholders and established networks. It also overlooks the role of intermediaries as mediators, facilitators, campaigners, and as stakeholders in their own right, and in particular the role of the media as an intermediary. There are three notable exceptions that consider some but not all of these aspects: Rowley (1997), Frooman (1999), and Rowley and Moldoveanu (2003) (see Sections 4.2.6, 4.5.1, and 4.5.2).

Frooman (1999: 198) analysed intermediaries in the organization–stakeholder relation through his consideration of indirect stakeholder strategies where 'the stakeholder works through an ally, by having the ally manipulate the flow of resources to the firm'. For Frooman, intermediaries are called upon in situations where the stakeholder has limited power, through resource control, to influence organization behaviour independently. He only considered intermediaries positively, as resource providers to augment limited resources of the direct stakeholders. This is a limited view. First, intermediaries are not necessarily allies. They can be representatives or influencing vehicles, such as the media. The media can be a double-edged sword, which cannot be perfectly controlled by organizations or stakeholder groups. Second, either side of the organization–stakeholder relationship can use intermediaries in an attempt to alter that relationship, not just the stakeholder. This is most commonly seen in the use that organizations make of the media as an intermediary but is also evident through alliances with NGOs, where the NGO is being used as an intermediary to change consumer opinion, through the endorsement of a product, or in the way organizations lobby regulators or government for change. Third, an intermediary does not necessarily have control over the flow of resources in the organization–stakeholder relation but instead may act as a facilitator or coordinator for a network that helps to mobilize stakeholder action.

Rowley (1997) presented a network theory of stakeholder influences. He recognized that stakeholders are likely to have direct relations with one another, not just relations with the organization. He used social network theory to analyse the interdependence of stakeholders, and how their position in the network influences their opportunities, constraints, and behaviours. Intermediary actors are those positioned between other actors. Like Frooman, Rowley suggested that actors occupying an intermediary network position have control over resource flow. The greater the organization's 'betweenness centrality, i.e. the extent to which it acts as an intermediary between its stakeholders', the greater the ability of the organization to resist stakeholder pressure. He viewed central actors (stakeholders or focal organization) as brokers or gatekeepers, since they facilitate exchanges between other actors and are able to manipulate information, by either preventing or biasing communication across the network. Rowley and Moldeveanu (2003) did not address intermediaries directly, but they did envision a field characterized by complex social networks in which intermediaries can facilitate coordination and communication among stakeholders, thereby contributing to the density of the social ties.

In this chapter first, we consider intermediaries in general. Intermediation of the organization–stakeholder relation is examined not only in terms of the flow of material resources, but also in terms of identity (Rowley and Moldoveanu 2003) and ideas (Friedman and Miles 2002). Second, we examine the role of the media as a particular type of intermediary. The media affects the flow of information, which may then indirectly affect the flow of material resources between the parties, by acting on identity and ideas, e.g. by removing public support. The role of the media is highlighted through several vignettes of examples of stakeholder (mis)management and through an in-depth case of the supplier relationship at the UK retailer Marks & Spencer (M&S).

8.2 Intermediaries in the organization–stakeholder relationship

It may be thought from reading the stakeholder literature that the consideration of organizations (and individuals) mediating the relationship between stakeholders and organizations is an esoteric subject applicable only in specific instances. We argue that *most* organization–stakeholder relations are mediated. Organization–stakeholder relations can be mediated by the following (with an illustration from organization–employee relations):

- *Individuals*: foreman negotiating better work conditions on behalf of the team.
- *Informal groups*: unelected workers acting as 'representatives' to negotiate conditions with management.
- *Formal groups*: elected workers negotiating conditions with management.
- Organiz*ations*: trade union representatives negotiating conditions with management.

The majority of intermediaries are organizations. The most easily recognized examples are environmental NGOs like Greenpeace or Friends of the Earth who 'represent' the interests of stakeholders affected by focal organizations. There are many intermediary organizations that represent the interests of specific stakeholders in organization–stakeholder relations, for example:

- *Employees*: trade unions, left-wing activist groups, and human rights groups.
- *Consumers*: consumer rights groups and government organizations such as the Office of Fair Trading in the UK.
- *Suppliers*: supplier associations and trade associations.
- *Local communities*: planning departments and action groups.

There are also intermediary organizations that represent focal organizations, such as trade associations and specific lobbying and research organizations. In this section such intermediaries are analysed in terms of their effects on the organization–stakeholder relation and comparisons are made between those that represent stakeholders and those that represent focal organizations.

8.2.1 INTERMEDIARIES SUPPORTING STAKEHOLDERS TO INFLUENCE FOCAL ORGANIZATIONS

Frooman presented the case of the Earth Island Institute's (EII) campaign to stop the cannery StarKist from sourcing tuna from fisheries that use 'dolphin unfriendly' nets (see Vignette 8.2) as an example of the use of an intermediary by a stakeholder to influence corporate behaviour. The ally (intermediary) identified was 'consumers', called on to boycott StarKist until the company changed its sourcing policy. EII is also an intermediary, as are all NGOs. This is how NGOs tend to constitute and present themselves: to claim to represent the interests of those affected by private organizations, governments, or natural disasters. However, they are not the same as those who they claim to represent. Similarly, trade unions are constituted and claim to represent employees, or certain groups of employees. They are intermediaries but also may be stakeholders in the relationship in their own right. However, they are a particular type of stakeholder.

Usually this distinction is masked by analyses of organization–stakeholder relations where the term stakeholder is thought of as individuals, groups of individuals, or even categories of individuals. The 'intermediary' may be consciously supported by those individuals, as in the case of a well-attended local trade union branch in the midst of an active dispute, but they may also be unrecognized or even unwanted by the individuals. Some NGOs claim to represent the interests of certain people without those people wishing it or even knowing of it. Nevertheless, the existence of a distinction between the aggregate of individual stakeholders in a category and the organization that represents, or purports to represent, that category of stakeholders does not by definition invalidate the NGO or compromise its efforts. However, it means that representative stakeholder groups need to be analysed as social entities (or organizations) in their own right with structures and cultures that may encourage those working for them (even in a voluntary capacity) to think and act in ways that preserve the security and enhance the development of those social entities. There may develop a conflict of interest, e.g. between the need for the social entity to finance itself and its need to expend resources in fighting for its constituency of stakeholder interests. In this sense we can consider stakeholder representative organizations as intermediaries. This opens issues such as the influence of individuals, or aggregates of individuals, on the stakeholder representative organization, the willingness and ability of the stakeholder representative organization to act, and particular strategies that it may pursue.

There may also be layers of stakeholder representativeness within focal organizations, as illustrated by the distinction between official strikes, official 'unofficial' strikes (sanctioned by shop stewards but not by relevant trade unions), and unofficial 'unofficial' strikes (sanctioned by neither shop stewards nor trade unions).

We may also consider other intermediaries for stakeholder influencing strategies. Governments can be powerful intermediaries supporting environmental stakeholders through environmental protection legislation. It may not be so helpful to think of stakeholder strategies to influence focal organization behaviour as either resource using or withholding when it is the government that is acting as the intermediary. Sanctions could be thought of as resource damaging rather than withholding or using. Similarly, when workers or NGOs engage in sabotage we have resource removal or destruction.

The SRI sector is characterized by the existence of a number of diverse, unusual intermediaries that support the SRI fund manager–corporate relation and actively seek to influence corporate behaviour (Vignette 8.1). The intermediaries pursue a range of strategies for influencing corporate behaviour including shareholder activism, constructive dialogue, screening, collectivism, promoting SRI to professional opinion formers, and lobbying for change in law.

Vignette 8.1 INTERMEDIARIES IN THE UK SOCIALLY RESPONSIBLE INVESTMENT SECTOR

The UK SRI sector has a range of interesting influential intermediaries. Their power to influence corporate behaviour is increasing due to the exponential growth of the sector and the changing nature of the intermediary–corporate relation. Defensive strategies such as boycotting investment are being complimented with two-way 'constructive dialogue'. It is believed that the latter has greater scope to influence corporate behaviour. The main intermediaries are:

(contd.)

Vignette 8.1 (*contd.*)

- UKSIF plays an important role in promoting SRI to professional opinion formers, including lobbying for and contributing to legislative change on various aspects of financial services. It was instrumental in the establishment of the All Party Group on Socially Responsible Investment,[1] and the Social Investment Taskforce.[2] Although UKSIF was unsuccessful in its campaign for a mandatory ruling to require independent financial advisers (IFAs) to ask clients 'the ethical question' prior to advice, the number of IFAs who did advise clients doubled between 1996 and 1998 (Drexhage 1998). The Pensions Review reforms were based on proposals from the Social Investment Taskforce to incorporate ethical considerations into pension investment decisions without sacrificing returns. Due to new rules requiring pension schemes to declare their SRI policy, the majority of UK pension funds now consider SRI issues and 'best of sector' engagement funds have emerged.
- EIRIS is Europe's longest-established ethical research provider. Established in 1983 as a collaborative research venture by a group of churches and charities, its global rating service boasts a database covering over 2,600 companies. Over 75 per cent of UK SRI funds subscribe to EIRIS. EIRIS provides its database via a software tool (Ethical portfolio manager), which allows fund managers to select positive and negative screens and engagement strategies on a flexible basis, thereby permitting experimentation with different benchmarks. A list of acceptable companies is then produced. Corporations are made aware of the areas that the SRI funds are interested in, and the level of tolerance permitted by the screens, through the questionnaire process.
- Pensions Investment Research Consultants (PIRC) provides a corporate governance service to pension and investment funds with combined assets of over £150 billion. They offer advice on establishing SRI policies and voting advice based on the assessment of corporate governance. PIRC runs a rating service on CSP. Together with UKSIF, PIRC actively lobbied (unsuccessfully) to lower the threshold required to lodge a shareholder resolution via the Company Law Reform. It provides a coordinating function for institutions interested in shareholder activism.

8.2.2 INTERMEDIARIES IN ORGANIZATION STRATEGIES TO INFLUENCE STAKEHOLDERS

Intermediaries do not just act for stakeholders. Corporations can contract out their stakeholder relations or use intermediaries as consultants on stakeholder relations. Corporations have also set up or contributed to the funding of lobbying and promotional organizations, which attempt to influence government and the general public. They can act to counter consumer boycotts, to lobby for the repeal or the reduction in rigour of environmental legislation, or for relaxation of employment legislation. Corporations do not usually act alone in this regard: groups of corporations in an industry set up and support trade associations and groups of corporations in particular cities set up and support chambers of commerce. These groups may directly attempt to influence 'powerful' stakeholder representative organizations like trade unions or global NGOs or 'neutral' institutions such as governments and the media. Alternatively, they may operate at arm's length from those they are trying to influence by establishing semi-independent think tanks, lobbying groups, or by funding research: aiming to mobilize consumers and voters through these second-step-removed organizations (Rowell 1996).

8.2.3 COMMONALITIES AND ASYMMETRIES BETWEEN INTERMEDIARIES ACTING FOR FOCAL ORGANIZATIONS AND STAKEHOLDERS

The use of intermediaries from the perspective of stakeholders influencing focal organizations and from focal organizations influencing stakeholders appears to be symmetric: trade unions are matched by trade associations; NGOs are matched by think tanks. Each side uses PR agencies or commissions research in order to ally the general public as voters, or as consumers, to influence resource allocation in their favour.

We can distinguish asymmetries in structural features between the two directions of intermediated activity based on characteristics that distinguish organizations from broad categories of their stakeholders. These structural asymmetries may affect strategies pursued by each as well as the effectiveness of those strategies. Stakeholders can be organizations that are of the same type of internal structural agency as corporations. For example, corporate suppliers and distributors are private profit-making corporations that simply occupy different positions along the value chain. Furthermore, some stakeholders are people, not organizations. In certain obvious and critical ways they are different from organizations and should be analysed distinctly. Apart from obvious distinctions (the emotional and ideational unity of people compared with the lack of 'soul' of organizations (see Section 2.2)) there are differences in power, strategic flexibility, and strategic consistency. On average, organizations are more powerful (control more resources) than individuals. The typical view of the corporate–stakeholder relation from the individual stakeholder perspective is of a large powerful corporation riding roughshod over the interests and feelings of a vast number of individuals. More to the point, ordinary consumers, citizens, voters, family members, and neighbourhood dwellers will often feel a sense of powerlessness in the wake of corporate action.

While the sum of the actions of large numbers of individual stakeholders can have substantial effects on organizations, individuals rarely perceive their isolated actions as having influence. We may not purchase a particular corporation's product because we are unhappy with aspects of its production process (the effect on animals, vulnerable people, or the natural environment), but without a way of feeling confident that a significant number match our actions, it is hard to see that our non-purchase will have much effect on the company. It is in relation to this problem that the degree of organization of groups of stakeholders becomes an important factor. This can be so, both for the degree to which a stakeholder group is organized (level, access, and permanency of communication; the existence of disciplinary mechanisms; or authority to enforce policies) and the degree to which people trust that espoused policies will be implemented, supported, and followed through.

In this sense we can say that the 'arrow of influence' running between corporation and individuals as stakeholders is different in nature between the arrow of influence running in the opposite direction. In order to carry out their purpose, corporations must act in a strategic, purposive, and deliberate manner.

- The corporation → stakeholder direction is a result of organized actions, i.e. actions based on collectively deliberative processes.
- The stakeholder → corporation direction occurs[3] through individuals acting on their own, at least initially.

Aggregative effects of stakeholder activities can have great influence on corporations. These effects are not based on organized deliberative (and by and large not on articulated) interests of the stakeholders as stakeholders. We may think of (deliberative) effects in the corporation → stakeholder direction as logically prior to those in the opposite direction. First, the usual pattern would be for the corporation to decide to make workers redundant or cut down trees to make room for a car park. Second, individual workers or people living with the trees as part of their neighbourhood will react to these initiatives. Stakeholders are one step behind the corporation in deliberative actions. They can catch up, but catching up may lead to corporations developing new ways of influencing stakeholders. Consequently, the gap in types of activities and degrees of deliberation, or rather elaboration, may widen and narrow at different times.[4]

In the organization–stakeholder relation individual people, as stakeholders, have some advantages. A crucial distinction is the ability of individuals to act strategically with great purpose, with single-mindedness and consistency, once they have articulated their interests to themselves. Individuals can act on beliefs and sentiments in ways that overcome the free rider problem. It is difficult to imagine corporations behaving in this manner (Rowley and Moldoveanu 2003). Corporations may be affected by the beliefs and sentiments of their top leaders, but actions based on these beliefs and sentiments will be constrained by the range of other people that must be relied upon to carry out such actions, and by the strict operating conditions required to keep corporations afloat.

Corporations can act in different ways at the same time and in ways that are contradictory: corporations have added problems of control over different individual actions within them. More of a problem is the relative inflexibility for changing strategies in response to new conditions: corporations are essentially bureaucratic structures that require internal procedures and processes to operate. There is a trade-off between consistency in actions and flexibility, which becomes more problematic as corporation size and complexity increases.

There are representative organizations of stakeholder interests, which are established not by individual people as stakeholders directly or at least not by a very large number of them. They are established by people dedicated to the idea of furthering the interests of a particular category of stakeholder. This is likely to be established in order to reduce, halt, or even redress a perceived loss or harm being done to particular stakeholders by a particular corporation or by a category of corporations (industry). As specialists in a particular relationship, such representative organizations may have an advantage that allows them to be more focused and more consistent, not only concerning all activities at any one point in time, but also over time. The lack of single-mindedness of most corporations in relation to their stakeholders is a source of asymmetry in the corporation–stakeholder relationship. This is particularly so if compared with the representative stakeholder organization, which is often perceived to be *the* stakeholders of the corporation (trade unions, consumer groups, environmental groups).

However, the distinction between the relative single-mindedness of a small representative stakeholder organization, or one that has been recently forged for this purpose, compared with corporations is likely to decline markedly as such organizations age, and particularly as they grow in size. Arguably, this happened to some extent to Greenpeace in the 1990s (Friedman and Miles 2002). It is common for campaigning organizations to lose a degree of radicalism or resolve as they grow, and enter into negotiation and power broking with focal organizations. Likewise, trade unions are commonly accused of 'selling out' to the bosses.

Representative groups may join together to form conglomerate representative stakeholder organizations, or federations of representative stakeholder groups. This is generally at a national level, though increasingly at a global level. In many countries such organizations become associated with political parties, such as National Farmers Unions and Labour Parties. In addition, representative stakeholder groups become focal organizations in their own right. At these higher levels of elaboration and complexity, more are likely to see themselves to be in corporate–stakeholder relations with these focal organizations. While corporations may be thought of as having both primary and secondary stakeholders, some stakeholders as individuals may also see certain corporations as their primary focal point or that their interests are primarily affected by certain organizations, and only secondarily affected by others.

8.3 (Mass) media as an intermediary

8.3.1 INTRODUCTION

The mass media plays a significant (and underanalysed) role in organization–stakeholder relations. The almost instantaneous international coverage of events facilitates the need for systems to be put in place to enable an immediate focal organization response. We argue here that the media can operate as intermediaries (Vignette 8.2). The media can play the role of arbiter, facilitating communication among stakeholders and providing counterarguments from different opinions (Marks and Kalaitzandonakes 2001).

Vignette 8.2 ROLE OF INTERMEDIARIES: EII AND STARKIST

Frooman (1999) analyses the role of intermediaries based on material resources rather than information or ideas, or reputation, which may be seen as a medium for material resources or may be seen as resources in themselves. His example of indirect stakeholder strategy involves four parties: EII (an environmental NGO), StarKist (a tuna cannery corporation), the foreign tuna fishing industry (which uses the kind of net EII objected to), and consumers (who EII called on to boycott StarKist). We distinguish a fifth party to the relationship: the television networks. According to Frooman, a eleven-minute EII video on the issue was aired by all major US television networks in March 1988. The video was then mass-produced and distributed to schools throughout the USA. 'During the rest of 1988 and 1989, first the environmental media and then, gradually, the general media began reporting on the story. By March of 1990, 60 percent of the public was aware of the issue and the call for a boycott of StarKist tuna' (Frooman 1999; citing Ramirez 1990). A month later StarKist announced that it could accede to the demand of EII that it only use tuna caught by an environmentally friendly method and that it could insist that ship crews were monitored by impartial observers.

The media is a double-edged sword. It cannot be perfectly controlled by corporations or stakeholder groups. In part this is because mass media follow their own logic. This is true of all intermediaries, but because for the most part mass media producers are not set up to act in this way, their use as intermediaries is even more likely to lead to unintended consequences for those who would attempt to use the media strategically. They are run by companies with their own stakeholder pressures and their own competitive environments and are staffed by individuals who have particular professional values and career ambitions.[5] The media appears to be primarily interested in bad news. Good, happy stories of effective, efficient, or even perfect stakeholder management do not sell newspapers. Nevertheless, focal organizations and particular stakeholder groups have used the media to get their messages across to other stakeholders and to the government. The effect of this trend has been to make the organization–stakeholder relation more visible. Another effect is the attention the media has given to a number of cases of poor stakeholder management, and subsequent attempts by many large corporations to show that they are actively working to manage their stakeholder relations. In the following sections we use a number of high-profile media cases of stakeholder mismanagement to illustrate difficulties in dealing with these questions. We first examine some general ideas about the relation between the media and its audience(s) derived from the broad field of media studies.

8.3.2 THEORIES OF THE (MASS) MEDIA

Originally mass media meant newspapers. According to 'free press theory', freedom of the press is a critical link supporting individual freedom and modern democracy, as the 'fourth estate' and a conduit for the voice of the people. The independent press is viewed as a neutral intermediary allowing the expression of diverse viewpoints and permitting an enlightened public opinion to be formed. In a free market economy, there is the presumption that the public will only buy papers that reflect their views and this will align owners' private interest to the public good and act as a check on the power of government, the Church, and the aristocracy (Thompson 1995: 238). Modern free press theory is associated with pluralism. Power is distributed among a plurality of competing groups representing different interests and values. None dominate. The State, through the law and through the assumed 'professionalism' of the politically neutral civil service, is assumed to act as an impartial referee among competing social groups. The media is then viewed as a conduit for the expression of proposals and opinions on proposals by the plurality of competing interest groups to the State as arbiter of these competing claims and views. Three critical assumptions behind the pluralist view are that:

1. the media has sufficient autonomy to fulfil its role;
2. the State is impartial;
3. different social groups are able to compete with one another by having adequate resource to express their views sufficiently 'loudly' to be 'heard' by the media.

These assumptions are challenged by the alternative 'propaganda model' (Herman and Chomsky 1988). In the twentieth century, particularly with the arrival of radio and television, came a view that the media constructs and promotes stereotypes (Lippmann 1922) and reproduces hegemony of the ruling class. In modern society people are anonymous and isolated. In these circumstances it is possible for a small elite to manipulate people en masse. This 'mass society theory' was given support by the use of mass media in Nazi Germany, Fascist Italy, and the rise of McCarthyism in the USA in the 1950s (Mills 1957). According to the propaganda theory of the media, five news 'filters'[6] interact and reinforce each other:

1. *Size, ownership, and profit orientation* of the mass media.
2. *Advertising* as the primary income source.
3. *Sourcing* news from government and business as well as experts funded and approved by them.
4. *Flak*: negative responses to a media statement or programme;[7]
5. *Anticommunism.*

For Herman and Chomsky these filters support a process of 'dichotomization' by which the regimes and the victims of regimes, which are regarded as the enemy, are treated in one way (regimes regarded as benign, victims of regime brutality regarded as unworthy of news attention) and those regarded as friends are treated in the opposite manner. In a footnote Herman and Chomsky (1988: 345) note that the same dichotomization applies to the treatment of welfare cheats (chiselers in the USA or scroungers in the UK) who are regarded as unworthy, compared with fraud and tax abuse by business and rich people, which is either ignored or even, in the case of tax evasion, regarded as acceptable or even laudable.

More recently the idea of the 'active audience' (Hermes 2002) or 'New Effects Research' (Kitzinger 2002) has been put forward to challenge the assumption that there is a simple and effective relationship between the intentions of message providers from the mass media and their audience. This work challenges what its proponents see as the traditional 'hypodermic model' of the mass media theorists, whereby messages directly enter the hearts and minds of the audience, like a drug injected into the bloodstream. Instead, they believe the audience will 'decode' messages from the media that are not those intended by the producers of media output (Hall 1981). The dominant meanings themselves need to be enforced and re-enforced by encouraging audiences to incorporate new events and new signs of events into a coherent mapping. Systematically different mappings are actively used by segments of the audience in ways that counteract the intentions of the producers of programmes.

8.3.3 A MODEL OF MASS MEDIA TO ANALYSE ORGANIZATION–STAKEHOLDER RELATIONS

Herman and Chomsky's model is limited in that it is directed towards the macro phenomenon of support for national interests as defined by the government and big business. If we focus on issues that are not so closely tied to 'the national interest', even from the perspective of government, the situation is less clear. For example, Herman and Chomsky define flak in general terms as negative responses to a media statement or programme, and consider it to be one of the five ways big business is able to use the media for its own ends. However, flak can also be used to react against stories that are pro-business, and arguably has often been used to turn news reports against big business when certain themes are involved, such as harming the environment. A potential filter not discussed by Herman and Chomsky is the 'entertainmentization' of the news. The news now receives high audience ratings and is increasingly presented as an entertainment.

8.3.3.1 Basic media model for analysing organization–stakeholder relations

We can begin by representing the position of a micro-level stakeholder and a single large-scale organization. There is no presumed prior relationship between the stakeholder and the media. The stakeholder in question can be an individual or an organization acting as the representative of a stakeholder group (Figure 8.1).

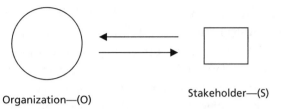

Organization—(O)

Stakeholder—(S)

Figure 8.1 Simple organization–stakeholder dyad

If the stakeholder (S) wishes to influence the organization (O) via the media, in order to stimulate a boycott of O's products, we can think of S's task as a five-step problem:

1. *Attention.* Penetrate the media by getting at least one mass media source to report on the issue.
2. *Affect encoding.* Get the message into the media; get the issue reported with the 'spin' S desires to come across to the audience.
3. *Affect message.* The text can be affected if S is able to provide 'camera ready' or 'storyline ready' material that can be lifted by the direct producers of the report.
4. *Affect decoding.* This may be done by alternative sources of media material hitting the audience with the same spin as S desires, say, by a sustained campaign containing a set of media interventions. The issue can be sustained in the minds of the audience if alternative experts are presented over a period of time.
5. *Audience-generated media attention.* The effect S desires in the audience (boycott) can be sustained and enlarged by the audience reacting to the first four steps of the process. There are clear reasons why this is not infinitely sustainable, but it is possible that a 'media frenzy' can be ignited, which will last for some time.

Figure 8.2 illustrates the situation of a group of stakeholders represented by an organizational intermediary facing the media as well as the focal organization with a media intermediary of its own.

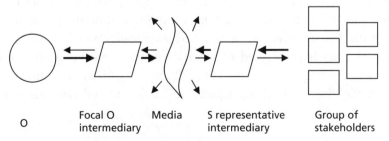

O

Focal O intermediary

Media

S representative intermediary

Group of stakeholders

Figure 8.2 Organization–stakeholder dyad with intermediaries and media

In this case there is more of an 'equality of arms' situation, or at least the power differential is more evened out. Here we must distinguish between stakeholder-representative intermediaries that are formed to deal with a particular issue and with a limited range of stakeholders (tightly defined as associated only with this particular focal organization), and large and powerful national or global organizations. The degree of equality of arms will be different if one of the latter organizations is carrying out the representative function. These organizations are presumably as sophisticated or even more sophisticated at getting their messages across to the media than focal organizations or even their intermediaries. In general, we would expect these types of inter-mediaries to be more sophisticated than either of the initial protagonists to the organization–stakeholder relation.

Even more legitimate than global stakeholder representative organizations are what are regarded as disinterested experts. A British Broadcasting Corporation (BBC) science correspondent is quoted by Anderson as stating:

[I]f scientists are fairly agreed that something serious is happening then I would take more notice of them than I would necessarily of an organization like Greenpeace claiming something's happening because it doesn't quite have the authority of some other organizations or that conventional scientists have. (1991: 463)

However, as evidenced from the Brent Spar incident of 1995 (Tsoukas 1999), Green-peace was able for a time to be treated by the media as the authoritative voice in spite of conflict with expert opinion commissioned by Shell on the best-known way of disposing of the oil platform.

As environmental issues moved up the 'newsworthiness' ladder as a broad category, certain changes occurred in the media itself. Not only did various newspapers and television networks employ more environmental specialists, but also the nature of coverage format changed. Anderson correctly predicted that environmental coverage would become increasingly politicized (1991: 473). She cited evidence that between the 1970s and the 1980s a gradual change in documentary programmes about the environ-ment occurred, from natural history style, divorced from social and political context, to programmes with a campaigning element. She predicted these programmes would become critical of government policy. This has certainly been borne out by reportage on foot and mouth disease (www.guardian.co.uk/footandmouth/), which dominated headlines in the UK for over five weeks, and genetically modified (GM) crops. The European media has been accused of sensationalizing the coverage of the GM food controversy and creating its own agenda to influence negative public opinion over GM foods, by highlighting some (bad) aspects of the debate and ignoring other (good) aspects (Vignette 8.3).

Vignette 8.3 REPORTING OF THE GM FOOD DEBATE IN THE MASS MEDIA

During 1995–6 a major campaign was launched by Europe-based NGOs against the acceptance of GM crops. Monsanto, a US-based corporation that had received import approval for some products in Europe, was singled out. Monsanto responded unsuccessfully, by launching an advertising campaign that highlighted the benefits of GM crops. This was perceived by many Europeans as an attempt to impose American processes on the European way of life (Krueger 2001: 212). The NGO campaign has been largely successful. Widespread negative public opinion has led to all major UK supermarkets increasing their range of organic foods and clearly labelling others 'GM free'. A similar movement did not occur in the USA. One explanation could be the manner in which this debate was reported in the press. Marks and Kalaitzandonakes (2001) examined the intensive media coverage of agrobiotechnology in three national US newspapers (*Wall Street Journal*, *Washington Post*, and *USA Today*) and two UK newspapers (*Times* and *Daily Telegraph*) over the period 1990–2001. Coverage in the USA was largely positive, emphasizing the potential benefits of new technology as a solution to world hunger, greater weed control, reduced production costs, and greater yields. Krueger (2001) stated that there was a strong US regulatory system for biotech approval and a strong belief that science would drive consumer acceptance of GM foods as products that benefited farmers and the environment. American NGOs, although not openly supporting GM crops, did not actively oppose it. Coverage in the UK, on the other hand, was negative, highlighting two main risks: food safety and potential damage to the environment. Benefits of GM crops were underreported. The European Union (EU) regulatory process was under scrutiny following the 'mad cow' crisis and the discovery of the human variant Creutzfeldt Jacob Disease. The media made links to bovine spongiform encephalopathy (BSE) adding to the perceived imminent danger of GM foods for human consumption.

8.4 Stakeholder mismanagement and the role of the media

For many focal organizations coverage by media can be disappointing. This is rarely the case when crisis erupts as crisis provides a focal organization with excessive publicity that would otherwise be difficult to generate. Indeed, some accidents can receive so much attention they become landmarks in the history of the industry. Accidents may reveal that some focal organizations are not as dependable as stakeholders first perceived. They bring to the attention of stakeholders the unflattering side of operations. Accidents often prompt investigations into their cause, and intense public scrutiny may highlight discrepancies or irregularities, which although fairly innocuous in themselves can further damage reputation.

Crisis is most frequently linked to environmental disasters, such as the Exxon Valdez oil spill, or accidents that result in a loss of human life, such as the Union Carbide disaster in Bhopal, India, in which over 25,000 died and over 200,000 were injured (Browning 1993). Jackson and Schantz (1993) suggested that crisis may occur as a result of boycotts, industrial accidents, hostile takeovers, potential bankruptcy, proposed changes in law, labour problems, product defects, patent infringements, production innovations, recession, government regulation, employee discrimination, or unfair competition. Even if the operational side of the crisis is handled effectively, a poorly handled media and stakeholder response can result in legal actions, a loss of shareholder confidence, and a falling market value. The impact may be widespread, resulting in joint reputation damage of industry members, despite the fact that the crisis concerned an isolated episode for a single corporation.

Stakeholders are the evaluators of the focal organization's reputation. Reputation can be the most important intangible asset and source of competitive advantage for an organization. Reputations usually take a long time to develop and cannot be replicated easily by competitors. However, even if an organization has a long history of a good reputation, dramatic events can cause significant and abrupt damage to it.

Some have examined the relationship between media attention and corporate reputation. Weinberger and Romeo (1989) found that negative media attention has negative impact on corporate reputation, whereas Fombrun and Shanley (1990) and Wartick (1992) suggested that there is no significant relationship, but the tone of media attention is a key factor associated with both the direction of the change in corporate reputation and the total movement of change. Zyglidopoulos (2001) stated that environmental damage impacts corporate reputation but damage to human life does not and that media attention does not have a significant impact on the reputation for social performance. Zyglidopoulos (2001) also noted that, following a crisis, various stakeholders could have different notions regarding the reputation of a firm, as each group is interested in different aspects of the firm and in different reputational dimensions. He called this stakeholder specificity. Therefore, the same accident would impact in different ways for different stakeholders due to the cognitive filters employed.

Stakeholders react emotionally to corporate accidents. Throughout a crisis, public and media perceptions are largely based on emotion fuelled by feelings and perceptions of risks, loss, tragedy, and corporate deception. Some incidents capture the imagination of stakeholders more than others: episodes of child exploitation or the unnecessary harm caused to dolphins from tuna fishing have commanded greater media attention than, say, inequitable supplier relations. For many focal organizations the degree of reputation damage stems from the way in which a crisis is handled (compare Vignettes 8.4 and 8.5).

Vignette 8.4 JOHNSON & JOHNSON AND TYLENOL

In 1992 seven US citizens died from cyanide poisoning after taking the painkiller Tylenol. Johnson & Johnson responded immediately by withdrawing all supplies of Tylenol from sale, despite the fact that the Federal Bureau of Investigation (FBI) advised them to take no action, on the basis that it was likely that the contamination was isolated to the Chicago area and the probability of further cases was remote. This decision is estimated to have cost $150 million.

Vignette 8.5 NIKE AND CHILD LABOUR

For many years Nike, the sportswear manufacturer, was at the centre of media attention over employing children in sweatshops in the Far East: in the media Nike became synonymous with sweatshops and child labour. Nike took a defensive stance towards accusations, disassociating itself from the exploitative conditions of the factories and the use of child labour because the work was subcontracted to local factory owners. Nike failed to see the connections between its brand that advocates honesty, competitiveness, and teamwork and the work conditions of its suppliers. Sales declined. Employees were embarrassed, disenchanted, and confused.

By putting the welfare of the customer first, Johnson & Johnson not only regained market leadership status but also benefited from increased market share due to *enhanced* reputation, despite the loss of life caused. Conversely, Nike's reaction that 'Nike did not own the sweatshops and therefore child labour was not Nike's problem' was seen as unacceptable and at odds with its brand and mission statement.

There is a wide literature on what focal organizations should do to establish and maintain an effective media plan. Jackson and Schantz (1993) suggested organizations attempt to understand stakeholder expectations and that the media not be regarded as an enemy but as a significant stakeholder that can shape the perceptions of an organization's performance during a crisis. As aforementioned, the media is not controllable, but there are certain predictable characteristics of how the media may react to crisis situations, for example, the media will seek explanations elsewhere if the state makes no comment, look for sensational or negative angles, and go with a story with good visuals.

Anderson (1991) noted clear differences in the approaches to the media from different global environmental groups. Greenpeace had their own cameraman and photographer and would send polished material to the media. This was reported to lead to resentment by environmental correspondents because news editors would accept this material and bypass them. On the other hand individual campaigners for Friends of the Earth established long-term contact with particular journalists and concentrated their efforts on well-researched reports. Some focal organizations and representative stakeholder organizations approach the media by using intermediary PR specialist organizations, some develop the capacity in-house. Representative stakeholder organizations have an advantage over focal organizations in that they are able to mobilize volunteers to carry out actions that are likely to attract media attention or in turn mobilize other intermediaries, such as organizing consumer boycotts or shareholder activism. Different environmental groups have different strategies when it comes to the media. Many have built their reputation on the basis of being scientific experts. The media can be a double-edged sword for these groups as well as for focal organizations. Vignette 8.6 presents a case where the environmental pressure group came off worse than the focal organization in the media. This was because the pressure group's reputation was entirely built on the basis of its expertise on environmental issues, which was challenged in this case.

Vignette 8.6 UNSUCCESSFUL STRATEGIC ALLIANCES: POLLUTION PROBE AND LOBLAWS (CANADA)

PP is a Canadian environmental NGO founded out of a student movement in 1969. Loblaws is Canada's largest food retailer. In January 1989, PP was paid directly for the endorsement of seven environmentally sound products launched by Loblaws under the label 'G.R.E.E.N.'. Friends of the Earth also endorsed two of the seven products. For PP the objective of the alliance was to educate the public about the environmental impact of particular products, with a view to promoting environmentally friendly lines. For Loblaws, the alliance was believed to bring heightened consumer confidence. Loblaws agreed to donate 1 per cent royalty on green product sales and $1 for each 'G.R.E.E.N.' sweatshirt and T-shirt sold. This was anticipated to be $150,000.

The connection was a disaster for PP. The deal was initially kept secret, which led Greenpeace Canada to accuse the partners of misleading the public. PP did not want to inform staff of the endorsement until the product prototypes could be exhibited. The product endorsement strategy was a major departure from PP's research-based approach and was not well received by their staff. Tension was heightened following the initial broadcast of Loblaws television advertisement in which the executive director of PP personally endorsed G.R.E.E.N. nappies. Internal strife was leaked to the media, which reported that a number of staff and volunteers resigned over the direction that the executive director was taking. The executive director resigned in July 1989, sensing a lack of support by board members (Ogilvie and Everhardus 2004).

Greenpeace attacked PP's endorsement after it analysed Loblaws' fertilizer, one of the products endorsed by PP, and found that it contained toxic substances (dioxins and furans). It demanded the product be removed from sale or rebranded. There was also criticism that the criteria for endorsing products were too narrow. For example, disposable diapers (nappies) were endorsed as 'green' because they were dioxin-free, while they still were not biodegradable (Gallon 1992). Environmentalists staged demonstrations outside Loblaws' supermarkets, denouncing G.R.E.E.N. products as 'pure G.R.E.E.D.'.

Eventually PP and Friends of the Earth withdrew their endorsements. With major funding withdrawn and depressed public support, PP had to lay off a sixth of its staff and cease publication of its magazine. As a consequence of the Loblaws deal, PP's reputation and credibility as a tough environmental NGO was considerably weakened (Stafford and Hartman 1996).

PP subsequently stated that three lessons were learnt from the Loblaws endorsement (Ogilvie and Everhardus 2004: 24):

1. By not testing all of the products it had decided to endorse, PP was unable to support all of the endorsement data and analysis.
2. Accepting royalties on endorsed products can be viewed as a conflict of interest by some stakeholders.
3. For a partnership to be credible and earn support, the process should be transparent to staff and key stakeholders.

We end this chapter with a case study of stakeholder mismanagement in relation to suppliers.

8.5 **Case study: suppliers as stakeholders at Marks & Spencer (UK)**

On 22 October 1999 Peter Salsbury, CEO of M&S, UK's largest retailer, gave six months' notice to David Suddens, CEO of William Baird, a large UK clothing manufacturer, that they were terminating their purchasing. The effect on Baird was catastrophic. Baird announced year-end losses of £93.5 million, closed sixteen factories, and laid off 4,500 employees. Suddens reported to the press that this decision came as 'a bolt from the blue' and that the move 'has put much of the industry in jeopardy'. Although Baird had no contract to supply M&S beyond six months, Suddens stated that he would seek 'compensation for losses that cannot be mitigated' and was 'taking legal advice on whether the length and nature of our relationship can be construed as a contract' (Osborne 1999). Baird had been supplying M&S for thirty years. The 1998 sales to M&S were £214.3 million.

Shares in M&S fell to 277p, a seven-year low. In January, soon after redundancy notices were issued to 6,000 workers at Baird and Daks Simpson (another UK supplier to M&S), the General Municipal Boilermakers (GMB) union (representing 70,000 textile workers) organized a demonstration outside M&S's flagship London store. It also wrote to M&S's major investors, including the Church of England Commissioners, asking them to intervene in the 'unethical' sacking of thousands of workers (Finch 2000). Baird sued M&S in the High Court for £53.6 million in costs and damages, claiming that its thirty-year relationship constituted a 'relationship contract' and deserved three years' notice rather than 'summary' termination (Osborne 2000). Baird were unsuccessful, but were granted permission to proceed to the Court of Appeal on the grounds that the dismissal amounted to a contradiction of M&S's past behaviour.

In May 2000 the dividend was cut for the first time in M&S history. Salsbury turned to his remaining UK suppliers, asking them to cut their profit margins. Coats Viyella, the third largest supplier to M&S, in an unheard-of step, stopped supplying them with almost immediate effect, which was claimed to cost M&S £6 million in lost knitwear sales (Bevan 2002: 227–8). In September 2000 Salsbury's departure from M&S was announced along with two other top executives. Baird's lawsuit dragged on into 2001, though in the end Baird were unsuccessful. Baird were taken over by a venture capital firm. M&S pre-tax profits continued to fall: £1,168 million (1998), £628 million (1999), £557 million (2000), and £481 million (2001).

M&S makes a fascinating case[8] but not as a straightforward lesson summarized as 'ignore your suppliers at your peril because they are important stakeholders'. M&S did not ignore their suppliers; on the contrary, the corporate–supplier relation was unique in British clothing retailing.

Soon after it floated on the London Stock Exchange in 1926, M&S introduced clothing into their general shops. The company was already a large-scale concern with

135 stores employing nearly 10,000 people. Breaking with tradition M&S offered clothing manufacturers highly profitable bulk orders in limited ranges. Manufacturers had to defy the then powerful Wholesalers Association and severely limit their customer base in order to deal with M&S, who branded these articles with their own 'St Michael' label. Not only did suppliers risk their businesses with one customer, they also had to accept severe scrutiny and intrusion from M&S. This included ideas on factory layout, machinery, raw materials sourcing, and strict quality control. In many cases M&S purchased raw materials directly for their suppliers. M&S benefited enormously by their relation with suppliers: through product and cost flexibility. They could call upon suppliers to 'make a contribution' in hard times: 'There would come that time when they would arrive and tell us it was time for the suppliers to "make a contribution",' reported Suddens (Bevan 2002: 56). They also expected suppliers to alter designs quickly and cheaply and to deliver product where it was wanted in good time. Due to their supplier relations M&S developed a reputation for stunning product quality control and for providing customers with the full range of sizes and colours of their products. Costs were reduced by cutting out wholesalers, relying on trust rather than formal supplier contracts, and by maintaining short communications channels through their 'buy British' policy (in 1980 80 per cent of M&S products were made in Britain, by 1998 it was 60 per cent, compared with the average of 25–30 per cent for British retailers).

The arrangement proved to be excellent for suppliers because M&S expanded almost continuously for the next seventy years. Throughout the period when the company was family-run and controlled (by the Marks and the Seiffs) a 10 per cent limit of profits on sales was adhered to. Extra potential profits were returned to customers through reduced prices or higher quality goods. Though floated on the stock market in 1926, the family controlled class A voting shares up to 1966 when all shareholders were given voting rights. For the next eighteen years while Edward and Marcus Sieff were chairmen, it was the power of the chairman/CEO that maintained resistance to taking more profits from the company for shareholders. The company was loyal to its suppliers, who figured prominently in the underlying principles of the business (Harris and Bower 1977):

1. To offer our customers a selective range of high-quality, well-designed, and attractive merchandise at reasonable prices.
2. To encourage our suppliers to use the most modern and efficient techniques of production and quality control dictated by the latest discoveries in science and technology.
3. With the cooperation of our suppliers, to enforce the highest standard of quality control.
4. To plan the expansion of our stores for the better display of a widening range of goods and for the convenience of our customers.
5. To foster good human relations with customers, suppliers, and staff.

These were not merely store window mission statements. The principles were religiously adhered to up to the 1980s and distinguished M&S from all other British retailers, as M&S wanted their suppliers to prosper with them:

Marks & Spencer wanted their suppliers to make a profit, Tesco didn't care whether they made a profit or not, Sainsbury didn't want them to make a profit and Asda didn't know whether their suppliers made a profit or not. (Bevan 2002: 105)

No suppliers had contracts longer than six months. Nevertheless, on the basis of a promise and a handshake, suppliers invested millions of pounds to supply M&S. It was an arrangement based on trust, and as long as the environment was benign or at least times were not too hard, it worked well.

M&S maintained a wide range of small suppliers until the 1980s. It became clear that many suppliers were too small to provide the long runs in key ranges that the company required. From 1980 a delicate cull of suppliers began, some were asked to reduce their capacity as M&S switched to larger suppliers, and some that would/could not adapt to the standards set were dropped. Those with long-standing relations were given as long as two years notice (Bevan 2002: 111). M&S clearly had a stronger relationship with the larger suppliers and contributed to the rationalization of the British textile industry by squeezing suppliers on one hand and offering those that could not survive such squeezes the solution of brokered mergers with larger suppliers. 'Observers dubbed the mergers shotgun marriages—if small suppliers did not agree to be taken over their custom would be terminated' (Bevan, 2002: 112). Richard Greenbury, then head of clothing (chairman and CEO, 1991–8), began to encourage consolidation of suppliers. From the early 1980s the British textile industry was in serious decline as more of M&S's competitors turned to cheaper foreign suppliers. Greenbury was slow to follow this lead because he was concerned about maintaining his links with heads of companies who had become close personal friends, and because 'he feared for the image of M&S with customers if he began ditching UK manufacturers' (Bevan 2002: 114). Rather he encouraged UK manufacturers to set up factories overseas in the 1990s.

In December 1998 Greenbury stepped down as CEO in favour of Salsbury, but remained non-executive chairman until June 1999. While there were clear differences in style and sensitivity to suppliers, essentially Salsbury carried on with the policies of Greenbury, though with greater vigour and urgency. Both generated a great deal of media ill-will. Not only were the suppliers upset by the change in policy, but also the media were badly handled.

The background of the 'shock' ditching of Baird was not of a company that misunderstood the importance of their supplier stakeholders. Rather, it was a company trying to change from a distinctive, strategic, and mutually beneficial relationship with this category of stakeholders towards a more traditional arm's length relationship by which suppliers were not treated as 'special' stakeholders. The case illustrates some of the problems corporations can have in withdrawing from strong and sophisticated stake-holder relationships in times of great market turbulence, and when corporations want to be flexible in terms of cutting off relations with certain stakeholders. It demonstrates the potential inflexibility of high investment in stakeholder relations. However, it may also be said that the problems M&S encountered were in part due to a lack of sensitivity and foresight in the manner in which suppliers were cut. Bevan attributes this to a lack of sensitivity at the top on the part of Salsbury, who paid for his mistakes with a quick termination of his reign at the company after less than a year.

☐ QUESTIONS/EXERCISES

1 Strategic use of intermediaries can be a double-edged sword. Consider this statement in relation to intermediaries used by focal organizations and any one category of stakeholder.

2 How would your answer to question 1 change according to the strategy to influence the focal organization pursued by the stakeholder? Consider in turn withholding, usage, voice, and damage strategies.

3 Consider the issue of the social responsibility of the media itself. Which stakeholders are likely to be more influential with the media? What strategies are more likely to influence the media?

☐ NOTES

1 Formed in January 1998 with sixty members from both houses of parliament to promote SRI debate and to ensure SRI issues are considered wherever relevant during the framing of legislation.

2 Established by the Chancellor in February 2000 to examine SRI to boost economic regeneration of deprived communities.

3 For those stakeholders that are individuals, not groups, such as potential and actual small-scale shareholders, consumers, people living near corporation sites, and employees.

4 The government may act as an intermediary to further the aims of one or the other side of the relationship. It may also at times act to develop the relationship itself: to secure or preserve it or to develop and clarifying regulations to promote mutual benefits (positive-sum game).

5 Their political and cultural aims are likely to be no more skewed than those of any other big businesses and the nature of their profit-making activity can lead them to broadcast views that are at variance with those of their owners.

6 These are routes by which special interests 'are able to filter out the news fit to print, marginalize dissent, and allow the government and dominant private interests to get their messages across to the public' (Herman and Chomsky 1988: 2).

7 Herman and Chomsky (1988: 26) claim: 'The ability to produce flak, and especially flak that is costly and threatening, is related to power.' They refer here to the government and big business.

8 Three Harvard Business School cases (Harris and Bower 1977; Montgomery 1991; Bower and Matthews 1994), independent books (Bahanda 1999, 2001; Bevan 2002), company-endorsed histories (Briggs 1984; Rees 1985), and leader biographies and memoirs (Bookbinder 1993; Sieff 1985, 1987) exist.

Part III
Policy and Management Education

The final part of this book examines two very different subjects. Neither is dealt with at the same level of comprehensiveness as the subjects covered in the first two parts of this book. This is due to some extent to the fact that the stakeholder concept is an emerging one and has as yet only limited influence on both these areas. Policy and management education are areas that we believe will attract considerable future research.

In Chapter 9 we arrange policy materials such as guidelines, regulations, and laws using a model that allows us to compare stakeholder policy initiatives in terms of two dimensions:

1. the level of stakeholder intervention (individual, organization, nation state, and international); and
2. the nature of stakeholder enforcement, i.e. the extent to which the policies are voluntary or are enforced through more or less severe penalties.

We also consider a third dimension: the effectiveness of policies. Numerous policies are described in the chapter (and in the extensive appendixes). These include guidelines on CSR, corporate governance, and CESER. A major case of policy failure is presented at the end of Chapter 9: the Enron and Arthur Andersen case.

In Chapter 10 we introduce a new subject for the stakeholder literature: assessment of the influence of the stakeholder concept on particular fields of management thought and education. This is a very preliminary investigation and is presented in the form of vignettes dealing with the influence of the stakeholder concept on the fields of strategy, accounting and finance, marketing, and HRM.

9 National and international stakeholder policies

9.1 Introduction

Regulations and guidelines pertinent to stakeholders are numerous. In addition to the array of geographical jurisdictions from which such guidelines emanate, the core focus can range from human rights, sustainable development, and employee practices to supply chain management. It is not the intention here to cover all such guidelines; however, we provide a framework in Section 9.2 by which the vast array of literature on policies, as well as the laws, regulation, and guidelines, can be categorized. It is intended to help make comparisons between policies and particularly in relation to the effectiveness of policies. Policies can be classified according to the agencies promulgating the policies. The nature of the sanctions that can be imposed for transgressing the policies is another basis for classification. In Section 9.2 we build a model that allows both these considerations to be compared in relation to the effectiveness of policy on protecting or furthering stakeholder interests.

There are strongly opposing views of how stakeholders may be best served by policy (Nuti 1997). One influential view is that market forces should be relied upon. However, this may still require broad legal support because the market may be subverted by purely strategic (opportunistic) considerations. This reliance can take different forms, depending upon whether emphasis is given to the market forces[1] or more specific legal sanctions. A market-orientated approach acknowledges the role of legislation as a background factor affecting strategic choice, but regards stakeholder interests as being best served by minimal public sector intervention. Adam Smith's invisible hand is thought to be the most important guarantor of the common good in a competitive economy. A more interventionist view sees government, or a regulator, through legislation or standards, as essential for representing stakeholders that may otherwise not influence the strategic decision-making process. Mandatory enforcement does have the advantage of fostering comparability and should raise the standard of the weakest performer, although the impact of regulation on the development of practices at the opposite end of the spectrum may be counterproductive, stifling advancement and creativity. That said, many organizations adopt policies that go beyond compliance.

Ethics or strategic motivators may drive this. For some, policies should allow ethical considerations to affect corporate actions in relation to stakeholders, and, based on instrumental stakeholder theory, regard strategic motivators as synergistic with ethical motivations. Organizations may attempt to pre-empt and/or shape regulations and thereby reap first-mover advantages. Taking actions beyond mere compliance with legal policies or regulations may also be a reaction to the expectations and pressures from those external institutions that provide the organization with legitimacy. Alternatively, such a strategy can raise the cost of market entry, as the threat of higher standards may lead to stringent regulations (Prakash 2001: 289).

Recent developments in relation to CSR, corporate governance, environmental stewardship, and sustainability may all be viewed as implementations of stakeholder theory (Zambon and Del Bello 2005). Interpretations of at least the most limited tenet of normative stakeholder theory are manifested in all these activities. Some express higher levels of normativity. These activities and the policies that support them are also implicated in the nature of the justification for normative stakeholder theories (typically those of the second kind normativity (see Section 3.2.4)). Consequently, the development, implementation, subsequent reporting, and benchmarking activities related to these actions in themselves become key elements in stakeholder management. Therefore this chapter focuses on legislation and initiative pertaining to CSR, corporate governance, corporate social reporting, and benchmarking. We focus primarily on the UK and the USA, and global guidelines that affect UK and US corporations. Occasionally, other countries are referred to where they have policies that are particularly strong or interesting in relation to stakeholders.

9.2 A framework for assessing national and international policy

Here we develop the last two of Stoney and Winstanley's five continua (2001) (see Section 5.7): levels of proposed intervention and degrees of enforcement advocated. These dimensions can be thought of as orthogonal. Figure 9.1 illustrates this by placing papers appearing in both of Stoney and Winstanley's continua 4 and 5 onto a single map.

The map may be more useful for understanding the significance of different policies if we explicitly consider a third dimension: policy effectiveness. Stoney and Winstanley clearly had this in mind because they defined their fourth continuum as 'the level at which stakeholding principles are established *in order to be effective*' (2001: 620, emphasis added). Mapping the level at which stakeholding principles are established *in order to be effective* can be interpreted in a number of ways. Does effective imply 'of use',

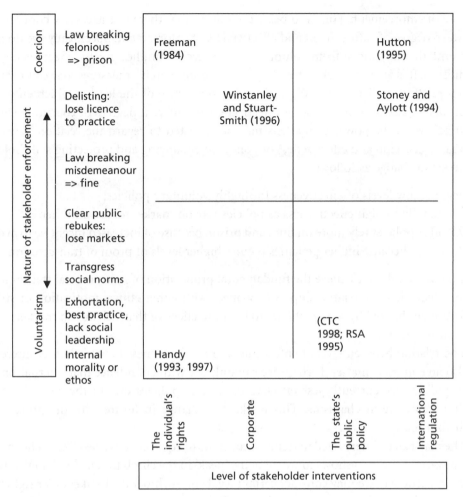

Figure 9.1 A framework for assessing national and international policy

'successful', or 'efficient'? For whom is it effective: the policymaker, the organization, or the stakeholder? The notion of Kantian rights, if embraced accordingly, should offer more effective protection to stakeholders than international policy. Yet, from a regulator's perspective, imposing minimal stakeholder protection through national or international policy may be more effective in cost–benefit terms. Here we separate the pure identification of the level of stakeholder intervention from the effectiveness of the intervention, and we propose that effectiveness be defined in terms of achieving the aims of normative stakeholder theory.

To make the difference between the mapped second dimension (corresponding to Stoney and Winstanley's fifth continuum) and effectiveness clear, we define the second dimension as nature of enforcement, distinguished by degree of *coercion* rather than degree of enforcement. This is to belay the notion that there is a necessary connection between degree of enforcement and effectiveness of enforcement. Specifically, we do not presume that any move from voluntarism to coercion implies greater effectiveness by definition. It is an empirical matter. In practice more coercive measures may or may not be more effective. The model highlights the importance of the level at which enforcement takes place as influencing the effectiveness of different degrees of coercion. Those who believe in the power of markets may be expected to regard the relation between increased coercion and effectiveness of policy for enhancing and protecting stakeholder interests to change as follows:

- begin at low levels of effectiveness for highly voluntary policies;
- rise rapidly to high effectiveness as policies rely on market forces; and then
- fall off as policies rely more on fines and prison because of increased incentive to avoid the law or because higher penalties require higher levels of proof of transgression.

But those who do not believe the fundamental proposition of instrumental stakeholder theory may view the relationship as U-shaped, with either ethical motivation or strict enforcement backed by stringent laws to be more effective than relying on markets and reputation factors.

The relation between level of enforcement and effectiveness for stakeholder interests is also an empirical matter. Perhaps we can only say with confidence that international-level policies are currently less effective than State policies due to the lack of international coercive mechanisms. This is likely to change in future with the process of globalization.

The map can be interpreted in terms of contours of equal effectiveness like a relief map. It may be that the map shows more than one 'peak' in the climb to stakeholder effectiveness. In particular, we may consider certain legal entrenchments of stakeholder rights as unenforceable in spite of the law, particularly if the laws are international ones. Similarly, we may note that voluntary codes, which are backed up by social strictures or stakeholder actions and which are viewed as legitimate by the media, may be more effective.

Before considering the vast array of national and international stakeholder policies using this map, we examine its two dimensions, the way they relate to Stoney and Winstanley's two continua, and finally provide a note on the third dimension, effectiveness of enforcement.

9.2.1 LEVEL OF STAKEHOLDER INTERVENTION

Stoney and Winstanley interpreted Freeman (1984), Weiss (1998), and Handy (1993, 1997) as proposing that the most effective level of intervention would be aimed at the Kantian notion of rights of individuals. At the opposite end of the spectrum Hutton

(1995, 1996) argued that international regulation is the most effective. Two further levels are included, the organization's corporate governance, emphasizing accountability, and the State's public policy. One way of distinguishing policies concerns the level or scope of the constituency to which the policy applies. Another is according to the level of the agency making the policy: some policies have been promulgated by international agencies, some by States, and some are developed as mission statements or codes developed by lower-level agencies such as trade associations, professional bodies, and individual organizations. Regulations aimed at the level of corporate governance may be promulgated by non-government agencies as well as States and international governments. Our dimension refers to the promulgator of the policy rather than to whom the policy is aimed: the level of intervention not the level of the targeted agent.

9.2.2 NATURE OF STAKEHOLDER ENFORCEMENT

This dimension is intended to capture the extent to which the stakeholder model is formally acknowledged and institutionalized within organizations and society, and in particular the nature of the sanctions supporting enforcements that have been legitimized. At one extreme lies 'coercion', through the legal entrenchment of stakeholder rights, backed by clear and substantial penalties for non-compliance. A distinguishing characteristic of this extreme is the sanction of depriving offenders of their liberty through prison sentences. At the other extreme is 'voluntarism' driven solely by an ethos or internal morality to do the right thing; here the sanction is purely optional.

From the extreme voluntarism end of the dimension, next to internal morality Stoney and Winstanley placed best practice and exhortation. The motivation for action differs between these types of enforcement. We have added lack of social leadership to this category. Stoney and Winstanley (2001: 622) placed exhortation nearer to voluntarism than best practice without further explanation. We note that the impulse to follow 'best' practice is moral, and the motivation for exhortation is also usually moral, though it can also be to gain a competitive advantage, i.e. doing well by doing good. This is even more the case with pioneer organizations, or what we call social leadership. We have interpreted this as including best practice guidelines as well as situations in which organizations make pioneering efforts towards greater transparency and accountability towards stakeholders that go beyond the efforts made by their peer group. Pioneer organizations explicitly state their commitment to their ethical policies and are judged accordingly, in that divergence should lead to public recognition of a lack of social leadership.

Further along the continuum Stoney and Winstanley have codes of conduct and directives towards greater coercion. We have placed situations in which organizations transgress social norms next, which is still at the voluntarism end of the dimension. Donaldson and Dunfee (1999) presented the notion of universal ethical principles or 'hypernorms' that are expected by society. These norms are regulated through the social contract (see Vignette 3.4) and organizations 'voluntarily' adopt the norms of the society in which they operate in order to retain their 'licence to operate' and hence their legitimacy in society. What distinguishes this from more purely voluntaristic models is that it is presumed that the others only involve the individuals concerned, feeling that they have transgressed or missed an opportunity to express their moral views. This type of enforcement involves the possibility of public opprobrium for those that do not reach a standard that is expected by society, even if the only coercive consequence is some form of unspecified public reproach, which may only be expressed by occasional media pieces or letters to editors.

The final 'voluntary' level involves situations in which irresponsible organizational behaviour leads to clear public rebukes, either through demonstrations, widespread negative media coverage, or consumer boycotts. Such public rebukes can lead to lost sales, a declining market share, and damage to brand and reputation.

The next three categories indicating increasing coercion relate to organizational breach of the rights of individuals, corporate governance regulations, and national or international law. Minor violations, or misdemeanours if recognized, are likely to result in a fine. Serious contraventions could result in delisting (loss of licence to practise) or imprisonment. The greater the extent of punishment, the greater is the degree of coercive enforcement.

9.2.3 EFFECTIVENESS OF STAKEHOLDER ENFORCEMENT

Just as level of intervention does not translate in a simple manner into effectiveness of enforcement, so the coerciveness of the enforcement does not simply translate into effectiveness. Effectiveness at the coercive end of the dimension will depend on both the degree of coercion in the form of the severity of the punishment for getting caught and the perceived risk of getting caught. For example, there may be a coincidence of these factors if law enforcement agencies are presumed to pursue more serious criminals more energetically. However, many of the different coercive methods rely on different enforcing agencies. How likely they are to take up an issue will depend on many factors, one of which is likely to be what may be termed a bubble effect or a frenzy. This is common in the national and global media. In this instance, campaigns against some organizations on certain issues may make it more likely that enforcement agencies will be more vigilant regarding transgressions by other organizations in a similar industry, or towards a similar group of stakeholders.

Figure 9.1 shows the position on our map of 'normative policy' contributions to the stakeholder literature. They are contributions that argue for a certain approach to policy on enforcement of active organization–stakeholder relations, which they believe will be effective. Figure 9.2 maps actual policies. It shows our positioning of the array of stakeholder guidelines, regulations, and laws that are discussed in this chapter. As noted above, neither map shows the effectiveness of policy, the effectiveness of proposed future policy, or the effectiveness of actual policies. Both maps are designed to provide a platform for consideration of effectiveness.

Both figures can be used to demonstrate where most enforcement effort is proposed and occurs. Conversely, they can be used to illuminate where there are gaps in proposed and actual efforts to support active stakeholder management and active influencing strategies by stakeholders. Figure 9.2 appears to show a positive relation between higher-level interventions and more coercive enforcement methods. Conversely, it shows no

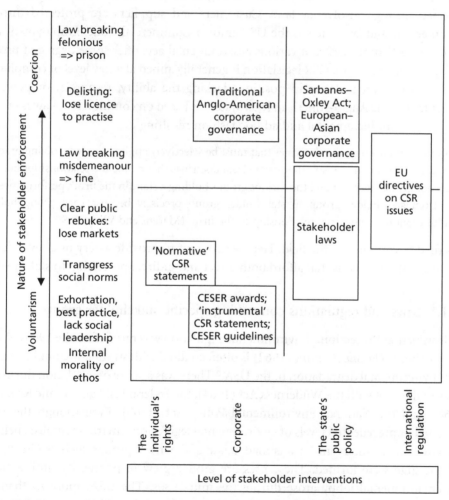

Figure 9.2 Nature of enforcement and level of interventions of stakeholder: mapping stakeholder laws, regulations, and guidelines

high-level policies enforced through voluntarism and rather few low-level coercive policies. A more comprehensive review of policies may lead to a less distinctive pattern.

9.3 Corporate social responsibility guidelines, laws, and regulations

9.3.1 NATIONAL AND INTERNATIONAL REGULATIONS

Many stakeholder groups are afforded a degree of protection in law. Creditors are protected through insolvency laws. Customers and suppliers are protected through consumer acts and laws such as the US Uniform Commercial Code. Employment laws aim to protect employees, and various environmental acts offer some degree of protection against degradation. CSR legislation is generally aimed at a low level of compliance, offering protection to those in positions lacking the ability, resources, or power to protect them. The Anglo-American legal system is based on common law. Law is created from cases in an incremental and ad hoc fashion resulting in

> often vague and overlapping doctrines that must be selectively applied towards solving practical business problems ... as a result the precise legal doctrines that define the relationships between top corporate management and the various groups holding a stake in the firm's performance will differ from stakeholder group to stakeholder group precisely because each group holds a different economic and social relationship to the firm. (Marens and Wicks 1999: 274)

This further complicates the field. Here we attempt to provide a very brief overview of the nature of regulations that afford both direct and indirect protection to stakeholders.

9.3.1.1 Laws and regulations concerning specific stakeholder groups

Environmental Protection. Environmental regulation was rare before the 1960s. Rachel Carson's book *The Silent Spring* (1962) is often credited with stimulating public concern over environmental degradation in the USA.[2] There was a surge of legislation during the 1960s in the USA with the Wilderness Act (1964), the Federal Wild and Scenic Rivers Act (1968), and the National Environmental Policy Act (1969). Even though the 1960s witnessed unprecedented levels of environmental legislation, environmentalists believed that government intervention was inadequate and activist groups such as Greenpeace and the EDF were formed. These pressure groups grew in popularity until a strong anti-environmental lobby arose during the mid-1980s. The USA, more so than any other country, witnessed a green backlash (Rowell 1996) through groups such as 'wise use' or 'sustainable use' that attempt to demonize the environmental movement and compromise its public support. These 'counter-groups' have enjoyed some success, turning the environmental debate in the USA towards the reversal of past environmental legislation rather than broadening and making more detailed legislation based on the progress achieved in the 1960s. Organizations such as the Global Climate Coalition, a consortium of fifty US trade associations and private corporations representing the majority of US corporations from high-polluting industries, have actively lobbied US Congress and campaigned to persuade the public that global warming is not a real threat and the issue is bad for business (Beder, Brown, and Vidal 1997; Kolk and Levy 2001). One clear example of legislative impact was rejection of the 1997 UN Kyoto Protocol by President Bush in March 2001 (La Guardia and Harnden 2001).

For many other nations environmental law developed rapidly as a direct response to the recognition of acid rain, global warming, and the depletion of the ozone layer in the early 1980s. In the UK much of the current environmental legislation is a direct result of EU Directives, many of which relate to the 1980s. Specific examples include the Environmental Protection Act, 1990; the Town and Country Planning Act, 1990; the Water Resources Act, 1991; the Environment Act, 1995; the Producer Responsibility Obligation (Packaging Waste) Regulations, 1997; the Countryside and Rights of Way Act, 2000; Waste and Emissions Trading Act, 2003; Sustainable Energy Act, 2003; and the Energy Act, 2004. These legislative requirements, although numerous, are not excessively onerous. Although non-compliance is subject to prosecution, the severity of punishment is inconsequential. Watson and Emery (2003) citing Gibbs (2001) report that the average fine imposed on the 694 corporations prosecuted in the UK in 2000 was only £8,532. It is not surprising that the Environment Agency tend to view prosecution as a last resort, adopting compliance strategies to persuade, negotiate, and cooperate instead of fining a corporate offender (Watson and Emery 2003). Gross polluters are punished more severely, e.g. Shell UK was fined approximately £1 million for polluting the river Mersey in the UK and ordered to pay £6 million in clean-up costs (Watson and Emery 2003). However, the level of protection afforded to the environment, despite the array of statutes, is rather low.

Human rights. The concept of human rights has continuously evolved. The first legal entrenchment of human rights can be seen in the British Magna Carta (1215), which granted the Church the right to be free from government interference and certain citizens the rights to own and inherit property and to be free from excessive taxes. It forbade bribery and official misconduct and established principles of due process and equality. The Magna Carta represented a very narrow view of human rights, affording protection to the privileged few and not to the masses. This remained the principal framework until the English Bill of Rights was declared in 1689. The French Declaration of the Rights of Man (1789) was born out of the French Revolution. The American Declaration of Independence in 1776 led to the American Bill of Rights in 1789. The latter instrument did not grant universal rights as it preserved the institution of slavery and did not recognize the rights of women as man's equal. The Geneva Convention (1864) was concerned with the laws of war and attempted to ameliorate conditions of the wounded on the fields of war. The first international declaration on general human rights, the Universal Declaration of Human Rights (1948), was adopted by the UN General Assembly following the Holocaust of the Second World War. It affords basic rights to citizens, such as the prohibition of discrimination, torture, slavery, and forced labour, the right to liberty and security, the right to a fair trial, the rights to respect for private and family life, the right to marry, and freedom of expression, thought, conscience, and religion. Other communities have adopted similar regulations such as the European Convention on Human Rights, which has been subsequently enacted into national law, for example, the (UK) Human Rights Act of 1998. In addition, there are a number of global voluntary guidelines advocated by AI and the UN that represent basic universal ethical principles aimed at corporations operating in nations where legislation is not explicit.

Employee protection. The rights of employees are protected in many developed societies by regulation on health and safety, equal opportunities, and the imposition of a minimum wage. In most countries these have evolved over a long period of legislation. For example, in the UK a series of acts from the Statute of Artificers of 1563 to the Master and Servant Act of 1824 made workers liable to imprisonment for breach of contract. From then on laws confining the activities of organized groups of employees were gradually relaxed. Employees are protected from exploitation through the Employment Act, 2002; Employment Relations Act, 2004; Minimum Wage Act, 2003; the Race Relations Act 1976; and the Health and Safety at Work Act, 1974. The latter act established the duty of care that employers have towards providing a safe workplace for their employees. It involves formal risk assessment and the formation of a risk policy. It also involves:

- adequate provision of protective clothing and equipment, safety signs, training, and first-aid facilities;
- ensuring that the workplace satisfies the health, safety, and welfare requirements for ventilation, temperature, lighting, and sanitary facilities;
- properly maintaining equipment, taking precautions against danger from inflammables or explosive hazards, electrical equipment, noise, and radiation.

Similar laws exist elsewhere. In the USA, principally the Civil Rights Act of 1964 established guidelines for equal employment opportunities. Individual laws such as the Occupation Safety and Health Administration Act and Fair Labor Standards Act cover specific areas. The number of specific acts is far greater than in the UK, reflecting the more litigious nature of US society.

Consumer rights. UK consumers are protected by the Sale of Goods Act, 1979 (amended by the Sale and Supply of Goods Act, 1994, and the Sale and Supply of Goods to Customer Regulations (Amendment Act), 1995). This is wide-ranging and applies to new and second-hand goods. It states that consumers are entitled to demand a refund if goods are not of satisfactory quality, are not 'as described', or are not fit for purpose. In addition, traders have a duty to supply safe goods and service providers have a duty of care to those they work for that their services are to a reasonable standard at a reasonable cost. There are additional regulations covering home selling. US and European regulation is similar. Additional specific US laws, such as the new car warranty legislations, commonly known as 'Lemon Laws', entitle consumers that purchase 'lemons' to receive a replacement car or full refund.

9.3.1.2 Laws and regulations to protect stakeholders as a general category

Indirect stakeholder regulations also exist. In Sweden, Norway, and Switzerland, pension fund trustees must consider CSR in addition to financial performance when screening corporations for potential investment. The UK pensions law was reviewed in 1999, but the resultant regulation fell short of the Scandinavian law in that it merely requires occupational pension schemes to declare their SRI policy but does not require such a policy to be implemented. This has had a positive impact on the UK pension market. By October 2000 a survey revealed that 48 per cent of the 171 UK pension funds sampled (representing £302 billion total assets) were desirous that fund managers take CSR into account (www.uksif.org). Engagement was also actively encouraged through the UK Company Law Reform. This required better corporate communication and improved disclosure of voting policy. The increase in transparency actively encourages institutional shareholders to vote at AGMs on specific resolutions and general corporate governance issues.

Thirty-two US states (as of December 2004) have direct stakeholder laws in that they have amended their General Corporation Laws to incorporate the stakeholder concept. These emerged from the case of *Paramount Communications v. Time Inc.* (1989) in which the US Chancery permitted the directors of Time Inc. to reject a takeover offer placed by Paramount despite the fact that it maximized shareholder returns. Consequently, corporate boards faced with a takeover situation need not sell to the highest bidder, but can take social factors into consideration. Several cases have tested the application of such stakeholder laws. The directors of Conrail Inc. were permitted to sell their corporation to CSX despite a significantly higher bid offered by Norfolk Southern, on the basis that the CSX deal was better for shippers and employees. It was ruled in the case of *Credit Lyonnais Bank NV v. Pathe Communications Corp* (1991) that directors do not owe duties to any single group (shareholders) but to 'the community of interests that the corporation represents' (cited in Letza, Sun, and Kirkbride

2004). Vignette 9.1 illustrates this through the recent sale of Ben & Jerry's, the US ice cream manufacturer to Unilever.

Vignette 9.1 STAKEHOLDER LAWS: BEN & JERRY'S

Ben & Jerry's is almost as famous for its strong ethos of CSR as it is for its ice cream. The company's founders, Ben Cohen and Jerry Greenfield, embedded strong ethical principles into the very fabric of the organization to the extent that it is frequently cited for its pioneering status in developing, operating, and executing a successful stakeholder model that has reaped strong business benefits. On 11 April 2000, the company was sold to Unilever. Since then 20 per cent of the staff have been made redundant, local GM free, organic suppliers have been supplanted with more competitive sources, and charitable donations have plummeted. Following the initial takeover bid, a consortium of social investors, called the Hot Fudge Corporation, made a counteroffer of $38 per share. This was marginally below the $40 Unilever bid, but Hot Fudge intended to continue the CSR philosophy of Ben & Jerry's. Unilever responded with a counter-counteroffer of $43.60, which was beyond the reach of Hot Fudge. The corporation was sold. When the CEO was asked why recourse through the General Corporation Laws of Philadelphia was not taken, he responded initially with shock, as he did not know such a law existed, and later with frustration that if a costly legal solution had been sought, victory could not be assured due to the imprecision of the law in failing to state the degree to which one may take social issues over financial issues.

Marens and Wicks (1999) examined a century of US legislation to demonstrate that there is no legal conflict for management advancing a stakeholder perspective. In examining the US stakeholder laws they reported that all but one of the stakeholder laws (Connecticut's) only *permit* directors to take the interests of customers, creditors, employees, or the community into consideration, they do not *compel* such concern. Nor has any court extrapolated such a right. Like Kelly (2003) they criticized such a statute for being unfamiliar, vague, little used, and consequently ineffective. Citing the example of 100,000 complaints of age discrimination that were filed with the Equal Employment Opportunity Commission in the USA during the 1990s, Marens and Wicks (1999: 284) stated: 'It seems highly implausible that no attorney would have attempted to sue on these statutes if there was a realistic hope that these statutes might be used to challenge, as well as defend, the policies pursued by corporate management.' They stated that the main impact of these laws is the informal reassurance for directors that they are not breaking the law in taking stakeholder interests into account. Consequently, Marens and Wicks argued that the practical implementation of stakeholder management would not imply such a radical overhaul of current legislation as some advocates might suggest.

According to our nature and level of enforcement framework, national and international policies are clustered in the middle of the right-hand quadrant (Figure 9.2), representing only moderate stakeholder enforcement. Surprisingly, it is the indirect stakeholder laws that seem to be more coercive and more effective. Scandinavian pension fund managers must take into account ethical considerations. In its current state, direct stakeholder law in the USA does not represent highly effective stakeholder protection, falling very short of what radical normative stakeholder theorists have called for. This is because:

1. the law only provides a minimum level of protection for stakeholders, if it provides any protection at all;
2. in practice recourse to the law is uncommon for the majority of stakeholders due to the ambiguity of the law and the excessive financial costs of bringing a case to court; and
3. in situations where recourse is pursued the penalties imposed on corporations are generally immaterial and do not act as a deterrent.

9.3.2 INTERNATIONAL VOLUNTARY CSR GUIDELINES[3]

CSR guidelines support the idea that businesses, as well as nations, other institutions, and individuals, have a duty to maintain the conditions under which stakeholder rights can be exercised. A number of initiatives have been developed in response to minimal regulation and a lack of government intervention following blatant examples of the abuse of corporate power over stakeholders. Examples of practices involving child labour (Nike, see Vignette 8.5), industrial accidents (Union Carbide Bhopal chemical leak, 1984, in which over 2,500 people were killed and a further 200,000 injured; Chernobyl, 1986, the worst nuclear power reactor accident in history), environmental accidents (Exxon Valdez oil spill, 1989, in which over 2,500 miles of coastline were polluted with 11 million gallons of oil, killing over 36,000 birds), and social and ecological injustices (Shell and the plight of the Ogoni in Nigeria, 1995) abound.

Appendix 9.1 briefly summarizes sixteen guidelines. Some of these we would classify as 'normative' CSR statements. They refer to what companies ought to do and we placed them at the level of transgressing social norms in Figure 9.2. They focus on individual rights, rather than corporate objectives and so are placed at the extreme left-hand side of the figure. Included in this category are the following from Appendix 9.1: AI; Caux Roundtable; Ethical Trading Initiative (ETI); the Global Sullivan Principles (GSP); Principles of Global Corporate Responsibility (PGCR); TNS; United Nations Global Compact (UNGC).

We have classified other statements as 'instrumental' CSR statements. These appeal to corporations in terms of how they can achieve traditional goals by being responsible, rather than what they ought to do for individuals or society in moral terms. We have placed them lower down the enforcement ladder in Figure 9.2 compared with normative CSR statements because they rely more on exhortation and social leadership than on transgressing social norms. Included in this category from Appendix 9.1 are Social

Accountability 8000 (SA8000); Business Impact Task Force (BITF); balanced scorecard (BSC); Excellence for Quality Management (EFQM); International Organization for Standardization (ISO series); Investors in People (IiP); International Chamber of Commerce (ICC); London Benchmarking Group (LBG); and Organization for Economic Cooperation and Development (OECD).

The most prominent initiatives are human rights 'declarations' (AI, BITF, ETI, GSP, the OECD guidelines, SA8000, PGCR, and UNGC) and environmental protection guidelines (BITF, Caux Roundtable, ICC, the ISO series, TNS, OECD, and UNGC). The more effective initiatives in terms of corporate uptake provide guidance on implementation, systems management, and monitoring processes. TNS, for example, has a far-reaching agenda, sustainability, but is fairly realistic in what it anticipates is achievable and encourages corporations to aim for 'low hanging fruit'. In so doing progress is evident and motivation maintained. At the opposite extreme lie guidelines such as PGCR, a church-based initiative that is very comprehensive in its aims to promote positive CSR 'consistent with the responsibility to sustain the human community and all creation', but is vague in terms of application, offering thirteen appendices of international guidelines for assistance. Such guidelines can be classified in the bottom left quadrant of the intervention–enforcement framework (Figure 9.2). These clearly advocate the individual's rights and voluntary adoption is predominantly based on the philosophy of doing right. However, many guidelines do not require certification or audit and so there is a risk that some corporations may only partially adopt, thereby reaping the PR benefits endowed to signatories, without the cultural commitment. Such corporations face the possibility of a fall from grace if it were subsequently revealed that such policies were not universally applied.

A number of guidelines aim to improve corporate performance through the adoption of a stakeholder focus. Two examples are the BSC and IiP. BSC proposes that an even-handed approach to managing financial aspects, customers, internal business processes, and learning and growth will enhance returns. IiP, an employee-focused initiative, is credited with enhancing motivation, lowering staff turnover, reducing absenteeism, and improving financial performance and customer satisfaction. Stoney and Winstanley (2001: 615) argue that such initiatives 'should be seen as a set of useful management tools for accounting and analysis rather than a concerted attempt to establish stakeholder rights and principles in corporate governance'. We agree but have included both on the basis that they widen the corporate remit to consider other aspects of performance other than the maximization of shareholder wealth. Gamble and Kelly (1996) argued that such models offer the best opportunities for stakeholding to permeate the corporate sector (cited in Stoney and Winstanley 2001). Clearly, the degree of stakeholder enforcement exhibited here is that of exhortation. In terms of the level of stakeholder intervention, this is unclear, which is perhaps why Stoney and Winstanley excluded such initiatives from their classification.

9.4 **Corporate governance**

Corporate governance relates to the way corporations are directed and controlled, the way directors run their corporations, and the way in which auditors monitor them. There are two broad styles of governance mechanisms: Anglo-American style and Continental European–Asian.[4] The Anglo-American system is enforced through professional pronouncements or stock market listing requirements, whereas the Continental–Asian system is enforceable through law. The Codetermination Law (Mitbestimmung), in Germany is often hailed as a stakeholder model (Vignette 9.2).

Vignette 9.2 CORPORATE GOVERNANCE: THE GERMAN CODETERMINATION LAW

In Germany, the supervisory board for all corporations with more than 2,000 employees is required to represent shareholders and employees in equal numbers. Under the two-tier board system, the supervisory board is responsible for appointing the board of directors, supervising management, approving the balance sheet, and making proposals for the distribution of profit (Lorsch 1991). In theory this gives employees and shareholders an equal voice on the supervisory committee. In practice, shareholders hold the majority as they appoint the supervisory board chairman, who has two votes in the event of a tie. Critics have indicated that the supervisory board meets infrequently (four times a year) and the management board, which the committee is empowered to oversee, selects the committee members. Although employee power in decision-making is limited, the format does provide for continuous dialogue.

The Anglo-American system is a market-based approach that has a shareholder interest maximization focus, based on fiduciary duties. In the UK the Combined Code of Corporate Governance provides general guidance on governance and internal control for any organization. It summarized the work of the Cadbury Committee (1992), Greenbury Committee (1995), Hampel Committee (1998), the Turnbull Committee (1999), and Higgs (2003). The Combined Code lays down fourteen principles of good governance and forty-five best practice provisions covering the make-up of the board, director's remuneration, shareholder relations, accountability and audit, and the promotion of exercising voting rights. It is a mixture of mandatory and voluntary performance principles, which attempts to promote transparency in corporate decision-making and governance. It takes a limited perspective on the inclusion of stakeholders in the governance of the corporation beyond that of the shareholders' AGM. Part of this process is risk management, incorporating the management of reputational risk. Corporations complying with the code should have systems in place to effectively manage such risks. Although not explicit in terms of what constitutes reputational risks, many organizations have inferred that ethical, social, and environmental risks should be incorporated. This would imply a widening of recognized stakeholders for many organizations, although not necessarily so. The utilities industry, as environmental stewards, should always recognize the implications of environmental degradation. Likewise, the retail industry should have in place management systems that recognize the importance of reputational damage and the power of consumer boycotts.

The dominant approach, the Anglo-American system, has come under great scrutiny following a string of high-profile corporate collapses, such as Enron (case 9.1) and WorldCom, associated with corporate fraud, abuse of managerial power, and social irresponsibility. This triggered a number of 'accelerated reviews' of governance frameworks and a resulting swell of practical pronouncements, together with operational changes geared towards increased transparency, verification, and accountability. The most pronounced was the Sarbanes–Oxley Act in the USA (Vignette 9.3). In terms of its impact on accounting and the audit profession it is the most comprehensive law since the Securities and Exchange Act (1934) (Burrowes, Kastantin, and Novicevic 2004). By taking what had been stock market guidelines into formal law, this represents a clear divergence from the UK model of corporate governance.

Vignette 9.3 THE US SARBANES–OXLEY ACT

The US Congress passed the Sarbanes–Oxley Act in July 2002 following concern over corporate accountability post Enron (case 9.1). Its main purpose is to increase accountability to investors and creditors. The act contains a number of provisions that affect the structure and governance of the accounting profession. According to Razaee (2005) the act requires accounting firms to:

1. be subject to oversight by a Public Company Accounting Oversight Board (PCAOB);
2. comply with auditing and other professional standards;
3. retain audit work papers for at least 7 years;
4. submit audits to second partner reviews;
5. rotate audit partners assigned to an audit engagement every 5 years;
6. be responsible to the audit committee and regularly report to the audit committee on accounting treatments;
7. cease offering non-audit services such as bookkeeping, system design, and internal audit outsourcing to public audit clients. As a result three out of the 'Final Four' have divested their consultancy practices (Burrowes, Kastantin, and Novicevic 2004).

Auditors are prohibited from auditing the accounts of a client whose main accounting or management staff were former employees of the audit firm at any time within the year preceding the audit. The PCAOB role is to ensure the adoption of auditing standards, quality control, and ethics as they relate to the audits of public corporations. It is empowered to investigate and discipline public accounting firms and accountants. There are monetary and non-monetary sanctions for those found guilty of violating the act's provisions. 'The monetary penalties seem not to fit the magnitude of the misdeeds . . . the non-monetary sanctions are professionally lethal . . . [in that a] person will be barred for life from serving in any financial capacity for any issuer in the United States' (Burrowes, Kastantin, and Novicevic 2004: 803).

The act also requires audit committees to (Razaee 2005: 291):

1. be directly responsible for the appointment, compensation, and oversight of the work of external auditors;
2. be composed of independent members of the board of directors;
3. have authority to engage auditors;
4. pre-approve any permissible non-audit services provided by the external auditors;

Vignette 9.3 (*contd.*)

5. establish procedures for employee whistle-blowers to submit their concerns regarding accounting and auditing issues;
6. disclose that at least one member of its audit committee is a financial expert;
7. receive regular reports from the independent auditors on accounting treatments;
8. receive corporate attorney's reports of evidence of a material violation of securities laws or breaches of fiduciary duties.

The act has been criticized for focusing too narrowly on the aspects of Enron: 'US Congress chose to attack the symptoms of the audit breakdown exhibited in the Enron case, while not engaging on a more serious effort to identify and treat the underlying disease of a lack of a sense of public duty and inadequate emphasis on audit competence in the audit profession's culture' (Cullinan 2004: 862). Razaee (2005) stated that the act does not address the core problems of auditor's conflicts of interest and has narrow implications because it only applies to public traded corporations and their associates.

The implications of Enron have further reinforced a global need for efficient and effective corporate governance. This triggered a core debate questioning the underpinnings of the Anglo-American framework as a shareholder-focused model. Some have called for restructuring to reflect the stakeholder-orientated philosophy underpinning the Continental European–Asian system. McLaren (2004) argued that focusing on increasing shareholder value in the short run causes corporations to emit toxic pollution rather than invest in pollution control, to transfer work to sites of cheap labour, or to buy cheaply from suppliers using forced or child labour. The Continental European–Asian system is not without problems. Widespread scrutiny followed the collapse of Parmalat, the Italian dairy foods giant (Vignette 9.4). Furthermore, European investors are likely to be hit by more Parmalat-style frauds because, like Parmalat, many European corporations are family-controlled through a chain of holding corporations, making corporate governance and supervision by regulators more difficult.

Vignette 9.4 GOVERNANCE AND PARMALAT (ITALY)

The decline of Parmalat, with $8.5–12 billion in vanished assets, represents one of the largest financial fraud scandals in history. Parmalat was the eighth largest industrial group in Italy, employing approximately 36,000 staff in over thirty-one countries. The accounts were scrutinized after a $185 million bond payment was defaulted in November 2003. Almost 40 per cent of corporate assets were supposedly held in a $4.9 billion account of a subsidiary in the Cayman Islands. No such account existed (Edmondson and Cohn 2004).

Parmalat shares were suspended on 27 December. The auditors, the Italian branches of Grant Thornton International (1990–9) and Deloitte Touche Tohmatsu (2000–2), failed to uncover blatant accounting fraud in which managers invented assets to offset as much as $16.2 billion in liabilities and falsified accounts over a fifteen-year period. Part of this was due to the use of derivatives and other complex financial transactions to shore up the balance sheet. By setting up some loan transactions as investments Parmalat hid its borrowing costs. Apart from $620 million that Tanzi, the CEO, confessed to misappropriating to cover losses in other family-owned corporations, the majority of the missing money has not been traced (Arie 2004). This collapse reveals an alarming lack of transparency. The US SEC has sued Parmalat for misleading investors in a 'brazen fraud'.

Proponents of the stakeholder model commenting on corporate governance have been modest in their proposals because of the overwhelming influence of shareholder protection in this area. They do not suggest that corporate governance should depart from ownership rights (Turnbull 1994, 1997, 1998) as property rights can be claimed by other parties in addition to shareholders (see Etzioni 1996, 1998, Section 3.4.3.3). The stakeholder system would suggest replacing the three-tiered approach to corporate governance (AGM, board of directors, and executive directors) by a structure characterized by stakeholder participation in decision-making, long-term contractual associations, trust relationships, and business ethics. Blair (1995) and Kelly and Parkinson (1998) predicted that stakeholder participation in corporate decision-making would generate more accurate and unbiased corporate information and thus enhance corporate efficiency. This is likely to be difficult to achieve in practice (Vignette 9.2).

9.5 Corporate environmental, social, and ethical reporting

Elevated stakeholder expectations for transparency are driving corporations to adopt beyond-compliance reporting of non-financial performance. Reporting provides a window into the organization and a means to disclose corporate commitments and performance. It can also be a cost-effective method for regularly delivering information to stakeholders in a consistent manner. Consequently, CESER is a major aspect of stakeholder management (see Section 6.6). A corporation can demonstrate its approach to CSR to its stakeholders by disclosing management strategies, systems, and policies relating to the environment, social, or ethical issues. Stakeholder engagement can be used to identify key areas of concern for different stakeholder groups, which can then be used as the focus for reporting, thereby strengthening stakeholder relations. However, the majority of corporations fail to disclose any information, and in instances where disclosure exists, formats, content, and quality vary dramatically.

Early attempts at CESER, in the 1980s, were predominantly an exercise in PR: a 'green glossy' account of how environmentally friendly and concerned corporations were. The data were largely qualitative, reported only good news, and were highly selective in scope of operations covered as corporations cherry-picked cases to highlight. Current reporting has moved on (Zadek, Pruzan, and Evans 1997), with some pioneers such as the Body Shop (UK) and Ben & Jerry's (USA) having a history of producing externally verified annual statements that report on the triple bottom line: the economic, the social, and the environmental. We argue that the progression and development of CESER is attributable to several factors, which are discussed at length below:

1. The development of national regulations
2. The development of formal voluntary guidelines
3. Corporate benchmarking and pioneer reporters
4. Professional benchmarking
5. CESER award schemes

9.5.1 NATIONAL CESER REGULATIONS

Historically, accounting regulators have only been concerned with the environment to the extent it impacted profits, e.g. the disclosure of contingent liabilities and provisions for environmental remediation (cleaning up and making good the damage done to the environment), and health and safety. Likewise, mandatory social reporting has been restricted to disclosing the extent of political and charitable donations, employment data, pension fund adequacy, employee involvement, employee share ownership schemes, employment of the disabled, and the period for payment of suppliers. Most of the little regulation that exists is directed towards reporting on environmental impact, rather than the social or ethical issues. A growing number of jurisdictions around the world are beginning to enforce some form of CESER (Vignette 9.5).

Vignette 9.5 MANDATORY CESER AROUND THE WORLD

A variety of legislative stances have been taken towards CESER around the world since the late 1990s. Some countries focus on the greatest polluters, some focus on the largest corporations, and others require all corporations to comply. Most of these laws relate to environmental reporting only.

Denmark (1996)
The largest corporations and the greatest polluters (approximately 20,000 corporations) are required to produce a standardized annual report on significant environmental impacts, pollution generated, and raw material used for each production site; a management report; information on the working environment; and employee involvement in reporting.

The Netherlands (1999)
The greatest polluters (approximately 300 corporations) are required to produce two environmental reports. The government report has stricter disclosure requirements than the public document. The former covers climate change, acidification, pollution, waste and waste disposal, groundwater depletion, and environmental management systems.

Sweden (1999)
All corporations that require an environmental permit are required to include environmental information in their annual report and accounts (AR&A).

(contd.)

Vignette 9.5 (*contd.*)
Norway (1992)

All corporations must state in their AR&A the extent of any significant environmental impact, and if significant, the measures taken. The act on the Right to Environmental Information (2002) affords all citizens the right to receive environmental information from private enterprises and public bodies upon request.

USA, Canada, and Australia (dates vary)

Limited reporting of emissions is required, primarily in order to produce a national toxic release inventory. Financial institutions in Canada with equity over $1 billion are also required to publish an annual report of their contribution to the Canadian economy and society.

France (1977 and 2002), Spain, and Switzerland (dates vary)

A social balance sheet is compulsory for all corporations with more than 300 employees. It must contain the main numerical data needed to assess employment and evaluate changes over the past three years. Similar reports are required in Spain and Switzerland. Modern versions attempt to cover the perspective of the workers and other interested groups (consumers, suppliers, creditors, public authorities, etc.) in addition to the owners. The 'new economics regulations' law (*nouvelles regulations économiques*) (2002) requires listed corporations to[1] publish information on the environmental and social impact of their activities in their financial statements: use of water and natural resources; energy consumption and emissions of greenhouse gases; effects of biodiversity; their efforts to reduce environmental risks and to educate employees about environmental management; and how companies cooperate with trade unions, civil society, neighbourhood communities, and NGOs (http://www.euractiv.com).

The UK government's 2005 White Paper on the future of company law (www.dti.gov/cld/review.html) assigns great importance to transparency and shareholder engagement, but fails to legislate. From 2006, all UK listed corporations (approximately 1,300) were expecting a compulsory requirement to file an operating and financial review (OFR). This was intended to show the main trends and factors underlying corporate development, performance, and position, now and in the future. This includes employee, environmental, social, and community issues; the strategies to manage them; the resources available; and the risks and uncertainties faced. In November 2005 the UK government decided to strike out plans to implement the OFR in an attempt to alleviate the regulatory burden on corporations. However, many corporations already provide OFRs and the Association of British Insurers have announced plans to push the requirements through the combined code of corporate governance in 2006.

A strong argument against the macro-level regulation of CESER is that the necessity to prescribe standards across diverse industries can only result in the achievement of minimum standards. This is evident in Scandinavia, which has a relatively long history of mandatory disclosure. With the exception of a few pioneers the quality and quantity of reporting remains weak when compared with voluntary practices in the UK and USA, as compliance with prescriptive Eco-Management Audit Scheme (EMAS) style statements in Scandinavia restricts creativity (Appendix 9.1).

9.5.2 VOLUNTARY CESER GUIDELINES

A plethora of reporting guidelines have emerged since the early 1990s. The majority of initiatives are international in scope and origin. Appendix 9.2 summarizes the main guidelines that have been developed. Some are industry-specific, such as the European Chemical Industry Council guidelines and the chemical industry's responsible care programme. Some are a direct reaction to natural disasters, such as the CERES principles that were drafted following the Exxon Valdez Alaskan oil spill. The Bellagio Principles were initiated as a direct result of the 1992 world conference on sustainability in Rio.

The aims and objectives of guidelines vary tremendously as does the level of detail prescribed. The ACCA and the UK DEFRA target new reporters, whereas sustainability initiatives, such as the Global Reporting Initiative (GRI), promote best practice. Few initiatives cover social and ethical performance (AA1000, the Bellagio Principles, BiC, GRI, Responsible Care, and SIGMA). Stakeholder engagement is emphasized by three initiatives: AA1000 considers it to be fundamental, the GRI encourages it as good practice, and SIGMA provides a dedicated management tool kit. AA1000 is further differentiated in that it doubles up as a risk management tool and is highly prescriptive in terms of assurance. Some guidelines such as SIGMA and ACCA refer to more detailed standards such as AA1000, GRI, or Responsible Care for further guidance. GRI is exceptionally comprehensive, being based on a life cycle approach, although emphasis is placed on environmental rather than social or ethical indicators. The United Nations Conference on Trade and Development (UNCTAD) claim their guideline is consistent with the GRI. However, it rejects the life cycle approach for being incongruent with financial reporting and therefore irrelevant to business. Instead, UNCTAD adopts the generally accepted accounting concepts from the International Accounting Standards Board's framework.

Complexity can be counterproductive, acting as a barrier to implementation. EMAS is not as popular as certification to ISO 14031 due to the level of detail prescribed. The difficulties involved in implementing the GRI were the motivation behind the development of the BiC model. Consequently, industry-based initiatives tend to lack detail, the Global Environmental Management Initiative (GEMI), for example, has a superficial dashboard approach, specifying few indicators.

We have placed voluntary CESER guidelines in Figure 9.2 at the level of enforcement relating to best practice and at the level of stakeholder invention relating to the corporate level. Given the plethora of different bases on which the guidelines have been designed, no clear social norms have yet emerged.

9.5.3 CORPORATE BENCHMARKING AND PIONEER REPORTERS

Corporations benchmark external stakeholder perspectives of corporate performance against multiple standards: from formal publicized monitoring protocols to informal review activities using published social reports of pioneer organizations or peers. Organizations learn from high-profile pioneering actions of others and incorporate aspects into their own internal systems. Interpretations of stakeholder theory that suggest those stakeholders that matter most to management will be attended to will be at best incomplete without an examination of wider benchmarking influences.

9.5.4 PROFESSIONAL BENCHMARKING

A combination of demand and the array of methodological issues involved in the assessment of a complex and dynamic subject have culminated in numerous bench-marking systems (Hammond and Miles 2004). Examples include UNEP/SustainAbility (1997), BiE (1999), Deloitte Touche and Tohmatsu (1997), PIRC (1999), CTC (1995), OXERA (2000), and GEMI (1992). Protocols have traditionally focused on environmental and not ethical or social disclosure, although a minority, such as UNEP/SustainAbility, are inclusive. Corporations are typically awarded for the disclosure of predetermined reporting ingredients, along with the scope, breadth, and depth of reporting, thereby enabling direct benchmarking between peers as an overall score is imparted. UNEP/SustainAbility is a pioneer of CESER assessment and forms the basis of many protocols. It documents progress against a five-stage model of CESER development (Figure 9.3) and highlights best practice, weaknesses, and strengths through international, longitudinal best practice surveys.

Reports are scored according to fifty attributes classified under six categories (Table 9.1): management policies and systems (receiving a 23 per cent weighting); inputs and outputs (weighted 37 per cent); finance (9 per cent); stakeholder relations and

1. Green glossy
2. One-off
3. Descriptive
4. State-of-the-art   4.1. Quantity
                          4.2. Quality
                          4.3. Comparability

5. Sustainability   5.1. Company responsibility
                          5.2. Government accountability
                          5.3. Market sustainability

Figure 9.3 A five-stage model of CESER assessment
Source: UNEP/SustainAbility (1997: 8–9).

Table 9.1 The UNEP/SustainAbility rating system of environmental reports

Main category	Specification		Per cent
Management, policies/systems	Top management statement Environmental policy Environmental management system Goals and targets Environmental auditing Management responsibility and accountability	Legal compliance Research and development Awards Verification Reporting policy Corporate context	23
Inputs and outputs	Inputs Material use Energy consumption Water consumption Process management Eco-efficiency/clean technology Health and safety Accident and emergency response Risk management and EIAs Land contamination and remediation Stewardship of local habitats and ecosystems	Outputs Waste minimization/management Air emissions Water effluents Noise and odours Transportation Products Life cycle design Environmental impact Product stewardship Packaging	37
Finance	Environmental spending Environmental liabilities Market solutions, instruments, and opportunities	Environmental cost Accounting Charitable contributions	9
Stakeholder relations and partnerships	Employees Politicians, legislators, and regulators Local communities Investors Suppliers and contractors	Environmental cost Accounting Charitable contributions	19
Sustainable development	Technology cooperation Global environment Global development issues	Global operating standards Visions, scenarios, future trends	10
Design/accessibility			2

Source: UNEP/SustainAbility, (1997: 30).

partnerships (19 per cent); sustainable development (10 per cent); and report design and accessibility (2 per cent). The inclusion of a reporting ingredient raises the score. To reflect fully the comprehensiveness with which a topic is addressed, the GEMI (1992) four-point system is used, except for awards and charitable contributions, which are either 0 or 1. Assessment covers all aspects of reporting, although environmental issues dominate. Ethical and social disclosure account for only 19 per cent of the total score. The relatively high weighting given to sustainability (10 per cent) reflects that this protocol was designed to assess best practice. Hammond and Miles (2004) suggest there is a close connection between good social performance and receiving a high score, due to the four-point scoring distinction, a 37 per cent weighting assigned to inputs and outputs, the focus on sustainability, and only a minor recognition for 'glossiness'.

In addition to the strict CESER assessment, some benchmarking systems look more widely at all aspects of corporate environmental responsibility. In the UK, BiE's 'Index of Corporate Environmental Engagement and Performance' is a major public peer benchmarking exercise as corporations are ranked according to overall position, FTSE position, and sector. BiE is highly regarded by corporations, partially due to its strong public profile and endorsement by the UK Government, the National Association of Pension Funds, and the *Financial Times*.

Hadley (1996) identified potential advantages of using such scoring systems. For stakeholders, scoring systems raise awareness of environmental and social issues and enable disclosure practices to be monitored over time. For corporations the principal benefit is benchmarking: to identify leaders within the peer group and those improving and/or moving up or down the ranks. This in turn increases competition between corporations to disclose more comprehensive information.

9.5.5 CESER AWARD SCHEMES AROUND THE WORLD

Annual CESER award schemes have evolved all over the world and are now emerging in lesser-developed nations such as Pakistan and Malaysia. Table 9.2 shows the sheer number of these awards. For many nations the driving force is an accounting organization such as the ACCA or the National Institute of Chartered Accountants. Corporations hold these awards in high regard. The competitions aim to highlight and reward best practice. They do not rank the CESER of all entrants. A scoring system may be used, but the details are not publicized and feedback is usually imparted via an overview, such as a report of the judges, highlighting strengths, weaknesses, and trends.

Gray, Owen, and Adams (1996) believe that the ACCA Environmental Reporting Awards (ERA) have been the major influence on the direction of environmental reporting in Europe (Figure 9.4). The rewards could be criticized for being too design-focused as 25 per cent of marks are awarded for communication. This is rated by an assessment of:

- layout and appearance;
- use and appropriateness of graphs;
- understandability;
- accessibility;
- innovation;
- the media adopted, with enhanced scores for using the Internet and referring to other websites.

Table 9.2 CESER award schemes around the world

Country	Award scheme and organizing institute(s)
Australia	ARA Annual Report Award, Annual Reports Awards Australia Inc.
Austria	Austrian Environmental Reporting Awards, Kammer der Wirtschaftstreuhänder
Belgium/Luxembourg	Instituut der Bedrijfsrevisoren (I.B.R.), RE-Institut des Reviseurs d'Enterprises
Canada	The Financial Post Annual Report Awards competition, the Canadian Institute of Chartered Accountants (CICA)
Denmark	Den Grønne Regnskabspris, Foreningen Statsautoriserede Revisor
Europe	The European Environmental Reporting Awards, co-organized by accountancy professional bodies in UK, Belgium, the Netherlands, Denmark, Germany, France, Finland, Switzerland, Italy, and Portugal
Finland	Environmental Reporting Awards, Elinkaari (A Finnish forum of environmental experts), KHT CGR
France	Trophée—La meilleure information pour le développement durable, CSOEC-Conseil Supérieur de l'Ordre des Experts-Comptables
Germany	Deutschen Umwelt-Reporting Award (DURA), Wirtschaftsprüferkammer
	Ranking Umweltberichte, Institut für Ökologische Wirtschaftsforschung (IÖW) future eV–Umweltinitiative von Unternehme(r)n, Deuche Bundesstiftung Umwelt
Hong Kong	ACCA Hong Kong Awards
Ireland	ACCA Environmental Reporting Awards, ACCA Ireland
Italy	Consiglio Nazionale dei Dottori Commercialisti (CNDC) and Federazione Relazioni Publione Italiana (FERPI)
Japan	Green Reporting Award, Toyo Keizai Inc., and the Green Reporting Forum
	Environmental Reporting Award, Zenkoku Kankyo Hozen Rengokai and supported by the Environment Agency of the Japanese government
Malaysia	Malaysia Environmental Reporting Awards, ACCA Malaysia
Netherlands	The ACC Award, NIVRA/VMA
New Zealand	Gilkison O'Dea Environmental Reporting Awards, Institute of Chartered Accountants of New Zealand/Gilkison O'Dea Ltd
Norway	Miljørapporteringspris, the GRIP Centre for Sustainable Production/ Den Norske Revisorening
Pakistan	ACCA—WWF Pakistan Environmental Reporting Awards
Portugal	ACC Award Portugal, Ordem dos Revisores Oficiais de Contas (OROC)
Singapore	Singapore Environmental Reporting Awards (SERA), ACCA Signapor
Spain	Instituto de Censores Jurados de Cuentas de Espana, The chartered accountant Institute in Spain and the 'Asociación Espanola de Contabilidad y Administración de Empresas', AECA
South Africa	WWF Annual Environmental Report Award, WWF (South Africa) and KPMG
Sweden	Årets miljöredovisning, Företagsekonomiska Institutet Affärsvälden
Switzerland	ÖBU–Preis, the Swiss Association of Environmentally Conscious Companies, St Gallen University's Institute for Economy and the Environment, Price Waterhouse Coopers and the business newspaper Cash
UK	ACCA UK Sustainability Reporting Awards
USA	CERES–ACCA Reporting Awards

COMPLETENESS   (40%)

- Corporate context
    - Major products and/or services   – Employment information
    - Financial performance   – Geographical location(s)
    - Key (direct and indirect) environmental impacts of business considered and explained
        - Environmental policy and management commitment
        - Rationale behind choice of environmental performance indicators used in report
        - Environmental targets and objectives
        - Product or service stewardship (e.g. design, LCA, disposal policies)
        - Supplier procurement policies and issues
        - Scope of the report (by entity)
        - Reporting and accounting policies (e.g. reporting period, consolidation)
        - Report audience identified
        - Linkages between environmental reporting and sustainability issues

CREDIBILITY   (35%)

Internal credibility:

- Headline environmental achievements in current period
- Named board member responsible for environmental issues
- Contact name and details for person in charge of report
- EMS and its integration into the business process
- Contingency planning and risk management
- Internal audit
- Compliance/non-compliance record
- Environmental impact data (absolute, normalized and comparative data with trends over time and within sector). For example (where appropriate):
    - Inputs (energy use, raw materials, water consumption, packaging)
    - Outputs (emissions to air, water, and land; product and waste output)
    - Transport (fleet description and fuel consumption)
    - Land contamination and remediation
- Conventional finance related data
- Environmental financial statements and full cost accounting

External credibility:

- ISO/EMAS accreditation/certification
- Adoption of reporting best practice (e.g. GRI, DEFRA's CO_2 indicator)
- Approaches to stakeholder dialogue
- Use of stakeholder feedback
- Third-party audit (remit and scope; sign of site visits/testing; data analysis; detection of data incorrectly omitted; independent comment on targets set/impacts identified; limitation and proposals).

COMMUNICATION   (25%)

- Layout and appearance
- Understandability, readability, accessibility, and appropriate length
- Frequency
- Communication, and feedback mechanisms
- Innovative approaches
- Availability of a summary report and/or executive summary
- Comprehensive navigation through report
- Use of Internet
- Referance to website and other report (e.g. financial, social)
- Appropriateness of graphs, Illustrations, and photos
- Integration with financial statements

Figure 9.4 ACCA UK Environmental Reporting Awards criteria

The two remaining categories are well-thought-out. Completeness is a recognized attribute of quality (Adams and Roberts 1995; Adams, Hill, and Roberts 1998) and ACCA ERA capture this more clearly than UNEP/SustainAbility, with a 40 per cent weighting. Instead of adopting a sliding score for all disclosure, such as the GEMI (1992) four-point system, credibility is weighted 35 per cent, capturing issues such as the scope of third-party verification and the reporting of absolute and normalized environmental impact data.

CESER awards are voluntary. Not all corporations are judged. A range of awards exist based on different criteria, some of which involve very limited and specific criteria. As a result some corporations that win awards on one set of criteria may not be judged as best practice according to other criteria. For example, the winners of the awards for first-time reporters and small and medium-sized enterprises (SMEs) would not be judged highly in a 'sustainability' category. As for CESER voluntary guidelines, we note that no clear social norms have yet emerged and we have therefore placed CESER awards at the level of exhortation and best practice in Figure 9.2.

9.6 **Case 9.1: Enron and Arthur Andersen**

Feudalism: You have two cows. Your lord takes some of the milk.

Fascism: You have two cows. The government takes both, hires you to take care of them, and sells you the milk

Communism: You have two cows. You must take care of them, but the government takes all the milk.

Capitalism: You have two cows. You sell one and buy a bull. Your herd multiplies, and the economy grows. You can sell them and retire on the income.

Enron capitalism: You have two cows. You sell three of them to your publicly listed company, using letters of credit opened by your brother-in-law at the bank, then execute a debt–equity swap with an option so that you get all four cows back, with a tax exemption for five cows. The milk rights of the six cows are transferred through an intermediary to a Cayman Island company secretly owned by the majority shareholder, who sells the rights to all seven cows back to your listed company. The Enron annual report says the company owns eight cows, with an option on one more.

Source: Swartz and Watkins (2003: 350–1)

In 1986 Houston Natural Gas and InterNorth merged to form the largest US natural gas pipeline corporation. The CEO, Ken Lay, christened it Enron. Fifteen years later Enron filed for bankruptcy. It was the biggest chapter 11 (US bankruptcy) filing to date, with

$62 billion in assets. Enron collapsed following the decision by credit ratings agencies to downgrade its outstanding bonds to junk status,[5] which triggered $690 million in accelerated debt obligations, cash that Enron did not have. As the joke cited above indicates, this was an accounting fraud, one of such proportions that it notoriously brought down with it one of the world's largest accountancy firms, Arthur Andersen. Reports suggest that the financial statements had been misstated by $24 billion (Barboza 2002). Below is a highly summarized version of events leading up to the bankruptcy.[6]

The first significant event was the concealment of $142–190 million of losses made from oil traders betting on the future oil price (Fusaro and Miller 2002: 22). The board of directors was apparently unaware of the losses, believing Enron Oil to be a star performer, which contributed $50 million to profits. The head of Enron Oil eventually went to prison for conspiracy to defraud and for filing false tax returns.

During the 1980s 75 per cent of sales in the deregulated US natural gas market were conducted through the highly volatile spot market. In 1989 Enron quickly capitalized on the need for risk transfer products and for reliable gas delivery at fixed and floating prices by becoming both the supplier and the gas bank. The gas bank involved making a market between buyers and sellers. Enron provided price stability through long-term contracts with suppliers (for which it charged a premium) and enabled customers to swap a fixed price for a floating price or vice versa, whilst Enron earned profits as a middleman. Enron was a pioneer in creating easy-to-understand standardized natural gas contracts. From basic swaps and options many forms of financial instruments were developed. Much of Enron's reputation as a world-class innovator came from the establishment of the gas bank. Unlike the stock market where a market maker strikes a deal between two parties and takes commission, all deals that went through Enron had Enron as the counterparty, exposing it to considerable risk. Wall Street required counterparties to have a high investment grade and appropriate capital locked in a subsidiary. Enron was heavily burdened with debt, lacked tangible assets and cash, and had a very low investment grade. As Enron relied on an investment grade rating to provide credibility and reassurance to clients, it resorted to creative ways to manage the working capital to fund the contracts by using off-balance-sheet financing[7] through Special Purpose Entities (SPEs). The first was created in 1993. Enron and CalPERS, the world's largest pension plan, formed the Joint Energy Development Investments (JEDI I). JEDI I was used legitimately to purchase power-generating assets off balance sheet.

The nature of the energy trading market meant that the bulk of profits from long-term contracts arise in the first two years, after which profits diminish. Therefore they are 'nonrecurring' (extraordinary) and excluded from the bottom line. Enron's solution was to make them appear to be recurring by investing in many new markets. In 1994 it started trading in electricity and quickly became the largest US marketeer. By 1995 it was the largest UK trader of natural gas and power and a major force across Europe. By 1997

Enron was dealing in commodities such as coal, pulp, paper, plastics, metals, chemicals, bandwidth, weather derivative products, and pollution rights.

In 1997 Enron wanted to sell part of Enron Energy Services (EES) to demonstrate its value in the market. CalPERS signed on the condition that Enron bought their $383 million investment in JEDI I. Enron had to agree as CalPERS's credibility was needed to reassure other investors. It had three options (Swartz and Watkins 2003: 161):

1. Buy CalPERS's investment via a loan for $383 million. This plus JEDI debt would increase balance sheet debt by $1 billion. This would be disastrous.
2. Find a third party to buy CalPERS's interest. This was improbable due to Skilling's impatience to announce investors in EES.
3. Create a SPE that could borrow money to buy out CalPERS. Chewco was born.

The legality of Chewco was questionable:

- Chewco needed to raise $11 million equity, financed by debt. For the debts of Chewco to be excluded from Enron's accounts, investors not associated with Enron must hold 3 per cent of the equity. Chewco was set up by Fastow (later to become chief financial officer (CFO)) to appear to meet this requirement, but Fastow supplied the 3 per cent capital. Nevertheless, Chewco remained 'off balance sheet'.

- Fastow intended to run Chewco through a subordinate, Michael Kopper, a role that required a waiver of Enron's code of ethics by the board. SEC disclosure was also required. Neither was gained. This also caused a conflict of interest. Fastow was a Chewco shareholder and was overseeing the negotiation of the purchase price to get the best deal for Enron.

Despite Fastow and Kopper pocketing vast sums from the deal, the CEO believed they had saved the day. Fastow was promoted to CFO in 1998.

Enron acquired 30 per cent of the shares in Rhythm NetConnections, a high-speed Internet service provider in March 1998 for $10 million. In April 1999 Rhythm went public at $21 per share, by the close of trading it reached $69, taking Enron's investment to $300 million. Enron booked the entire $290 million in profits. Prohibited from divestment until late 1999, Enron faced the risk of substantial losses if Rhythm's share price declined. Enron was unable to hedge this risk with a third party due to their poor credit rating and the large percentage of shares held. Fastow's solution was to create an SPE, called LJM, which he would own and run. It would use forward contracts Enron had as a hedge for the Rhythms transaction. Enron had contracts to buy Enron stock at a set price; share price had risen so, in theory, it could exercise the contracts and make $250 million.[8] The structure of LJM was inherently unstable and not in the best interest of Enron stakeholders. Enron was essentially insuring itself, so there was no insurance. If both stocks fell, LJM would go bust unless Enron rescued it. If the insurance was never needed, Fastow could pocket the premium. Also, there was a clear conflict of interest since Fastow was serving both as Enron's CFO and the owner of LJM. Without this hedge, profits would potentially be slashed and Enron would face humiliation on Wall Street. Despite the irregularities, Enron's board, lawyers, and Arthur Andersen condoned the SPE. Enron entered into over twenty distinct transactions with LJM during 1999. Later that year a second SPE, LJM2, was created.

In November 1999 EnronOnline was launched, simplifying trading further and enabling higher turnover to compensate for low margins. By mid-2000, 5,000 transactions per day were processed in 1,800 different products (Fusaro and Miller 2002: 75–7). Profits soared from $40 billion (1999) to $100 billion (2000), although much of this was due to how the trades were accounted for. As each involved Enron as counterparty, the entire amount of each sale was booked as income, rather than only booking the spread. Although legitimate, this was hardly a fair presentation of events.

As CFO, Fastow was able to build an empire of dubious SPEs without interference from Enron and in the process was able to misappropriate $40 million for himself and for those who had assisted him (Fusaro and Miller 2002: 37). The first 'Raptor' partnership was formed in April 2000. Three similar deals followed, all equally complex and involving convoluted deals with further SPEs, in which LJM2 invested. Once again Enron was hedging with itself. Once again the SPEs were created to benefit LJM2 more than Enron shareholders. These partnerships enabled Enron to hide $1 billion in losses. The Raptor deals accounted for 80 per cent of $650 million earnings for the last two quarters of 2000. By 2001 Enron was the seventh largest corporation in the world with sales of $100 billion. At the peak of the 'dot.com' market, Enron unsuccessfully invested billions of dollars in the broadband market. To artificially inflate income, sham deals were created to give the illusion of liquidity. Commodities were sold at a profit in return for overvalued assets. A profit was realized but no cash exchanged, and the true value of the commodities acquired was not disclosed. The SEC was later to investigate a $500 million broadband swap between Enron and Qwest during the third quarter for 2001.

Six months before bankruptcy, Skilling was declared CEO and Lay became chairman. Enron was trading at fifty-five times its earnings, over twice the P/E ratio of its competitors. For the first quarter, 2001 earnings were up 18 per cent at $425 and revenues up 280 per cent. This was not translated into cash: operations had cost $464 million. The balance sheet and cash flow statements were not released, creating concern that the directors were hiding something. Share price fell below $59.78 on 5 May, triggering loan obligations of $2.4 billion. The second quarter earnings were up 40 per cent to $823 million but cash from operations was negative $1.337 billion. Skilling resigned 'for personal reasons' and Lay resumed his position as CEO. On 5 September, share price fell below $34.13, triggering further loan repayments. In the eighteen months up to Skilling's departure, Lay had sold $100 million of Enron shares, yet, to boost staff morale, declared that shares were an 'incredible bargain'. Thirty lawsuits naming Skilling were to follow. The third quarter results included a $1.01 billion write-down to reflect the deteriorating conditions of many of its businesses, especially broadband, resulting in a loss ($618 million). This triggered an SEC investigation into Enron's related party transactions (16 October). In full knowledge of the investigation, the following day Arthur Andersen employees began shredding Enron-related documents. The SEC elevated its enquiries to a formal investigation into Enron's financial dealings six days later. Enron responded by forming a committee of the board to investigate the partnerships (The Powers Report). By 31 October share price had fallen to $11.

Enron restated its 1997–2001 accounts on 8 November after deciding that it should have consolidated Chewco and a related partnership. This reduced net income by $586 million and increased debt by $2.6 million. Arthur Andersen's competence was questioned. The following day the US corporation Dynergy offered to buy Enron for a share exchange worth $8.9 billion. On 20 November, Enron warned that credit worries, declining asset values, and reduced trading could impact third quarter results negatively. A week later Enron's credit ratings fell below investment grade, triggering debt repayments of $690 million. Share price fell to $1. Dynergy failed to negotiate a better deal and withdrew their offer. With all major lifelines gone, the credit rating agencies downgraded Enron's bonds to 'junk status'. The Bush administration could not bail Enron out over concerns of potential charges of corruption being levelled at the presidency as Lay and Bush are close friends. Enron filed for bankruptcy on 2 December 2001. Four thousand employees were laid off. Enron was sold on 18 January to UBS Warburg for one-third of future profits. Ken Lay stepped down on 23 January. It was later discovered that $55 million had been paid in bonuses the week before bankruptcy. Twenty executives received 75 per cent of the outlay. This was on top of $50 million paid to key traders in November.

On 14 January 2002 David Duncan, head of Arthur Andersen's Houston office, was fired for ordering the destruction of Enron documents, including some that had been subpoenaed by the SEC. Eichenwald and Glater (2002) indicated that Duncan overruled concerns of a number of Andersen staff over the accounting treatment of some of the transactions in Enron's accounts. By signing off repeatedly on the dubious SPEs Andersen became part of the scandal. By shredding documentation it laid itself open to federal prosecution. A firm of chartered accountants cannot function with a felony conviction. Over 85,000 employees worldwide have lost their jobs. Andersen's chairman, Joseph Berardino, argued that as the $52 million in fees from Enron was less than 1 per cent of Andersen's $9.3 billion revenues the money had not corrupted it. Cullinan (2004) stated that Arthur Andersen actively searched for a solution to Enron's problems by working with management to structure a deal to offset some of the losses. On 15 June 2002 a jury found Arthur Andersen guilty of obstruction of justice: the abrupt end of an eighty-eight-year-old accounting firm. It also brought into question the ethics of other accounting firms. The first criminal charges against an Enron insider came in August 2002, when Kopper pleaded guilty to two felonies arising from his dealing with Enron partnerships.

☐ QUESTIONS/EXERCISES

1 Consider Figure 9.1 as a relief map and draw how you think the lines of equal effectiveness of policy would be shaped. Justify your drawing.

2 Consider Figure 9.2 in a similar manner. What information would you need in order to draw lines of equal effectiveness on this map?

3 Compare Figures 9.1 and 9.2 and discuss reasons why the pattern of quadrants filled are different.

4 Given the details of the Enron case, what types of guidelines or regulations do you think would be most effective in ensuring this case is not repeated?

Appendix 9.1 Corporate social responsibility guidelines: A summary of aims, content, and stakeholder orientation

Guideline	Scope and goal	Stakeholders	Contents	Comment
Amnesty International's Human Rights Guidelines for Corporations (AI 1998), www.amnesty.org.uk	Basic framework for developing human rights policies.	Concerns all individuals affected by a corporation's actions.	Performance areas with minimum expectations: 1. corporation policy on human rights; 2. security; 3. community engagement; 4. freedom from discrimination; 5. freedom from slavery; 6. health and safety. Guidance is given on strategic planning and policy framework, personnel policies and practices, improving human rights, and overall implementation and monitoring.	Directly linked to the Universal Declaration of Human Rights and offers a framework of implementation.
Balanced Scorecard (BSC) (Kaplan and Norton 1996), www.bscol.com	A performance measurement tool that links strategy to four aspects: financial; customer; internal business processes; and learning and growth.	Investors, customers, employees. Stakeholder engagement via customer and employee surveys.	Organizations develop their own key performance indicators (KPI) and respective targets. A number of KPIs and targets should be set for each of the four areas. The assessment should be balanced, with equal weighting assigned.	A well-structured model, which facilitates application. It implies that corporate survival is dependent upon balancing stakeholder interests, yet offers no support in relation to conflicts.
Business Impact Task Force (BITF 1998) 'Winning with integrity: a measure of progress', www.business-impact.org	To treat employees fairly, operate ethically and with integrity, respect basic human rights, be a caring neighbour, and sustain the environment.	Investors and owners, customers, employees and suppliers, environment, and community.	Performance areas: 1. purpose and values; 2. workforce; 3. marketplace; 4. environment; 5. community; 6. human rights; 7. guiding principles. Phase 1 involves securing a commitment, identifying external concerns, and reviewing current practice. Phase 2 involves defining and implementing a strategy, measuring and reporting on performance, and interacting with external parties.	This comprehensive standard links corporate performance to the means to manage and measure it.

(contd.)

Appendix 9.1 (*contd.*)

Guideline	Scope and goal	Stakeholders	Contents	Comment
Caux Roundtable Principles for Business ((CRPB 1986), www.cauxroundtable.org	To help reduce trade tensions.	Customers, employees, owner/investors, suppliers, competitors, and communities. One of the few standards that recognize competitors as a stakeholder.	Seven core principles: 1. the responsibility of businesses: beyond shareholders towards stakeholders; 2. the economic and social impact of business; 3. business behaviour: beyond the letter of law towards a spirit of trust; 4. respect for rules; 5. support for multilateral trade; 6. respect for the environment; 7. avoidance of illicit operations.	Good mix of general business principles with stakeholder specific details. It is vague in terms of its practical application. Little alignment with internationally recognized standards, e.g. UN or ILO guidelines.
Excellence for Quality Management Excellence Model (EFQM 1991), www.efqm.org	Quality management tool aimed towards achieving sustainable excellence.	Excellence is dependent upon balancing and satisfying the needs of all relevant stakeholders.	The underpinning concepts include: customer focus; leadership and constancy of purpose; continuous learning, innovations, and improvement; partnership development; people development; and involvement and public responsibility. The process weights nine areas of management: 1. leadership; 2. policy and strategy; 3. people; 4. partnerships and resources; 5. processes; 6. customer results; 7. people results; 8. society results; 9. key performance results.	A true stakeholder model, albeit a relatively narrow definition of stakeholder is adopted.
The Ethical Trading Initiative (ETI 1998), www.ethicaltrade.org	Global standard on employment and working conditions.	Employees and suppliers.	Nine key principles: 1. employment is freely chosen; 2. freedom of association and the right to collective bargaining is respected; 3. working conditions are safe and hygienic; 4. child labour shall not be used; 5. living wages are paid;	There are additional commitments to awareness raising and training and to take corrective action. It is based on sound guidelines (ILO and the UN Declaration of

		6. working hours are not excessive; 7. no discrimination is practised; 8. regular employment is provided; 9. no harsh or inhumane treatment is allowed. Members are expected to monitor, report, and independently verify disclosure.	Human Rights and Rights of the Child).
Global Sullivan Principles (GSP 1970), www.globalsullivanprinciples.org	Economic, social, and political justice by corporations where they do business.	Covers: human rights; equal opportunities; freedom of association; basic pay; skill improvement; health and safety; quality of life; training, development; and community involvement.	Sound principles. There is a lack of tangible indicators and no mechanisms to provide independent assurance. Adopted by the UN in 1999.
International Chamber of Commerce (ICC 1990) 'Business Charter for Sustainable Development', www.iccwbo.org	To improve environmental performance and to measure and report on it via sixteen principles.	Stakeholder focus on principles: customers, suppliers, employees, and the environment. Sixteen principles: 1. environmental management and policies; 2. integration of policies into all management functions; 3. continual improvement; 4. employee education; 5. prior assessment of environmental impacts; 6. development of environmentally sound products/services; 7. customer advice; 8. eco-efficiency; 9. support of environmental research; 10. adopting a precautionary approach; 11. promotion of principles down the supply chain; 12. emergency preparedness; 13. contribute to the transfer of environmentally sound technology; 14. contribute to the development of public policy on environmental awareness; 15. Openness with employees; 16. Measure, audit and report on performance.	ICC, UNEP, and the International Federation of Consulting Engineers have a developed a toolkit to enable enterprises to integrate the principles in environmental management systems. Recommended by Chapter 30 of the business and industry Agenda 21.

(contd.)

Appendix 9.1 (contd.)

Guideline	Scope and goal	Stakeholders	Contents	Comment
Investors in People (IiP 1993), www.iipuk.co.uk	Promotion, quality assurance, and development of personnel in line with organizational objectives.	Employees.	External assessors review four key principles (subdivided into twelve indicators): 1. commitment to invest in people; 2. planning how skills, individuals, and teams are to be developed to achieve goals; 3. taking action to develop and utilize skills; and 4. evaluating the outcomes of training and development for an individual's progress.	Associated benefits include improved productivity and profitability, reduced costs and waste, improved motivation through greater involvement, personal development, and customer satisfaction.
ISO Series, the International Organization for Standardization (dates vary). There are over 11,000 standards covering 130 countries, www.iso.ch	To achieve quality management systems in the delivery of products and services (ISO 9000 series) and environmental management (ISO 14000 series).	Staff suppliers and customers. For ISO 14000 stakeholders have a role in assessing the significance of activities as they affect each environmental aspect (air, water, land, natural resources, etc.).	ISO 9001 requires corporations to establish customer needs and to undertake a commitment to meet them through defined policies and appropriate audited systems and to review and amend the system where necessary. ISO 14000 requires that significant environmental impacts be considered in setting objectives; systems developed; and targets set, systematically audited, and reviewed. An environmental policy must be documented, implemented, maintained, and communicated.	The standards are very detailed. Corporations must gain independent certification to each. Implementation is associated with enhanced performance. The standards are very bureaucratic and may result in corporations aiming to satisfy the ISO assessor rather than striving for continuous improvement.

London Benchmarking Group (LBG 1994). Founded by community affairs managers from BP, Diageo, IBM, Marks and Spencer, NatWest Group and Whitbread. www.corporate-citizenship.co.uk	To define measures of efficiency and effectiveness of all types of community involvement activity by benchmarking.	Communities, staff, suppliers, and customers. Reporting is not an integral part of the model, restricting stakeholder involvement.	No specific performance standards. It defines 'charity', 'community investment', 'commercial initiatives', and the core activities in meeting society needs for goods/services in a socially, ethically, and environmentally responsible manner. It assigns a monetary value to the input costs and assesses the output between social impact, business benefit, and additional external resources provided.	Widely recognized in the UK as important. High level of detail provided in respect of the indicators used. A US group, The *Measuring Corporate Citizenship Project*, was formed around the same time by sixteen US corporations.
The Natural Step (TNS 1989). Founded by Dr Robért, licensed by Forum for the Future in 1997. www.naturalstep.org.uk	Non-certified step-by-step sustainability guideline.	Not directed towards specific stakeholders. Emphasizes environmental sustainability, with little inclusion of stakeholder dialogue.	To reduce dependency on fossil fuels; to use materials more efficiently; to replace persistent and unnatural compounds with those that break down more easily; to draw resources only from well-managed ecosystems; and to live using fewer resources.	The framework encourages to start with 'low hanging fruit' in order to motivate participants towards 'sustainability' but focuses on environmental issues. It has many signatories.
OECD Guidelines for Multinational Enterprises (MNEs) (OECD), (1991), www.oecd.org/daf/investment/guidelines/mnetext.htm	This aims to ensure that MNEs: operate in line with regulations; support sustainability; strengthen the MNEs/local community relation.	MNEs should fully take into account the established policies of host countries and consider the views of other stakeholders.	It includes guidance on: reporting; employee and industrial relations; environmental management; combating bribery; consumer interests; science and technology; competition and taxation; human rights; local capacity building; corporate governance; self-regulation.	Many aspects of sustainable development are covered. It forms the basis for other guidelines, e.g. UNGC and GSP.
Social Accountability 8000 (SA 8000) (1998), Social Accountability International, www.cepaa.org/SA8000/SA8000.htm	To develop, maintain and enforce policies and procedures in relation to labour and employment issues.	Employees and suppliers. Some benefit is apparent for trade unions, NGOs, consumers, and investors.	Guidance is given on: child and forced labour; freedom of association; collective bargaining; health and safety; minimum wage; living wage; discrimination and disciplinary practices; working hours; and training. Certification includes verification. Compliance to additional regulations is required (Universal Declaration of Human Rights and the UN Convention on the Rights of the Child).	It provides a robust approach to labour and employment issues but is less effective in ensuring similar principles are applied throughout the supply chain. Quality is essentially dependent upon the standard of the individual auditor.

(contd.)

Appendix 9.1 (contd.)

Guideline	Scope and goal	Stakeholders	Contents	Comment
The Principles for Global Corporate Responsibility (PGCR) (amended 1998), founded by the Interfaith Center for Corporate Responsibility, the Ecumenical Council for Corporate Responsibility in Great Britain and the Taskforce on the Churches and Corporate Responsibility in Canada. www.iccr.org	To promote positive corporate social responsibility consistent with the responsibility to sustain the human community and all creation.	Communities, customers, employees, suppliers, and contractors, shareholders and the environment. Corporations should use corporate governance policies that balance the conflicting interests of managers, employees, shareholders, and other corporation stakeholders.	The actions are required on four areas. 1. *Communities*: compliance with international standards on human rights, labour, health and safety; identification of impact on local communities. 2. *Employees*: engage in collective negotiations; regulate employment terms and conditions; provide social support to enhance women's economic empowerment and the payment of living wages. 3. *Customers, suppliers, and contractors*: ensure that products meet customer expectations; use its purchasing power to encourage good corporate citizenship. 4. *Protection of the environment*.	Thirteen appendices of international codes are included on areas such as human rights, sustainable development, advertising, racial discrimination, and boards of directors. Amendments in 1998 include benchmarking assessment. It is generic and it is unclear how it could be implemented in practice.
UN Global Compact (UNGC) (1999) www.unglobalcompact.org	Advancement of responsible corporate citizenship for human rights, labour, and the environment.	Promotes a non-confrontational approach to engagement and partnership between UN, governments, corporations, labour, and civil society.	Based on the Universal Declaration of Human Rights, The Fundamental Principles and Rights at Work of the ILO, and the Earth Summit Agenda 21. Signatories must work towards implementing these principles into their strategies, cultures, and day-to-day operations	No demonstrable performance improvements are required as monitoring and verification is not undertaken. Signatories can gain advantage of membership without true commitment.

Appendix 9.2 Voluntary CER guidelines: a summary of scope and contents

CER guideline	Scope and goal	Stakeholders	Contents	Comment
ACCA: An introduction to environmental reporting (2001), www.accaglobal.com	Environment reporting: increased transparency as a dimension of corporate governance.	Encourages stakeholder surveys and stakeholder engagement as part of CESER process.	Components of an ideal report include organization profile; environmental policy statement; targets and achievements; performance and compliance; management systems and procedures; and an independent verification statement. A balanced and comprehensive view is sought.	The report lacks detail, being written for those new to reporting. Users are referred to global examples of best practice. It supports GRI.
AccountAbility 1000 (AA1000) (2000), ISEA, www.AccountAbility.org.uk	A global standard to improve social accountability and performance by learning through stakeholder engagement	A quality process of social accounting is governed by accountability to anybody that is affected by or affects an organization. Integrates stakeholder engagement processes into everyday activities	Governed by the principles of accountability, inclusivity, completeness, materiality, and responsiveness in relation to stakeholders. Four stages: 1. *Planning*: establish commitment and governance procedures; identify organizational stakeholders; define and review objectives, policies, and values. 2. *Accounting*: identify issues; determine scope of process; identify indicators of performance; collect and analyse information; set targets; and develop improvement plan. 3. *Auditing and reporting*: prepare reports; audit report; communicate results and obtain feedback. 4. *Embedding*: establish and embed systems for continuous improvement. AA1000S offers additional modules on: verification; stakeholder engagement; integrating accountability in existing systems; governance and risk management; and accountability management for small organizations.	The standard has been used for reporting; assurance; as a risk management tool for investors and corporate governance; standards; awards development; and training. It is one of the few standards that place stakeholder engagement at the heart of the process.

(contd.)

Appendix 9.2 (contd.)

CER guideline	Scope and goal	Stakeholders	Contents	Comment
Bellagio principles (1997) International Institute for Sustainable Development	To provide a clear guidance for undertaking and improving performance towards sustainable development.	Stakeholders are not explicitly mentioned.	Ten elements are included: 1. Vision and goals; 2. a holistic perspective (completeness, good and bad news, monetary and non-monetary disclosure); 3. Essential elements of a social, ecological, and economic perspective; 4. Adequate scope; 5. practical focus (link goals to indicators, standardize measurement, aid comparability through target setting, and disclosure of trends); 6. openness (accessibility and transparency); 7. effective communication that addresses user needs; 8. broad participation; 9. ongoing assessment; 10. Institutional capacity (assign tasks, enable data collection, maintenance, and documentation).	Practical advice for the whole process (system design, identification of indicators, measurement, interpretation, and communication). Illustrated via cases. Base level standards to reflect realism. Driven by Agenda 21.
Business in the Community (BITC), Corporate Impact Reporting (2001), www.bitc.org.uk	To provide useful business information in addition to data of interest to stakeholders.	Customers, employees, suppliers, community, and the environment.	Indicators cover customer issues (satisfaction levels, retention, and complaints); ecological issues (energy consumption, prosecutions, level of recycling); employee data (staff profile, absenteeism, grievances, turnover, and training); community issues; and human rights issues. Progression from new reporters (baseline data) to those wishing to move beyond basic commitment (performance and impact data), and to corporations aiming at further performance improvements (qualitative and quantitative data).	Simplified framework that identifies core issues. Created out of a demand from business, which felt that GRI requirements were too complex. A UK initiative but exploring links with EU businesses.
Department for Environment, Food, and	How to produce a good quality	Audience suggested employees, suppliers,	Six stages are included: 1. identify audience;	Aimed at new reporters. Detailed guideline is

				given on formulating KPIs and advice is given on the cost of reporting.
Rural Affairs (DEFRA 2001), Environmental reporting: general guidelines, www.defra.gov.uk/environment/envrp/index.htm	environmental report	customers, funders/shareholders, government, academics/commentators, local community, and neighbours.	2. review and identify main environmental impacts; 3. prepare an environmental policy; 4. incremental approach in considering what to report; 5. how to report; 6. assurance arrangements. Report contents should include CEO statement; environmental policy; organization profile; description of the management system; key environmental impacts; environmental KPIs; targets for improvement; progress against targets; and legal compliance.	
Eco-Management and Audit Scheme (EMAS 1992, 1995, 2001), adopted by the European Council on 29.6.1993, www.emas.org.uk	To reduce pollution, ensure sound management of resources; use clean(er) technology; achieve sustainable growth; and provide relevant information to the public.	Potential audience identified (local community, customers, employees, financial institutions, investors, consumers and their interest groups, and NGOs). The environmental policy must be effectively communicated to staff, the general public, and other stakeholders.	An independently verified environmental statement designed for public use (concise, comprehensible, transparent, and comparable) is required. Structure is not specified but report changes should be highlighted. The environmental management scheme must conform to ISO14001. Six recommendations are included: 1. give a clear understanding of the corporation and its activities, products, and services; 2. Present policy commitments and outline how these are implemented; 3. Give a picture of significant environmental aspects and explain the environmental consequences of its activities, products, and services. 4. describe the environmental objectives and targets for significant environmental impacts; 5. Report significant environmental impacts against legal provisions; 6. State who has verified the environmental statement and when.	EMAS is less popular than ISO14001 due to disclosure requirements. Implementation cost may be too high for SMEs. It encourages little stakeholder engagement above staff training and awareness-raising. Although it is prescriptive, it is narrow as it focuses on pollution at the site level.

(contd.)

Appendix 9.2 (*contd.*)

CER guideline	Scope and goal	Stakeholders	Contents	Comment
Global Environment Management Initiative (GEMI 1990, 2004) Transparency a pathway to public trust. www.gemi.org	Identification of an effective transparency strategy. To determine the business case for action.	Model similar to Savage et al. (1991) is used to determine stakeholders. A comprehensive list is provided. Stakeholder engagement is actively encouraged through a process of establishing integrity, building credibility, earning respect, and developing trust.	Three key aspects of transparency are leadership and governance, stakeholder relations, and reporting practices. The five-step process is aligned to each area. 1. Understand the context in which the corporation operates; to consider strengths and weaknesses, principles and mission, opportunities and risks, and stakeholder expectations. 2. Set strategic commitment. 3. Take action via stakeholder engagement and reporting. Stakeholders should inform reporting. Characteristics of quality financial accounting are applied (timely, consistent, relevant, etc.). Develop indicators and verification processes. 4. Measure and report results according to the three areas. 5. Evaluate, learn, and adjust. Guidance is provided on the key elements of corporate transparency: corporate governance, stakeholder relations, and performance reporting. Case study illustrations are provided.	Formed by a group of US multinationals. GEMI commission Deloitte Touche Tohmatsu International to develop the principles in response to the ICC principles. Detail is superficial. Dashboard approach to help synthesize data into a few KPIs.
Global Reporting Initiative (GRI), the Guideline on Sustainable Reporting, originated in 1997 from CERES. Independent status achieved in 2002 with strong support from UNEP, www.globalreporting.org CERES Principles, Coalition for environmentally responsible economies (CERES), 1989, updated in 2002 to align principles with GRI.	Environment, social, and economic.	Multi-stakeholder process of open dialogue and collaboration in designing a commonly accepted voluntary framework for corporations.	A set of reporting indicators across the environmental, economic, and social triple bottom line. Recommended structure: 1. CEO statement. 2. Profile and financial performance. 3. Executive summary and KPI. 4. Vision and strategy. 5. Policies, organization, and management systems. 6. Performance. There are five reporting principles. 1. Underlying principles: clear definition of boundaries. 2. Qualitative characteristics of reporting: relevance, reliability, clarity, comparability, timeliness, and verifiability.	Provides comprehensive guidance on what should be reported and how. Environmental indicators are more robust. Takes a life cycle approach (which includes assessing responsibility for both upstream and downstream activities in the supply chain). Encourages accountability and

		3. Classification of performance-reporting elements into three elements: categories (social, economic, and environmental); aspect (information related to categories such as greenhouse emissions); indicators (e.g. tonnes of emissions). 4. Ratio indicators. 5. Disclosure of reporting policies.	learning. Focuses on reporting and may detract attention from performance.
ISO 14031, ISO series, the International Organization for Standardization (dates vary) www.iso.ch	To establish environmental performance indicators in three core areas: management, operational, and environmental evaluation.	This includes planning environmental performance evaluation; management considerations; selecting indicators for the three evaluation areas; collecting, analysing, and evaluating data; reporting and communicating information; reviewing and improving the process. The required disclosure includes number of employed participated in environmental training programmes; number of specific activities (environmental audits and emergency drill); number of products undergoing life cycle assessment; the use of natural resources and energy; emissions to air, water, and soil; greenhouse effect; ozone layer depletion, and acidification.	Emphasis is placed on practical usability, cost effectiveness, objectivity, verifiability, reproducibility, and comparability. A more holistic approach than EMAS. Acts as an enabler rather than being prescriptive.
Public Environmental Reporting Initiative (PERI 1993). Founded by Amoco, BP, the Dow Chemical Corporation, Du Pont, IBM, Nortel, Phillips Petroleum, Polaroid, Rockwell, and United Technologies, www.ibm.com	A reporting framework for a balanced perspective on environmental policies and practices	Encourages reporting and provides framework with ten core components. 1. Corporate profile. 2. Environmental policy. 3. Environmental management. 4. Environmental releases. 5. Resource conservation. 6. Environmental risk management. 7. Environmental compliance. 8. Product stewardship. 9. Employee recognition. 10. Stakeholder involvement. Corporations may choose the components applicable to their operations.	Simple and non-prescriptive to permit flexibility. Represents an evolving statement of best practice. Compatible with other initiatives such as Responsible care, CEFIC, and EMAS.

Stakeholder involvement is explicit. Customers, employees, shareholders, environmentalists, government agencies, and the media are identified as potential users.

Focus on environmental reporting.

(contd.)

Appendix 9.2 (*contd.*)

CER guideline	Scope and goal	Stakeholders	Contents	Comment
Responsible Care (1985), European Chemical Industry Council Reporting (CEFIC), www.icca-chem.org	To drive improvement in health, safety, and environmental performance in the worldwide chemical industry and to open communication about activities and achievements.	Stakeholder are not specified. Performance data is directed towards employee and environmental disclosure. There is also a commitment to dialogue and working with stakeholders	A rigorous system of checklists, KPIs, and verification procedures. Common structure for CESER is proposed including: introductory section (CEO statement, environmental policy, and methodology for reporting); production facilities and products; corporation plans (qualitative and quantitative objectives). Performance data on issues such as safety at the workplace indicators; distribution incidents; emissions to water, air, and land; energy consumption and CO_2 emissions; and occupational illness frequency rate. Threshold levels for reporting emissions to air and water of key substances are provided. Updates include guidance on product stewardship (2002) and examples of activities to illustrate implementation.	Run in forty-seven countries and adopted by 116 corporations (2003). Internationally recognized for making a significant contribution to sustainable development. Recommended by Agenda 21.
SIGMA Project 8 (1999, 2003), 'Sustainability Integrated Guidelines'. The British Standards Institute, Forum for the Future and ISEA, www.projectsigma.com Sponsored by the UK Department for Trade and Industry	To develop, deliver, monitor, and report on strategy and performance relating to five aspects of capital (natural, social, human, manufactured, and financial) encompassed by accountability.	Stakeholder focus in determining strategy. Stakeholder identification and engagement is recommended.	This includes a management framework and a toolkit for direction on management challenges, such as stakeholder engagement and verification. It has four phases: 1. leadership and vision. 2. planning. 3. delivery. 4. monitor, review, and report. It suggests key activities, useful resources for how these could be achieved, and possible outcomes.	Users are taken through the process but referred to other documentation for further detail, e.g. ISO14001, IiP, ISO9000, and AA1000. Compatible with UNGC, GSP, OECD guidelines, and AI.
United Nations Conference on Trade and Development (UNCTAD 1999, 2000, 2004).	To define, recognize, measure, and disclose	Users are taken from IASB framework: investors, employees, creditors, suppliers,	The measurement, recognition, and disclosure of environmental elements (water and energy use, global warming contribution, ozone-depleting substances, and waste) are required. Each element should be further	Supports existing guidelines such as GRI. It rejects the life cycle approach for being

Source	Purpose	Stakeholders	Content	Comments
Manual for the preparers and users of eco-efficiency indicators, www.unctad.org	environmental and financial information within an accounting framework.	customers, governments and their agencies, and the general public.	detailed into items or groups of items, such as the source of energy consumed, and progress on each item tracked via indicators.	incongruent with financial reporting.
World Business Council for Sustainable Development (WBCSD, 1992, 2000). Measuring eco-efficiency: a guide to reporting corporation performance, www.wbcsd.ch	To improve business performance and monitor performance with measures which are transparent and verifiable.	Management, employees, boards of directors, investors, accountants, shareholders and analysts, bankers and insurers, international standards bodies, communities, customers, and interest groups.	Eight principles are included. 1. Be relevant and meaningful with respect to protecting the environment and human health, and improving the quality of life. 2. Inform decision-making to improve corporate performance. 3. Recognize the inherent diversity of business. 4. Support benchmarking and monitoring over time. 5. Be clearly defined, measurable, transparent, and verifiable. 6. Be understandable and meaningful to identified stakeholders. 7. Be based on an overall evaluation of a corporation's operations, products, and services. 8. Recognize relevant and meaningful issues related to upstream (supplier) and downstream (product use) aspects of corporate activities. A limited number of eco-efficiency measures are proposed in order that reports are not made unnecessarily complex.	Guidance on generic and industry indicators, implementation, and communication is offered. Tested with twenty-two corporations from ten industrial sectors and fifteen countries. Guidance is fairly detailed offering advice on developing indicators, measurement, and common problems experienced.

⬚ NOTES

1 This will appeal to many as a voluntary approach, though underpinned by broad legal supports based on clarifying responsibility for the consequences of harming certain stakeholder interests that appear to be little different from the general principles that underlie the justice system.

2 For example, the US environmental group EDF was founded out of a fund honouring Carson in 1967.

3 By guidelines we refer to published statements that have no clear legal penalties attached to their transgression. In the human rights field such statements are generally called declarations. In the corporate social and environmental reporting field they are generally called principles or initiatives. In all the other fields we discuss they are generally called guidelines. However, these terms are used interchangeably as can be seen by the titles of the human rights guidelines summarized in Appendix 9.1.

4 Hawley and Williams (1996) identified four corporate governance models: finance, stewardship, stakeholder, and the political model. Blair (1995) and Keasey, Thompson, and Wright (1997) proposed four different models: principal–agent (or finance), myopic market, the abuse of executive power, and the stakeholder model. Some argue that the UK and the US models are diverging due to the Sarbanes–Oxley Act (2002) in the USA.

5 Rating agencies classify investments unworthy of an investment grade rating as 'junk'. Price falls after classification because many pension fund trustees are legally bound to hold only investment-grade bonds.

6 See Cruver (2003), Fox (2003), Fusaro and Miller (2002), Prashad (2002), or Swartz and Watkins (2003) for more in-depth accounts.

7 Off-balance-sheet financing involves raising funds without recording them on the corporation's balance sheet. This is a form of creative accounting and goes against the principle of fair representation.

8 Accounting rules do not permit corporations to profit from transactions in their own stock. There are no rules prohibiting corporations from using such deals as collateral (Swartz and Watkins 2003: 170).

10 The stakeholder concept and fields of management thought

10.1 Introduction

The stakeholder concept is popular with management theorists and has influenced several management disciplines. Theory development, academic debate, and management education are influenced by managerial practice and therefore a review of theory development can indicate future directions in management thought and action. At the time of writing (May 2005), a simple search in Ingenta, the social science electronic catalogue, returned 1,678 academic articles with title, keyword, or abstracts containing the word stakeholder. Some disciplines, such as marketing and HRM, have looked towards the stakeholder concept as a possible solution to a rapidly changing environment. Others, such as corporate planning, governance, and reporting, have explored the concept in the context of scandal or failure. The sphere of influence is wide, but for most management disciplines it is not deep. There are two exceptions: strategy and business ethics. In both these disciplines stakeholder thinking forms a core component of modern textbooks.

We regard this as an interesting field of study, which warrants rigorous research. In this chapter we first examine the field that Freeman's seminal work emerged from twenty years ago: strategy. We then examine three core subjects of most standard management degrees: accounting and finance, marketing, and HRM. The intention is only to provide an exploratory investigation, a preliminary taste of what can be done in this area. Other core areas of MBAs and undergraduate management degrees, such as information systems, managing innovation and change, and entrepreneurship (along with correlative subjects such as law and economics), could also be explored. Furthermore, the importance for management theory and practice, of ideas related to the stakeholder concept (such as CSR), could also be examined through an investigation of the extent and nature of their treatment in management textbooks. Questions/exercises at the end of this chapter provide a further indication of how this may be investigated in future.

10.2 The influence of the stakeholder concept on fields of management thought

We would distinguish different fields of study within business and management in terms of:

1. Whether they are outward- or inward-facing in terms of the organization. Inward-facing management subjects concern the understanding and proliferation of techniques related to the transformation of inputs into outputs, and administration aspects of the organization. Outward-facing subjects concern connections between the organization and stakeholders;

2. Whether they concern a single stakeholder or a broad range of stakeholders. Subjects like HRM are mainly concerned with a single primary set of stakeholders (employees), while subjects like strategy concern the organization's relation with its environment, defined at the outset as a range of stakeholders (competitors and potential competitors, suppliers and distributors, customers), such as suggested by Porter's five competitive forces analysis (Porter 1980).

Traditionally, some subjects, such as accounting and marketing, have primarily concerned a single stakeholder group: shareholders and customers, respectively. There are two ways in which the importance of attention to other stakeholders can be formulated and justified: either as derivative stakeholders that acquire their justification for attention due to their influence on the primary stakeholder group, or by raising the importance of secondary stakeholders as part of a redefinition of the overall purpose of the subject area. For marketing, we consider it to be the former. Charter (1992) refers to an enormous range of stakeholders that marketeers ought to take into account.[1] However, these stakeholders are only important as they affect customer perception of the organization and its products. For accounting, we consider both factors to be important. On one hand, secondary stakeholder relations with the organization can affect risk and reputation, as these in turn affect shareholder value. However, secondary stakeholder relations can also be raised to primary status if the whole purpose of accounting is reconceived in terms of social accountability and transparency rather than fulfilling fiduciary duties to shareholders.

Vignettes 10.1–10.4 illustrate these propositions. We present the vignettes in order of the extent to which the stakeholder concept appears to be embedded in the respective fields of management thought.

Vignette 10.1 STRATEGY AND THE STAKEHOLDER CONCEPT

The field of (business) strategy is inherently about how the organization deals with its environment in order to achieve its aims and objectives. The connection between the organization and its environment may be thought of in many different ways: as a set of forces as for Porter's five-forces analysis (Porter 1980), as a set of issues in terms of opportunities and threats, and as a set of market configurations (Henderson 1979). Most of these frameworks predate Freeman's work. What Freeman contributed was a framework that focused on viewing the organization's connection with its environment as a set of relationships with particular agents (usually categories of people).

Two decades later, Johnson, Scholes, and Whittington in their (2005) core strategy text for many MBA and undergraduate strategy courses present a stakeholder perspective on par with the other key strategy approaches. They discuss stakeholder mapping (identifying stakeholder expectations and power to assess political priorities) as a key concept concerned with assessing the suitability of strategic options on par with 'PESTEL', 'scenarios', 'five forces', 'strategic groups', 'core competences', 'value chain', and 'cultural web'. They argue that an important element of strategic position is to decide which stakeholders the corporation should serve and to assess stakeholder expectations in the light of strategy formation. To assess how stakeholders might influence the success of a particular strategy, they differentiate (2005: 180):

1. 'Market stakeholders' (identified from the five-forces framework and governance chain) such as suppliers, competitors, distributors, and shareholders that can influence the value creation process.
2. 'Social/political stakeholders' such as policymakers, regulators, and government agencies that can influence the social legitimacy of a strategy.
3. 'Technological stakeholders' such as key adopters, standards agencies, and owners of competitive technologies that may influence the diffusion of new technologies and the adoption of industry standards.

Johnson, Scholes, and Whittington (2005) discuss conflict and the need for compromise at some length, providing vignettes to illustrate cases. For them power and the level of stakeholder interest are the determinants of salience. They suggest a strategic matrix, which is similar to Freeman's generic stakeholder strategies matrix (see Figure 4.3).

This strategic tool is designed to assess which stakeholders may oppose or welcome a strategy and how managers should respond. It may also identify situations where maintaining a stakeholder's level of either interest or power may be essential. Additionally, they identify situations where repositioning stakeholder groups are desirable or feasible. Johnson, Scholes, and Whittington (2005) also suggest that accountability to stakeholders has a major influence on the strategy development process. For example, if a wide range of stakeholder interests needs to be explicitly considered, the timescale for the adoption of strategies will need to be lengthened accordingly, and plans adjusted, as stakeholder engagement and dialogue is a time-consuming activity. Despite the fact that Freeman is not widely cited in the strategy literature, it is clear where accepted, standard discourse originated.

Strategy is the area of management thought that is most suited to a reconceptualization based on the stakeholder concept. Strategy is not confined to consideration of a single stakeholder. Rather, it concerns the overall aims and objectives of the organization, however defined. How those aims and objectives are defined can easily be formulated in terms of balancing stakeholder interests. When things are going well, it is easier to see how an organization can afford the luxury of attending to only the most powerful stakeholders, whether they be managers or shareholders. This can be dangerous. Arguably, stakeholder analysis was incorporated into strategic planning as a reaction to failure. According to Mintzberg, 'every failure [of strategic planning] led to the inclusion of new factors.... When political forces were deemed the problem, "stakeholder" planning was added,... as the competition from Japan became severe... cultural planning became the imperative' (1994: 141).

Bryson (1988: 52, cited in Mintzberg 1994: 142) showed how to systematically calculate the wants and needs of different corporate influencer groups and factor them into the planning process. He suggests that for a complete stakeholder analysis, a planning team needs identification of:

- organization stakeholders;
- their stake in corporation or its output;
- criteria to judge corporate performance;
- how well the corporation performs against these criteria;
- how stakeholders influence the corporation;
- how important various stakeholders are.

Vignette 10.2 ACCOUNTING AND FINANCE AND THE STAKEHOLDER CONCEPT

Traditional accounting and finance have been governed by the fiduciary duties of managers and the objective to maximize shareholder wealth. However, there are areas in which stakeholder consideration has always been applied and others in which this is a growing concern. Professional accounting bodies play an important role in accounting education, by active accreditation of university courses, through examination of trainee accountants at the professional levels, and continuing professional development through courses and conferences. Many of these bodies have produced reports on stakeholder reporting and on measuring the business value of stakeholder relationships (CICA 2001; AICPA 2002), or have a dedicated research agenda on stakeholder-related issues, which informs their education agenda. Furthermore, such bodies support global consortiums, such as AccountAbility (2002) and the ICC (see Appendix 9.1), which are currently driving the production of stakeholder-focused guidelines for reporting and practice. This structural elaboration of educational activity indicates that the stakeholder concept is embedded in accounting and finance education and is likely to continue. An indicator of this filtering into practice in the UK is the voluntary disclosure of many UK listed companies of an OFR (see Section 9.5.1). The OFR includes employee, environmental, social, and community issues; the strategies to manage them; the resources available; and the risks and uncertainties faced.

Financial reporting is concerned with providing financial corporate information to interested external parties (stakeholders). This begs two questions.

1. What are the boundaries for reporting? This has been long debated in the accounting literature (Hindes 1988). Professional pronouncements suggest an 'end of pipe' assessment (Stone 1995) whereby corporations only consider contingent liabilities for potential clean-up costs or lawsuits. The extension of accountability to legitimate stakeholders has been restricted by cost estimation and audit verification difficulties. As accounting has developed on a firm-centred, rather than societal-level-based analysis (Roberts and Mahoney 2004), the stakeholders are identified from an instrumental, and not a normative perspective. However, for some corporations this is changing, as indicated by the increase in voluntary CESER (see below).

2. Who are the users of financial statements? US and UK reports were commissioned in the early 1970s to identify the users of financial statement, their needs, and how these needs might be met (AICPA 1973; ASSC

Vignette 10.2 (*contd.*)

1975). A range of 'stakeholders' was identified. Primary focus was given to shareholders and little account-ability, beyond legal requirement, was afforded to other groups in practice. A similar exercise was repeated in the late 1980s, culminating in the publication of an international conceptual framework (IASC 1989). Although widely regarded as a stakeholder model, this has resulted in only a marginal increase in stake-holder disclosure.

The Anglo-American accounting standard setting process may be viewed as one of negotiating and balancing various interests (Weetman 1999). Prior to the release of a standard, an exposure draft is issued and widely circulated to stakeholders for comment. The standard setting process for various accounting standards has been examined (Aranya 1979; Mumford 1979; Hope and Gray 1982; Power 1992). For example, Nobes (1992) identified five political stakeholders that influenced the development of the UK goodwill standard: managers, auditors, users (shareholders, creditors, and employees), government, and the International Accounting Stand-ard Committee (IASC).

Corporate environmental, social, and ethical reporting. There are several theoretical bases that justify or support voluntary CESER: political economy theory, legitimacy theory, agency theory, and stakeholder theory (Gray, Owen, and Adams 1996). Gray, Owen, and Adams distinguish two models that are based on stakeholder theory. The accountability model is based on the idea that the organization–stakeholder relationship is embedded in organizational practice. It proposes a moral responsibility and transparency in dealings with all stakeholders (as determined by society) by virtue of the widespread damage that corporations can perpetrate. This approach is similar to the normative version of stakeholder theory and offers little descriptive or explanatory power for CESER. The organization-centred model is based on the idea that stakeholders are identified by the organization to the extent to which it believes that each group needs to be managed in order to further corporate interests. The more important the stakeholder to the organization, the greater the effort placed on managing the relationship. This approach is similar to instrumental stakeholder theory. Ullmann (1985) developed a stake-holder-centred model in which CESER is viewed as a function of the organization's economic performance, strategic posture towards social responsibility, and the intensity of stakeholder pressure. Roberts (1992) tested this with positive results. The form of stakeholder theory that has been applied to CESER is basic and lacks the refinement of theory development that has occurred in mainstream management journals throughout the last decade. For example, it is implied that salience is chiefly derived from power. Urgency is ignored and legitimacy is only paid lip service, via initial stakeholder identification.

Management accounting and finance are concerned with the use of accounting information for decision-making. Historically, this has emphasized the maximization of shareholder funds. Standard textbooks such as Drury (2004) state that decisions purely based on financial considerations are at best incomplete and an assessment of 'qualitative factors' should be considered with respect to how the decision impacts on corporate stakeholders, although the actual term stakeholders may not be used. This is a defensive approach, viewing stakeholder assessment in terms of risks, threats, and costs. The extent to which such considerations are made in practice is unclear and requires further research. Brenner (1995) examined the degree of consistency between a range of management techniques and stakeholder theory. Total quality management and customer focus were found to be most consistent with stakeholder theory, followed by codetermination, management by walking around, multifunctional teams, and participatory management. Capital budgeting was the least consistent, despite the attention given in textbooks to stakeholder impact where this technique is described. The BSC (Kaplan and Norton 1996) was created to address the short-term and narrow focus of traditional approaches. Other 'new' practices (activity-based costing, life cycle costing, just-in-time inventory management, total quality management, target costing, value chain analysis, employee empowerment, continuous improvement, etc.) are sufficiently flexible to accommodate stakeholder factors. Problems of data collection and exact costing infor-mation need to be solved before such techniques can become widely used as part of a stakeholder framework.

The distinction made in Section 10.1 between a field of education embracing a range of stakeholders, either through enhancing the role of their derivative importance to the traditional primary stakeholder group or by stimulating a redefinition of the purpose of the field itself, can be most clearly seen in the two CESER models described above. Accounting may be viewed as a lens through which stakeholders judge the corporation. The credibility of accounting has been called into question following many recent accounting scandals, such as WorldCom and Parmalat (see Vignette 9.4). This is particularly so in the case of Enron (see Section 9.6) due to the fatal impact it had on Arthur Andersen (one of the 'Big 5' global accountancy firms at that time). This has led to a partial reconception of the field of accounting, involving increasing attention given to corporate governance, CESER, transparency, stakeholders, and ethics in general.

The reconceptualization is less pronounced in management accounting and finance. This is partially because these systems are viewed as internal to the organization. It is also partly because current management accounting systems are not flexible enough to deal with dedicated stakeholder analysis, reporting, or engagement. Many stakeholder impacts on decision-making are intangible and are difficult to assess, e.g. the indirect economic advantages of prevention. Such costs and benefits tend to be underestimated or overlooked, resulting in poor-quality decision-making information. This is despite agencies such as the US Environmental Protection Agency actively encouraging organizations to modify management accounting systems to fully account for environmental costs and to actively use that information in decision-making, including capital budgeting (EPA 1994).

Vignette 10.3 MARKETING AND THE STAKEHOLDER CONCEPT

Marketing appears inconsistent with stakeholder management. It has historically focused on one stakeholder, the customer, with maxims such as 'the customer is king' and 'the customer is always right' forming the cornerstone of the marketing concept. Jackson (2001) suggested that such attitudes are not helpful and calls for marketeers to dismiss them. In 1991 Miller and Lewis concluded that stakeholder theory had yet to catch on in marketing. This appears to be changing (Coddington 1993; Greenley and Foxall 1996; Menon and Menon 1997; Slater 1997; Charter and Polonsky 1999). Stakeholder influences range from general recommendations to distinct approaches such as market-orientated strategic planning, relationship marketing, green marketing, and cause-related marketing. Charter (1992: 27–8) outlined the development of the field and proposed that this recent call for a stakeholder approach stems from stakeholder pressure, particularly a marked growth in environmental and social criteria used to make personal buying decisions. This could be viewed as the latest in a number of variations on the traditional marketing concept that has witnessed the emergence of 'the human concept', 'the intelligent consumer concept', 'the ecological imperative concept', 'the ecological marketing concept', and 'the societal marketing concept'.

It is common for marketing textbooks to advise marketeers to be aware of stakeholder relationships, as each can influence customer value by providing or withholding brand support. Marketeers are recommended to ensure mutually productive relations with stakeholders, identifying interests, motivations, and conflicts (Adcock, Halborg, and Ross 2001; Charter 1992). A consequence of these recommendations is that the marketing

Vignette 10.3 (*contd.*)

department should work with other departments, and even relinquish budgets if resources are better spent to address stakeholder priorities elsewhere. In different situations, different stakeholder groups take priority. In a brand crisis the media take priority but in corporate restructuring it should be the employees. Polonsky (1996) proposed that stakeholders can directly threaten, directly cooperate, or indirectly influence the marketing function. He identified four stakeholder marketing strategies (isolationist, aggressive, adapting, and cooperative), which are heavily influenced by Freeman (1984). Miller and Lewis (1991) used stakeholder theory and value exchange theory (relating to the creation and delivery of value) to provide a framework for marketeers. For each stakeholder group, marketeers are advised to identify the nature of the value exchange, the methods of influence, how groups react towards each other, where balance/imbalance exists, and how strong, or at risk, is the state of (dis)equilibrium. Koiranen (1995) recommended moving stakeholders up a 'ladder of stakeholder loyalty', rather than focusing on the building of new relationships. Strategies are formulated on the basis of the gap between the actual and the desired position of a stakeholder on the ladder and the current state of relationship, whether potential, actualized, or de-actualized. The evolutionary stage of the relationship is of importance: discovery, initialization, stabilization, or development. Polonsky, Schuppisser, and Beldona (2002) argued that it is not efficient to place all stakeholders at the top of the ladder.

Market-orientated strategic planning recommends that marketeers need to incorporate external cues and stimuli into their decision-making. Kotler (2003) argued that unless other stakeholders are 'nourished', the business may never earn sufficient returns for shareholders. Corporations can deliver to any stakeholder on three levels of satisfaction: threshold, performance, or excitement. For example, to delight customers, to perform well for employees, but to only deliver a threshold satisfaction for suppliers.

Relationship marketing focuses on building and maintaining 'a chain of relationships' that will benefit the corporation and its customer. It recognizes that customers' needs require contributions from other stakeholders, which have the potential to add value or harm the corporation–customer relation. As such, the effective alignment of the corporation's capabilities with stakeholder expectations is important for marketeers. Gordon (1998) argued that it may not be easy to bring capabilities into alignment but called for corporations to recognize the relationships as a fundamental and explicit component of strategy and to focus on how to add value through relationships.

Green marketing recommends that corporate responsibilities extend beyond corporate boundaries into the next generation, making issues such as life cycle analysis, environmental audit, and impact assessment central to the marketing function. As 'environmentally friendly' products doubled in the early 1990s marketeers quickly reacted to the potential for the 'green pound'. Many corporations jumped on the green bandwagon, only to be later disgraced, as consumers and NGOs differentiated between real and spurious claims. This was particularly so for the recipients of Friends of the Earth 'Green Con of the Year Awards'. Marketeers are rarely environmental experts and tend to be inward-looking according to Polonsky, Rosenberg, and Ottman (1998). They suggested that marketeers belittle, discount, or totally ignore ideas from outside the corporation. They called for the development of a more open culture that is willing to listen to and learn from new ideas from external stakeholders, especially special interests groups. Developing strategic green alliances may be effective in maintaining green stakeholder support and may enhance the marketeer's limited environmental knowledge. In practice, very basic methods are used to include stakeholders (Polonsky, Rosenberg, and Ottman 1998).

Cause-related marketing strategies appear to be congruent with increasing stakeholder value. It involves the purchase of a product from a corporation that pledges to donate a percentage of the price to a good cause. Sponsorship occurs irrespective of sales. Historically, disease-based causes have been favoured. Partnerships have been formed between the Body Shop and AIDS, Coca-Cola and Guide Dogs for the Blind, and Mercedes Benz and Multiple Sclerosis. Sophisticated campaigns have focused on diseases where the primary target group

(*contd.*)

Vignette 10.3 (*contd.*)

has the same profile as the target consumer groups. For example, many corporations manufacturing products aimed at women (*Cosmopolitan*, Estée Lauder, Revlon, Avon) have promoted campaigns in support of breast cancer. Such campaigns have proved very successful but over time cynicism can result in a consumer backlash. Friedman and Kouns (1997) identified a major weakness of these approaches: that 90 per cent of customers cannot link specific philanthropic efforts with particular corporations. As an alternative, some corporations are integrating strategic philanthropy[2] with the marketing function. McAllister and Ferrell provided numerous examples and argued that this is becoming widespread.

Though there are some calls to define marketing as a field of study to encompass a wider stakeholder perspective, it seems clear from Vignette 10.3 that those who argue for a wider stakeholder perspective are primarily thinking of this in terms of the importance of all stakeholders being derived from their influence on the primary stakeholder target of marketing: customers.

Vignette 10.4 HUMAN RESOURCE MANAGEMENT AND THE STAKEHOLDER CONCEPT

The stakeholder concept has impacted HRM through the recognition of employees as 'stakeholders'. This is presented as an answer to a lack of job security and poor workplace relationships characterized by lack of trust, respect, and commitment. Ackers (2001) stated that employees cannot be expected by management to be committed to the corporation unless management demonstrates that it is committed to them. Management should recognize their contribution *as stakeholders*, through the development of a 'psychological contract' by being honest; treating people fairly, justly, and consistently; keeping its word; and showing willingness to listen to the comments and suggestions made by employees. Monks (1998: 174) went further by proposing a four-prong approach to developing corporate–employee partnerships, one of which includes giving employees a voice in how the corporation is run, and the right to information and consultation on strategic issues. He advocated that employees must be able to express collective views, and that consultation must be meaningful, fair, comprehensive, and unbiased.

The best-known descriptive models of HRM are consistent with the stakeholder approach: the Harvard Model (Beer et al. 1984) and the Massachusetts Institute of Technology (MIT) model (Kochan, Katz, and McKersie 1986). These are concerned with management's role in balancing competing interests and in identifying choice and the factors that affect choice. The Harvard Map indicates that HRM policies are influenced by:

1. *Stakeholder interests*, which should inform HRM policies, otherwise 'the enterprise will fail to meet the needs of these stakeholders in the long run and it will fail as an institution' (Beer et al. 1984).
2. *Situational factors*, which may constrain the development of and be influenced by HRM policies. Situational factors include the state of the labour market, the calibre and motivation of staff, management style, production technologies, working methods, the form of ownership, and to whom management are accountable.

The effectiveness of HRM policies should be evaluated according to the commitment and competence of employees, congruence (between employees and organizational goals), and cost-effectiveness (of HRM practices). HRM policies should seek to increase the level of each factor. The Harvard Map attempts to link HRM policy with competitive strategy and calls for line managers to accept greater responsibility for assuring their alignment. This was deemed necessary to facilitate the development of HRM as a management discipline that was no longer solely linked to the mundane and instrumental tasks of recruitment and selection, training,

> **Vignette 10.4** (*contd.*)
>
> appraisal, and maintenance of employee records. The model is relatively flexible and can accommodate different employment structures, managerial styles, and cultural differences. It has been received more favourably in the UK than in the USA, due to stronger union structures and labour traditions. Criticisms include variables are difficult to measure and identify, cost-effectiveness and congruence may conflict, and technology or working conditions may obstruct the ability to increase the level of some factors. The model has been developed further (Hendry and Pettigrew 1986, 1990; Guest 1987, 1989, 1990). In all subsequent revisions less focus has been given to stakeholder interests. The BSC is also viewed as an HRM stakeholder model, with HRM practices falling under the 'learning and growth' perspective. Maltz, Shenhar, and Reilly (2003: 197) have developed the scorecard by including a 'people development dimension' that explicitly recognizes the critical role of employees in organizational success.

The call to reconceptualize this field has not led to its effective widening to take into account the interest of multiple stakeholders in HRM policy, but instead has led to a call for an empowerment of employees to be viewed as stakeholders, rather than mere input costs. This is little different from the Human Relations approach to employee relations advocated by Mayo and others at Harvard Business School in the 1930s.

We would not expect the stakeholder concept to influence the field of HRM as much as the fields of strategy, accounting, or even marketing because, as noted in Section 10.1, HRM is inherently a more inward-looking subject. Certainly, the move from personnel towards HRM, and particularly strategic HRM, has been stimulated by an attempt to raise the status of this function in the boardroom. However, the move can be supported by other means than embracing consideration of multiple stakeholders, e.g. by embracing information systems techniques. Vignette 10.4 shows that this is a field where the extent to which educationalists and practitioners take up the stakeholder concept may well be merely a fad and perhaps a short-lived one.

10.3 **Conclusion**

In this chapter we have indicated that the stakeholder concept has permeated management education differentially in different fields. In some, such as HRM and marketing, it has been incorporated in only a very patchy and possibly a superficial manner. It may be that the stakeholder concept represents only a passing fad and textbook writers are correct in being wary of giving it much space or depth of discussion. However, in the field of strategy the stakeholder concept is firmly embedded, though it has complemented, rather than replaced, other frameworks. In some ways the accounting field is the most interesting. The stakeholder concept is less explicitly and less widely considered than in the strategy field. However, the rise of the stakeholder concept as a replacement for the stockholder concept in this field is associated with a broad reconceptualization of the field itself.

Finally, we suggest it is important for advocates, particularly of *normative* stakeholder theory, to address the role of education and consider how the stakeholder concept could impact on the core subjects of management. We note that what is being called for is only at the level of the third kind of normativity, as indicated in the model of normative stakeholder theories presented in Chapter 3 (see Figure 3.3). Laws and institutions do not need to change (second kind of normativity) in order to make an impact on management thinking and practice. Management education, through textbooks, can be an effective lever to achieve greater consideration of stakeholders and greater influence of stakeholders on organizations.

☐ QUESTIONS/EXERCISES

1 Compare any strategy textbook with Johnson, Scholes, and Whittington (2005). How do their treatments of stakeholder analysis compare in terms of:
   (a) Importance attributed to stakeholder analysis?
   (b) Integration of stakeholder analysis with other strategic analysis techniques?
   (c) Extent to which recommended treatment of stakeholders is sensitive to type of stakeholder, life cycle conditions of either stakeholders, corporations, or issues at stake?

2 Consider the extent that the stakeholder concept has been incorporated into any corporate governance textbook. How strongly does the text recommend incorporation of stakeholder considerations into
   (a) Fundamentals of risk management?
   (b) As part of the structuring of actual corporate governance procedures?

3 Consider a standard text in marketing. Briefly summarize its references to the stakeholder concept. Evaluate the extent to which stakeholders other than customers are considered in their own right, compared with their potential impact on customers.

☐ NOTES

1 The media, politicians, environmental pressure groups, the parent company, the board of directors, senior management, employees, customers, the community, legislators, investors, suppliers, pressure groups, competitors, trade unions, trade associations, professional bodies, non-regulatory bodies, and academics.

2 Strategic philanthropy is 'the synergistic use of organizational core competencies and resources to address key stakeholders' interests and to achieve both organizational and social benefits' (McAllister and Ferrell 2002: 690).

☐ REFERENCES

AccountAbility (2002). *AA1000 Assurance Standard: Guiding Principles*. London: AccountAbility.

Ackers, P. (2001). 'Employment Ethics', in T. Redman and A. Wilkinson (eds.), *Contemporary Human Resource Management*. Harlow, UK: Financial Times/Prentice-Hall, pp. 377–403.

—— and Payne, J. (1998). 'British Trade Unions and Social Partnership: Rhetoric, Reality and Strategy', *The International Journal of Human Resource Management*, 9/3: 529–50.

Adams, C. A. and Roberts, C. B. (1995). 'Corporate Ethics: An Issue Worthy of Report?' *Accounting Forum*, 19/2–3: 128–42.

——, Hill, W., and Roberts, C. B. (1998). 'Corporate Social Reporting Practices in Western Europe: Legitimising Corporate Behaviour?' *British Accounting Review*, 30/1: 1–21.

Adcock, D., Halborg, A., and Ross, C. (2001). *Marketing: Principles and Practice*. Harlow, UK: Financial Times/Prentice-Hall.

Agle, B. R., Mitchell, R. K., and Sonnenfeld, J. A. (1999). 'Who Matters to CEOs? An Investigation of Stakeholder Attributes and Salience, Corporate Performance and CEO Values', *Academy of Management Journal*, 42/5: 507–25.

Ahlstedt, L. and Jahnukainen, I. (1971). *Yritysorganisaatio Yhteistoiminnan Ohjausjaerjesteimaenae*. Helsinki: Weilin and Göös.

AICPA (American Institute of Certified Public Accountants) (1973). *Report of a Study Group on the Objectives of Financial Statements (The Trueblood Committee)*. New York: AICPA.

AICPA (American Institute of Certified Public Accountants) (2002). *Reporting to Analysts and External Stakeholders*. New York: AICPA.

Alkhafaji, A. F. (1989). *A Stakeholder Approach to Corporate Governance; Managing in a Dynamic Environment*. Westport, CT: Quorum Books.

Alchian, A. and Demsetz, H. (1972). 'Production, Information costs, and Economic Organization', *American Economic Review*, 62: 488–500.

Ambler, T. and Wilson, A. (1995). 'Problems of Stakeholder Theory', *Business Ethics: A European Review*, 4/1: 30–5.

Anderson, A. (1991). 'Source Strategies and the Communication of Environmental Affairs', *Media, Culture and Society*, 13/4: 459–76.

Andrews, K. (1980). *The Concept of Corporate Strategy*. Homewood, IL: Richard D. Irwin.

Andriof, J., Waddock, S., Husted, B., and Rahman, S. S. (eds.) (2002). *Unfolding Stakeholder Thinking. 1: Theory, Responsibility and Engagement*. Sheffield, UK: Greenleaf Publishing.

—— —— —— —— (eds.) (2003). *Unfolding Stakeholder Thinking. 2: Relationships, Communication, Reporting and Performance*. Sheffield, UK: Greenleaf Publishing.

Ansoff, H. I. (1965a). *Corporate Strategy*. New York: McGraw-Hill.

—— (1965b). *Strategic Management*. New York: John Wiley & Sons.

Aoki, M. (1984). *The Co-operative Game Theory of the Firm*. Oxford: Clarendon Press.

Aranya, N. (1979). 'The Influence of Pressure Groups on Financial Statements in Britain', in T. A. Lee and R. Parker (eds.), *The Evolution of Corporate Financial Reporting*. Sunbury-on-Thames, UK: Nelson.

Archer, M. S. (1995). *Realist Social Theory: The Morphogenic Approach*. Cambridge: Cambridge University Press.

Argandoña, A. (1998). 'The Stakeholder Theory and the Common Good', *Journal of Business Ethics*, 17: 1093–102.

Argenti, J. (1993). *Your Organization: What Is It for?* New York: McGraw-Hill.

—— (1997). 'Stakeholders: The Case Against', *Long Range Planning*, 30/3: 442–9.

Arie, S. (2004). 'Parmalat Dream Goes Sour', *The Observer*, 4 January.

Arnstein, S. R. (1969). 'A Ladder of Citizen Participation', *American Institute of Planners Journal*, 35 (July): 216–24.

Ashforth, B. E. and Kreiner, G. E. (1999). 'How Can You Do It? Dirty Work and the Challenge of Constructing a Positive Identity', *Academy of Management Review*, 24: 413–34.

ASSC (Accounting Standards Steering Committee) (1975). *The Corporate Report*. London: ASSC.

Aupperle, K. E., Carroll, A. B., and Hatfield, J. D. (1985). 'An Empirical Investigation of the Relationship Between Corporate Social Responsibility and Profitability', *Academy of Management Journal*, 28: 446–63.

Axelrod, R. (1984). *The Evolution of Cooperation*. New York: Basic Books.

Bacharach, S. (1989). 'Organizational Theories: Some Criteria For Evaluation', *Academy of Management Review*, 14: 496–515.

Bahanda, S. (1999). *Marks & Spencer: The Rocky Road to Recovery*. London: Deutsche Bank.

—— (2001). *On Your Marks*. London: Deutsche Bank.

Barboza, D. (2002). 'Its Assets May Have Been Misstated by $24 Billion, Enron Discloses', *The New York Times*, 23 April.

Barney, J. B. and Ouchi, W. G. (1986). *Organizational Economics*. San Francisco: Jossey-Bass.

Barry, N. (1998). *Business Ethics*. London: Macmillan.

Baudrillard, J. (1981). *Simulacres et Simulation*. Paris: Galilée. Translated in 1994 by Ann Arbor, MI: University of Michigan Press.

Bauman, Z. (1993). *Postmodern Ethics*. Oxford: Blackwell.

Beauchamp, T. L. and Bowie, N. E. (eds). (1983/1988/1993/1997/2004). *Ethical Theory and Business*. Englewood Cliffs, NJ: Prentice-Hall.

Becker, L. C. (1978). *Property Rights*. London: Routledge.

—— (1992). 'Property', in L. C. Becker and C. B. Becker (eds.), *Encyclopedia of Ethics, Vol. 2*. New York: Garland, pp. 1023–7.

Beder, S., Brown, P., and Vidal, J. (1997). 'Who Killed Kyoto?' *The Guardian*, 29 October: 4.

Beer, M., Spector, B., Lawrence, P., Quinn Mills, D., and Walton, R. (1984). *Managing Human Assets*. New York: Free Press.

Berle, A. A., Jr. (1931). 'Corporate Powers as Powers in Trust', *Harvard Law Review*, 44/7: 1049–74.

—— (1932). 'For Whom Are Corporate Managers Trustees: A Note', *Harvard Law Review*, 45: 1365–72.

—— and Means, G. C. (1932). *The Modern Corporation and Private Property*. New York: Macmillan.

Berman, S. L. (2000). 'Managerial Opportunism and Firm Performance: An Empirical Test of Instrumental Stakeholder Theory', *Research in Stakeholder Theory, 1997–1998: The Sloan Foundation Minigrant Project*. Toronto: The Clarkson Center for Business Research.

—— Wicks, A. C., Kotha, S., and Jones, T. M. (1999). 'Does Stakeholder Orientation Matter? The Relationship Between Stakeholder Management Models and Firm Financial Performance', *Academy of Management Journal*, 42/5: 488–506.

Best, S. and Kellner, D. (1991). *Postmodern Theory: Critical Interrogations*. New York: Guilford.

Bevan, J. (2002). *The Rise and Fall of Marks & Spencer*. London: Profile Books.

Bhaskar, R. (1975). *A Realist Theory of Science*. Leeds, UK: Leeds Books.

BiE (Business in the Environment) (1999). *Performance: Sustaining the Business Revolution: Business in the Environment Index of Corporate Environmental Engagement 1999 Survey*. London: BiE.

Bigelow, B., Fahey, L., and Mahon, J. F. (1991). 'Political Strategy and Issues Evolution: A Framework for Analysis and Action', in K. Paul (ed.), *Contemporary Issues in Business Ethics and Politics*. Lewiston, NY: Edwin Mellen Press, pp. 1–26.

—— —— —— (1993). 'A Typology of Issue Evolution', *Business & Society*, 32/1: 18–29.

Bishop, J. D. (2000). 'A Framework for Discussing Normative Theories of Business Ethics', *Business Ethics Quarterly*, 10/3: 563–91.

Bizjak, J. M. and Marquette, C. J. (1998). 'Are Shareholder Proposals All Bark and No Bite? Evidence from Shareholder Resolutions to Rescind Poison Pills', *Journal of Financial and Quantitative Analysis*, 33/4: 499–521.

Blackmore, S. (1996). 'Memes, Minds and Selves'. Lecture at the London School of Economics, 28 November, www.memes.org.uk/lectures/mms.html.

Blair, M. M. (1995/1998). 'Whose Interests Should Corporations Serve?' in Brooking Institution, *Ownership and Control: Rethinking Corporate Governance for the Twenty-first Century*. Washington, DC: Brooking Institution. Reproduced in M. B. E. Clarkson (ed.) (1998), *The Corporation and Its Stakeholders: Classic and Contemporary Reading*. Toronto: University of Toronto Press.

Blair, T. (1994). *Financial Times*. 11 June: 12.

—— (1996). Speech to the Singapore Business Community, 8 January, cited in Stoney and Winstanley (2001: 606).

Blyton, P. and Turnbull, P. (1994). *The Dynamics of Employee Relations*. London: Macmillan.

Boatright, J. R. (1994). 'Fiduciary Duties and the Shareholder–Management Relation: Or What's So Special About Shareholders?' *Business Ethics Quarterly*, 4/4: 393–407.

Bookbinder, P. (1993). *Simon Marks, Retail Revolutionary*. London: Weidenfeld & Nicolson.

Bowen, H. R. (1953). *Social Responsibilities of the Businessman*. New York: Harper & Row.

Bower, J. and Matthews, J. (1994). 'Marks & Spencer: Sir Richard Greenbury's Quiet Revolution', discussion paper, Harvard Business School, August.

Bowie, N. E. (1988). 'The Moral Obligations of Multinational Corporations', in S. Luper-Foy (ed.), *Problems of International Justice*. Boulder, CO: Westview Press, pp. 97–113.

—— (1998). 'A Kantian Theory of Capitalism', *Business Ethics Quarterly*, The Ruffin Series, Special Issue No. 1: 37–60.

—— (1999). *Business Ethics: A Kantian Perspective*. Oxford: Blackwell.

Braverman, H. (1974). *Labor and Monopoly Capital*. New York: Monthly Review Press.

Brenner, S. N. (1993). 'The Stakeholder Theory of the Firm and Organizational Decision-making: Some Propositions and A Model', *Proceedings of the International Association for Business and Society*, 205–10.

Brenner, S. N. (1995). 'Stakeholder Theory of the Firm: Its Consistency with Current Management Techniques', in J. Näsi (ed.), *Understanding Stakeholder Thinking*. Helsinki: LSR-Julkaisut Oy, pp. 75–96.

Briggs, A. (1984). *Marks & Spencer 1884–1984: A Centenary History*. London: Octopus Books.

Brown, G. (1975). *Sabotage: A Study in Industrial Conflict*. Nottingham: Spokesman Books.

Browning, J. (1993). 'Union Carbide Disaster at Bhopal', in J. A. Gottschalk (ed.), *Crisis Response: Inside Stories on Managing Under Siege*. Detroit, MI: Visible Ink Press.

Bryson, J. M. (1988). *Strategic Planning for Public and Nonprofit Organizations*. San Francisco, CA: Jossey-Bass.

Burrowes, A. W., Kastantin, J., and Novicevic, M. M. (2004). 'The Sarbanes-Oxley Act as a Hologram of Post-Enron Disclosure: A Critical Realist Commentary', *Critical Perspectives on Accounting*, 15: 797–811.

Burton, B. K. and Dunn, C. P. (1996). 'Feminist Ethics as Moral Grounding for Stakeholder Theory', *Business Ethics Quarterly*, 6/2: 133–47.

Cadbury Committee (1992). *Report on the Committee on the Financial Aspects of Corporate Governance*. London: Gee.

Calton, J. M. (1991). 'The Dark Side of Commitment: Is the Literature on Organizational Commitment an Ideological Blackhole?' in K. Paul (ed.), *Contemporary Issues in Business Ethics and Politics*. Lewiston, NY: Edwin Mellen Press, pp. 69–99.

—— and Kurland, N. B. (1995). 'A Theory of Stakeholder Enabling: Giving Voice to an Emerging Postmodern Praxis of Organisational Discourse', in D. M. Boje, R. P. Gephart, and T. J. Thatchenkery (eds.), *Postmodern Management and Organization Theory*. London: Sage, pp. 154–77.

—— and Lad, L. J. (1995). 'Social Contracting as a Trust-Building Process of Network Governance', *Business Ethics Quarterly*, 5/2: 271–95.

Campbell, D. (2003). 'Intra- and Intersectoral Effects in Environmental Disclosures: Evidence for Legitimacy Theory?' *Business Strategy and The Environment*, 12/6: 357–71.

Canham, J. (2001). 'Screening for Green Investment', *The Financial Times*, 26 January, London.

Carroll, A. B. (1979). 'A Three-Dimensional Conceptual Model of Corporate Social Performance', *Academy of Management Review*, 4: 497–505.

—— (1989/1993). *Business and Society: Ethics and Stakeholder Management*. Cincinnati, OH: South-Western Publishing.

—— and Näsi, J. (1997). 'Understanding Stakeholder Thinking: Themes from a Finnish Conference', *Business Ethics*, 6/1: 46–51.

Carroll, W. K. and Ratner, R. S. (1996). 'Master-Framing and Cross-Movement Networking in Contemporary Social Movements', *Sociological Quarterly*, 37: 601–25.

Carson, R. (1962). *The Silent Spring*. New York: Fawcett Crest.

Carter, J., Stockdale, M., Roman, F. P., and Lawrence, A. (1995). 'Local Peoples Participation in Forest Resource Assessment: An Analysis of Recent Experiences, with Case Studies from Indonesia and Mexico', *Commonwealth Forestry Review*, 74/4: 333–42.

Chapman, J. and Fisher, T. (2000). 'The Effectiveness of NGO Campaigning: Lessons from Practice', *Development in Practice*, 10/2: 151–65.

Charter, M. (ed.) (1992). *Greener Marketing: A Responsible Approach to Business*. Sheffield: Greenleaf Publishing.

—— and Polonsky, M. J. (eds.) (1999). *Greener Marketing: A Global Perspective on Greening Marketing Practice*. Sheffield: Greenleaf Publishing.

Child, J. W. and Marcoux, A. M. (1999). 'Freeman and Evans: Stakeholder Theory and the Original Position', *Business Ethics Quarterly*, 9: 207–24.

CICA (Canadian Institute of Chartered Accountants) (2001). *Measuring the Business Value of Stakeholder Relationships*. Toronto: CICA.

Clarkson Center for Business Ethics (1999/2002). *Principles of Stakeholder Management*. Toronto: University of Toronto. Reproduced in 2002, *Business Ethics Quarterly*, 12/1: 256–64.

Clarkson, M. B. E. (1988). 'Corporate Social Performance in Canada, 1976–86', in L. E. Preston (ed.), *Research in Corporate Social Performance and Policy*, Vol. 12. Greenwich, CT: JAI Press, pp. 331–58.

—— (1991). 'Defining, Evaluating and Managing Corporate Social Performance: A Stakeholder Management Model', in J. E. Post (ed.), *Research in Corporate Social Performance and Policy*. Greenwich, CT: JAI Press, pp. 331–58.

—— (1994). *A Risk-Based Model of Stakeholder Theory*. Toronto: The Centre for Corporate Social Performance & Ethics.

—— (1995). 'A Stakeholder Framework for Analyzing and Evaluating Corporate Social Performance', *Academy of Management Journal*, 20/1: 92–118.

Coase, R. H. (1960). 'The Problem of Social Cost', *Journal of Law and Economics*, 3: 1–4.

Coddington, W. (1993). *Environmental Marketing: Positive Strategies for Reaching Green Consumers*. New York: McGraw-Hill.

Cohen, M. D., March, J. G., and Olsen, J. P. (1972). 'A Garbage Can Model of Organizational Choice', *Administrative Science Quarterly*, 17/1: 1–25.

Coke, E. (1613). *10 Coke Report 1a, 77 Eng. Rep. 937* (Exchequer Chamber).

Commons, J. (1924). *Legal Foundations of the Capitalism*. New York: Macmillan.

—— (1931). 'Institutional Economics', *American Economic Review*, 21: 648–57.

Cook, P. (1990). 'The Silent Strike: Causes and Solutions', Address to the Conference on Absenteeism and Employee Turnover, Centre for Industrial Relations and Labour Studies, University of Melbourne.

Cooper, R. (2004). *The Timewaster Letters*. London: Michael O'Mara Books.

Corlett, J. A. (1989). 'The "Modified Vendetta Sanction" as a Method of Corporate Collective Punishment', *Journal of Business Ethics*, 8: 937–42.

Cornell, B. and Shapiro, A. C. (1987). 'Corporate Stakeholders and Corporate Finance', *Financial Management*, 16: 5–14.

Coser, L. A. (1956). *The Functions of Social Conflict*. London: Routledge & Kegan Paul.

Cragg, W. (2002). 'Business Ethics and Stakeholder Theory', *Business Ethics Quarterly*, 12/2: 113–42.

Cruver, B. (2003). *Enron: Anatomy of Greed: The Unshredded Truth from an Enron Insider*. London: Arrow.

CTC (Centre for Tomorrow's Company) (1995). *Sooner, Sharper, Simpler: A Lean Vision of an Inclusive Annual Report*. London: CTC.

—— (1998). *Inclusiveness and Sustainable Business Success: The Research Evidence*. London: CTC.

Cullinan, C. (2004). 'Enron as a Symptom of Audit Process Breakdown: Can the Sarbanes-Oxley Act Cure the Disease?' *Critical Perspectives in Accounting*, 15: 853–64.

Cummings, J. F. (2001). 'Engaging Stakeholders in Corporate Accountability Programmes: A Cross-Sectoral Analysis of UK and Transnational Experience', *Business Ethics: A European Review*, 10/1: 45–52.

Cyert, R. M. and March, J. G. (1963). *A Behavioral Theory of the Firm*. Englewood Cliffs, NJ: Prentice-Hall.

Darnall, N. and Jolley, G. J. (2004). 'Involving the Public: When Are Surveys and Stakeholder Interviews Effective?' *Review of Policy Research*, 21/4: 581–93.

Davidson, D. K. (1995). 'Ten Tips for Boycott Targets', *Business Horizons*, 38 (March–April): 77–80.

Davis, K. (1973). 'The Case for and Against Business Assumption of Social Responsibilities', *Academy of Management Journal*, 16/2: 312–22.

—— and Blomstrom, R. L. (1975). *Business and Society: Environment and Responsibility*, 3rd edn. New York: McGraw-Hill.

Dawkins, R. (1976). *The Selfish Gene*. Oxford: Oxford University Press.

—— (1989). *The Selfish Gene*, 2nd edn. Oxford: Oxford University Press.

Deegan, C. and Gordon, B. (1996). 'A Study of the Environmental Disclosure Practices of Australian Corporations', *Accounting and Business Research*, 26/3: 187–99.

Deetz, S. (1995). *Transforming Communication, Transforming Business: Building Responsive and Responsible Workplaces*. Cresskill, NJ: Hampton Press.

Della Porta, D. and Mario, M. (1999). *Social Movements: An Introduction*. Malden, MA: Blackwell.

Deloitte Touche and Tohmatsu (1997). *Corporate Environmental Report Score Card*. Denmark: Deloitte Touche and Tohmatsu.

Derrida, J. (1978). *Writing and Difference*, A. Bass (trans.). London: Routledge & Kegan Paul.

—— (1980). *Of Grammatology*, G. C. Spivak (trans.). Baltimore, MD: The John Hopkins University Press.

Dewey, J. (1885/1967). 'Psychology', reprinted in J. A. Boydston (ed.), *The Early Works: 1882–1989*. Carbondale, IL: Southern Illinois University Press.

Dicey, A.V. (1914). *Lectures on the Relationship Between Law and Public Opinion in England During the Nineteenth Century*, 2nd edn. London: Macmillan.

Dickson, M. (2001). 'Of Ethics, Indices and the Wisdom of the Easter Bunny: A Flurry of Events Over the Past Few Days Demonstrates That Companies Will Have to Pay Increasing Attention to Their Social Responsibilities, Whether They Like it or Not', *The Financial Times*, 14 April: 11.

Dill, W. R. (1958). 'Environment as an Influence on Managerial Autonomy', *Administrative Science Quarterly*, 2: 409–43.

Dobson, J. (1996). 'The Feminine Firm: A Comment', *Business Ethics Quarterly*, 6/2: 227–32.

Dodd, E. M., Jr. (1932). 'For Whom Are Corporate Managers Trustees?' *Harvard Law Review*, 45: 1145–63. Reproduced in M. B. E. Clarkson (ed.) (1998), *The Corporation and Its Stakeholders: Classic and Contemporary Reading*. Toronto: University of Toronto Press.

Dodge, H. J. and Robbins, J. E. (1992). 'An Empirical Investigation of the Organizational Life Cycle Model for Small Business Development and Survival', *Journal of Small Business Management*, 30/1: 27–37.

Donaldson, T. (1999). 'Response: Making Stakeholder Theory Whole', *Academy of Management Review*, 24/2: 237–41.

—— and Dunfee, T. W. (1994). 'Towards a Unified Conception of Business Ethics: Integrative Social Contracts', *Academy of Management Review*, 19/2: 252–84.

—— —— (1999). *Ties That Bind: A Social Contracts Approach to Business Ethics*. Cambridge, MA: Harvard Business School Press.

—— —— (2000). 'Précis For: Ties That Bind', *Business and Society Review*, 105/4: 436–43.

—— and Preston, L. E. (1995). 'The Stakeholder Theory of the Corporation: Concepts, Evidence and Implications', *Academy of Management Review*, 20/1: 65–92.

Donovan Commission on Industrial Relations (1968). *Report of the Royal Commission on Trade Unions and Employers' Associations 1965–1968*. Cmnd 3623. London: HMSO.

Dore, R. (1983). 'Goodwill and the Spirit of Modern Capitalism', *British Journal of Sociology*, 34: 359–82.

Drexhage, G. (1998). 'There's Money in Ethics', *Global Investor*, 109: 56.

Drisco, C. and Starik, M. (2004). 'The Primordial Stakeholder: Advancing the Conceptual Consideration of Stakeholder Status for the Natural Environment', *Journal of Business Ethics*, 49/1: 55–74.

Drury, C. (2004). *Management and Cost Accounting*. London: Thomson.

Duncan, T. and Moriarty, S. (1997). *Driving Brand Value: Using Integrated Marketing to Manage Profitable Stakeholder Relationships*. New York: McGraw-Hill.

The Economist (1990). 'Boycotting Corporate America', *The Economist*, 26 May: 69–70.

Edmondson, G. and Cohn, L. (2004). 'How Parmalat Went Sour', *London BusinessWeek*, 12 January.

Edmunds, D. and Wollenberg, E. (2001). 'A Strategic Approach to Multistakeholder Negotiations', *Development and Change*, 32: 231–53.

Edwards, R. (1979). *Contested Terrain: The Transformation of the Workplace in the Twentieth Century*. New York: Basic Books.

Eichenwald, K. and Glater, J. (2002). 'Andersen Hinted of Risk, But Sounded No Alarm', *New York Times*, 14 February.

EIRIS (Ethical Investment Research Information Services) (1996). *Money and Ethics*. London: EIRIS.

Emerson, R. M. (1962). 'Power-Dependence Relations', *American Sociological Review*, 27: 31–41.

EPA (Environmental Protection Agency) (1994). *Stakeholders' Action Agenda: A Report of the Workshop on Accounting and Capital Budgeting for Environmental Costs* (December 5–7). Washington, DC: May.

EPE (European Partners for the Environment) (1997). *Building Trust Through EMAS: What Can We Learn from Responsible Care?* Report of the Dow Europe/EPE Workshop. Brussels: EPE.

Etzioni, A. (1964). *Modern Organizations*. Englewood Cliffs, NJ: Prentice-Hall.

—— (1996). *The New Golden Rule. Community and Morality in a Democratic Society*. New York: Basic Books.

—— (1998). 'A Communitarian Note on Stakeholder Theory', *Business Ethics Quarterly*, 8/4: 679–91.

Evan, W. M. and Freeman, R. E. (1988/1993). 'A Stakeholder Theory of the Modern Corporation: Kantian Capitalism', in T. L. Beauchamp and N. E. Bowie (eds.), *Ethical Theory and Business*. Englewood Cliffs, NJ: Prentice-Hall, pp. 75–84.

Fama, E. F. and Jensen, M. C. (1983). 'Separation of Ownership and Control', *Journal of Law and Economics*, 26: 301–26.

Finch, J. (2000). 'M&S Does Not Need to Cut Jobs, Says Union', *The Guardian*, 7 January: 27.

Fineman, S. and Clark, K. (1996). 'Green Stakeholders: Industry Interpretations and Response', *Journal of Management Studies*, 33/6: 715–30.

Fiske, S. and Taylor, S. (1984). *Social Cognition*. New York: McGraw-Hill.

Fleetwood, S. and Ackroyd, S. (eds.) (2004). *Critical Realist Applications in Organisation and Management Studies*. London: Routledge.

Foley, S. (2003). 'How the Cat Lost the Cream at Britain's Biggest Drugs Firm', *The Independent*, 20 May: 4.

Follet, M. P. (1918). *The New State: Group Organization, the Solution of Popular Government*. New York: Green.

Fombrun, C. and Shanley, M. (1990). 'What's in a Name? Reputation Building and Corporate Strategy', *Academy of Management Journal,* 33: 233–58.

Fox, A. (1966). 'Industrial Sociology and Industrial Relations', *Royal Commission Research Paper No.3.* London: HMSO.

—— (1974). *Beyond Contract, Work, Power and Trust Relations.* London: Faber & Faber.

Fox, L. (2003). *Enron: The Rise and Fall.* Hoboken, NY: John Wiley & Sons.

Foucault, M. (1972). *The Archaeology of Knowledge and the Discourse on Language,* A. M. Sheridan Smith (trans.) London: Tavistock.

—— (1973) *The Order of Things.* New York: Vintage Books.

Frank, R. H. (1988). *Passions Within Reason: The Strategic Role of Emotions.* New York: Norton.

Frederick, W. C. (1998). 'Creatures, Corporations, Communities, Chaos, Complexity: A Naturological View of the Corporate Social Role', *Business & Society,* 37/4: 358–89.

—— Post, J. E., and Davis, K. (1988). *Business and Society: Corporate Strategy, Public Policy, Ethics,* 6th edn. New York: McGraw-Hill.

Freeman, R. E. (1984). *Strategic Management: A Stakeholder Approach.* Boston, MA: Pitman.

—— (1994). 'The Politics of Stakeholder Theory: Some Future Directions', *Business Ethics Quarterly,* 4/4: 409–21.

—— (1999). 'Response: Divergent Stakeholder Theory', *Academy of Management Review,* 24/2: 233–36.

—— (2004). 'A Stakeholder Theory of the Modern Corporation', in T. L. Beauchamp and N. E. Bowie (eds.), *Ethical Theory and Business,* 7th edn. Upper Saddle River, NJ: Pearson/Prentice-Hall, pp. 55–64. Note: this article appeared in 5th (1997) and 6th (2001) editions.

—— and Evan, W. M. (1990). 'Corporate Governance: A Stakeholder Interpretation', *Journal of Behavioral Economics,* 19: 337–59.

—— and Gilbert, D. R. (1987). 'Managing Stakeholder Relationships', in S. P. Sethi and C. M. Falbe (eds.), *Business and Society: Dimensions of Conflict and Cooperation.* Lexington, NY: Lexington Books, pp. 397–423.

—— —— (1992). 'Business Ethics and Society: A Critical Agenda', *Business & Society,* 31/1: 9–17.

—— and Reed, D. L. (1983). 'Stockholders and Stakeholders: A New Perspective on Corporate Governance', *California Management Review,* 25/3: 88–106.

Friedman, A. L. and Miles, S. (2001). 'Socially Responsible Investment and Corporate Social and Environmental Reporting in the UK: An Exploratory Study', *British Accounting Review,* 33: 523–48.

—— —— (2002). 'Developing Stakeholder Theory', *Journal of Management Studies,* 39/1: 1–21.

—— and Phillips, M. (2005). 'Model for Governance of Professional Associations', *Nonprofit Management & Leadership,* 15/2: 187–204.

Friedman, M. (1962). *Capitalism and Freedom.* Chicago, IL: The University of Chicago Press.

—— (1970). 'The Social Responsibility of Business Is to Increase Its Profits', *The New York Times Magazine,* 13 September: 33.

—— (1991). 'Consumer Boycotts: A Conceptual Framework and Research Agenda', *Journal of Social Issues,* 41/1: 149–68.

Friedman, S. and Kouns, C. (1997). 'Charitable Contribution: Reinventing Cause Marketing', *Brand Week,* 27 October.

Frooman, J. (1999). 'Stakeholder Influence Strategies', *Academy of Management Review,* 24/2: 191–205.

Froud, J., Haslam, C., Suckdev, J., Shaoul, J., and Williams, K. (1996). 'Stakeholder Economy? From Utility Privatisation to New Labour', *Capital and Class*, 60/Autumn: 119–34.

Fusaro, P. C. and Miller, R. M. (2002). *What Went Wrong at Enron? Everyone's Guide to the Largest Bankruptcy in US History.* Hoboken, NJ: John Wiley & Sons.

Gallon, G. (1992). 'The Green Product Endorsement Controversy: Lessons from the Pollution Probe/Loblaws Experience', *Alternatives*, 18/3: 17–25.

Gamble, G. and Kelly, G. (1996). 'Stakeholder Capitalism and One Nation Socialism', *Renewal*, 4/1: 23–32.

Garrett, D. E. (1987). 'The Effectiveness of Marketing Policy Boycotts: Environmental Opposition to Marketing', *Journal of Marketing*, 51: 46–57.

GEMI (Global Environment Management Initiative) (1992). *Environment Self-Assessment Program, Publication No. SAP-102.* London: GEMI.

Gerlach, M. and Lincoln, J. (1992). 'The Organization of Business Networks in the United States and Japan', in N. Nohria and R. Eccles (eds.), *Networks and Organizations: Structure, Form and Action.* Boston, MA: Harvard Business School Press, pp. 491–520.

Gibbs, G. (2001). 'Penalties Too Low to Deter Polluters Says Agency', *The Guardian*, 29 September.

Gibson, K. (2000). 'The Moral Basis of Stakeholder Theory', *Journal of Business Ethics*, 26: 245–57.

Gillan, S. L. and Starks, L. T. (2000). 'Corporate Governance Proposals and Shareholder Activism: The Role of Institutional Investors', *Journal of Financial Economics*, 57: 275–305.

Gilligan, C. (1982). *In a Different Voice.* Cambridge, MA.: Harvard University Press.

Gioia, D. A. (1999*a*). 'Response: Practicability Paradigms and Problems in Stakeholder Theorizing', *Academy of Management Review*, 24/2: 228–32.

—— (1999*b*). 'Gioia's Reply to Jones and Wicks', *Academy of Management Review*, 26/4: 624–5.

Godward, E. (1998). 'The Privatization of British Rail 1994–1997', *Proceedings of the Institution of Mechanical Engineers, Journal of Rail and Rapid Transit*, 212/F3: 191–200.

Goodpaster, K. E. (1991). 'Business Ethics and Stakeholder Analysis', *Business Ethics Quarterly*, 1/1: 53–73.

Gordon, I. (1998). *Relationship Marketing.* Etobicoke, Ontario: John Wiley & Sons.

Gouldner, A. W. (1955). *Wildcat Strike.* London: Routledge & Kegan Paul.

Graves, S. B., Rehbein, K., and Waddock, S. (2001). 'Fad and Fashion in Shareholder Activism: The Landscape of Shareholder Resolutions, 1988–1998', *Business and Society Review*, 106/4: 293–314.

Gray, J. (1989). 'Against Cohen on Proletarian Unfreedom', in E. F. Paul, F. D. Miller, and J. Paul (eds.), *Capitalism.* Oxford: Basil Blackwell.

Gray, R. H., Kouhy, R., and Lavers, S. (1995). 'Corporate Social and Environmental Reporting: A Review of the Literature and a Longitudinal Study of UK Disclosure', *Accounting, Auditing and Accountability Journal*, 8/2: 47–77.

—— Owen, D. L., and Adams, C. (1996). *Accounting and Accountability: Changes and Challenges in Corporate Social and Environmental Reporting.* Hemel Hempstead, UK: Prentice-Hall.

Greenbury Committee (1995). *Directors' Remuneration: Report of a Study Group.* London: Gee.

Greenley, G. E. and Foxall, G. R. (1996). 'Consumer and Nonconsumer Stakeholder Orientation in UK Companies', *Journal of Business Research*, 35/2: 105–16.

—— —— (1997). 'Multiple Stakeholder Orientation in UK Companies and the Implication for Company Performance', *Journal of Management Studies*, 34/21: 259–84.

Gribben, C. and Faruk, A. (2004). *Just Pensions: Will UK Pension Funds Become More Responsible?* London: Ashridge Centre for Business and Society.

Gruchy, A. G. (1972). *Contemporary Economic Thought*. London: Macmillan.

Grunig, J. E. and Grunig, L. A. (1989). 'Towards a Theory of Public Relations Behavior of Organizations: Review of a Program of Research', in J. E. Grunig and L. A. Grunig (eds.), *Public Relations Research Annual*, Vol. 1. Hillsdale, NJ: Lawrence Erlbaum, pp. 27–63.

Grzybowski, C. (2000). 'We NGOs: A Controversial Way of Being and Acting', *Development in Practice*, 10/3–4: 436–44.

Guest, D. (1987). 'Human Resource Management and Industrial Relations', *Journal of Management Studies*, 24/5: 503–21.

—— (1989). 'Human Resource Management: Its Implications for Industrial Relations', in J. Story (ed.), *New Perspectives in Human Resource Management*. London: Routledge, pp. 41–55.

—— (1990). 'Human Resource Management and the American Dream', *Journal of Management Studies*, 27/4: 378–97.

Habermas, J. (1984). *The Theory of Communicative Action*. Boston, MA: Beacon Hill.

—— (1987). 'Philosophy as Stand-in and Interpreter', in K. Baynes, J. Bohman, and T. McCarthy (eds.), *After Philosophy*. Cambridge, MA: MIT Press.

—— (1990). *Moral Consciousness and Communicative Action*. Cambridge: Polity.

—— (1993). *Justification and Application: Remarks on Discourse Ethics*. Cambridge, MA: MIT Press.

—— (1996). *Between Facts and Norms: Contributions to a Discourse Theory of Law and Democracy*. Cambridge, MA: MIT Press.

Hadley, M. (1996). 'Putting a Price on Environmental Risk', *Environmental Information Bulletin*, 57: 10–12.

Hainsworth, B. E. (1990). 'The Distribution of Advantages and Disadvantages', *Public Relations Review*, 16/1: 33–9.

Hall, S. (1981). 'Encoding and Encoding in the Television Discourse', in S. Hall, D. Hobson, A. Lowe, and P. Willis (eds.), *Culture, Media, Language: Working Papers in Cultural Studies, 1972–79*. London: Hutchinson, pp. 197–208.

Hammond, K. and Miles, S. (2004). 'Assessing Quality Assessment of Corporate Social Reporting: UK Perspectives', *Accounting Forum*, 28: 61–79.

Hampel Committee (1998). *Committee on Corporate Governance: Final Report*. London: Gee.

Handy, C. (1993). 'What is a Company For?' *Corporate Governance: An International Review*, 1/1: 14–16.

—— (1997). *The Hungry Spirit*. London: Hutchinson.

Harris, C. and Bower, J. L. (1977). 'Marks and Spencer, Ltd', discussion Paper, Harvard Business School, revised.

Harrison, J. and St John, C. (1996). 'Managing and Partnering with External Stakeholders', *Academy of Management Executive*, 10/2: 46–60.

Haselhoff, F. (1976). 'A New Paradigm for the Study of Organizaional Goals', in I. Ansoff, R. Declerk, and R. Hayes (eds.), *From Strategic Planning to Strategic Management*. New York: John Wiley & Sons, pp. 15–27.

Hasnas, J. (1998). 'The Normative Theories of Business Ethics. A Guide for the Perplexed', *Business Ethics Quarterly*, 8/1: 19–42.

Hawley, J. P. and Williams, A. T. (1996). *Corporate Governance in the United States: The Rise of Fiduciary Capitalism—A Review of the Literature.* (Available at http://www.lens-library.com/info/competition.html.)

Hay, C. (1996). 'A State of Disarray? Huttonomics, New Labour and the Contemporary British Impasse', *Renewal*, 4/3: 40–50.

Hayes, R. and Abernathy, W. (1980). 'Managing Our Way to Economic Decline', *Harvard Business Review*, 58/4: 67–77.

Hazlitt, W. (1822/1910). *Table Talk, Essays on Men and Manners.* London: Bell, Bohn's.

Henderson, B. (1979). *Henderson on Corporate Strategy.* Cambridge, MA: Abt Books.

Hendry, C. and Pettigrew, A. M. (1986). 'The Practice of Strategic Human Resource Management', *Personnel Review*, 15/5: 3–8.

—— —— (1990). 'Human Resource Management: An Agenda for the 1990s', *International Journal of Human Resource Management*, 1/1: 17–43.

Hendry, J. (2001). Economic Contacts Versus Social Relationships as a Foundation for Normative Stakeholder Theory', *Business Ethics: A European Review*, 10/3: 223–32.

Herman, E. S. and Chomsky, N. (1988). *Manufacturing Consent: The Political Economy of the Mass Media.* New York: Pantheon.

Hermes, J. (2002). 'Active Audiences: The Active Audience', in A. Briggs and P. Cobley (eds.), *The Media: An Introduction*, 2nd edn. London: Pearson/Longman, pp. 282–93.

Heugens, P. P. M. A. R., Van Den Bosch, F. A. J., and Van Riel, C. B. M. (2002). 'Stakeholder Integration: Building Mutually Enforcing Relationships', *Business & Society*, 41/1: 36–60.

Heydebrand, W. (1989). 'New Organization Forms', *Work and Occupations*, 16/3: 323–57.

Hicks, J. R. (1932). *The Theory of Wages.* London: Macmillan.

Higgs, D. (2003). *Review of the Role and Effectiveness of Non-executive Directors.* Available at http://www.dti.gov.uk/cld/non_exec_review/pdfsphiggsreport.pdf.

Hill, C. W. L. and Jones, T. W. (1992). 'Stakeholder-Agency Theory', *Journal of Management Studies*, 29/2: 131–54.

Hindes, R. D. (1988). 'Financial Accounting: In Communicating Reality We Construct Reality', *Accounting, Organisation and Society*, 13/3: 251–61.

Hirschman, A. O. (1970). *Exit Voice and Loyalty: Response to Decline in Firms, Organizations and States.* Cambridge, MA: Harvard University Press.

Hobbes, T. (1651/1958). *Leviathan, Parts I and II.* New York: Liberal Arts Press.

Hobsbawm, E. J. (1968). *Labouring Men: Studies in the History of Labour.* London: Weidenfeld & Nicolson.

Honore, A. M. (1961). 'Ownership', in A. G. Guest (ed.), *Oxford Essays in Jurisprudence.* Oxford: Clarendon Press.

Hope, T. and Gray, R. (1982). 'Power and Policy Making: The Development of an R&D Standard', *Journal of Business Finance and Accounting*, 9/4: 531–58.

Hosseini, J. and Brenner, S. N. (1992). 'The Stakeholder Theory of the Firm: A Methodology to Generate Value Matrix Weight', *Business Ethics Quarterly*, 2/2: 99–119.

Hutton, W. (1995). *The State We Are In.* London: Jonathan Cape/Random House.

—— (1996). 'The 30/30/40 Society: The Economic and Fiscal Implications', Third Cantor Lecture on the Future of Work. *RSA Journal*, March: 32–6.

Hyman, R. (1972). *Strikes.* London: Fontana/Collins.

IASC (International Accounting Standards Committee) (1989). *Framework for the Preparation and Presentation of Financial Statements*. New York: IASC.

Jackson, C. and Bungård, T. (2002). 'Achieving Quality in Social Reporting: The Role of Surveys in Stakeholder Consultation', *Business Ethics: A European Review*, 11/3: 253–9.

Jackson, J. E. (2001). 'Prioritising Customers and Other Stakeholders Using the AHP', *European Journal of Marketing*, 35/7–8: 858–71.

—— and Schantz, W. T. (1993). 'Crisis Management Lessons: When Push Shoved Nike', *Business Horizons*, January–February: 27–35.

James, W. (1890). *Principles of Psychology* (2 volumes). New York: Holt.

—— (1907). *Pragmatism: A New Name for Some Old Ways of Thinking: Popular Lectures on Philosophy*. New York: Longmans Green.

Jasanoff, S. (1997). 'NGOs and the Environment: From Knowledge to Action', *Third World Quarterly*, 18/3: 579–94.

Jawahar, I. M. and McLaughlin, G. L. (2001). 'Towards a Descriptive Stakeholder Theory: An Organizational Life Cycle Approach', *Academy of Management Review*, 26/3: 397–414.

Jensen, M. C. (2002). 'Value Maximisation, Stakeholder Theory and the Corporate Objective Function', *Business Ethics Quarterly*, 12/2: 235–56.

—— and Meckling, W. H. (1976). 'The Theory of the Firm: Managerial Behaviour, Agency Costs and Ownership Structure', *Journal of Financial Economics*, 3 (October): 305–60.

Jevons, S. (1871/1970). *The Theory of Political Economy*, with an introduction by R. Collinson-Black. Harmondsworth: Penguin.

Johnson, G., Scholes, K., and Whittington, R. (2005). *Exploring Corporate Strategy: Text and Cases*, 7th edn. Harlow: Prentice-Hall/Financial Times/Pearson Education.

Johnson, H. L. (1971). *Business in Contemporary Society: Framework and Issues*. Belmont, CA: Wadsworth.

Jones, T. M. (1995). 'Instrumental Stakeholder Theory: A Synthesis of Ethics and Economics', *Academy of Management Review*, 20/2: 404–38.

—— and Wicks, A. C. (1999a). 'Convergent Stakeholder Theory', *Academy of Management Review*, 24/2: 206–19.

—— —— (1999b). 'Letter to AMR Regarding "Convergent Stakeholder Theory"', *Academy of Management Review*, 26/4: 621–3.

Kaplan, R. S. and Norton, D. P. (1996). *The Balanced Scorecard*. Boston, MA: Harvard Business School Press.

Karpoff, J., Malatesta, P., and Walking, R. (1996). 'Corporate Governance and Shareholder Initiatives: Empirical Evidence', *Journal of Financial Economics*, 42: 365–95.

Keasey, K. Thompson, S., and Wright, M. (eds.) (1997). *Corporate Governance: Economic and Financial Issues*. Oxford: Oxford University Press.

Kelly, G. and Parkinson, J. (1998). 'The Conceptual Foundations of the Corporation: A Pluralist Approach', *Corporation, Financial and Insolvency Law Review*, 2: 174–97.

—— , Kelly, D., and Gamble, A. (eds.) (1997). *Stakeholder Capitalism*. Basingstoke, UK: Macmillan.

Kelly, M. (2003). 'Why Social Mission Gets Squeezed Out of Firms When They're Sold, and What To Do About It', *Business Ethics: Corporate Social Responsibility Report*, Summer, 17/2.

Kerr, C., Dunlop, J. T., Harbison, F., and Myers, C. A. (1964). *Industrialisation and Industrial Man*. Oxford: Oxford University Press.

Kenner Thompson, R. (1988). 'Union Use of Public Proxy Resolutions', *Labor Studies Journal*, Fall: 40–57.

King, W. and Cleland, D. (1978). *Strategic Planning and Policy*. New York: Van Notrand Reinhold.

Kitzinger, J. (2002). 'Impacts and Influences, Media Influence Revisited: An Introduction to "New Effects Research"', in A. Briggs and P. Cobley (eds.), *The Media: An Introduction* (2nd edn). London: Pearson/ Longman, pp. 272–81.

Klein, J. G., Craig Smith, N., and John, A. (2002). 'Exploring Motivations for Participation in a Consumer Boycott', *Advances in Consumer Research*, 29: 363–9.

Knowles, K. G. J. C. (1952). *Strikes: A Study in Industrial Conflict*. Oxford: Blackwell.

Kochan, T. A. and Rubinstein, S. A. (2000). 'Towards a Stakeholder Theory of the Firm: The Saturn Approach', *Organization Science*, 11/4: 367–86.

—— , Katz, H., and McKersie, B. (1986). *The Transformation of American Industrial Relations*. New York: Basic Books.

Koiranen, M. (1995). 'Custopreneurship Coalitions in Relationship Marketing', in J. Näsi (ed.), *Understanding Stakeholder Thinking*. Helsinki: LSR-Publications, pp. 184–94.

Kolk, A. and Levy, D. (2001). 'Winds of Change: Corporate Strategy, Climate Change and Oil Multinationals', *European Management Journal*, 19/5: 501–9.

Kotler, P. (2003). *Marketing Management: Analysis, Planning, Implementation and Control*, 11th edn. Upper Saddle River, NJ: Prentice-Hall.

Kriesi, H., Koopmans, R., Duyvendak, J. W., and Guigni, M. G. (1995). *New Social Movements in Western Europe*. Minneapolis, MN: University of Minnesota Press.

Krueger, R.W. (2001). 'The Public Debate on Agrobiotechnology: A Biotech Company's Perspective', *AgBioForum*, 4/3–4: 209–20.

Kujala, J. (2001). 'Analysing Moral Issues in Stakeholder Relations', *Business Ethics: A European Review*, 10/3: 233–47.

La Guardia, A. and Harnden, T. (2001). 'Bush Defies Europe Over Pollution: US Rejects Kyoto as "It Makes No Sense"', *The Daily Telegraph*, 30 March: 1.

Lampe, M. (2001). 'Mediation as an Ethical Adjunct of Stakeholder Theory', *Journal of Business Ethics*, 31: 165–73.

Langtry, B. (1994). 'Stakeholders and the Moral Responsibilities of the Firm', *Business Ethics Quarterly*, 4/4: 431–43.

Laski, H. J. (1916). 'The Personality of Associations', *Harvard Law Review*, 20/4: 404–26.

Laudan, L. (1977). *Progress and its Problems*. Berkeley, CA: University of California Press.

—— (1981). 'A Problem-Solving Approach to Scientific Progress', in I. Hacking (ed.), *Scientific Revolutions*. Oxford: Oxford University Press, pp. 144–55.

Lawler, E. J. and Bacharach, S. B. (1987). 'Comparisons of Dependence and Punitive Forms of Power', *Social Forces*, 66: 446–62.

Lea, D. (2004). 'The Imperfect Nature of Corporate Responsibilities to Stakeholders', *Business Ethics Quarterly*, 14/2: 201–17.

Leader, S. (1999). 'Participation and Property Rights', *Journal of Business Ethics*, 21: 97–109.

Lee, K. (1993). *Compass and Gyroscope: Integrating Science and Politics for the Environment*. Washington, DC: Island Press.

Letza, S., Sun, X., and Kirkbride, J. (2004). 'Shareholding Versus Stakeholding: A Critical Review of Corporate Governance', *Corporate Governance*, 12/3: 242–62.

Levy, A. and Merry, U. (1986). *Organizational Transformation*. New York: Praeger.

Lewicki, R. J. and Bunker, B. B. (1994). 'Developing and Maintaining Trust in Work Relationships', *Working Paper series 94–49*. Akron, OH: Max M. Fisher College of Business, The Ohio State University.

Lewis, A. and MacKenzie, C. (2000). 'Support for Investor Activism Among UK Ethical Investors', *Journal of Business Ethics*, 24/3: 215–22.

Lindblom, C. K. (1994). 'The Implications of Organizational Legitimacy for Social Corporate Performance and Disclosure'. Presented at the Critical Perspectives on Accounting Conference.

Lippmann, W. (1922). *Public Opinion*. New York: Harcourt Brace.

Lipsey, R. and Chrystal, A. (2003). *Economics*. Oxford: Oxford University Press.

Logsdon, J. M. and Wood, D. J. (2002). 'Business Citizenship: From Domestic to Global Level of Analysis', *Business Ethics Quarterly*, 12/2: 155–88.

Lorsch, J. W. (1991). 'The Workings of Codetermination', *Harvard Business Review*, July–August: 107–8.

Lovejoy, A. O. (1963). *The Thirteen Pragmatisms and Other Essays*. Baltimore, MD: Johns Hopkins Press.

Low, M. B. (1991). 'Stockholder Versus Stakeholder: How Managerial Attitudes Affect Goal Consensus Between Groups', *Academy of Management Proceedings*, 336–40.

Luoma, P. and Goodstein, J. (1999). 'Research Notes: Stakeholders and Corporate Boards: Institutional Influences on Board Composition and Structure', *Academy of Management Journal*, 42/5: 553–63.

Lyotard, J. (1984). *The Postmodern Condition*. Minneapolis, MN: University of Minnesota Press.

McAdam, T. W. (1973). 'How to Put Corporate Responsibility into Practice', *Business and Society Review/ Innovation*, 6: 8–16.

McAllister, D. T. and Ferrell, L. (2002). 'The Role of Strategic Philanthropy in Marketing Strategy', *European Journal of Marketing*, 36/5–6: 689–705.

McCarthy, J. D. and Zald, M. N. (1977). 'Resource Mobilization and Social Movements: A Partial Theory', *American Journal of Sociology*, 82: 1212–41.

MacIntyre, A. (1967). *A Short History of Ethics*. London: Routledge.

—— (1981). *After Virtue*. Notre Dame, IN: University of Notre Dame Press.

Mackenzie, C. (1998). 'The Choice of Criteria in Ethical Investment', *Business Ethics: A European Review*, 7/2: 81–6.

McLaren, D. (2004). 'Global Stakeholders: Corporate Accountability and Investor Engagement', *Corporate Governance*, 12/2: 191–201.

MacRae, D. and Whittington, D. (1997). *Expert Advice for Public Policy Choice*. Washington, DC: George-town University Press.

Mahoney, J. (1994). 'Stakeholder Responsibilities: Turning the Ethical Tables', *Business Ethics: A European Review*, 3/4: 31–5.

Maltz, A.C., Shenhar, A. J., and Reilly, R. R. (2003). 'Beyond the Balanced Scorecard: Refining the Search for Organizational Success Measures', *Long Range Planning*, 36: 187–204.

Marcoux, A. M. (2000). 'Business Ethics Gone Wrong', *Cato Policy Report*, 22/3, Washington, DC: The Cato Institute.

—— (2003). 'A Fiduciary Argument Against Stakeholder Theory', *Business Ethics Quarterly*, 13/1: 1–24.

Marens, R. and Wicks, A. (1999). 'Getting Real: Stakeholder Theory Management Practice and the General Irrelevance of Fiduciary Duties owed to Shareholders', *Business Ethics Quarterly*, 9/2: 273–94.

Marinetto, M. (1998). 'The Shareholders Strike Back: Issues in the Research of Shareholder Activism', *Environmental Politics*, 7/3: 125–33.

Marks, L. A. and Kalaitzandonakes, N. (2001). 'Mass Media Communiations About Agrobiotechnology', *AgBioForum*, 4/3–4: 199–208.

Marris, R. (1964). *The Economic Theory of 'Managerial Capital'*. London: Macmillan.

Mars, G. (1982). *Cheats at Work: An Anthropology of Workplace Crime*. London: Allen & Unwin.

Marshall, A. (1890/1910). *Principles of Economics*, 6th edn. London: Macmillan.

Marx, T. (1986). 'Integrating Public Affairs and Strategic Planning', *California Management Review*, 29/1 (Fall): 141–7.

Mathieu, E. (2000). *Response of UK Pension Funds to the SRI Disclosure Regulation*. London: UKSIF.

MEB (Management Institute for Environment and Business) (1995). *The Power of Environmental Partnerships*, F. Long and M. Arnold (eds.), Fort Worth, TX: Dryden Press.

Mendleson, N. and Polonsky, M. J. (1995). Using Strategic Alliances to Develop Credible Green Marketing', *Journal of Consumer Marketing*, 12/2: 4–18.

Menon, A. and Menon, A. (1997). 'Enviropreneurial Marketing Strategy: The Emergence of Corporate Environmentalism as a Marketing Strategy', *Journal of Marketing*, 61/1: 51–67.

Metcalfe, C. E. (1998). 'The Stakeholder Corporation', *Business Ethics: A European Review*, 7/1: 30–36.

Meznar, M. B., Chrisman, J. L., and Carroll, A. B. (1991). 'Social Responsibility and Strategic Management: Toward an Enterprise Strategy Classification', *Business and Professional Ethics Journal*, 10/1: 47–66.

Miles, S. and Friedman, A. L. (2004). 'The Social Construction of Stakeholder Management in the UK', *Governance and Accountability Group Working Paper*, 04/01. Oxford: The Business School, Oxford Brookes University.

—— , Hammond, K., and Friedman, A. L. (2002). *ACCA Research Report No. 77: Social and Environmental Reporting and Ethical Investment*. London: Certified Accountants Educational Trust.

Miller, D. and Friesen, P. H. (1980). 'Momentum and Revolution in Organizational Adaptation', *Academy of Management Journal*, 23: 591–614.

Miller, R. L. and Lewis, W. F. (1991). 'A Stakeholder Approach to Marketing Management Using the Value Exchange Models', *European Journal of Marketing*, 25/8: 55–68.

Mills, C.W. (1957). *The Power Elite*. Oxford: Oxford University Press.

Mintzberg, H. (1994). *The Rise and Fall of Strategic Planning*. London: Prentice-Hall.

Mitchell, R. K., Agle, B. R., and Wood, D. J. (1997). 'Towards a Theory of Stakeholder Identification and Salience: Defining the Principle of Who and What Really Counts', *Academy of Management Review*, 22/4: 853–86.

Monks, J. (1996). 'The TUC's Stake in Mr Blair', *The Times*, 17 January: 16.

—— (1998). 'Trade Unions, Enterprise and the Future', in P. Sparrow and M. Marchington (eds.), *Human Resource Management: The New Agenda*. London: Pitman, pp. 171–9.

Montgomery, C. A. (1991). 'Marks and Spencer', discussion paper, Harvard Business School, May.

Mumford, M. (1979). 'The End of a Familiar Inflation Accounting Cycle', *Accounting and Business Research* (Spring): 98–104.

Munzer, S. R. (1992). *A Theory of Property*. New York: Cambridge University Press.

Murphy, D. F. and Bendell, J. (1997). *In the Company of Partners: Business, Environmental Groups and Sustainable Development Post-Rio*. Bristol: The Policy Press.

Murphy, P. and Dee, J. (1992). 'Du Pont and Greenpeace: The Dynamics of Conflict Between Corporations and Activist Groups', *Journal of Public Relations Research*, 4/1: 3–20.

Murray, A. (2001). *Off the Rails*. London: Verso.

Näsi, J. (1995). 'What is Stakeholder Thinking? A Snapshot of Social Theory of the Firm', in J. Näsi (ed.), *Understanding Stakeholder Thinking*. Helsinki: LSR-Julkaisut Oy, pp. 19–32.

Neligan, C. (2003). *Increasing Accountability Through External Stakeholder Engagement*. London: One World Trust, Houses of Parliament.

Nobes, C. W. (1992). 'A Political History of Goodwill in the UK: An Illustration of Cyclical Standard Setting', *Abacus*, 28/2: 142–67.

Noddings, N. (1984). *Caring: A Feminine Approach to Ethics and Moral Education*. Berkeley, CA: University of California Press.

Nozick, R. (1974). *Anarchy, State and Utopia*. Oxford: Blackwell.

Nussbaum, M. and Hurley, S. (1993). 'Non-relative Virtues: An Aristotelian Approach', in M. Nussbaum (ed.), *The Quality of Life*. Oxford: Clarendon Press, pp. 242–78.

Nuti, D. M. (1997). 'Democracy and Economy: What Role for Stakeholders?' *Business Strategy Review*, 8/2: 14–20.

O'Brien, D. P. (1986). 'Divestiture: The Case of AT&T', in J. Coyne and M. Wright (eds.), *Divestment and Strategic Change*. Oxford: Philip Allan/Barnes & Noble Books, pp. 166–201.

O'Dywer, B. (2002). 'Managerial Perceptions of Corporate Social Disclosure: An Irish Study', *Accounting, Auditing and Accountability Journal*, 15/3: 406–36.

Ogden, S. and Watson, R. (1999). 'Corporate Performance and Stakeholder Management: Balancing Shareholder and Customer Interests in the UK Privatized Water Industry', *Academy of Management Journal*, 42/5: 526–36.

Ogilvie, K. B. and Everhardus, E. (2004). *ENGO-Business Partnerships: Lesson Learned*. Toronto: Pollution Probe.

O'Riordan, T. (1981). *Environmentalism*, 2nd edn. London: Pion.

ORR (Office of the Rail Regulator) (1999). *Railtrack's Stewardship of the Network*. London: ORR, November. Available at www.rail-reg.gov.uk.

Orts, E. W. and Strudler, A. (2002). 'The Ethical and Environmental Limits of Stakeholder Theory', *Business Ethics Quarterly*, 12/2: 215–34.

Osborne, A. (1999). 'Clothes Sector Reels as M&S Sacks Suppliers', *The Daily Telegraph*, 23 October: 29.

—— (2000) 'City: Marks Rejects Contract Move for Suppliers', *The Daily Telegraph*, 12 January: 31.

OXERA (Oxford Economic Research Associates) (2000). *Accounting for the Environment: An Analysis of the Quality of Environmental Reporting Across the Food and Retail, Oil and Gas, Utilities, and Banking Sectors*. Oxford: OXERA Environmental.

Page, C. G. (2002). 'The Determination of Organization Stakeholder Salience in Public Health', *Journal of Public Health Management and Practice*, 8/5: 76–84.

Palgrave, R. H. I., Eatwell, J., Milgate, M., and Newman, P. (eds.), (1992). *The New Palgrave Dictionary of Money and Finance*. London: Macmillan.

Pearson, R. (1989). 'Business Ethics as Communication Ethics: Public Relations Practice and the Idea of Dialogue', in C. H. Botan and V. Hazelton (eds.), *Public Relations Theory*. Hillside, NJ: Lawrence Erlbaum, pp. 111–31.

Peteraf, M. and Shanley, M. (1997). 'Getting to Know You: A Theory of Strategic Group Identity', *Strategic Management Journal*, 18: 165–86.

Peters, T. and Waterman, R. (1982). *In Search of Excellence*. New York: Harper & Row.

Pfeffer, J. (1972). 'Interorganizational Influence and Managerial Attitudes', *Academy of Management Journal*, 15: 775–90.

—— (1982). *Organizations and Organization Theory*. London: Pitman.

—— and Leong, A. (1977). 'Resource Allocations in United Funds: An Examination of Power and Dependence', *Social Forces*, 55: 775–90.

—— and Salancik, G. R. (1978). *The External Control of Organizations: A Resource Dependence Perspective*. New York: Harper & Row.

Phillips, R. (1997). 'Stakeholder Theory and a Principle of Fairness', *Business Ethics Quarterly*, 7/1: 51–66.

—— (2003a). 'Stakeholder Legitimacy', *Business Ethics Quarterly*, 13/1: 25–41.

—— (2003b). *Stakeholder Theory and Organizational Ethics*. San Francisco, CA: Berrett-Koehler Publishers.

PIRC (Pensions & Investment Research Consultants) (1999). *The 1999 Survey of Environmental Reporting at FTSE 350 Companies*. London: PIRC.

Plato (1981). *Five Dialogues: Euthyphro, Apology, Crito, Meno, Phaedo*, G. M. A. Grube (trans.). Indianapolis, IN: Hackett.

Polonsky, M. J. (1996). 'Stakeholder Management and the Stakeholder Matrix: Potential Strategic Marketing Tools', *Journal of Market Focused Management*, 1/3: 209–29.

—— Rosenberger, P. J. III, and Ottman, J. (1998). 'Developing Green Products: Learning From Stakeholders', *The Journal of Sustainable Product Design*, 5: 7–21.

—— Schuppisser, S. W., and Beldona, S. (2002). 'A Stakeholder Perspective for Analysing Marketing Relationships', *Journal of Market Focused Management*, 5/2: 109–26.

Poole, M., Mansfield, R., and Mendes, P. (2001). *Two Decades of Management*. London: Institute of Management.

Porter, M. (1980). *Competitive Strategy: Techniques for Analyzing Industries and Competitors*. New York: Free Press.

Post, J. E. (1978). *Corporate Behavior and Social Change*. Reston, VA: Reston.

—— Preston, L. E., and Sachs, S. (2002). *Redefining the Corporation: Stakeholder Management and Organizational Wealth*. Stanford, CA: Stanford University Press.

Power, M. (1992). 'The Politics of Brand Accounting in the UK', *The European Accounting Review*, 1/1: 39–68.

Prakash, A. (2001). 'Why Do Firms Adopt "Beyond Compliance" Environmental Policies?' *Business Strategy and the Environment*, 10: 289–99.

Prashad, V. (2002). *Fat Cats & Running Dogs: The Enron Stage of Capitalism*. London: Zed.

Preston, L. E. and Sapienza, H. J. (1990). 'Stakeholder Management and Corporate Performance', *Journal of Behavioural Economics*, 19: 361–75.

Ramirez, A. (1990). 'Epic Debate Led to Heinz Tuna Plan', *New York Times*, 16 April: D1, 6.

Rawls, J. (1971). *A Theory of Justice*. Cambridge, MA: Harvard University Press.

Razaee, Z. (2005). 'Causes, Consequences, and the Deterrence of Financial Statement Fraud', *Critical Perspectives on Accounting*, 16/3: 277–98.

Reed, D. (1999). 'Stakeholder Management Theory: A Critical Theory Perspective', *Business Ethics Quarterly*, 9/3: 453–83.

—— (2002). 'Employing Normative Stakeholder Theory in Developing Countries', *Business & Society*, 41/1: 166–207.

Rees, G. (1985). *St Michael: A History of Marks & Spencer*. London: Pan Books.

Rhenman, E. (1964). *Foeretagsdemokrati och foeretagsorganisation*. Stockholm: Thule.

Robbins, J. (2003). 'Stakeholders and Conflict Management: Corporate Perspectives on Collaborative Approaches', in J. Andriof, S. Waddock, B. Husted, and S. Sutherland Rahman (eds.), *Unfolding Stakeholder Thinking 2: Relationships, Communication, Reporting and Performance*. Sheffield, UK: Greenleaf Publishing, pp. 162–80.

Roberts, R. W. (1992). 'Determinants of Corporate Social Responsibility Disclosure: An Application of Stakeholder Theory', *Accounting Organizations and Society*, 17/6: 595–612.

—— and Mahoney, L. (2004). 'Stakeholder Conceptions of the Corporation: Their Meaning and Influence in Accounting Research', *Business Ethics Quarterly*, 14/3: 399–431.

Robinson, D. and Garratt, C. (1996). *Ethics for Beginners*. Cambridge: ICON Books.

Rosenau, P. M. (1992). *Postmodernism and The Social Sciences: Insights, Inroads, and Intrusions*. Princeton, NJ: Princeton University Press.

Ross, S. (1973). 'The Economic Theory of Agency: The Principal's Problem', *American Economic Review*, 63: 134–9.

Rothschild, W. (1976). *Putting it All Together*. New York: AMACOM.

Rowell, A. (1996). *Green Backlash: Global Subversion of the Environmental Movement*. London: Routledge.

Rowley, T. J. (1997). 'Moving Beyond Dyadic Ties: A Network Theory of Stakeholder Influences', *Academy of Management Review*, 22/4: 887–910.

—— (2000). 'Does Relational Context Matter? An Empirical Test of a Network Theory of Stakeholder Influences', *Research in Stakeholder Theory, 1997–1998: The Sloan Foundation Minigrant Project*. Toronto: The Clarkson Center for Business Research.

—— and Moldoveanu, M. (2003). 'When Will Stakeholder Groups Act? An Interest and Identity Based Model of Stakeholder Group Mobilization', *Academy of Management Review*, 28/2: 204–19.

RSA (Royal Society for Arts) (1995). *Tomorrow's Company: The Role of Business in a Changing World. Final Report*. London: RSA.

Ruder, D. S. (1965). 'Public Obligations of Private Corporations', *University of Pennsylvania Law Review*, 114: 209–29.

Ruf, B. M., Muralidhar, K., Brown, R. M., Janney, J. J., and Paul, K. (2001). 'An Empirical Investigation of the Relationship Between Change in Corporate Social Performance and Financial Performance: A Stakeholder Theory Perspective', *Journal of Business Ethics*, 32: 143–56.

Salancik, G. R. (1979). 'Interorganizational Dependence and Responsiveness to Affirmative Action: The Case of Women and Defense Contractors'. *Academy of Management Journal*, 22/2: 375–94.

Samuelson, P. A. (1947). *Foundations of Economic Analysis*. Cambridge, MA: Harvard University Press.

Savage, G. T., Nix, T. W., Whitehead, C. J., and Blair, J. D. (1991). 'Strategies for Assessing and Managing Organizational Stakeholders', *Academy of Management Executive*, 5/2: 61–75.

Sayer, A. (2000). *Realism and Social Science*. London: Sage.

Schelling, T. C. (1956). 'An Essay on Bargaining', *The American Economic Review*, XLVI/3: 281–306.

Schiller, F. C. S. (1915). 'Realism, Pragmatism, and William James', *Mind*, 25/4, 516–24.

Schilling, M. A. (2000). 'Decades Ahead of Her Time: Advancing Stakeholder Theory Through the Ideas of Mary Parker Follett', *Journal of Management History*, 6/5: 224–42.

Schlegelmilch, B. B. (1997). 'The Relative Importance of Ethical and Environmental Screening: Implications for the Marketing of Ethical Investment Funds', *International Journal of Bank Marketing*, 15/2: 48–53.

Schlossberger, E. (1994). 'A New Model of Business: Dual-Investor Theory', *Business Ethics Quarterly*, 4/4: 459–74.

Schonberger, R. (1992). 'Total Quality Management Cuts a Broad Swath Through Manufacturing and Beyond', *Organizational Dynamics*, 20/4: 16–27.

Schumpeter, J. A. (1934). *The Theory of Economic Development*. Cambridge, MA.: Harvard University Press.

—— (1942). *Capitalism, Socialism, and Democracy*. New York: Harper Brothers.

Scott, S. G. and Lane, V. R. (2000). 'A Stakeholder Approach to Organizational Identity', *Academy of Management Review*, 25/1: 43–62.

Second Vatican Council (1965). 'Gaudium et Spes', *Acta Apostolicae Sedis*, 58 (1966): 1048–9.

Sen, S., Gürhan-Canli, Z., and Morwitz, V. (2001). 'Withholding Consumption: A Social Dilemma Perspective on Consumer Boycotts', *Journal of Consumer Research*, 28: 399–417.

Sharma, S. and Starik, M. (2004). *Stakeholders, the Environment and Society*. Cheltenham, UK: Edward Elgar.

Shiochet, R. (1998). 'An Organization Design Model for Nonprofits', *Nonprofit Management & Leadership*, 9/1: 71–88.

Shipp, S. (1987). 'Modified Vendettas as a method of punishing corporations', *Journal of Business Ethics*, 6: 603–612.

Sieff, I. (1985). *The Memoirs of Israel Sieff*. London: Weidenfeld & Nicolson.

—— (1987). *Don't Ask the Price: The Memoirs of the President of Marks & Spencer*. London: Weidenfeld & Nicolson.

Skorecki, A. (2001) 'Top Companies Under Pressure on the Environment', *Financial Times*, 10 April.

Slater, S. F. (1997). 'Developing a Customer Value-Based Theory of the Firm', *Journal of the Academy of Marketing Science*, 25/2: 162–7.

Smillie, I. and Helmich, H. (eds.) (1999). *Stakeholders: Government–NGO Partnerships for International Development*. London: Earthscan.

Smith, A. (1776). *The Wealth of Nations*. Republished in 1933. London: Dent.

—— (1790). *The Theory of Moral Sentiments*. Republished in 1976. Oxford: Clarendon Press.

Smith, K. G., Mitchell, T. R., and Summer, C. E. (1985). 'Top Management Priorities in Different Stages of Organizational Life Cycle', *Academy of Management Journal*, 28: 799–820.

Smith, N. C. and Cooper-Martin, E. (1997). 'Ethics and Target Marketing: The Role of Product Harm and Consumer Vulnerability', *Journal of Marketing*, 61: 1–20.

Snow, C., Miles, R., and Coleman, H. (1992). 'Managing 21st Century Network Organizations', *Organizational Dynamics*, 20/3: 5–19.

Social Investment Forum (1997). *SEC Shareholder Rights Analysis: The Impact of the Proposed SEC Rules on the Resubmission of Shareholder Resolutions*. Washington, DC: Social Investment Forum.

Stafford, E. and Hartman, C. L. (1996). 'Green Alliances: Strategic Relations Between Business and Environmental Groups', *Business Horizons*, 39/2: 20–59.

Stainer, L. (2004). 'Ethical Dimensions of Management Decision-making', *Strategic Change*, 13: 333–42.

Starik, M. (1993). 'Is the Environment an Organizational Stakeholder? Naturally!' Paper presented at the 4th annual conference of the International Association for Business and Society. San Diego, CA: IABS.

—— (1994). 'Essay by Mark Starik: The Toronto Conference: Reflections on Stakeholder Theory', *Business & Society*, 33/1: 89–95.

—— (1995). 'Should Trees Have Managerial Standing: Towards Stakeholder Status for Nonhuman Nature', *Journal of Business Ethics*, 14: 207–17.

Steadman, M. E. and Green, R. F. (1997). 'An Extension of Stakeholder Theory Research: Developing Surrogates for Net Organizational Capital', *Managerial Auditing Journal*, 12/3: 142–7.

Sternberg, E. (1994). *Just Business: Business Ethics in Action*. Boston: Little, Brown.

—— (1996). 'Stakeholder Theory Exposed', *The Corporate Governance Quarterly*, 2/1: 4–18.

—— (1997). 'The Defects of Stakeholder Theory', *Corporate Governance: An International Review*, 5: 3–10.

—— (2000). *Just Business: Business Ethics in Action*. Oxford: Oxford University Press.

Stittle, J. (2003). *Annual Reports: Delivering Your Corporate Message to Stakeholders*. Aldershot, UK: Gower.

Stone, D. (1995). 'No Longer at the End of the Pipe, But Still a Long Way from Sustainability: A Look at Management Accounting for the Environment and Sustainable Development in the United States', *Accounting Forum*, 19/2–3: 95–110.

Stoney, C. and Aylott, N. (1994). 'Tomorrow's Company?' *Renewal*, 4 (October): 56–65.

—— and Winstanley, D. (2001). 'Stakeholding: Confusion or Utopia? Mapping the Conceptual Terrain', *Journal of Management Studies*, 38/5: 603–26.

Strickland, D., Wiles, K., and Zenner, M. (1996). 'A Requiem for the USA: Is Small Shareholder Monitoring Effective?' *Journal of Financial Economics*, 40: 319–38.

Strong, K. C., Ringer, R. C., and Taylor, S. A. (2001). 'THE* Rules of Stakeholder Satisfaction (*Timeliness, Honesty, Empathy)', *Journal of Business Ethics*, 32/3: 219–30.

Sturdivant, F. D. (1979). 'Executives and Activists: Test of Stakeholder Management', *California Management Review*, 12/1: 53–9.

Suchman, M. C. (1995). 'Managing Legitimacy; Strategic and Institutional Approaches', *Academy of Management Review*, 20/3: 571–611.

Sutherland-Rahman, S., Waddock, S., Andriof, J., and Husted, B. (2002). *Unfolding Stakeholder Thinking: Theory, Responsibility and Engagement*. Sheffield, UK: Greenleaf Publishing.

Svendsen, A. (1998). *The Stakeholder Strategy: Profiting from Collaborative Business Relations*. San Francisco, CA: Berrett-Koehler Publishers.

Swanson, D. L. (1999). 'Towards an Integrative Theory of Business and Society: A Research Strategy for Corporate Social Performance', *Academy of Management Review*, 24/3: 506–24.

Swartz, M. and Watkins, S. (2003). *Power Failure: The Rise and Fall of Enron*. London: Aurum.

Swift, T. (2001). 'Trust, Reputation and Corporate Accountability to Stakeholders', *Business Ethics: A European Review*, 10/1: 16–26.

Targett, S. (2000). 'Worth Going That Extra Mile: Shareholder Value Added?' *Financial Times*, 30 March.

Taylor, B. (1971). 'The Future Development of Corporate Strategy', *The Journal of Business Policy*, 2/2: 22–38.

Thayer, H. S. (1968). *Meaning and Action: A Critical History of Pragmatism*. Indianapolis, IN: Hackett.

Thompson, J. K. (1995). *The Media and Modernity*. London: Polity Press.

—— , Wartick, S. L., and Smith, H. L. (1991). 'Integrating Corporate Social Performance and Stakeholder Management: Implications for a Research Agenda in Small Business', *Research in Corporate Social Performance and Policy*, 12: 207–30.

Thompson, T. A. and Davis, G. F. (1997). 'The Politics of Corporate Control and the Future of Shareholder Activism in the United States', *Corporate Governance*, 5/3: 152–9.

Tilly, C. (1978). *From Mobilization to Revolution*. New York: Random House.

Treviño, L. K. and Weaver, G. R. (1999*a*). 'Response: The Stakeholder Research Tradition: Converging Theorists—Not Convergent Theory', *Academy of Management Review*, 24/2: 222–7.

—— —— (1999*b*). 'Treviño and Weaver's Reply to Jones and Wicks', *Academy of Management Review*, 26/4: 623–4.

Tsoukas, H. (1999). 'David and Goliath in the Risk Society: Making Sense of the Conflict Between Shell and Greenpeace in the North Sea', *Organization*, 6/3: 499–528.

Turnbull Committee (1999). *Internal Control: Guidance for Directors on the Combined Code*. London: The Institute of Chartered Accountants in England and Wales.

Turnbull, S. (1994). 'Stakeholder Democracy: Redesigning the Governance of Firms and Bureaucracies', *Journal of Socio-Economics*, 23: 321–61.

—— (1997). 'Stakeholder Governance: A Cybernetic and Property Rights Analysis', *Corporate Governance*, 5: 180–205.

—— (1998). 'Should Ownership Last Forever?' *Journal of Socio-Economics*, 27: 341–64.

Tversky, A. and Kahneman, D. (1981). 'The Framing of Decisions and the Psychology of Choice', *Science*, 211: 453–8.

Ullmann, A. E. (1985). 'Data in Search of a Theory: A Critical Examination of Relationships Among Performance, Social Disclosure and Economic Performance of US Firms', *Academy of Management Review*, 10/3: 540–7.

UNEP/SustainAbility (1997). *Engaging Stakeholders: The 1997 Benchmark Survey: The Third International Progress Report on Company Environmental Reporting*. London: UNEP/SustainAbility.

—— (1999). *The Social Reporting Report*. London: UNEP/SustainAbility.

Unerman, J. and Bennett, M. (2004). 'Increased Stakeholder Dialogue and the Internet: Towards Greater Corporate Accountability or Reinforcing Capital Hegemony?' *Accounting Organisations and Society*, 29: 685–707.

Utterback, J. M. (1979). 'Environmental Analysis and Forecasting', in D. E. Schendel and C. W. Hofer (eds.), *Strategic Management: A New View of Business Policy and Planning*. Boston, MA: Little, Brown.

Valasquez, M. G. (1992). 'International Business Morality and the Common Good', *Business Ethics Quarterly*, 2/1: 27–40.

Van Buren, H. J. III, and Paul, K. (2000). 'Company Reactions to Socially Responsible Investing: An Empirical Analysis', *Research in Stakeholder Theory, 1997–1998: The Sloan Foundation Minigrant Project*. Toronto: The Clarkson Center for Business Research.

Vaughan Switzer, J. (1997). *Green Backlash: History and Politics of Environmental Opposition in the US*. Boulder, CO: Lynne Rienner.

Veblen, T. (1904). *The Theory of the Business Enterprise*. New York: Macmillan.

—— (1923). *Absentee Ownership and Business Enterprise in Recent Times: The Case of America*. New York: B. W. Huebsch.

Vinten, G. (2001). 'Shareholder Versus Stakeholder: Is There a Governance Dilemma?' *Corporate Governance*, 9: 36–47.

Votaw, D. (1973). 'Genius Becomes Rare', in D. Votaw and S. P. Sethi (eds.), *The Corporate Dilemma: Traditional Values Versus Contemporary Problems*. Englewood Cliffs, NJ: Prentice-Hall, pp. 11–45.

Wah, L. (1998). 'Treading the Sacred Ground', *Management Review*, 87: 18–22.

Wahal, S. (1996). 'Public Pension Fund Activism and Firm Performance', *Journal of Financial and Quantitative Analysis*, 31: 1–23.

Wallace, W. A. (1977). *The Elements of Philosophy: A Compendium for Philosophers and Theologians*. New York: Alba House.

Walras, L. (1874). *Elements D'economie Politique Pure ou Théorie de la Richesse Sociale* [Elements of Pure Economics or the Theory of Social Wealth]. Lausanne, Switzerland: Corbas.

Wartick, S. L. (1992). 'The Relationship Between Intense Media Exposure and Change in Corporate Reputation', *Business & Society*, 31: 33–49.

Watson, M. and Emery, A. T. (2003). 'The Emerging UK Law on the Environment and the Environmental Auditing Response', *Managerial Auditing Journal*, 18/8: 666–72.

Weaver, G. R. and Treviño, L. K. (1994). 'Normative and Empirical Business Ethics', *Business Ethics Quarterly*, 4: 129–44.

—— —— and Cochran, P. L. (1999). 'Integrated and Decoupled Corporate Social Performance: Management Commitments, External Pressures and Corporate Ethics Practices', *Academy of Management Journal*, 42/5: 539–52.

Weetman, P. (1999). *Financial and Management Accounting: An Introduction*. London: Pitman.

Weinberger, M. G. and Romeo, J. B. (1989). 'The Impact of Negative Product News', *Business Horizons*, 32/1: 44–50.

Weiner, P. P. (1973–74). 'Pragmatism', in Weiner P. P. (ed.), *The Dictionary of the History of Ideas: Studies of Selected Pivotal Ideas*, Vol. 3. New York: Charles Scribner's Sons, pp. 551–70.

Weiss, J. W. (1998/2003). *Business Ethics: A Stakeholder and Issues Management Approach*. Quebec: Thomson South-Western.

Weyer, M. V. (1996). 'Ideal World', *Management Today*, September: 35–8.

Whysall, P. (2000). 'Addressing Ethical Issues in Retailing: A Stakeholder Perspective', *International Review of Retail, Distribution and Consumer Research*, 10/3: 305–18.

Wicks, A. C. (1998). 'How Kantian a Theory of Capitalism?' *Business Ethics Quarterly*, Special Issue No. 1: 61–74.

—— and Freeman, R. E. (1998). 'Organization Studies and the New Pragmatism: Positivism, Anti-positivism, and the Search for Ethics', *Organization Science*, 9: 123–40.

—— , Gilbert, D. R., Jr., and Freeman, R. E. (1994). 'A Feminist Reinterpretation of the Stakeholder Concept', *Business Ethics Quarterly*, 4/4: 475–97.

Wijnberg, N. M. (2000). 'Normative Stakeholder Theory and Aristotle: The Link Between Ethics and Politics', *Journal of Business Ethics*, 25: 329–42.

Williamson, O. E. (1975). *Markets and Hierarchies*. New York: Free Press.

—— (1985). *The Economic Institutions of Capitalism*. New York: Free Press.

Wilson, I. (1975). 'What One Company Is Doing About Today's Demands on Business', in G. A. Steiner (ed.), *Changing Business–Society Interrelationships*. Los Angeles: Graduate School of Management, UCLA.

Wilson, W. (1913). *The New Freedom: A Call for the Emancipation of the Generous Energies of a People*. New York: Doubleday, Page & Co.

Winstanley, D. and Stuart-Smith, K. (1996). 'Policing Performance: The Ethics of Performance Management', *Personnel Review*, 25/6: 66–84.

Wolmar, C. (2001). *Broken Rails*, 2nd edn. London: Aurum.

Wood, D. J. (1991). 'Corporate Social Performance Revisited', *Academy of Management Review*, 16/4: 691–718.

—— and Jones, R. E. (1995). 'Stakeholder Mismatching: A Theoretical Problem in Empirical Research on Corporate Social Performance', *The International Journal of Organizational Analysis*, 3/3: 229–67.

Wood, M. M. (1992). 'Is Governing Board Behavior Cyclical?' *Nonprofit Management & Leadership*, 3/2: 139–63.

WWF-International (World Wildlife Fund for Nature) (1996). *Marine Stewardship Council Newsletter*, No. 1. Godalming: WWF-International.

Zadek, S. and Raynard, P. (2002). 'Stakeholder Engagement: Measuring and Communicating the Quality', *Accountability Quarterly*, 19: 8–17.

—— , Pruzan, P., and Evans, R. (1997). *Building Corporate Accountability: Emerging Practices in Social and Ethical Accounting, Auditing and Reporting*. London: Earthscan.

Zambon, S. and Del Bello, A (2005). 'Towards a Stakeholder Responsible Approach: The Constructive Role of Reporting', *Corporate Governance: The International Journal of Business in Society*, 5/2: 130–41.

Zöller, K. (1999). 'Growing Credibility Through Dialogue: Experiences in Germany and the USA', in M. Charter and M. J. Polonsky (eds.), *Greener Marketing: A Global Perspective on Greening Marketing Practice*. Sheffield, UK: Greenleaf Publishing, pp. 196–206.

Zyglidopoulos, S. C. (2001). 'The Impact of Accidents on Firms' Reputation for Social Performance', *Business & Society*, 40/4: 416–41.

☐ INDEX